T0291403

Decisions, Preferences, and Heuristics

"The economist may attempt to ignore psychology, but it is sheer impossibility for him to ignore human nature ... If the economist borrows his conception of man from the psychologist, his constructive work may have some chance of remaining purely economic in character. But if he does not, he will not thereby avoid psychology. Rather, he will force himself to make his own, and it will be bad psychology."

John Maurice Clark, 1918
(Text cited in Thaler, 2016: 1578)

Decisions, Preferences, and Heuristics

An Introduction to Economic Psychology and
Behavioral Economics

Pere Mir-Artigues

Professor of Microeconomics, University of Lleida, Spain

Cheltenham, UK • Northampton, MA, USA

Original Publication – Decisions, preferències i heurístiques. Una introducció a la psicologia econòmica published by Edicions de la Universitat de Barcelona

Published by
Edward Elgar Publishing Limited
The Lypiatts
15 Lansdown Road
Cheltenham
Glos GL50 2JA
UK

Edward Elgar Publishing, Inc.
William Pratt House
9 Dewey Court
Northampton
Massachusetts 01060
USA

A catalogue record for this book
is available from the British Library

Library of Congress Control Number: 2023939586

This book is available electronically in the **Elgar**online
Economics subject collection
http://dx.doi.org/10.4337/9781035315277

Printed on elemental chlorine free (ECF)
recycled paper containing 30% Post-Consumer Waste

ISBN 978 1 0353 1526 0 (cased)
ISBN 978 1 0353 1527 7 (eBook)

Printed and bound in the USA

Contents

Preface and acknowledgments

This book is an introduction to economic psychology, a discipline primarily concerned with understanding decisions, preferences, and heuristics. Although more than half a century old, this field of research is still little known among economists, whether professionals or academics. This shortcoming has worse consequences for those who follow courses in economic or business management. This group can also include all people interested in how economic decisions are made. In the search for information about economic psychology, all these people have to overcome two obstacles: the small number of academic books available, with the first handbooks published only about 15 years ago, and the particular orientation of the books aimed at the general public sold throughout the world. These latter works focus on denouncing the many biases and mental errors that, according to their authors, people systematically commit. These books, therefore, project the spectrum of irrationality on everyday judgments and choices, whether in the private or the work domain. However, analysis and results from authors, schools, and research in economic psychology show that the priority given to mental biases is also biased dissemination of the results of the discipline. To begin the exploration of this territory with better prospects, after the introduction, Chapter 2 contains a brief history of the economic view of rationality and, more especially, a description of the two research programs, sometimes convergent, often divergent, that coexist in economic psychology. Then, in Chapter 3, the most common terms of decision theory, i.e., preferences, heuristics, and algorithms, are discussed. Chapter 4 first proposes a simple framework of the main elements influencing economic decision-making processes and, second, deals with the treatment of risk and uncertainty, followed by a description of empirical results and models designed in the analysis of inter-temporal preferences. Once the major factors driving the economic decisions have been identified, Chapter 5 systematizes the main patterns, methods and, above all, algorithms that determine decisions. This chapter draws, though not exclusively, on the results of the research program called ecological rationality, a term that has to be interpreted as contextual rationality. Chapter 6 suggests a tentative model of the interaction of preferences, heuristics, and other psycho-social factors driving consumption decisions, and a long section discusses preference manipulation techniques. The book closes with a brief epilogue and a bibliography. All this forms a long path that has endeavored to include all the important points and that has not hesitated to be prolix when the subject deserved it.

The book introduces the basic concepts and topics of economic psychology. It aims is to be a complete and orderly map, indispensable for moving through the territory of economic psychology. However, it is also true that this goal implies ignoring many details and not going deeply enough into the connections between the many aspects dealt with. In addition, the book is intended to be a launching pad for current students considering making their contribution to behavioral economics research in the not-too-distant future. The reader is encouraged to explore and delve deeper into the various issues mentioned throughout the book by browsing the bibliography. Many of the references are freely available on the Internet. Furthermore, with a little more effort, many more can undoubtedly be found, since economic psychology is one of the fastest-growing fields of economics.

This book is an adapted, translated, and improved version of the one published in September 2022 by the University of Barcelona, under the title *Decisions, preferències i heurístiques. Una introducció a la psicologia econòmica.* The original Catalan text benefited from the comments and suggestions of Alfons Barceló and Josep González Calvet (University of Barcelona), and Pablo del Río (IPP-CSIC, Madrid). These colleagues kindly read the text when it was still in progress, that is when the reader would surely find an unrefined style, bibliographic deficiencies, and many misleading ideas. Moreover, two anonymous reviewers from the University of Barcelona contributed with some ideas and references that improved that first edition of the book. Concerning this English version, the author would like to thank Gerd Gigerenzer, Director of the Harding Center for Risk Literacy (Max-Planck-Institute for Human Development, Berlin) and Mario Morroni, Department of Political Science (University of Pisa) for their helpful comments, as well as an additional anonymous reviewer. However, the author is solely responsible for any errors and omissions that the text may still contain.

December 2022

1. Introduction

Economic psychology studies the processes of choice between options of an economic character, coupled with the great variety of judgments, and their determinants, that encompass them. Whether in private or in professional life, people often have to choose amongst alternatives with more or less salient economic implications.[1] Sometimes, the decision has an undoubtedly economic nature such as, for example, purchasing consumer goods, contributing to a retirement plan, launching a business project or replacing an obsolete machine. In others, decisions have an identifiable but indirect economic flavor, as is often the case when enrolling in an educational activity, becoming a member of a social club, or moving to a more exclusive neighborhood. In contrast, deciding whether to reconcile with someone with whom I am angry, or choosing whether or not to go on a diet, do not seem to be decisions with significant economic effects, either at the time of making the choice or afterward, whether with a one-off or long-lasting effects.

Economic decision-making processes always involve numerous psychosocial elements and are always affected by contextual circumstances. Therefore, economic psychology focuses on the cognitive capacities that people activate and their correspondence with the context in which a given decision is made. Economic psychology assumes that everyone works to shape his or her own life, according to the options offered by the context and how these are interpreted. On the one hand, people make choices motivated by reasonable goals, i.e., that they are neither ludicrous nor extravagant, and that they are intelligent enough to correctly perceive and understand the options available to them. On the other hand, economic psychology shows that many of the decisions ultimately aim at adapting to the social reality that surrounds people.[2] People constantly interact with each other, and they are thus inevitably influenced by the beliefs and behaviors of others (Aronson, 2008: 6–7). However, the adaptive drive could not be expressed to its full potential if humans did not have a brain with an extraordinary capacity to learn and store experiences and knowledge. This is a requirement for people to be able to readjust their behavior in response to more or less anticipated changes in the environment (Morgado, 2017: 24).

Since the 18th century, if not earlier, the analysis of decision-making processes (What judgments drive them? How are the consequences evaluated? What does risk entail? Etc.) has been mixed up with speculation about the nature of human rationality. Thus, much of the economic discourse considers that only decisions that provide maximum satisfaction to individuals deserve the label of rational. Exercising rationality would therefore consist of identifying and choosing the option that best suits motivations and consequences. However, the study of decisions focused on results implies, on the one hand, ignoring the limitations and also, paradoxically, the flexibility of the human mind and, on the other hand, avoiding many of the conditioning factors imposed by social reality.[3] There is an alternative conception of rationality that emphasizes decision procedures. Its priority is to analyze the adequacy between the method of choosing and the specific features of the context in which the decision is made, while the outcome obtained becomes a second-order issue.[4] As mentioned, this approach is more realistic with the aptitudes and plasticity of the human mind and, at the same time, can be connected with the vision of rationality held by other human and social disciplines such as psychology, sociology, and anthropology.

The common meaning of rationality points in the direction of knowing how to give convincing explanations: an action can be considered rational if the person who has carried it out can credibly justify why they have acted the way they did. Rationality requires good reasons for what has been decided and done (Aronson, 2008: 182–183). The subjects have to be able to persuade others and themselves that they have acted coherently and expectedly. This explanation does not presuppose any moral evaluation, although they cannot indefinitely escape it. It should also be borne in mind that the result obtained is not necessarily related to the intensity of the motivation (Elster, 2010: 84). In a nutshell, rational behavior connotes (self-)control: the individual is aware of the motivation that has triggered the choice, knows that they are immersed in it (disengagement is not possible) and, as is often the case, the choice can be justified in a sufficiently plausible way. In contrast, the foolish choice and the mental state of obfuscation are two sides of the same coin. It is not surprising that third parties are astonished (or demand an apology) when someone has acted toward them (or another person) in a way that is difficult to understand, i.e., without knowing quite why they have done what they have done. Although harmless consequences may lessen the concern, they do not change people's minds about the action taken.

Similarly, economic decisions can be considered rational if the individual chooses in a way that is congruent with the known reality (which includes information on the opportunities, means, and time available) and remains alert throughout the process (which implies a minimum discernment of their motivations and the capacity to evaluate the consequences). At present, this definition sets aside any scrutiny of the volume of cognitive resources involved and eludes measuring the degree of satisfaction achieved. In this conception of human rationality, making mistakes in decision-making processes is quite normal. Sooner or later everyone makes mistakes. Even so, human beings do not make systematic mistakes; rather, they are irregular and scattered over time. There is also no shortage of successes during this time. Making mistakes can be explained by factors such as arbitrary appraisals, contradictory objectives, unexpected events, lack of attention, and a long etcetera. All this, however, does not reflect a presumed deficient design of the mind, but rather the influence of inclinations and circumstances. Unfortunately, taking care of gathering information and processing it does not guarantee that the judgments associated with a decision will be sound and, hence, that the decision made will lead to the best possible consequences. An expectation, for example, may be unfounded. Finally, it should not be forgotten that a person's will is not always firm on executing a decision.

As pointed out, a relevant feature of the human mind is its capacity for rationalization. People want to appear reasonable, i.e., they strive to have admissible explanations for what they have decided and done, both to themselves and third parties. This impulse is present at the moment of making a decision and often afterward, especially if, because of the results, it is necessary to revise the justifications imagined and/or given. Whatever it may be, the quest for rationalization is never exhausted. This observation opens the door to a caveat: the reasons given to explain the choices made may not necessarily be the real ones. For example, someone may claim to be dieting for health reasons when, in reality, they are doing it out of vanity, i.e., to remain physically attractive according to the current aesthetic canons. This motivation is not made explicit for fear of being branded as ridiculous. Strictly speaking, any motivation attached to a choice is also a choice (Elster, 1991: 46–47): why does this person say what they say about the decision taken? Although authentic motivations are not easy to uncover, there may be indiscreet statements that are sufficiently revealing (such as the well-known open microphone trap), or ways of behaving that make it obvious. In any case, humans are masters in the art of disguising the real motivations behind their decisions (and actions).

The environment in which human rationality operates contains two characteristics that stand out: the intense interaction between people and the uncertainty that pervades many decisions. Since it is not possible to directly read the minds of others, people devote much interest and time to observing and understanding the opinions expressed and actions taken by others. This impulse transforms humans into a kind of amateur detective: they constantly make inferences about the social reality unfolding around them. This reality includes, on the one hand, the behavior of others, which is interpreted according to the following three pieces of information: the coherence of the action undertaken (do they always behave the same in this type of situation?), the degree of consensus (does everyone behave like this in the same circumstances?) and what makes it unique (what is particular about their behavior?)

(Aronson, 2008: 120). For example, if someone is seen kissing somebody else, the action will be interpreted very differently depending on the answers to such questions. However, it is not enough to capture the behavior of others; it is also necessary to predict it (Hogg and Vaughan, 2014: 82–83). On the other hand, people also pay close attention to the lifestyles[5] of others. People spare no effort to learn about them and, if necessary, assimilate them while internalizing social norms. This is a lifelong process of imitation and learning.[6] The eagerness to conform to the observed or assumed behavior of people is valued positively by society, even though it can sometimes make it difficult to face new and imperative situations.

Generically speaking, social influences come from the following five sources:

- The family understood as a dwelling unit or household, and the circle of relatives, as well as the members of the closest social environment in which daily life takes place.
- The various groups that emerge in the course of people's lives, such as classmates, co-workers, etc.
- All kinds of professionals such as teachers, doctors, plumbers, lawyers, mechanics, clergymen, and a long etcetera, whose opinions may deserve great respect and/or credibility.
- Images and messages, whether or not advertisements, disseminated by the media.
- Social networks in which people of a presumably close personal and/or social profile, although unknown, disseminate their points of view.

Leaving aside closed communities, these influences tend to share the same broad cultural patterns, which does not prevent certain social groups from claiming certain singularities (for reasons of origin, religion, language, etc.).

Social norms have a considerable impact on people's behavior. They have shared rules, either explicit or tacit, on how to behave, especially in public. Their assimilation begins in childhood. They range from rules concerning the distances that, depending on the occasion and the degree of trust, people have to keep from each other, to (quasi) moral principles (unconditional, such as the prohibition of incest, or conditional, such as congratulating only those who congratulate you on your birthday). They also include certain ancestral cultural values (such as the insistence in patriarchal societies that women's highest aspiration is to have children and take care of them), good civic practices (not throwing papers on the floor, standing in line), rules of etiquette (how to act at the table, how to dress according to the occasion), conventions (which side of the road to drive on, when and what to tip), local traditions (what holidays to celebrate, how to establish first names and surnames), etc. (more information in Elster, 1991: 102–107 and 2010: 387–390; Nolan et al., 2008; Eibl-Eibesfeldt, 2012: 318–320 and 335; and Sorokowska et al., 2017).[7] This series of conventions and obligations gives the group identity and ensures that the behavior of its members is adequately predictable. However, the reasons for and moments of their creation are often difficult to pinpoint. In addition, their fulfillment does not necessarily please or satisfy, or bring well-being to every person who complies with them. Anyway, strict compliance is not usually required. If non-compliance is slight, the disobedience will hardly be rebuked. At most, it will be the motive for mockery. As a general rule, it is sufficient to conform to social norms, since it seems that the majority also accept and follow them.[8] If non-compliance is serious, the person may be ostracized and, in some cases, severely penalized or expelled from the group. At this point, since social norms are key elements of human groups' identity, their members prevent problems by submitting, even reluctantly (Aronson, 2008: 23; Eibl-Eibesfeldt, 2012: 315).

This last idea opens the door to identifying three types of responses to social influences (Aronson 2008: 35–41):

- Submission to avoid retaliation, or to obtain a reward. Obeying is the response to power. However, to the extent that compliance may be apparent, nonconformity may emerge in unsupervised spaces.
- The lazy identification or adoption of the beliefs, norms, and behaviors encouraged by the group: observance drives people to adjust their behavior, but normally without this requiring blind faith in it.
- The internalization or complete assimilation of the ideas and behaviors of the group. People end up convinced of their suitability and solidity: they consider without hesitation that they are the right thing to do.

Interestingly, people also tend to believe that conformism is a matter for others, while at the same time defending their unique personalities. They consider that others are motivated by being highly valued, while they are only moved by doing the right thing. This pushes people to pay special attention to what (presumably) knowledgeable or experienced people say and do. This reflects the human desire for certainty, which is closely associated with the consolidation of one's own beliefs. In this process, the person trusts that their qualities of intelligence, honesty, and goodness will be widely recognized.

The permanent scanning of the lifestyles of others, either directly or indirectly, facilitates the establishment of reference points (including aspirations).[9] The importance of relative comparisons, whether cross-sectional or longitudinal, cannot be overemphasized. The former are usually interpersonal: an individual feels better off being paid more than their colleagues, despite low salaries, than receiving a high salary but in a work environment where the others are paid even more (Ariely and Kreisler, 2017: 202). Social comparisons over time are much more subtle, since they mix previous personal history and expectations, as reflected in the so-called tunnel effect (Hirschman and Rothschild, 1973). It turns out that people whose income is increasing become interested in the goods and services usually consumed by the members of the attained status level. Some consumption choices are directly copied while others are interpreted and partially modified. As time goes by, people even end up assimilating the aspirations of the reached social group. If, unfortunately, a setback occurs, people try to maintain as long as possible the previous lifestyle, including the level of consumption. Any relative downturn is experienced with bitterness. They are confident that they will fully recover the lost position once the upward trend returns, i.e., when the exit from the tunnel is in sight. Something similar happens in a traffic jam. When all lanes (in a given direction of travel) are full of stopped cars, the fact that the neighboring lane starts to move does not provoke the anger of the drivers still waiting. Satisfaction is their initial reaction: the fact that some people are moving forward is interpreted as a sign that everybody will soon be moving forward. Drivers only become angry when time passes and their lane remains stationary. With a steering wheel stroke, they will then try to pass into the lane that is moving. The longer they have been waiting the more aggressive this reaction will be. This vicissitude, easily transferable to the socioeconomic domain, underlines the strength of expectations and relative positions: discomfort at seeing some people improve their position with respect to ours is modulated by the speed at which progress is spreading. At the same time, stagnation, or even certain backwardness, does not provoke anger if it is a general problem (or at least affects the circle of acquaintances). Whatever it may be, people are reluctant to lose the socially recognized position attained. In short, comparisons over time extend across a range in which the lower boundary is occupied by the lifestyle already achieved and the upper one is open according to personal expectations.

An intricate aspect of social relations is their possible strategic character. A simple tale could illustrate this (from Gigerenzer, 1991: 21): in a small village, there was a man who was judged a fool because, when offered the choice between a €1 coin and a 10 cents coin, he always chose the latter. This fact ratified that he was an idiot. Really? Quite the contrary. If the story is carefully observed, it is easy to realize that the stupid choice has the effect of encouraging others to continue with the game. In this way, the sum collected will end up being greater than what would have been gained if the €1 coin had been chosen. The evidence that the man is smarter than he seems would have immediately stopped the offers. This story highlights the ability of people to anticipate the course of events and, therefore, to adjust their decisions promptly (more information in Chapter 5, section 5.1.5).

The previous paragraphs, despite their brevity, are enough to give an idea of the powerful influence of the social environment on decisions and, in general, on the behavior of people: when someone looks in a certain direction nobody pays attention, but if only a small group do so, many others stop to look at the same place; those who have fat friends are very likely to end up obese; the effort made by students depends a great deal on the effort made by their friends, and so on.[10]

As noted a few paragraphs ago, making economic decisions has another basic characteristic: the consequences are embedded in uncertainty. Obtaining precise information on future consequences is very difficult, if not impossible, regardless of the number of options involved. The suspicion that there are some still to be discovered further complicates the matter. Fortunately, the human mind has developed stratagems to even make decisions blindly. As is evident, people try to avoid uncertainty whenever possible. However, if this is not feasible, people decide by relying on mental levers that, pending further details, can be described as intuitions. They may also resort to emotions and, why not, to magic. Whatever the case, uncertainty does not paralyze decision-making. There is no doubt that one of the primary objectives of economic psychology has been to identify and analyze all of these stratagems.

The above considerations have left one question unanswered: what is irrationality? It can be defined as the actions that a subject undertakes against their physical integrity, psychological stability, or social identity. It includes all those decisions that threaten one's own safety (including health) and personal autonomy. Not infrequently, they also have detrimental effects on third parties. The reasons for such behavior can be an incorrect or inadequate understanding of the situation or being dominated by unbridled emotions. As illustrated by the antihero in Fyodor Dostoyevsky's great novel, *Notes from Underground*, irrational actions are perfectly possible if the people are immersed in situations such as the following:

- Strong anguish and other very intense emotional states push them to be reckless and to rush, while also feeding all kinds of obsessions (such as anorexia) and phobias (Elster, 2007: Chapter 3).
- In the same vein, factors such as excessive tiredness or strong pressure (stress) should also be mentioned (Wilkinson, 2008: 409, 423).
- Unhealthy (excess) self-esteem, or narcissism, which usually hides an insecure personality.
- Weakness of will as when, at the turn of the year, we make a firm resolution to give up smoking, a commitment that lasts only two minutes until someone offers us a cigarette; or when we break the promise to go on a diet just when the dessert menu appears; two common cases of lack of self-control.

- A serious socialization problem: since belonging and being recognized by others is a desire deeply rooted in the human condition, the feeling of being rejected can lead to self-destruction. People overwhelmed by this dynamic often make absurd or counterproductive decisions, which often aggravate their isolation.[11]

Among the economic behaviors that denote a lack of self-control, compulsive buying stands out. Everyone has bought something on impulse. There are incentives such as, for example, placing sweets when near the checkouts in supermarkets (Solomon, 2015: 80, 181). These are, however, one-off actions involving modestly priced things and, therefore, without remarkable consequences. It is only a sign of psychoticism if it is a continuous behavior that ends up involving significant economic amounts, an uncontrolled craving that reflects a pathological weakness of will. It seems that this problem only affects, and not persistently, 3–6% of the population (Szmigin and Piacentini, 2015: 23, 401).[12]

This book does not deal with psychotic behaviors identified after careful diagnosis and even less so pathological ones. It is always assumed that decisions are made by healthy people, with their undoubted virtues and inevitable defects, and with their moments of parsimony and urgency. People make mistakes (involuntary, due to overconfidence, etc.) and experience successes, sometimes the result of dedicated work, sometimes completely unforeseen. Humans, in short, are neither impeccably rational nor incorrigibly irrational, but rather reasonably rational (an idea suggested in Wilkinson and Klaes, 2012: 138). This conclusion, when studying economic decision processes, appeals to procedural control, correspondence to the context, the achievement of good enough satisfaction, and the possibility of error (Altman, 2017b: 5–6). These postulates constitute the backbone of this book.

Before closing this introduction, a minimal neuroscientific excursion is in order. As is evident, it is not a matter of explaining the physiological basis of the mental processes underlying decision-making, i.e., indicating the biochemical triggers and specific brain areas that are activated when making a choice. This is beyond the scope of this book and the expertise of its author. Even so, when dealing with decision-making processes, although many neuroscientific results could be taken into account, these pages only highlight those that provide conceptual precision, especially about memory or, better, the types of memory that the human mind harbors (as discussed in Chapter 4, section 4.1.4).

To begin with, rationality should not be confused with consciousness. The latter is an important property of the mind: emerging from a collection of interconnected brain states, consciousness enables the individual to become aware of their own and other people's reality. Or, in other words, it unfolds subjective life as a narrative that is singular to each individual but at the same time susceptible to being shared. No wonder the human species is a great confabulator: people tell stories all the time, to themselves and others. Stories are important for people to have the feeling that each one is a unit and that their life is under control. Although details remain to be elucidated, no one can avoid building and telling such stories. Perhaps this is because of the stakes involved: being aware of who we are includes identifying one's abilities and skills, recalling past experiences, formulating expectations for the future, detailing one's origins and social position, and recognizing the attributes of one's character, and so on. In a nutshell, to be conscious is to remember the past, live in the present and be able to think about the future (Bunge, 2010: Chapter 11). On the one hand, consciousness can operate at different levels: in a routine and repetitive task, it goes into autopilot mode; when faced with an intentional effort or the need to face an unforeseen situation, it focuses attention. In both cases, consciousness plays a key role in monitoring decisions: it controls mental and motor activity, which is a necessary condition to legitimize them, i.e. to associate them with one's own will.[13] On the other hand, although decision-making processes range from detailed forethought to impulsive action, they are never unconscious. They mobilize cognitive capacities that outline representations of reality based on emotions and accumulated experience, although the influence of repeated behaviors and habits can also be observed. However, instinctive reactions such as immediately pulling hands away from a hot surface, responding by bending the body to what may be an imminent impact after a sudden blow or shout, especially if it was behind one's back, or fleeing without thinking when one sees that others are also fleeing, are quite another matter. Body movements while sleeping are also unintentional (Reiss, 2013: 30).

The final aspect to retain is that the mind constantly scans the environment, sending to its conscious part the stimuli that affect the person. As an example, anyone focused on a conversation in the middle of a rather noisy environment (because of traffic, a crowd, etc.) instantly turns towards the place where someone has just called their name a few meters away (Nisbett, 2016: 76). This reaction also means that being awake is a requirement for being conscious (Morgado, 2019: 57–58). This waking state does not manage to cancel the subtle role of the non-conscious part of the mind, which gathers and submits to the permanent reconstruction of all kinds of appetites (some deeply rooted in the biological bases of human existence), desires and wishes, longings, emotions, etc. Whatever it may be, neuroscience is making progress in understanding *what* happens in general terms in the brain, that is, what interactions occur within and between the brain and the rest of the body, and the external world, although it has great difficulty in knowing *how* this happens. Although the brain processes the stimuli it receives through discharges of neurons arranged in complex networks, some innate and others developed throughout life, there are innumerable details that remain completely unknown (Cobb, 2020: xii, 321 and 354). There is no doubt that the intricate relationship between brain and mind and, more specifically, between consciousness and unconsciousness, are complex and exciting subjects, but are beyond the scope of research in economic psychology.

NOTES

1. In this book, priority is given to the term economic psychology, although without rejecting the behavioral economics one. As is well known, the latter concept identifies the research program on cognitive biases and the limitations of heuristics (see Chapter 2, section 2.2). However, there is also the research program on ecological rationality and several particular contributions at the frontier between economics and psychology (see Chapter 4, section 4.1, Chapter 5, section 5.1.6, and Chapter 6, section 6.2). As these approaches combine cognitive and psychosocial elements, they have a broader scope. Consequently, the term economic psychology encompasses the term behavioral economics.
2. The role of the natural environment should not be underestimated. Living near the Arctic Circle is not the same as living in the Mediterranean basin or the depths of the equatorial rainforest. For example, the existence in temperate climates of several weeks of low temperatures greatly reduces the number of pathogens in the environment, which is good for human proliferation, but at the same time makes shelter conditions more difficult and requires food storage. On these pages, the influence of climate and other natural factors, which are very important from the point of view of human evolution, are left aside.
3. Not to mention physical, chemical, and biological constraints: no one can stop time, foresee the future in detail or make personal plans for the 25th century.
4. It should be emphasized that both approaches to rationality are primarily practical. There is also a more conceptual outlook: rationality can be understood as the predisposition to consider arguments from different sources and the eagerness to learn from experience, as well as the ability to integrate all into daily life. Practical and conceptual approaches complement each other.
5. The term can be loosely understood as the general pattern in which an individual allocates their time and resources (cognitive, economic) (Solomon, 2015: 477). It encompasses habits and beliefs. The former are the sum of everyday customs (including ritualized manifestations such as outward appearance), work routines, and preferences (especially in consumption). The latter are particular visions of the world (see Chapter 4). All these give rise to relatively stable behaviors and are made up of similar acts repeated over and over again. Lifestyles and their components are learned.
6. Social psychology distinguishes between the group to which one belongs according to objective criteria, an external designation or social consensus, and the aspirational reference group. The former, as just suggested, is a source of conformism and the latter a source of arousal (Hogg and Vaughan, 2014: 237).
7. Certain legal norms can be derived from social norms. For example, the compulsory wearing of helmets. Turning off the cell phone seems to follow the same path.

8. Modern societies gather huge volumes of population. As anonymity prevails, these societies have a comparatively greater relaxation in following such norms. This favors creativity and the expression of people's talents (Eibl-Eibesfeldt, 2012: 175 and 618–619).

9. It should be pointed out that aspirations are not illusory desires or dreams. As a general rule, they are a modest improvement concerning the daily situation, just a step ahead of one's own reality. Aspirations change depending on what is observed (in relatives, neighbors, etc.) and on recent experiences of successes (or failures). Achieving them encourages people to set more ambitious ones, while failure often does not imply their abandonment. As long as the chances of success seem to outweigh the chances of failure, people will persist with extra efforts if necessary. Abandonment comes only after repeated frustrations.

10. Susceptibility to the social environment can itself be a business. In Cialdini (2007: 138), it is explained that, around 1820, the company *L'Assurance des Succés Dramatiques* was created. It aimed to guarantee the success of theatrical performances. The firm paid spectators to start the applause and thus encourage the rest of the hall. It also offered different rates to the show's sponsors according to the duration of the ovation, the addition of "bravo," standing up and shouting in euphoria, and so on.

11. As can be seen, the so-called cognitive errors (see below) have not been included among the symptoms of irrationality (cf. Ariely, 2009: xvii–xix, Elster, 2010: 19–20 and 259). As explained throughout the text, many of these misconceptions are not symptoms of irrationality, while others result from the desire to confuse or mislead people.

12. Despite being a small fraction, this has not prevented some pharmaceutical companies from proposing drugs to treat this syndrome. The attempt to correct the manifestations of irrationality can also be a business model.

13. Will is not always free, nor do people act according to their own judgment. People may be pushed to make choices under various constraints (Bunge, 2010: Chapter 11, section 11.9).

2. Brief history of the relationship between economics and psychology

Throughout the history of economic thought, many authors have made contributions with psychosocial aspects. To collect them exhaustively would require an entire book, and therefore only the key facts of the relationship between economics and psychology will be described here. This journey spans from the last third of the 18th century to the present day. Three stages can be distinguished (adaptation of Skořepa, 2011: 58–71):

- From the beginning of the 19th century up to the interwar period, many researchers worked on the subjective approach to the value of commodities. Although there were precedents dating back to the previous century, the psychophysical research of the last third of the 19th century was an important source of inspiration for this line of work. For example, this influence was behind the search for a cardinal measure of utility. Although it was later harshly rejected due to its immature character, the effort made by the first marginalists to approach the psychology of their time should be recognized, although it contained just a handful of precarious knowledge. These economists also took up the postulates of the probability theory developed since the Enlightenment.
- The axiomatic orientation triumphed in the middle decades of the 20th century, years of strong expansion of economic analysis, both in terms of the growth of academic activity and the number of researchers. Agents endowed with unlimited rationality became the protagonists of choice models which, embedded in strong normative principles, explicitly banished any relationship with the other social sciences, especially psychology and sociology. This discourse, animated by a strong desire for singularity barely broken by borrowing certain mathematical tools, ended up being the reference point for many decision analysts. Thus a field of study emerged that had blurred boundaries and in which mainly economists and engineers coexisted. The key work of these years was *The Theory of Games and Economic Behavior* (1944), a book written by mathematicians John von Neumann (1903–1957) and Oskar Morgenstern (1902–1977). Its content notably influenced strategic studies and military planning and, to a lesser extent, decision analysis and economic theory.

• In the mid 1950s, the situation began to change with the important contributions of the unclassifiable Herbert A. Simon (1916–2001) and the publication of works by psychologist Ward Edwards (1927–2005). From the late 1970s onwards, a growing group of researchers consolidated and expanded the study of decision-making under real-life conditions. As a result, although the axiomatic approach is still dominant, it is indisputable that the years between the 20th and 21st centuries show signs of a certain reconnection between economics and psychology. This rapprochement takes the form of contributions that are still quite local, which can either extend and create a solid bridge between the two disciplines, or fail in the attempt to break the academic inertia that keeps them apart. All this takes place in a context in which neuroscience is advancing at full speed. The timid renaissance of economic psychology presents, however, a complex landscape: it unfolds in two research programs, one known as "heuristics and biases" and the other as "fast-and-frugal heuristics." Although the labels that identify them are somewhat confusing and their conclusions are sometimes indistinguishable, their important theoretical and praxeological differences weigh more heavily. Their postulates are opposed on many fundamental questions.

This chapter briefly reviews the above stages with a reference to the main authors and hypotheses. This is an essential step in an introductory text on economic psychology.

2.1   PRECEDENTS

To recover a couple of ideas from Adam Smith (1723–1790) is the best way to start a history of the relationship between economics and psychology. The first one states the intricate nature of human relationships, a mixture of egoism and empathy. While in his work *An Inquiry into the Nature and Causes of the Wealth of Nations* he argued that,

> ... it is not from the benevolence of the butcher, the brewer, or the baker, that we expect our dinner, but from their regard to their own interest. We address ourselves, not to their humanity but of their self-love, and never talk to them of our necessities but of their advantages ... (Smith, 1981: 26–27),

in his other book, *The Theory of Moral Sentiments*, he wrote:

> How selfish soever man may be supposed, there are evidently some principles in his nature, which interest him in the fortune of others, and render their happiness necessary to him, though he derives nothing from it except the pleasure of seeing it. (Smith, 1994: 9)

This represents a fascinating duality between competition and cooperation that, unfortunately, was forgotten for decades and decades. It is only a few years since it has once again been retrieved. Smith's second idea was to associate the value of commodities with their capacity to satisfy human needs. This property, called utility, is present from the ingestion of food and water to sustain the biochemical cycles of life, to the purchase and display of gold jewelry, precious stones, and diamonds. In the latter case, however, their high values do not come from functionality, but from their extraordinary rarity, which awakens a powerful desire for elitist exhibition (Dmitriev, 1968: 214). The concept of value as subjective appreciation had already been advanced some years before Smith by Étienne Bonnot de Condillac (1714–1780) and Ferdinando Galiani (1728–1787), authors who distinguished between the level of satisfaction obtained by meeting a specific need linked to a given social and historical framework, and how the level of utility evolves when it is pursued continuously (Dmitriev, 1968: 215–216). In both cases, the greater the sensation of need (a subjective urgency, not always physiological), the more the good that satisfies it is appreciated and, hence, the more economic value it deserves.

In the 18th and 19th centuries, the main interest of economic commentators was the identification of the driver, or the engine, of the economic changes that were taking place in the most dynamic countries of Europe, with the United Kingdom at the forefront. The spotlight was placed on local or regional entrepreneurs striving to make a profit in a remarkably open competitive environment. This reality was interpreted as a ruthless race in which cunning, intuition, or strategic calculation were the key winning tools. The ambition of these pioneers was immediately considered the most genuine depiction of human behavior. Although some authors disagreed, most thinkers accepted the postulate that the pursuit of one's own interests is the most powerful force that has ever existed for social and economic transformation (Hunt, 1992: 153–157; Arnsperger and van Parijs, 2000: 29–30). This epic vision of individuality as a factor of social rupture/renewal was mixed with the well-known principle of utilitarian philosophy: the main motivation of human beings is to enjoy pleasures and obtain an advantageous position while avoiding falling into misfortune, calamity, or unhappiness.

Utilitarianism was a kind of social reform program initiated by Jeremy Bentham (1748–1832), an author known above all for his book *An Introduction to the Principles of Morals and Legislation* (1780).[1] In this work it is argued that the purpose of decision-making, both in personal life and especially in public affairs, is to bring maximum happiness to all people, or the greatest possible number. From a moral point of view, utilitarianism valued human actions in terms of whether they had good consequences, equated with pleasure, or a state of mind in which happiness prevails over pain, or whether they unfortunately had harmful effects. Hedonistic calculus, therefore, emerges as the most suitable tool to drive behavior: people must pursue pleasure (or reward) and avoid pain (or loss). Since everyone pursues maximum happiness, legal reforms and, in general, social policies have to be satisfactory for the greatest number, which presupposes that all preferences are legitimate and comparable. Policymakers have to carefully evaluate the pros and cons of decisions, aggregating and comparing happiness and pain, which assumes that there is a universal unit of measurement of utility. In practice, utilitarianism became a doctrine that proposed paternalistic social policies, i.e., dressed in indulgence (Reichlin, 2013: 7–9; Sandel, 2009: Chapter 2; and Aronson, 2008: 121).

Only five years elapsed between Bentham's aforementioned work and the demolishing critique of utilitarian morality by Immanuel Kant (1724–1804) in the book *Groundwork for the Metaphysics of Morals*. Although the blow was fatal, the utilitarian doctrine would survive in social sciences such as economics and political theory, areas of knowledge in which decision-making processes have always received exceptional attention (see Kant, 2018: xxi–xxiii, 10–16, and 43; Sandel, 2009: Chapter 5).

In the book *On Liberty*, published in 1859 by John Stuart Mill, the utilitarian corpus would adopt the individual dimension that Bentham ignored (Sandel, 2009: Chapter 2). According to Mill, the hedonistic calculus is the most appropriate tool for achieving maximum *individual* utility. The application of this criterion presupposes that the individual can choose (or do) whatever she wishes (of course, without harming others either immediately or in the long run). Only people know how to formulate and evaluate what is best for them. However, this elitist postulate forgets that experiences are always contingent, that is, framed by numerous individual, social and cultural factors. For example, a few centuries ago the way of accumulating utility (whether measured in terms of the emotional intensity experienced or, as eventually prevailed, in simple monetary values) was excelling in riding and fighting on horseback, key skills for social success, while today it is sportsmen who kick or bounce a ball who obtain a large amount of utility. These factors can change even within a human lifetime.

The hedonistic individual imperative of utilitarian philosophy faded over the years (only traces remained behind the later aseptic definitions of utility and preference), but it paved the way for considering self-interest as the main driver of human behavior. The weak foundation, whether philosophical or psychological, of hedonistic calculus, would be obviated: the only important thing is that it is the criterion for bringing people closer to the best possible outcome, i.e., to achieve the best (economic) result.

More focused on economic discourse, Jean Baptiste Say (1767–1832) based the relative price of goods on their value of use. Therefore, enterprises create utility. Entrepreneurs make this possible due to their frugality: investments are nothing more than consumption that has been forgone and, consequently, profits are the corresponding compensation (Hunt, 1992: 165). Nassau Senior (1790–1864) should also be mentioned in this vein. This economist of conservative ideas was convinced that selfishness is the ultimate explanation of human behavior. He added, on the one hand, that human cravings have no limit. He argued that humans never have enough. People are never satisfied (Hunt, 1992: 169–185). On the other hand, he considered that the comparison of the utility perceived by different people is meaningless since the subjective experience of desires is not the same for everyone. This postulate corrected a paradox: by arguing that extra utility decreases as the point of satiety approaches, people with fewer resources, by the simple fact of consuming fewer units of the different goods, would enjoy the greatest increase in satisfaction. By extension, widespread frugality would result in a happier society. The insistence on the singularity of each consumption experience neutralized this curious bottom-up egalitarian bias of utility theory (Robinson, 1962: Chapter 3, section 3.4, Reichlin, 2013: 9). Along with the notion that abstinence is the origin of capital and its profitability, Senior added that the instinctive pursuit of profit is a basic constituent of one's self-esteem. Even vanity could be useful, provided it takes root in fertile soil. Finally, some ideas of Claude Frédéric Bastiat (1801–1850) can be mentioned. He was a great advocate of initiative and private property. These are two requisites for exchange between equals, i.e., that which is beneficial to all parties. He also shared the notion that desires are the basis of human behavior. Unfortunately, they are insatiable so they surpass the means to be satisfied (Hunt, 1992: 218–220).

All these postulates were intended to reflect the hard task that awaited the new entrepreneurs. Given that growing a business project is not easy, frugality (coming from resisting the temptation of immediacy) and a proven capacity for leadership and risk-taking, emerge as the key factors for success. These ideas were attractive to the economic pioneers who, from the first third of the 18th century in Atlantic Europe, were trying to carve out a social and economic niche for themselves among the landed gentry and the great merchants. It is worth remembering that this century witnessed spectacular speculative bubbles, and the subsequent collapse, of the securities of colonial companies (such as the British South Sea Company) and associated banks (such as the French Banque Royale). These projects were sponsored by the highest spheres of power and aimed at quick and easy profits (Goetzmann, 2017: 320–381). As a reaction to this deplorable state of affairs, the aforementioned authors praised the bottom-up initiative and the individual accumulation of capital in a highly competitive environment.

Concerning the above-mentioned incipient proposals of hedonistic calculation, it is now known that, among the functions of the brain, there is the control of actions addressed to the maintenance of the internal stability (homeostasis) of the organs and physiological systems of the body. This is an essential condition for performing their functions without problems. The maintenance of these internal balances, coupled with the preservation of cognitive abilities, requires sleep and the regular intake of water and food. As long as the vegetative nervous network shows no signs of problems, individuals perceive pleasant physical well-being, a common sensation in young people. Seen from an evolutionary perspective, this enjoyment encourages people to take the appropriate conscious actions to underpin homeostasis. Thus, the pleasure of drinking or eating is like a catalyst for not neglecting to attend to these basic needs. Therefore, pleasure has a survival value. However, this sensation is so powerful that it can become autonomous: one ends up drinking or eating not out of real need but for the pleasure they provoke (Morgado, 2019: 17–20). This pursuit of pleasure for pleasure's sake can acquire the character of addiction, that is, an impulse that is never satiated. Based on this knowledge, it can be concluded that utilitarianism considered the pursuit of profit as a form of pleasure and, consequently, as the most effective incentive to stem ingenuity and, hence, to win in the competitive struggle. The quest for economic enrichment was thus placed at the core of human nature (read psychology). It was a proclamation in favor of the self-made *homme entrepreneur* which anticipated the well-known *homo œconomicus*.[2] Its survival for almost two centuries leads us to suspect that it is inherent in the discourse prone to capitalist accumulation (Arnsperger and van Parijs, 2000: Chapter II, sections II.1–II.4, Mirowski, 2013: 75–77).

Some years later, authors such as John Stanley Jevons (1835–1882) or Edgeworth would mix the postulates of utilitarian philosophy with the results of psychophysics, a kind of pioneering research in experimental psychology. Two results attracted their attention:

- The so-called law of (Gustav Theodor) Feschner (1801–1887) and (Ernst Heinrich) Weber (1795–1878), was initially proposed in 1860. These authors considered that mental phenomena can be quantified from the perceived sensation of certain sensory stimuli. Specifically, they concluded that the perception of stimuli of increasing intensity is gradually decreasing. For example, if 25 kilograms are being carried and another kilogram is added, the sensation of carrying a larger weight is less than if only five kilograms were being carried initially (Heukelom, 2014: 51). A trivial case linked to consumption may be the flood of intense and pleasurable sensations unleashed by the first sip of exquisite wine, subsequent sips of which always have a much more modest gustatory impact.
- Introspection is the most suitable source of access to subjective experiences, as explained by the psychologist Wilhelm Wundt (1832–1920) in a book published in 1874. This postulate was pleasing to the ears of

utilitarian authors since it allowed the interpretation of utility as a type of intimate satisfaction, despite its vagueness.

The Weber-Fechner "law" seemed to provide empirical support for the principle of diminishing marginal utility associated with the consumption of goods and services. Let us, therefore, refer to Figure 2.1 concerning the hypothetical relationship between utility and the intensity of the stimulus (Dmitriev, 1968: 244): when the latter is minuscule, there is no reaction; the stimulus must exceed a certain threshold to cause positive utility; as its intensity increases, utility reaches a maximum and then begins to fall; and, for very strong stimuli, the sensation becomes annoying (or negative utility). This evolution opens the door to plotting a marginal utility curve which, after the initial zero values, presents increasing positive, then progressively decreasing, and finally negative values.

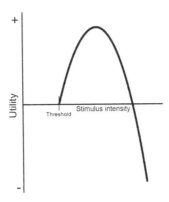

Figure 2.1   Total utility and stimulus intensity

The interpretation of Figure 2.1 poses, however, some problems (Dmitriev, 1968: 239–240):

- The psychophysical "law" relates objective stimuli (lightness, weight, density, etc.) above a certain threshold to the factual expression of psychological sensations, while the utility is a completely subjective variable.
- At best, this figure could reflect the immediate and direct impact of the consumption of tangible goods and personal services on the physical state of people. Utility theory assumes, however, that the consumption of all kinds of aesthetic, moral, and so on contents also brings satisfaction.

- There is no reason why the (total and marginal) utility curves should be continuous.
- While it seems plausible that there is a finite quantity of material goods at which marginal utility is canceled out, the possibility of negative values causes perplexity: is the analysis heading towards the swampy terrain of pathological behavior?

These observations did not dissuade economists from going much further: they did not hesitate to try to quantify utility, since it is an essential step in establishing the economic value (and hence prices) of commodities.

Jevons defined utility from a real-time hedonistic perspective: it is the intrinsic property of goods that reveals the pleasure experienced during the act of consumption (Georgescu-Roegen, 1977: 562). The utility is, therefore, the lever that makes it possible to express the value of use quantitatively. Utility sustains, exclusively and exhaustively, the theory of value, since buying and selling operations are nothing but comparisons of it. Furthermore, as expected, the pursuit of a maximum individual utility arises as the economic motivation par excellence. In this process, a key element is the utility coming from the last unit consumed, which is directly linked to prices. The golden rule of rational economic calculation thus emerges: maximum utility is obtained when the ratio of marginal utilities and prices coincides. In this vein and following Bentham, Edgeworth, while ratifying that utility is good in itself, although humans differ in the way they experience it, proposed the "hedon" or the minimum unit of perceptible pleasure, a sensation assimilated to utility (Robinson, 1962: Chapter 3, section 3.1, Barbé, 2006: 182, Reichlin, 2013: 159). At this point, not denying reasons for mathematical tractability, he also added the assumption that the utilities coming from different goods are commensurable and, hence, compensable by each other (Berg and Gigerenzer, 2010: 14). In other words, given a vector $(x_1, x_2, ..., x_n)$ which represents quantities of goods, for any pair of these goods k and j, $k \neq j$, in the event of an amount of decrease of the jth commodity, there is an additional quantity of the kth one which compensates for the lost utility. This assumption implies that none of the goods, or the attributes that identify them, dominates the rest: for instance, when choosing an apartment the fact that it has one less room may be perfectly compensated for by having a bus stop nearby.[3] Edgeworth was confident that the conceptual basis he proposed would propel the progressive unfolding of a deep, solid and articulated theoretical framework on economic activity. It would represent an evolution in the likeness of the then reference science, physics. This pretension was, however, unfocused and excessive (see Mirowski, 1989; Roncaglia, 2005: Chapter 10, section 10.4). Beyond the problem of empirically substantiating cardinal utility, especially concerning qualitative variables, a minimum inspection of the trade-off assumption reveals another serious problem: as the number of objects and attributes increases, so does the number of two-by-two comparisons. To undertake this process, the individual must have time and great cognitive capacities. In particular, for n options each with k attributes, exhausting all possible two-by-two comparisons, a necessary condition to achieve maximum utility, must be carried out,

$$\frac{nk(n-1)}{2}$$

comparisons. For example, for modest $n = 5$ and $k = 5$, there are 50 comparisons. A great deal of will, dedication, and time will be necessary.

It is also worth mentioning Carl Menger (1840–1921) for having insisted on including needs in the analysis of people's economic behavior. Inspired by the postulate of diminishing marginal utility, he argued that people satisfy their needs following a decreasing order of importance. He illustrated this with the case of a peasant living in an isolated property who satisfies his needs starting with the most basic (food) and then moving on to satisfy the secondary and successive needs, provided that the harvested amount allows it. Unfortunately, the hierarchy of needs is imprecisely laid out (it lacks a clear-cut structure), although it is not amorphous. In fact, rather than discussing how needs are ordered (whether as a pyramid or a branched structure), what is critical is to scrutinize their properties (see Georgescu-Roegen, 1977: 584–585, Lavoie, 1992: 61–85, and Doyal and Gough, 1991). Irreducibility is one of the most relevant: jewelry is not a substitute for shelter or, more generally, needs are not interchangeable. This postulate, which should have occupied a central place in the theory of consumer choice, was displaced by the indifference one associated with a weighting and adding algorithm[4] (see below).

Despite the thousand and one objections that can be made to the theory of utility, it cannot be denied that drawing inspiration from the postulates of psychophysics was reasoning in the right direction. In time, if the analysts had persisted in following the results of cognitive and social psychological research, it might have been possible to build a solid and contrasting theory of economic behavior. Unfortunately, the bridges between economic theory and psychology were never built. The subjective theory of value was developed not to deepen the analysis of decision-making processes and their psychosocial aspects, but as a reaction to the postulates of classical political economy after the turn that Karl Marx (1818–1883) gave to the labor theory of value initiated by Adam Smith and developed by David Ricardo (1777–1823). This happened, moreover, at a historical stage in which the class conflict was growing, entering an acute phase between the Commune of Paris (1871) and World War I. All this upset, to put it euphemistically, the small academic community and, by extension, the rest of the elites of 19th-century society. Therefore, priority was given to a foundation of the theory of value that would downplay the distributive conflict and emphasize the role of individual initiative in economic prosperity.

The last third of the 19th century witnessed the gradual emergence of the large corporation. Decision-making was left in the hands of waged managers, while the pioneering entrepreneurs, or their now-wealthy heirs, adopted a lifestyle reminiscent of that of the old land rentiers. The heroic discourse, a mixture of intuition and determination, was being left behind. It was argued that, in an oligopolistic environment, the enormous amount of resources that projects require and the caution with which response times must be adjusted, required, rather than sagacious managers, those who were capable of systematically and exhaustively evaluating the different options. The study of the peculiarities of human behavior was losing interest in the face of the organizational challenges posed by the bureaucratic and technocratic complexity of large companies. Rather than trying to imitate the unique cognitive capacities and social skills of unrepeatable people, it pointed toward the convenience of having universal rules to guide, and exhaustive protocols to implement, with parsimony, decision-making processes. Moreover, it should not be forgotten that the professionals in charge of management were responsible in the eyes of the owners. Therefore, to prevent actions that could be considered negligent, these managers regarded as necessary, though not sufficient, the existence of standardized and rigorous management procedures. Indeed, to comply with these rules would act as a safeguard in case of failed decisions. As for the rest of the (administrative) staff, strict assignment of tasks coupled with efficient methods of working (writing and calculating),[5] made formal educational qualifications a basic hiring requirement.

In this new context, economic analysis ended up forgetting psychophysical ideas. Despite the fact that the proposed models became resistant to empirical tests, at the same time they strove to incorporate all kinds of mathematical tools (from simple order relations to complex functional forms). Over the years this methodological mix has characterized the development of the subjective theory of value. An important step along these lines was taken by Walras who, by linking the amount of utility attained by people only to the number of goods consumed, discarded any possible satisfaction obtained from other sources. Under this assumption, the motivations and aspirations of people, two key elements subject to personal idiosyncrasies and social influences, became irrelevant. This postulate also overlooked human empathy,[6] as well as the hierarchy of needs. It is not surprising that money ended up being considered a proxy measure of utility: satisfaction is proportional to the amount of money people are willing to pay to obtain it (Georgescu-Roegen, 1977: 570, 585; Grall, 2003: 88–95). Marshall too worked to disconnect utility from any psychological reference: in his interpretation, it was a manifestation of the inscrutable force of a non-specific incitement that pushes people to acquire goods and services. Utility was loosely defined as a subjective but not fully psychological fact. Utility became an abstract, universal and one-dimensional magnitude arising from the non-quantifiable, only orderable, comparison of mere sensations perceived in the consumption processes. The circularity of the argument would not be perceived as an obstacle to the foundation of the exchange value (Robinson, 1962: Chapter 3, section 3.1; Roncaglia, 2005: Chapter 10, section 10.2).[7]

As mentioned, the cardinal measure of utility, a key element of the first marginalist theory, was replaced with the ordinality postulate: although it is not possible to discern the precise magnitude of utility, it is plausible to know which good provides more (or less) of it than another. Unfortunately, ordinality is also a weak postulate. No one has ever been able to design a graduated and universal "hedometer," similar to the Richter scale for comparing earthquake intensities and damages. It is not surprising that, on the one hand, ordinality came to be seen as a strictly individual matter and that, on the other hand, the concept ultimately faded behind that of preferences.

Perhaps the most important author in the first stage of the history of the relationship between economics and psychology is Vilfredo Pareto (1848–1923). Although he held both psychology and sociology in high esteem, he defined economics as the science of optimization, which distanced it from the rest of the social sciences. Among the methodological and theoretical features of his proposal, the following should be highlighted (adapted from Bruni and Sugden, 2007; Berg and Gigerenzer, 2010: 29; and Reichlin, 2013: 160):

- There is no room for interdisciplinarity: each science has to develop its conceptual tools. The quest for inspiration never justifies borrowing concepts from other disciplines and, even less, sharing research fields between them.
- The economic analysis aims to identify the logical coherence between actions and their drivers, an indispensable step for optimal choice. Even so, understanding the decision-making process as a logical matter does not deny the role of learning. Indeed, it must be borne in mind that many economic decisions are repeated. Despite Pareto's nuance, the position of Knut Wicksell (1851–1926) eventually prevailed at this point: any possible psychosocial clue, however small it might be, should be banished from the analysis.
- Preferences are defined as subjective feelings that, when compared, generate rankings. Since the latter stem from rational calculations, they are not necessarily hedonistic. He suggested representing such orderings by

indifference curves (Georgescu-Roegen, 1977: 562, 577; Roncaglia, 2005: Chapter 12, section 12.3).[8]

In the 1920s and 1930s, disregarding the tendency of economic theory to dispense with empirical testing, the psychologist Louis Leon Thurstone (1887–1955) observed how people choose between sets of goods presented two by two. His goal was to identify indifference curves. Combining, for example, shoes and hats, the experimenter applied a compensatory algorithm to detect the indifference between quantities of one good and the other. Unfortunately, the results were disappointing (Edwards, 1954: 384–387; Lenfant, 2012: 127–130; Heukelom, 2014: 13–17). In 1942, Allen Wallis (1912–1988) and Milton Friedman (1912–2006) would disqualify this research because "it is probably not possible to design a satisfactory experiment for deriving indifference curves from economic stimuli applied to human beings" (words of Wallis and Friedman mentioned in Lenfant, 2012: 139). According to them, such controlled experiments do not correctly reflect the actual conditions under which people make choices. For example, they ignore constraints and many other determinants. Incidentally, this criticism highlights the illusory nature of the indifference curve: it is a simple characterization of what is (presumably) directly observed in everyday life, evidence that requires no further scrutiny. However, if it is not testable, the concept will likely end up in the bin of fiction. These authors should not have closed the door to postulating it as a characteristic curve of the observed relationship between variables, in imitation of what is usual in the natural sciences and technical disciplines. This would have turned the indifference curve into an empirical basis for the formulation of hypotheses. For this reason, his expertise aside, Thurstone was doing what had to be done. Strictly speaking, the lack of satisfactory results should have pushed theorists to refine their experiments and, if necessary, rethink the concept of indifference. Thurstone's attempts were quickly forgotten.[9]

The second stage indicated at the beginning of this chapter began with the diffusion of the revealed preference model. Since the late 1930s, the concepts of utility and preferences lost any psychological trace and, consequently, became mere labels. Even though both continued to be very present in economic theory, from the perspective of these pages the use of these concepts became common rhetoric. It is no surprise that the revealed preference approach considered the nature and subjective content of preferences as analytically irrelevant: only what is observed matters, i.e., the choice made. The existence of preferences is ephemeral: their life begins and ends at the very moment they are revealed. They are nothing more than what people choose. This decision only concerns them. It is not denied that psychology may be interested in knowing why a person has chosen what she has chosen, but this is outside the field of economic theory, now qualified as pure. The processes of formation and modification of preferences are not an economic matter. However, marketing, one of the branches of the vast tree of economic knowledge, has never ceased to ask questions in this respect, with undoubted success (Solomon, 2015: 69).

The revealed preference approach has been widely criticized. Without claiming to be exhaustive, the following points should be highlighted (from Hausman, 2012: 24–27 and Reiss, 2013: 34):

- It is not uncommon for individuals to choose not to choose. An experiment consisted of observing consumer behavior at a grocery store: one week six different varieties of jams were offered while another week there were 24. The result was that people browsed more in the latter case, but bought more in the former (reported in Nisbett, 2016: 133). In general, an offer is more eye-catching the more options it contains. Still, as the variety increases, the more difficult it is to know which one to choose (assuming that the consumer does not know exactly what she is looking for). In the end, the profusion of variants can lead consumers to buy nothing. This effect is called choice overload. Although consumers may frown upon a poor assortment, they are overwhelmed by a large number of options. This circumstance suggests that the anticipation of possible regret powerfully affects consumer decisions (Gigerenzer, 2014: 55). Since the revealed preference model disregards underlying appetites, non-choice can only be attributed to a lack of preferences, which is a ridiculous diagnosis.[10]
- Preferences are not unrelated to beliefs (see Chapter 5). At the end of the play, Romeo takes his own life believing that Juliet is dead when, in fact, she is only fast asleep. This is a drastic decision since, with Juliet being dead, the preferred option of running away with her is no longer possible. However, from the revealed preference approach, it must be concluded that Romeo prefers death since this is what he has chosen. This is an absurd interpretation of having ignored that choices do not necessarily reveal preferences. It is not difficult to find examples in which, given people's attitudes,[11] it can be suspected that their preferences have been upset: do children want to go to school day after day? Has someone who smokes suddenly changed their preferences when wanting to give up?
- People interact strategically. Making decisions in a social environment usually implies that the others' preferences (in the form of intentions) should be anticipated assuming that, in turn, these people are also trying to forecast ours. This implies a complex interconnection of beliefs that gives rise to intricate decision-making processes (Schelling, 2006a, Hausman, 2012: 30). On having ignored the autonomous existence of preferences, the revealed preference model does not capture any of this. For example,

it cannot address the behavior of stock speculators, since they are always alert to what appear to be the decisions of others.

For years, this approach caused the study of preferences to remain on standby. Moreover, the next step was to consider preferences as immanent[12] and immutable. The successive bricks of the prodigious and isolated building of a self-contained economic theory were thus being laid (Ekeland and Elster, 2011: 5–19). This project would reach its zenith in the 1940s and 1950s with the work of authors such as, for example, John Hicks (1904–1989), Roy G. D. Allen (1906–1983) or Paul A. Samuelson (1915–2009), and, for the specific effort he devoted to it, John Harsanyi (1920–2000).

The book by von Neumann and Morgenstern (1953: 24–29) contained and discussed an initial list of the axioms of rational choice. This set of principles made it feasible to formalize, and represent graphically, in a very rigorous manner, the individual choices according to the utility frame. However, the book neither intended to model economic behavior,[13] nor aspired to be an instruction booklet, i.e., specifying how to undertake an individual action to obtain optimal results. The book was even ambiguous concerning a normative interpretation of the axioms (Gigerenzer, 2021: 3548). Maybe for these reasons, Leonard "Jimmie" Savage (1917–1971) completed and systematized the formal-logical requirements that must be met by decisions for the maximization of expected utility.[14] This author interpreted the axioms as the requirements that, in a premeditated effort, have to comply with preferences to perfectly attain the pursued objectives (Heukelom, 2014: 20–23). Whatever their content, preferences lead to an optimal result if they fulfill, among others, the following principles (Wilkinson, 2008: 87; Hausman, 2012: 13–14, 19):

- Completeness: for any x, y of a given set of options, people manifest that $x > y$, or $y > x$, or that they are indifferent.[15]
- Transitivity: for any x, y and z of a given set of alternatives, if $x > y$ and $y > z$, then, $x > z$. The principle also holds in the case of weak preference ($\geqslant$) and indifference.
- Context independence: if for an individual $x > y$, this preference holds in any situation.
- The factor determining the choice: the choice always falls on the affordable option that most strongly satisfies the preference.

Failure to comply with the completeness condition means that individuals are not able to make comparisons, which prevents them from reaching any maximum of utility. Transitivity guarantees the coherence of the evaluation process. The third axiom ensures that the agent remains firm in their choices in any situation and context. Finally, the principle of determination implies not choosing x when option y can be chosen, which, all things considered, is undoubtedly better. These axioms are the most characteristic of perfect (or unlimited) rationality, that is, they identify minds whose decision-related judgments are logically coherent. The supreme role given to this coherence gives ground to think that rationality is either perfect or it is not: there is no room for debate, no room for nuances. What is not completely rational is irrational. Therefore, to prevent greater evils, it is assumed that people behave as if they were rational (see below). This assumption allows for the rapid deduction of all kinds of propositions that, when deemed appropriate, certain empirical approaches will validate (see below). This rigidity sends any version of rationality that is inevitably less strict to the wastebasket. Such versions are considered ambiguous, naive, or tendentious (Berg et al., 2008, Arkes et al., 2016).

The axiomatic effort made by von Neumann and Morgenstern was an improvement to the decision criterion of mathematical expectation, the origin of which dates back to the 17th century. It turns out that, in the case of simple lotteries in which money can be won according to certain probabilities, the expected value (EV) of gains is given by the expression

$$EV = \sum_{i=1}^{n} p_i \cdot x_i$$

where p_i is the probability of each outcome x_i, and $i = (1, 2, ..., n)$. This model soon ran into the St. Petersburg paradox. To overcome this hurdle, Daniel Bernoulli (1700–1782),[16] partially inspired by Gabriel Cramer (1704–1752), modified the format in 1731 to the form,

$$U(A) = \sum_{i=1}^{n} p_i u(x_i)$$

In general, on the one hand, there is a function $U(\cdot)$ that transforms a set of possible consequences, x_i, into utility levels, $u(x_i)$. The latter evokes the degree to which the consequences are desirable for a given person. Therefore, this function reflects a specific subjective disposition that can be expressed through suitable mathematical functions, i.e., designed to show a certain eagerness to obtain utility.[17] On the other hand, probabilities represent states of the world. If it is not possible to determine them objectively, they can be established subjectively. In this latter case, it is assumed that it reflects the individual's beliefs about such states. Probabilities (or beliefs) about states of the world are the most flexible factor of the model, given that preferences are given and that the goal of utility maximization is out of the question.

The work of von Neumann and Morgenstern, characterized by a strong formalist orientation and inspired by the metaphor that economic decisions are a kind of gamble (Lane et al., 1996: 46), was enthusiastically received by many economists. The main reason was the consequentialism it conveyed, that is, the analytical primacy was placed in the decisions' outcome. This issue was undoubtedly a priority in the sphere of economic management (Hausman, 2012: 44–45). However, while convergence between the subjective conception of value and decision analysis was widely welcomed, from the 1950s onwards three positions could be distinguished (Heukelom, 2014: Chapter 2):

- Savage's followers considered the axioms as an approximation to the behavior of people, albeit an idealized one. Since they were not exactly a description, these principles did not have to be empirically contrasted. Their validity was confined to and confirmed by the fulfillment of the predictions held up by them (a thesis advanced by Friedman). This is a criterion that requires that preferences remain stable, at least in the short run. On the one hand, this enables the labeling of the cases of non-compliance as irrational and, on the other hand, it restrains the analysis from entering the realm of psychology. However, it runs up against a serious methodological problem: everyone has to agree that the events that have occurred either confirm the prediction, or do not. Setting aside simple lab experiences, this is an exceptional situation: normally, social and economic facts are interpreted in very different and often opposing ways. There is also the temptation to twist the argument until what has happened fits, or at least appears to conform to the prediction. Therefore, establishing the success of the prediction as a criterion of validity is both weak and naive (Tetlock, 2005).
- Other authors interpreted the expected utility model as a description of how rational beings should decide. This view, supported by economists such as William Baumol (1922–2017), placed expected utility maximization at the top of economic decision algorithms. The main task of researchers then became to make suggestions of formal variants of the utility function, which had to manifest properties of interest. These proposals were empirically tested, often through simple lotteries. This line of work was boosted by the publication of a book by Abraham Wald (1902–1950), *Statistical Decision Functions* (1950). This text linked decision theory and statistical inference (Heukelom, 2014: 49).
- Axioms are the normative benchmark against which to compare the actual behavior of people. In everyday life, people's judgments suffer from biases due to the presence of systematic and predictable cognitive blunders. Unfortunately, when making decisions, people ignore the postulates of expected utility, as well as the laws of logic, the rules of Bayesian inference

[created by Thomas Bayes (1701–1761)], and so on. The reason would be profound: the faulty configuration of the human mind. Analysts devote themselves to the search for more and more cognitive errors in the hope that, when they are noticed, people will stop making them. Many authors in behavioral economics share this view (more details later in this chapter).

A common element of these three approaches is to consider that, in the application domain, the expected utility model has no rival. Posed as a universal characterization of human behavior and nurtured with formal rigor and logical consistency, its hegemony seems unquestionable. In the validity domain, which is included in the previous one, authors show crucial differences: some strive to reveal the maximizing intentions behind any economic decision, if necessary by resorting to labyrinth arguments, and others, as recently pointed out, make the axioms merely the ideal reference for measuring biases in the observed decisions. These latter researchers consider the results of cognitive psychology very relevant (Gigerenzer, 2020: 1370). All in all, over the years a myriad of contributions has ended up shaping the perfectly rational economic agent: a theoretical creation of compact design protected by numerous assumptions, among which the following should be highlighted (Motterlini and Guala, 2015: 6):

- The expected utility maximization criterion can be applied to any environment, be it stable, turbulent, or highly uncertain.
- People seek to maximize their utility, that is, they look out for their own interests. People can hide this rational selfishness under very sophisticated appearances.
- The accumulated utility depends only on the number of goods consumed, measured at their respective prices. In addition, the welfare of people is measured by the variety of goods and services available to them.
- Preferences are the filter of decision processes: they are equivalent to the expectations of people regarding the gains and losses of options. Whereas the origin of preferences does not matter (it is not an economic problem), they must be exhaustively defined and comply with the axioms. Furthermore, they should not waver in the face of different representations and/or contextualizations of the same object.
- Under uncertainty, the agent makes decisions according to the postulates of Bayesian statistics. Specifically, the individual undertakes the systematic calculation of the potential utility derived from every possible alternative or, more generally, from the multiple paths of action. First, this implies that the agent has the cognitive capacity to analyze any volume of information. Since they proceed with the systematic evaluation of the relationships between all the informative elements, it is ensured that all discarded con-

tents are irrelevant. Second, people always have probabilistic beliefs, even about circumstances that are not accurately known by them. People are able, therefore, to generate well-formed subjective appraisals. Finally, all new information is integrated into the decision-making process, updating it (Gilboa et al., 2004: 3–5; Gilboa et al., 2012: 14–15).

The model contains an extensive interpretation of the postulates of Bayesian statistics. This makes it easier to approach any socioeconomic decision without delay. Indeed, on the one hand, uncertainty has vanished, since any course of action without antecedents (or identified probability) has been discarded. On the other hand, the arrival of new evidence is not a problem either: the value of the antecedents is updated based on subjective beliefs, without ever asking how they have been formed and what influences they may have undergone during the process.

This last point is disturbing because psychological experiments have made it clear how easily memories can be routed. Let us take the following case (reported to Aronson, 2008: 147–148): a group of people watch images of cars driving down a street; one of them shows a green car passing by the point where a pedestrian was hit; everything suggests that this car is responsible, although this is not entirely obvious. Then, half of the participants are asked if the *blue* car that passed by has skis on its roof, while no color is mentioned to the other half. Finally, they are asked for the color of the car allegedly involved in the accident. The first half tends to indicate they saw a blue car, but not the second half. Therefore, the judgment has been modified by an additional detail subtly introduced. Consequently, although according to Bayes' guidelines it is possible to quantify the degree of ambiguity of the witnesses' memories, there is no guarantee that the very process of revealing has not altered them in a certain sense.

The model of rational calculation contains more assumptions that are often not made explicit. Among these is the willingness of people to use their boundless cognitive capacity: it is not enough to have it, people must want to make use of it. Luckily, it is argued that obtaining the optimum is always an irresistible incentive. Another assumption is that the stability of the world guarantees that deviations are always random and occasional and, as a result, they are diluted within the aggregate. Because they are not systematic, perturbations never have major consequences. They always end up being neutralized. There is also an implicit and particularly problematic assumption: the decision that is beneficial for an individual is also beneficial for the group. Unfortunately, this is simply not true: in a company, the pursuit of maximum short-term profit may be attractive to the current managers, who are probably interested in receiving good bonuses, but it may compromise the viability of the firm in the medium and long term. Managers behave rationally, but their decisions are detrimental to the interests of the other stakeholders.

Protected by numerous assumptions, the analysis of decisions focused on expected utility constitutes a colossal theoretical building.[18] Its structural core is formed by a family of utility functions appreciated for their capacity to obtain stereotyped results (or, also, for complying with the requirement of "good economic behavior"). Nonetheless, this edifice began to crack very early on. Thus, at the beginning of the 1950s, in the *Journal of Political Economy*, an article authored by Baumol indicated that most people prefer less risky lotteries to others with larger prizes. This empirical observation, which was in collision with the axioms, did not please Friedman and Savage. In their 1952 reply, they argued that the axioms do not claim to describe reality, and therefore any anomaly does not jeopardize their soundness. More important was the fissure detected by the French engineer and economist Maurice Allais (1911–2010). This researcher was interested in rational choice models but viewed expected utility theory with suspicion. Allais discovered that people overvalue sure outcomes over others that are bigger but, at the same time, riskier. He suspected that behind this lay the anticipation of regret if nothing is obtained, mainly due to having had a smaller, albeit certain, prize within reach; for example, between winning a guaranteed €30 or participating in a lottery in which there is an 80% chance of winning €45 and a 20% chance of winning nothing (thus, the mathematical expectation is $0.8 \cdot €45 + 0.2 \cdot €0 = €36$), the vast majority take the €30.

In a series of letters since 1951, Allais argued to Savage that the postulates of von Neumann and Morgenstern had to be understood as just a first attempt to approximate how people make decisions. The latter replied with the afore-mentioned argument that the axioms have no empirical vocation. Fortunately, the two economists coincided at the *Colloque International sur le Risque* held in Paris between May 12 and 17, 1952. It is explained that, during a meal, Allais presented to Savage the following two decision problems (here rounded off in euros) (Heukelom, 2014: 55; see also Wilkinson, 2008: 91: Motterlini and Guala, 2015: 23; and Cartwright, 2018: 102–105):

1. Which of the two lotteries do you prefer?
    (a) one with a 100% probability of winning €152,000;
    (b) another one with an 89% chance of winning €152,000, a 1% chance of receiving nothing and a 10% chance of winning €762,000.
2. And which of the following two?
    (a) a probability of 89% of winning nothing and 11% of winning €152,000;

(b)   a 90% chance of receiving nothing, and a 10% of chance of winning €762,000.

Savage chose options 1(a) and 2(b). A predictable choice: 1(a) is preferred because of risk aversion even though it does not maximize the potential gain (which is just over €211,000); while 2(b) is the option that gives more money (€76,200 versus €16,720) without the difference in probability being significant (just 1%). However, as Allais pointed out, these choices were contradictory to the theory: the same person can either pursue maximum profit or not. This violates the axiom of independence. Initially puzzled, Savage ended up considering that his choice did not invalidate the axioms of rational choice. On the contrary, Allais thought that this anomaly was of sufficient size to justify revising the postulates of expected utility. In 1953, Allais submitted an article with his points of view to the journal *Econometrica*. Savage dismissed this work as a minority: he knew of nobody else who advocated such views. Nonetheless, Savage, in his book *The Foundations of Statistics*, insisted on the distinction between the normative and empirical readings of the postulates of perfect rationality.

A few years later, in 1961, Allais's paradox was joined by Ellsberg's paradox, formulated by Daniel Ellsberg (1931–2023) (drawn from Angner, 2012: 136–139; see also Gilboa et al., 2012: 17; and M. Baddeley, 2013: 129–130). This anomaly erodes the assumption that people transform uncertainty into probabilistic beliefs. Let us consider the following case: an opaque urn contains 90 balls of the same size, texture, and temperature; 30 are known to be red, while the other 60 are either black or white with no way of knowing how many of each there are. The following games are then proposed:

- Choose between (a) winning €100 if a red ball is drawn, or (b) winning €100 if a black ball is drawn. Once the game mode is chosen, a single draw is performed.
- Choose between (c) winning €100 if the ball is red or white, or (d) winning €100 if the ball is black or white. As before, there is only the possibility of a single draw.

Between (a) and (b), most choose (a) in an attempt to obtain a red ball, plausibly because they know that there is a prize 1/3 of the time (30/90 balls). In contrast, in option (b) there is no way to approximate the proportion of times the ball drawn will be black. In the second game, the second possibility (d) is chosen, since there is a 2/3 probability that the drawn ball will be black or white. Table 2.1 shows the winnings according to the color of the drawn ball. If (a) or (b) is chosen, drawing a white ball means losing in both cases. However, if you choose between (c) and (d), drawing a white ball always means winning €100. The white ball means a certain loss in the first game and

Table 2.1   *Ellsberg paradox: money won*

Option/ball	Red	Black	White	Probability
(a)	€100	€0	€0	1/3
(b)	€0	€100	€0	?
(c)	€100	€0	€100	?
(d)	€0	€100	€100	2/3

a guaranteed win in the second one. Thus, the choices depend only on the first two columns, which are equal as shown in the table. Ignoring the white balls, (a) and (c) are identical choices, as are (b) and (d). Still, (a) and (d) are chosen because they have clear expectations of winning, while (b) and (c) are entirely uncertain alternatives. Therefore, ambiguity causes uneasiness. Perhaps not everyone experiences it with the same intensity, but it seems that there are no people who find uncertainty encouraging. Ellsberg's paradox suggests that people prefer to dodge uncertainty than to assign subjective probabilities to it (more information in Chapter 4, section 4.2).

2.2   THE EMERGENCE OF BEHAVIORAL ECONOMICS

While the theoretical framework of unlimited rationality was being consolidated in academic circles, and its flaws largely ignored, the landscape was already changing. Albeit timidly at first, the third stage of this story expanded in the 1950s and 1960s. A pioneering author in the study of human behavior far from rational calculation postulates was George Katona (1901–1981). For years he was the director of the Institute of Social Research at the University of Michigan, where the term "behavioral economics" was coined in the late 1940s (Heukelom, 2014: 4, 75, Gigerenzer, 2015: 249). Among the many contributions of this economist, the following should now be highlighted (for more information see Wärneryd, 1982 and Curtin, 2017):

• He was not interested in the outcomes of decisions, but rather in the traits of decision-making procedures (Curtin, 2017: 19).
• He considered that the selling techniques and product promotion stratagems invented in the last third of the 19th century by department stores and shopping malls provided relevant information on people's economic behavior. Not surprisingly, he fostered the Survey Research Center, a forerunner in empirical studies on consumption.
• Framed by the growing interest in macroeconomic issues throughout the 1950s, Katona was interested in the connection between aggregate magnitudes (especially consumption and savings) and people's perception of the

advancement of their personal affairs (and of the economy as a whole). He aimed to integrate to the aggregate function of consumption not only past and present consumption, but also people's expectations and aspirations (Curtin, 2017: 20–23, Hosseini, 2017: 133–134; Tomer, 2017: 102–109).

During these years, other relevant contributions came from the so-called Carnegie School (linked to the Carnegie Institute of Technology, later Carnegie-Mellon University), including the economist Richard Cyert (1921–1998), the sociologist James G. March (1928–2018), and Simon (Earl, 2017: 8; Sent, 2017). Studying how decisions are made in large companies and institutions, they found that everyday routines and a lot of simple decision rules predominated, while the appeal to grand principles played a ceremonial role. Moreover, decision-making in organizations is directly influenced by institutional design and work climate. Simon, probably the most influential author of those mentioned, challenged the attributes of *homo œconomicus*, such as unlimited cognitive capacity, unbreakable will, total self-control, and absolute priority to the systematic defense of one's own interests (Simon, 1955 and 1959; Hertwig and Pedersen, 2016, Berg, 2014a: 385). He insisted that the conditions that facilitate the implementation of the axioms of perfect rationality (all options are known, as well as their consequences and probabilities) do not occur in reality, except in "small world" cases, as Savage described the simplest decisions under conditions of certainty.[19] Simon, rejecting the idea that axiom violations were a manifestation of irrationality, wondered how people make decisions. He then developed an approach that, combining cognitive and contextual aspects, has left a strong imprint on economic psychology (Gigerenzer et al., 2011: xviii–xix).

In the strict field of psychology, the years following World War II witnessed the collapse of the psychoanalytic approach, a circumstance that led to a renewed interest in research on perception, memory, and the formulation of judgments. Cognitive psychology emerged as a wide-ranging reflection on the capacities of the human mind. In this field, two names stand out: the aforementioned Edwards, and Donald Marquis (1908–1973). Edwards, in an article published in 1961 under the title "Behavioral decision theory," which was in addition to another from 1954, made a careful summary of the theory of utility, with its stages and main concepts, plus a presentation of the economic postulates on risk. Written in a markedly descriptive tone, these articles aimed to facilitate psychologists' access to such a theoretical corpus, while simultaneously encouraging them to relaunch research in economic psychology to overcome the empirical weakness he observed in the conventional approach (Heukelom, 2014: 81). Even so, communication between psychologists and economists has never been easy, either then or now:[20] the former have often found that humans violate the axioms, a fact that the latter have attributed to a lack of learning and the modest value at stake.[21] However, many psychologists recall that, without fairly frequent experience and immediate feedback, there is little room for learning (Thaler, 2015: 50). For example, driving more cautiously in the future often requires the accumulation of several warnings (i.e., fines) and/or shocks (i.e., traffic incidents). Unfortunately, in life some decisions are made once or very rarely, such as finding a partner, choosing a career, or changing jobs. Moreover, although there are specific areas or situations in which experience speeds up problem-solving or decision-making actions, people are not immune to overconfidence. Let us look at this.

Overconfidence is a psychological bias of undoubted economic importance, which is a reason for devoting a few paragraphs to it. Five different phenomena could be included under this name (according to Gigerenzer, 1991: 4–6; Mousavi and Gigerenzer, 2011; and Chabris and Simons, 2015: 124, 144). The first two deal with the calibration error often illustrated by double questions on general knowledge such as the following:

* Which city is at a higher latitude, Rome or New York?
* How confident are you in your answer: 50%, 60%, 70%, 80%, 90% or 100%?

The responses obtained can be analyzed in two ways:

* The gap between the actual degree of correctness and the degree of confidence declared by the different participants is noted. Applied to questions with different levels of intrinsic difficulty, the gap obtained shows that the most difficult questions lead to a lack of confidence, i.e., the mean value of the answers to the second question is below the mean number of correct answers to the first question, while the opposite is true for the easiest questions, i.e., people show overconfidence.
* When a large group of people answers this type of dual question, it is observed that the answers show the following regularity: the real degree of correctness is always below the declared level of confidence, whatever the latter may be. For some authors, this overconfidence should be considered a mental bias. However, if the experiment questions are not selected (to be misleading) but are a representative sample (say, for example, of all large cities), the overconfidence for the declared number of correct answers vanishes. All that remains is the carelessness with which people usually answer many questions, something that can cause contrariness but cannot be considered a mental flaw.

In real life, it seems that people opt for informed inferences, i.e., based on what they believe to be solid evidence with respect, for example, to the climate of certain cities. As many more images of New York under snow have been seen than of Rome, most people infer that the North American city is further north. However, it is Rome that is at the higher latitude (about one degree). What happens is that the information used to make the inference is not complete: climate also depends on many particular geographical circumstances.

The third meaning of overconfidence is the tendency to forecast too narrow confidence intervals. For instance, when experts are asked to indicate the interval of the interest rate values with a high probability, say 90%, next year, real data often fall outside (either above or below) the suggested ranges. It can be concluded that the more people wish to demonstrate that they know something in depth, the more they tend to make tight predictions.

The fourth type of overconfidence is related to skills: people consider themselves to be more skillful than they are, often above the average of the reference group. This is not necessarily a mistake, since it has to be contextualized: seeing oneself as a better driver than average is true for the vast majority of drivers if the variable at stake is the number of accidents suffered. The distribution of this variable is very asymmetric because a very high proportion of drivers have a below-average number of accidents. This might not be the case if the variable were the number of engine breakdowns. Moreover, this is a matter in which qualitative aspects often abound. Consequently, the (absolute and relative) metrization is never quite clear: what exactly does it mean to be a teacher with talent above, or below, average?

The fifth meaning of overconfidence is related to the degree of self-control over personal tasks and projects. This belief is combined with the self-serving bias or the feeling of firmly being in control of the course of one's own life (Aronson, 2008: 173). This perception cannot be separated from self-esteem. If at the beginning of the course, students are asked in which decile they think their final grade will be, only a few think they will probably be below the median. More than half expect to be actually within the two highest deciles (whatever the distribution of grades). The same is true for new entrepreneurs involved in small businesses such as stores, restaurants, etc. Even though the failure rate over a reasonable time frame exceeds half, they consider the probability of succeeding to be extremely high. Unfortunately, humans often lose sight of the fact that, in addition to the things they control and/or know, there are certainly many other things that elude them. Being motivated and convinced of one's own effort does not eliminate either the unforeseen events or the reaction of those harmed (the rest of the stores in the street) by the new business project.

Complacency predisposes people to attribute their successes to effort, willpower, clairvoyance, and other internal factors, while failures are caused by external, usually contingent, circumstances. For example, it is common for students to claim to have passed on their own merits, while failures are the fault of the teacher (Motterlini, 2010: 40). Fans also attribute their teams' victories to the skills of the players, the good atmosphere in the dressing room or the genius of the coach, among others. This is a series of causes internal to the club. Defeats, however, are explained by external factors: injuries caused by opponents, referee decisions, bad luck, etc. This perception has a curious variant, known as the attribution error: the tendency to impute the reprehensible behavior of others to their intrinsic character or predisposition, that is, to their way of being ("He spilled the drink because he is clumsy," "He spoke rudely because he is aggressive in nature," etc.) while, as just mentioned, one's own inexcusable behavior is largely said to be dependent on contextual factors. However, if it is a question of the successes of others, people emphasize the help (presumably) received from surrounding circumstances (Hogg and Vaughan, 2014: 93, 97; Aronson, 2008: 160–162, 170). As can be observed, successes and setbacks are imputed in opposite ways depending on whether they are their own or those of others.

Overconfidence has just been the appetizer of the many results with which psychology can enrich the economic discourse. Unfortunately, for many economists, especially if they think the economic theory has to be prescriptive, the details of the real behavior are just noise (Heukelom, 2014: 60, 86).[22]

Over the last 40 years, despite starting almost from zero, economic psychology has become one of the most dynamic areas of research. Dozens of authors, seminars and congresses, specialized journals, multiple published books (with several addressed to the general public), and, significantly, a handful of Nobel Prize winners in economics, namely Herbert A. Simon in 1978, Reinhard Selten (1930–2016) in 1994, Daniel Kahneman in 2002, and Richard H. Thaler in 2017,[23] have disseminated and given prestige to economic decision-making processes combined with psychological factors. Even so, from the very beginning economic psychology has been divided into two major research programs, namely (Earl, 1990; Sent, 2004; Mousavi et al., 2017; Altman, 2017b: 1–3; Tomer, 2017: 16–28):

• The study focuses on pervasively biased judgments. Once detected, people are warned to avoid them since they imply choices with poor results. Among the causes explaining this deplorable state of affairs should be remarked the tendency to rely on heuristics, a concept that can be provisionally defined as simple and informal choice rules: for example, on deciding at which roadside restaurant to stop for lunch, always choose the first one with a good number of parked vehicles (see Chapters 3 and 5). This research program, known as "heuristics and biases," argues that deciding to follow an elaborate blueprint is always better, but, unfortunately, cognitive biases are numerous and recurrent.[24] These biases are inherent in the design of the human mind, which is incredibly complex and very fickle at the same time. Therefore, errors of judgment are not trivial mistakes due to lack of attention or interest, distraction, shyness, or bluster. Mental illusions also actually occur when concentration is at its highest and when people's preparedness is beyond any doubt.[25] This shows that the human mind is not capable of following, at all times and in all circumstances, the rules of logic and, more specifically, those of rational economic calculus (Tversky and Kahneman, 2018b). Therefore, the postulates of perfect rationality are established as a normative benchmark. The analysis then focuses on the evaluation of deviations from this reference. Simultaneously, the audience (students, professionals, managers, etc.) is warned of the high costs involved in the use of heuristics. Therefore, they are invited to reject them. Unfortunately, it is only partially successful to disclose common mistakes as a first step to starting to think suitably. Sooner rather than later, people fall back into the same cognitive errors. In short, in this program, the economic assumption that humans behave as if they were rational becomes a pretension: people behave as if they were trying to be rational.

- It is clear from the outset that there are two main types of decisions: those that are simple, i.e., with a small number of options, prior experience, and no unforeseen events, and those that are fraught with complexity and uncertainty, the consequences of which often overwhelm any exhaustive and careful inspection. In the first case, people easily compare the foreseeable results of their choices. In the second one, they often rely on heuristics, a kind of cognitive expedients that are as simple as they are powerful. The consequences may not be innocuous, but only very rarely does the use of heuristics harm the physical integrity of people, reduce their well-being level, entail economic losses, or lead to a shorter life (Berg, 2003; Berg et al., 2008; Arkes et al., 2016). The purpose of the "fast and frugal heuristics" program is to clarify the role of heuristics in judgment formation and decision-making. Their degree of effectiveness depends on certain basic characteristics of the context in which they are applied. Therefore, the analysis tries to identify the situations in which the suitability of a given heuristic outweighs the efficacy/effort ratio of other decision criteria and, conversely, the contexts in which it is not recommended. Anyway, these cognitive shortcuts do not reflect any alleged poor design of the human mind. Heuristics is rather one of its most genuine and powerful manifestations (Gigerenzer, 2014: 14). Since heuristics have an adaptive value, especially as regards the social circumstances of the people, this program has also coined the term "ecological rationality," or "environment-consistent rationality."

Psychologists Kahneman and Amos Tversky (1937–1996) can be considered the founders of the heuristics and biases program (Heukelom, 2017b). It all started in the 1960s with Kahneman's study of the influence of sensory perception on judgments, even though he did not relate it to decision theory. He concluded that so-called cognitive errors were caused by the imperfect perception of the corresponding stimulus. However, later he began to suspect that the propensity of humans to make such errors was persistent and not occasional. For his part, in several experiments, Tversky found that violation of the axioms of perfect rationality was systematic rather than anecdotal. He then proposed to abandon these axioms, but on working later with Kahneman he agreed to keep them as a benchmark. By equating rational with normative, the two researchers consolidated the term cognitive biases (Heukelom, 2014: 98–99, 102, 104). This approach experienced a boost in the 1980s when, first, the Alfred P. Sloan Foundation (in the period 1984–1989) and, later, the Russell Sage Foundation (1986–1992) generously funded the organization of scientific meetings, publications, grants, etc. (Sent, 2004: 742–750; Heukelom, 2014: 149–154 and 2017a: 103).

As explained in Thaler (2015: 149), Kahneman and Tversky's theses were received by some economists with curiosity, especially if they were at the beginning of their academic career, even if very few adopted them, and the annoyance of authors focused on pure axiomatic work as they understood that these postulates only highlighted the irrational side of people. There were also those who reacted with indifference. Although a debate held in October 1985 at the University of Chicago revealed the huge gap between supporters and opponents, the approach of the two psychologists gradually gained acceptance among economists. This could be explained by the following reasons (adapted from Kahneman, 2005; Wilkinson, 2008: 57–70 and 155; Heukelom, 2014: 125; and Tomer, 2017: 33–39, 120):

- Although it is understandable to feel uncomfortable highlighting alleged manifestations of irrationality, the fact of maintaining the axioms as a reference, i.e., as a standard measure of empirical results, actually reinforces the conventional approach. It can be added that basic concepts, such as utility, are not abandoned either. In this case, the following are rather deployed: anticipated utility, transaction utility, acquisition utility, diagnostic utility, etc. (Prelec and Bodmer, 2003; Kahneman, 2006; Thaler, 2015: 59). All this shows the willingness to give the term utility a certain psychological basis. This claim is not new.
- The required controls of statistical quality in empirical work are well known to economists. At the same time, questionnaires are not difficult to design and access to respondents, often students, is immediate and inexpensive.
- By setting aside the non-cognitive aspects of decisions, especially the social context, the research program on biases and heuristics borders on the

realm of cognitive psychology. In doing so, its results acquire a glaze of universality, as this is understood in rational economic analysis.

- The inherent and persistent nature of biases makes them difficult to correct. Nevertheless, given the costs they can entail for people, it is worth trying to correct them mainly through learning (Motterlini and Guala, 2015: 99–100). Therefore, the approach fits perfectly into the business of coaching.[26] In turn, it has also given rise to the social technique of nudging (Thaler and Sunstein, 2008; Motterlini, 2014; Chetty, 2015; Tomer, 2017: Chapter 7). This consists of subtly and appropriately modifying some elements of the environment in which people make easy decisions. According to its proponents, this contributes to people's well-being (Halpern, 2015). Several governments have created and maintain active administrative agencies dedicated to the design and dissemination of messages that, for example, encourage people to take the stairs instead of elevators, try to take advantage of the demonstration effect to prevent tax fraud, and so on. However, this social technique has been criticized from conservative positions for supposedly restricting people's choices; a criticism that Thaler and Sunstein have been quick to refute. From diametrically opposed positions, it has been criticized for ignoring primary causes of the behaviors to be adequately modified and the possibility of collective actions to change the current state of affairs. For example, messages are launched to combat obesity, but the advertising of highly processed foods in the media is not curbed, and the right to a retirement pension is addressed as a design flaw in the system of incentives for individual contributions, instead of encouraging collective action in favor of the universal right to a pension. In any case, the weakness of nudging is its reliance on people's cognitive biases. If it turns out that many of the biases actually are not really biases, the sustained effectiveness of nudging will be doubtful.[27]

Reluctance has not prevented the heuristics and biases research program from taking root in the academic world. There is no doubt that the renewal of the mainstream theory it encourages (Lavoie, 2014: 85) opens up a whole new line of inquiry with, why not, promising academic careers (Selten, 1991; Rabin, 1998 and 2013; and Nagel et al., 2017). Anyway, the approach still has a limited role in the curricula of the countless economics and management training centers scattered all over the world. With the turn of the century, the first courses appeared and, hence, some textbooks such as Wilkinson (2008), Wilkinson and Klaes (2012), Angner (2012), Just (2014), and Cartwright (2018).

The approach has also reached the general public. Examples are the pioneering book by Piattelli-Palmarini (1996) and the subsequent books by Motterlini (2006 and 2010) and Ariely (2009, 2010 and 2012). Some of them have achieved the level of international bestsellers, such as Lehrer (2009) and, most notably, Kahneman (2011).[28] To close this brief review, it should be mentioned that the dissemination of the postulate of biases and heuristics also includes cases of opportunistic exploitation, such as:

- The appeal to cognitive errors to divert attention and dispense with liability for damages in cases of negligence, deceit, corruption, etc. For example, the company Exxon Valdez managed to reduce the high fine for the 1989 Alaska oil spill, arguing that the jurors had not shown the necessary mental skills to understand the situation (Gigerenzer, 2018).
- It has been proposed to use the results of the program to manipulate consumers (see, e.g., Shotton, 2018).

An unintended consequence of the insistence on the bias would have been to promote reliance on computer programs designed to make decisions instead of people. As is well known, mathematical algorithms are currently being promoted for personnel selection, parole granting, allocation of all kinds of resources, etc. Presumably, these automated systems would choose without bias. They would be unobjectionable because of the large number of variables considered and data processed. They would therefore be free from psychological bias. However, such programs may incorporate the biases of their developers, as well as those coming from the users that have commissioned them (O'Neil, 2016).

While the research program pushed by Kahneman, Tversky, and their followers moved away from Simon's postulates, other researchers maintained their proximity (Sent, 2004: 740–742; Hogg and Vaughan, 2014: 43). The first step in this direction was psychologist John W. Payne's article, "Heuristic search processes in decision making," published in 1976. Since the 1990s it has been the psychologist Gerd Gigerenzer, linked to the Max Planck Institute (Germany), who has been encouraging the research program on fast and frugal heuristics. This program focuses on the several inferences that people used in making decisions in their daily lives (personal, family, and work). This analysis is key to assessing the appropriateness of decision-making procedures based on heuristics and their adaptive value. As is known, the inference is understood as the reasoning extended from one or more propositions initially accepted as true (or false) and endowed with a certain degree of precision, to another proposition, whose value is not unrelated to that of the initial premises. In psychology, the inference is simply the process of generating judgments about reality and its circumstances (Gigerenzer and Gaissmaier, 2011: 454). People typically make two types of inferences (Gigerenzer et al., 2008: 233–234):

- Those that rely on the information stored in the memory. Once the options of the decisions in progress have been instantaneously or progressively identified, people estimate their value and validate the choice.
- Those coming from cues detected in the options to be chosen. Their agile inspection settles the value of such alternatives, determining the choice.

The ecological rationality program presents the following methodological singularities (from Gigerenzer et al., 2011: xx; Tomer, 2017: 30; Lavoie, 2014: 87–88; and Schilirò, 2017):

- The analysis is focused on the correspondence between the decision procedures and the basic characteristics of the environment (as detailed in Chapter 5). Therefore, the establishment of an unappealable benchmark for assessing the effects of decision procedures is not necessary. The normative quality of a given procedure is not a logical matter but stems from the fact that, when implemented, such heuristics obtain sufficiently good results in a given class of situations.
- The effectiveness of heuristics is evaluated through careful field experiments and mathematical simulation techniques. Models with heuristics must be computable to identify in which type of context they succeed or fail. One of the most relevant exercises is to compare various decision criteria, to observe which ones best predict the observed choices (Berg and Gigerenzer, 2010: 143–144). Therefore, the adaptive value of heuristics is measured by the robustness of the behavioral predictions relied on,[29] and not by the fit of a given formal model to the available data (Roberts and Pashler, 2000).
- In practice, people choose heuristics depending on:
  - The information stored in memory (which, in turn, reflects lived experiences and accumulated knowledge).
  - The differences in their personality and abilities (they are not equally intuitive, nor do they manifest the same degree of anxiety, for example).
  - The feedback mechanism: a successful heuristic is more likely to be chosen again.

The analysis, therefore, contributes to the design of heuristics (and decision methods in general) aimed at improving the decision-making process in fields such as health, business, personal life, courts, etc. (Gigerenzer and Brighton, 2009: 129).

Leaving for the fifth chapter the description of the most common heuristics in economic decision-making, it should be stressed that the program of ecological rationality insists that complex decisions do not necessarily require complicated procedures. This idea has ancient roots: many people are wary of convoluted procedures for making everyday life decisions. However, pointing towards simple rules does not mean suggesting simplistic ones. The greater the uncertainty, the number of alternatives, and the volume of data, the less operational sophisticated procedures are. Therefore, simple methods are necessary since less can be more (Gigerenzer, 2014: 97).

The two research programs in economic psychology maintain important differences. The following paragraphs describe perhaps the three most relevant ones: those relating to the conception of heuristics, the reparative nature of the heuristics and biases program, and the nature of the results obtained. To begin with, when Kahneman and Tversky incorporated heuristics in the early 1970s, they considered them as stable components of the mind aimed at decision-making, but usually imperfect. They were considered to be cognitive tools that hinder discernment and, therefore, the choice of the best options. At best, heuristics lead to a second-best option (Gigerenzer and Brighton, 2009: 109). This interpretation differed from that of Simon and his followers enrolled in the ecological rationality program: heuristics are intelligent shortcuts for decision-making, i.e., they require few resources and are an example of the creativity and insight of the human mind.

Secondly, the heuristics and biases program manifests great concern for the statistical fit of the available data to the models. This has pushed its designers to add more and more free parameters (Berg and Gigenrenzer, 2010: 4–6). As explained a few pages back, the St. Petersburg paradox forced an initial modification of the mathematical expectation criterion. Years later the model collided with the Allais paradox. This new hurdle was overcome with the Prospect Theory (see Kahneman and Tversky, 1979; Tversky and Kahneman, 1986 and 1992; Wilkinson, 2008: 95–126; Wakker, 2010; Cartwright, 2018: 115–126; Wilkinson and Klaes, 2012: 161–185; Heukelom, 2014: 121–122; and Tomer, 2017: 40–43). Leaving details to one side, the expected utility model applied to simple lotteries is conveniently modified by incorporating into it some functions referred to the probabilities and values at stake. Thus, objective probabilities are transformed according to the "decision weight" function, $\pi(\pi_1)$, and the utility function becomes a particular type of value function, $v(x_i)$. All of this leads to the expression

$$V(A) = \sum_{i=1}^{n} \pi(p_i) \cdot v(x_i)$$

The value of a lottery, $V(A)$, is associated with two S-shaped[30] functions which, as is evident, add some more free parameters to the previous model. As is well-known, this strategy usually improves the fit between the model and the data sample, which currently comes from field experiments. This refinement does not mean, however, that the model will have better predictions if a different data sample is used.[31] Moreover, the greater complexity of prospect theory also implies that economic agents have enormous cognitive capacities (Gigerenzer, 2002 and 2014; Berg and Gigerenzer, 2010: 5; Lavoie, 2014: 72–82). Without a doubt, they are larger than those required by the expected utility model.

The evolution from Bernoulli's model to prospect theory is a good example of successive repairs: models are rebuilt over and over again without the slightest concern about their increasing complexity. To address the emerging anomalies it is also common to incorporate variables with a psychological flavor, even if they do not necessarily stem from a deep understanding of the underlying psychological (cognitive and psychosocial) factors involved (Brandstätter et al., 2006, Berg and Gigerenzer, 2010). The result is a patchwork of mathematical formats and a diversity of parameters whose purpose is to achieve a high degree of fit.

This research plan has been termed "Ptolemaic," after Claudius Ptolemy (*c.* AD 90–168), a mathematician and astronomer from Alexandria (Egypt), known for his cosmological model (see Elster, 2007: Chapter 2; Gigerenzer, 2020: 1370; Gigerenzer et al. 2011: xx). In Ptolemy's most famous work, the *Almagest*, a model of the planetary system is proposed in which, on the one hand, the Sun, each planet (up to Saturn, the last then known), and the rest of the stars of the sky (only those visible to the naked eye) orbit the Earth, the celestial body fixed in the center. On the other hand, the planets' orbits result from the combination of two uniform circular displacements: one called deferent and centered on the Earth, and the other known as an epicycle, or smaller radius rotation embedded inside the previous one. This mixture of motions was able to explain the observed approach and departure of celestial bodies, their moments of apparent motionlessness, and retrograde displacements. Ptolemy's model, as opposed to the heliocentric model that had existed since the fourth century BC, was the reference work in astronomy for more than a millennium. It was not until the publication of Copernicus' work in the mid-sixteenth century that the model began to be abandoned.

In these pages, Ptolemy's work is of interest not for its content, but as an example of analytical development. At this point, it should be noted that this model was successful for three reasons (Russo, 2004: 78–93):

- It agreed with the postulates of philosophers such as Pythagoras, Plato, and Aristotle, all renowned, but none dedicated to astronomical observation.

- The combination of deferent and epicycle gave a convincing description of the motion of the planets. Increasing the number of epicycles made the model extremely convoluted, but it seemed to match the observed data.
- With a ruler, a protractor, and a compass, the most common tools used at the time to make geometrical calculations, there was enough to describe the motions of the considered celestial bodies.

In other words, it respected the criterion of authority, the explanation it provided was effective and it only required common tools and calculation operations. The increasing complexity of the model was not judged a problem: anomalies only reflect the magnificence of the Creator's work. Reality is complicated and the model could do nothing but mirror it. However, today this conclusion would convince no one: the criterion of Occam's razor, by its propagator William of Occam (*c.*AD 1288–1347), holds that the entities present in a model (or in a theory) should never be multiplied unnecessarily. Scientific discourse prefers parsimony and simplicity. Before proceeding to construct complex and intricate explanations, probably coupled with a lot of assumptions, it is advisable to approach the issue differently. This is a heuristic principle that does not always work (when, for example, there are several equally simple explanations), but that scientific research should never forget.

Third, the heuristics and biases program has been criticized for its superficial identification of heuristics. They are given vague labels (availability heuristics, representativeness heuristics, etc.) without further specification, and they can therefore serve to explain very different psychological phenomena.[32] There is no doubt that the consideration of heuristics as a poor decision tool is not unrelated to this simple and imprecise identification. As an alternative, the research program on fast and frugal heuristics opts for describing the components that make up the heuristics and for testing them systematically under different conditions. This empirical work is characterized by the following features (as explained by Marewski et al., 2010a; Gigerenzer and Gaissmaier, 2011: 459; and Gigerenzer, 2018):

- Fieldwork is designed with the greatest care.
- The results are incorporated into computer simulation programs, the flexibility of which makes it possible to evaluate the accuracy of heuristics and other choice criteria, including random choice, under different conditions (see Chapter 5, section 5.1.7).

An important outcome of the ecological rationality program is the less-is-more effect. This effect is related to heuristics applied, according to Savage's nomenclature, in "large world" situations, i.e., in circumstances in which only partial information is available and consequences are permeated with uncertainty. Figure 2.2 (inspired by Gigerenzer and Brighton, 2009: 110; Gigerenzer and Gaissmaier, 2011: 453; and Gigerenzer, 2015: 108 and 2021: 3556) shows the relationship between precision and volume of information in such cases. As can be seen, inferences lose accuracy when the amount of information handled exceeds a certain threshold. The postulate does not indicate that having less information is always better: it only warns that there is a point beyond which collecting more data is detrimental to decision-making, regardless of the cost of gathering them. The proposition, therefore, is not marginalist in nature: it does not propose to collect information until the additional cost of doing so exceeds the value of the extra content. It is not a rule to manage (optimize) the accuracy/effort trade-off. It is the experience of applying a particular heuristic that opens the door to the suspicion that continuing to accumulate and manage more information may be counterproductive.

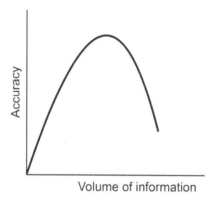

Figure 2.2   *The less-is-more effect*

The less-is-more effect has its origin in the fairly stable relationships that the elements (and the signals they emit) present in a given context tend to maintain with each other. Although noise may lead people to think that reality is chaotic, a more careful inspection allows us to detect the properties that structure it. For the study of decision-making processes, the following should be highlighted (adapted from Gigerenzer and Gaissmaier, 2011: 457):

- People realize that reality displays a certain number of particular signals. The attempt to consider them all may run up against the availability of resources and time, as well as the limits of human rationality. A not necessarily arbitrary selection is required. Previous experiences, what has been learned, the person's objectives, and so on, are the factors that determine such a selection. Normal, healthy people have no trouble noticing these cues. People are smart enough to examine them according to some criteria to decide on a choice. There are several ways, or algorithms, to do this: the signals are weighted and summed, they are arranged in a hierarchy, etc.

- The cues are correlated with each other, which gives some degree of redundancy to the different contexts. This term, commonly used in engineering, refers to the duplication of key components or functions of a system to increase its reliability under normal conditions, or to sustain its performance in case of unforeseen events.[33] Thus, machines, vehicles, digital networks, etc. have critical elements repeated two or more times. Redundancy can also affect the output of a system, as when an operation is repeated several times: for example, sending several copies of a message one after the other. In economics, routine (repeated cycles of the same action, such as daily shopping) is the most prominent source of redundancy (Gigerenzer, 2015: 115). These actions take place in an environment that is also redundant, given that the same cues are being reiterated in the same elements (such as the attributes that characterize different brands of a product class) (more information in Rieskamp and Dieckmann, 2012). Redundancy occurs, however, to varying degrees: the eating habits of an exotic place may at first come as a surprise ("you have to get used to it," it is explained), while fast food chains offer the same menu in the same way all over the world.
- The presence of uncertainty. The past is irrevocable, while the course of future events is unknown, especially at a greater distance from the present. Although reality exhibits all kinds of cycles, this regularity is not imperturbable, without denying the possibility of new things appearing. In any case, the accuracy of predictions is inevitably limited. Although this issue will be dealt with in detail in a later chapter, what should be emphasized here is the impossibility of observing in advance the consequences of the decisions to be taken.

It is necessary to insist that although social and economic realities present an enormous dispersion of elements and signals, most of them maintain strong correspondences with each other. The various (sub)systems that make up reality (kinship circles, companies, administrations, etc.) bring together in the same milieu a series of elements regularly intertwined with each other. People perceive and scan the signals to understand their nature and relationships with others. The goal is to adapt, not to dilute. This explains why, at any given time and place, there are long-lasting human societies and, in turn, multiple lifestyles. People share some attributes (social norms, aspirations, etc.) and hold others in particular (tastes, beliefs, etc.).

In short, the ecological rationality program rejects that people behave as if they were solving a more or less complex optimization problem with restrictions, under the focus of Bayesian beliefs and pursuing their interests. This type of decision is only feasible in small world situations because of the predominance of certainty and the assumption that, in the meantime, reality will not undergo any relevant mutation. To grasp the importance of this last assumption, let us look at the following example (adapted from Gigerenzer, 1991: 107–108): a tribe in the middle of the jungle lets children swim in the river, instead of climbing trees, because only the oldest people remember hearing about someone being eaten by crocodiles, while everyone knows of children killed by falling from trees; however, one day a person arrives in the village explaining that, in another settlement, a child was attacked by a crocodile a few days earlier. The question is, what should be done? Applying Bayes' rule, the new information has not changed things: since this is an isolated attack, the least risky option is still swimming in the river. Nonetheless, there is no doubt that children will be forbidden from going down to the river. The new information pushes adults to think that its conditions have changed: the attack was not a fatality attributable to an episodic crocodile patrolling the river, but it is suspected that crocodiles have invaded new stretches of the river. Therefore, no one else will swim until it is certain that the stability of the river, hitherto observed, has been restored. In general, beyond the difficulty in capturing the changes of state, axioms and the algorithms connected to them will fail in decisions with conflicting objectives, incommensurable attributes, and with the presence of unknown options and/or characteristics (Gigerenzer, 2001: 41–42). When the principles of rationality applied do not systematically guarantee the success of decisions, they cannot be the benchmark either. At best, the rational calculation can only aspire to be, after a severe adaptation that many will consider blurs it completely, one more procedure for decision-making (as explained in Chapter 5). Heuristics would be its main alternative.

This brief presentation of the vicissitudes of the relationship between psychology and economics cannot be closed without referring to the enormous experimental work carried out by the two major research programs mentioned.[34] This empirical effort has taken one of the following three broad forms (adapted from Skořepa, 2011: 72; Angner, 2012: 6–7; Wilkinson and Klaes, 2012: 36–42; and Tomer, 2017: 115, 126–134):

- Interviews and questionnaires in which people are asked for their opinion about certain facts, or their reaction to a given situation. These experiences are not difficult to design, can be applied in a simple way, and results are obtained immediately. The main problems are control of the conditions under which the experiment is carried out and the representativeness of the sample. It is also important that participants, who risk nothing personally, respond honestly. It should be taken into account that, in real life, many economic decisions involve one's own resources and, consequently, even if the consequences are small, the choice would be influenced by this fact. For example, for a psychological impact to occur, a purchase does not need to lead to bankruptcy: a bad experience of a few euros can hurt for months and be remembered for years, thus affecting subsequent consumption. All in all, analysts must remember this in designing experiments and not forget that knowing what is decided is not the same as knowing why.[35]

- The direct and unobtrusive observation of actual behavior. This includes, for example, spying on how people do shopping or observing how gamblers behave in a casino. In the same vein, social network users' reactions to certain messages, or choice proposals, are analyzed. Such contents are dumped on the network without prior notice and the responses are then evaluated according to the profile of the participants. Non-response is also significant. The analysis is carried out by algorithms that, in their most advanced versions, are capable of automatically reformulating themselves so as not to lose track of the users. Since the size of these experiments is colossal (even a tiny proportion of respondents involves hundreds of thousands of people), the Internet has become the all-time largest laboratory. Along with their speed, such experiments have aroused the avidity of all kinds of interests. As expected, many misgivings have been raised about invading privacy and keeping the intentions of their promoters opaque (Christl and Spiekermann, 2016; O'Neil, 2016; Foer, 2017).

- The use of neurological scanning devices.[36] Such research, whether on laboratory animals or humans, often requires expensive equipment and its implementation is cumbersome (people wear electrodes all over their heads and/or have to endure preparatory sessions). In recent years, the fMRI technique, which measures brain activity through the level of oxygen in the bloodstream, has been widely used as it is non-invasive. The aim is to identify which areas of the brain are particularly activated by stimulus or by undertaking a given cognitive operation. However, the following observations should be kept in mind (from Eklund et al., 2015 and Cobb, 2020: Chapter 14):

  - It is not easy to separate the background activity of the brain from the activity under study. The processing of the received signals is not error-free.
  - The illuminated brain areas are only correlated with the received stimuli. Different regions are permanently more or less active, and the same area can be excited under very different circumstances. Moreover, it should not be forgotten that, however small the area under study may be, it contains millions and millions of neurons with hundreds of biochemical components involved.
  - The number of people scanned is still modest. Robust results require mass scans.

Although the collected data are decisive for the advancement of neuroscience and cognitive psychology, these results are of less interest to economic psychology. No one doubts the importance of elucidating the physiological basis of mental processes. For example, in applying these techniques to economic decisions, they have detected that impulsive and routine purchases activate different brain regions. Nonetheless, economic psychology focuses on the connection between socio-biographical aspects and features of the contexts in which people make economic decisions (as emphasized in Chabris and Simons, 2015: 214 and Bunge, 2010: Chapter 9).

It should again be noted that experiments in economic psychology have a great sensitivity to the specific conditions in which they are conducted: the volume of resources involved, the presence or not of the supervisor, the nature and representativeness of the participants, and so on. Many variables are difficult to control and lead to acute debates about whether the measurement is correct. Consequently, the generalization of results is always problematic (Reiss, 2013: 180 and 187).

NOTES

1. Often presented as a philosopher, it is more pertinent to consider him as a jurist given his activity in compiling and bringing coherence to the then scattered and generally arbitrarily applied British common law. He perceived moral philosophy as a set of principles whose origin is neither religion nor any mythical story, but which arise from the natural world. Therefore, these principles are open to empirical analysis, as previously suggested by Anglican theologians and French Enlightenment philosophers. The work of John Stuart Mill (1806–1873) would consolidate the utilitarianism corpus (Reichlin, 2013: 10–24, 27, 93–97).
2. This term was perhaps used for the first time by the English economist Charles Stanton Devas (1848–1906) and then by the German historicist school. The British authors of the 19th century, when referring to the effort to generate and accumulate wealth, used the concept of the Economic man. When this term came to connote the agent focused on maximizing utility, it began to be criticized. Francis Ysidro Edgeworth (1845–1926) and Alfred Marshall (1842–1924) already considered such criticism to be unfair since, according to them, the expression does not intend to deny other dimensions of human lives (Cremaschi, 1998). However, the connection between these spheres is so close that such a distinction can only be a provisional methodological stratagem. At this point it is worth recalling the comment sent, on October 1, 1901, by the mathematician and physicist Jules Henri Poincaré (1854–1912) to Léon Walras (1834–1910) about his book *Éléments d'économie politique pure* (1899): while the hypothesis that people behave selfishly may be accepted at first approximation, the assumption that they are perfectly rational is entirely misleading (Ingrao and Israel, 2015). As time went by, the assumptions about *homo œconomicus*, rather than enveloping the concept in the interim, ended up shielding it.
3. From the outset, the compensatory criterion causes important doubts (see Chapter 5) and could become absurd when non-material attributes are involved:

what compensates for the loss of a good friend? Knowing that gratifying social interaction are a primary source of quality of life, what can replace them? (Berg and Gigerenzer 2010: 142).

4.   The concept, profusely used in these pages, comes from the Latinized surname of the mathematician and astronomer Muhammad ibn Musa al-Khwarizmi. Born in the territory of present-day Uzbekistan, he was a scholar in Baghdad in the first half of the 9th century AD. In these pages, an algorithm is a criterion to specify a given choice. Its formalization is not indispensable (but see Skořepa, 2011: 22, 128–184).

5.   At this point we can recall the names of the business consultant F. W. Taylor (1856–1915), the industrialist Henry Ford (1863–1947), and the engineers Frank B. Gilbreth (1868–1924) and his wife Lillian M. Gilbreth (1878–1972). All of them developed methods and systems of work control aiming to increase performance.

6.   This is the faculty to understand and share the emotions of others. Empathy encourages people to let themselves be carried away by the laughter, sadness, etc. that they observe or imagine. It is a powerful emotion. It is easy to witness how, in a conversation, people synchronize expressions and gestures, a mimicry that reinforces the quality of the interaction. Even further: people cry at the sight of the hardships of the main characters of a movie, despite knowing that it is pure fiction.

7.   In this period, some economists, however, followed a very different trajectory. One example was Thorstein Veblen (1857–1929). Strongly influenced by the studies of the French psychologist Gabriel Tarde (1843–1904), he studied the mechanisms of imitation and social emulation, especially in the affluent sectors of society.

8.   The indifference curve is closely associated with a compensatory algorithm, which guarantees that it will be asymptotic to the coordinate axes. It was designed to reflect the choice of goods and services by social groups with enough income to satisfy needs beyond basic ones. The presence of superfluous needs leaves room for individual preferences to be expressed. On the other hand, when income is low, as was the case at the time for manual workers, estimating demand was quite simple due to its inflexible and irreducible character.

9.   Forgotten, of course, by economists, but not by psychologists. Thurstone's psychometric postulates and experiments can be traced to the present day. See Brown and Maydeu-Olivares (2011 and 2012) and Bürkner et al. (2019).

10.   This experiment also casts doubt on whether preferences may be innate: if so, the number of options would not affect the choice process.

11.   Attitude can be understood as the relatively stable subjective evaluation (positive or negative) of a given object, which in principle pushes people to act in a certain way. Therefore, attitudes are a component of motivation, although not a good predictor of behavior (see Wilkinson and Klaes, 2012: 70; Hogg and Vaughan, 2014: 150–158; and Solomon, 2015: 336).

12.   At first sight, the property of immanence excludes the possibility of preferences being endogenous and influenced by the social context. However, it is also possible to assume that this does not alter them. In any case, multiple field experiences indicate that preferences are not alien to the environment. For example, paid blood donation provokes greater rejection than voluntary donation (Sandel, 2013: 125–127).

13.   The authors never refused to submit the axioms to empirical screening. Nonetheless, they thought this was not their business. Over the years, the Cowles Commission, the Ford Foundation, the Rand Corporation, and the Pentagon funded numerous studies on the contribution of axioms to the improvement of the decision-making processes (Mirowski, 2002: 116–129, Heukelom, 2014: 66–67, Roncaglia, 2005: 617).

14.   It should be noted that von Neumann was a mathematician very worried about the logical foundations of his work. This explains the axiomatic effort made in *The Theory of Games and Economic Behavior*. Concern for the logical foundations of mathematics had been widespread since the 19th century, although for many mathematicians the most important point is that the formal models work in practice. There is no doubt that this concern for logical consistency subsequently motivated many theoretical economists.

15.   The relation $x > y$ indicates that x is preferred, or that it is better than y. The expression $x \geqslant y$ denotes that x is never worse than y (or, in other words, either x is preferred to y, or x is as good as y). See Skořepa (2011: 36) for a complete list of relations and symbols.

16.   The first person to suggest the paradox was, in 1713, Nicholas Bernoulli (1687–1759), Daniel's cousin.

17.   In economics it is still common to associate people with certain utility functions, although it is rarely stated what other personality traits justify this attribution and how it changes depending on the context and the time passing. It should be noted that psychology abandoned the rigid typology of personalities years ago. Inspired by factorial analysis, current personological models consider only five general traits ("the Big Five") which, as has been amply demonstrated, take on particular and changing configurations (see Moffitt, 1993; B. Roberts et al., 2006; and Gigerenzer, 2020: 1369).

18.   Some authors extended rational economic postulates to the analysis of any manifestation of human behavior. This imposture, seen in perspective, is just another case of economism (Fine and Milonakis, 2009). Even some authors of economic psychology have fallen into the trap. For example, Thaler (2015: 20–21) explains the paradox of a person who does not buy an object (watch, clothes, etc.) on display in a shop window because of its high price but is happy to receive it later as a gift from their partner (under the assumption that they share expenses). This fact is qualified as incoherent. However, a gift is not a simple economic transaction, but a manifestation of attachment. For this reason, sincere gifts are priceless, as everyone has known since time immemorial (Morson and Schapiro, 2017: 125–126, 280; Sandel, 2013: 101). There is no puzzle to solve, despite what is assured by Wilkinson (2008: 7). Something similar happens with brides' wedding dresses: they are a large expenditure for a single use. This is a surprising fact from an economic point of view, but not from a sociocultural perspective.

19.   Technically, the small world category gathers future states of the world that are exhaustive and mutually exclusive, features that are also shared by the consequences. This definition excludes, on the one hand, surprises and uncertainty (see Chapter 4, section 4.2.2) and, on the other hand, decisions that involve a computationally intractable number of states. At this point, Savage suggested as an example the game of chess, given that it contains around 10^{120} sequences of movements, a figure that exceeds the estimated number of atoms in the universe (Gigerenzer, 2021: 3548–3551). The axioms of optimal rationality cannot be applied in either case.

20. In stark contrast to the bulk of psychologists, anthropologists have always une-
     quivocally rejected the postulates of perfect rationality (Heukelom, 2014: 180).
21. In other words, instead of rationality conditioned by circumstances and uncer-
     tainty, there are poorly trained minds and the habit of paying scant attention
     to unimportant decisions. Therefore, increasing bets will presumably motivate
     a more optimizing behavior. However, as suggested in Thaler (2016: 1583), what
     in all likelihood increases with the magnitude of reward or loss, is nervousness
     and anguish.
22. Since the 19th century, this normative view has been part of a broad program
     of personal and social engineering, especially active in the United States. It is
     an effort to strengthen the (cognitive and/or social) capabilities of people in the
     workplace, especially if the task involves the control of complex human and/
     or technical systems. This drive for productivity has led to developments in
     ergonomics, interface design, management models, etc. See Mirowski (2002),
     Backhouse and Fontaine (2010: 186–189, 206–207 and 216–221), and Heukelom
     (2017b: 124).
23. Thomas C. Shelling (1921–2016), who received the award in 2005, could also
     be added. This mathematician proposed several models of human behavior, as
     related in section 5.1.6.3. Finally, George A. Akerlof, awarded in 2001, and
     Robert J. Shiller, awarded in 2013, should be mentioned for specific contribu-
     tions with behavioral content, such as the famous work on information asymme-
     try in the used car market (Akerlof, 1970) or the analysis of the psychological
     factors that fuel speculative bubbles in the real estate and financial markets
     (Akerlof and Shiller, 2009).
24. Type "List of cognitive biases" in a browser to ascertain it. This source contains
     over 200 biases, a number so high that many researchers of the heuristics and
     biases program probably reject it. See also M. Baddeley (2013: 106–119), and
     Tversky and Kahneman (2018a).
25. At this point, it should be warned that Thaler's analogy between visual and
     cognitive illusions is misleading (Berg and Gigerenzer, 2010: 145–146; Berg,
     2014a: 387–388; Chater et al., 2018: 799–801; and Gigerenzer, 2018). Images
     are captured in two dimensions, with the brain adding the third dimension. In
     this process, the mind attaches information so that it is possible to deceive it.
     However, this is not an easy task: the human brain is the result of millions of
     years of evolution, which explains its ability to make excellent guesses. Not
     surprisingly, visual illusions are very elaborate traps.
26. Cognitive bias detection and correction have also found their way into self-help
     books.
27. More information on the timeliness and/or effectiveness of this social technique
     can be found in Bovens (2009), HL (2011), Hausman (2012: 101), Reiss (2013:
     278 and 286–296), and Mousavi (2017: 90). Instead of nudging, authors such as
     Hertwig and Grüne-Yanoff (2017) propose to undertake actions to stimulate, or
     boost, people's competences, and the diffusion of transparent information. These
     actions are known as BRAN (bounded rational adaptive nudging) (see Viale,
     2018: 176–197).
28. This book collects the main contributions of its author in an informative format.
     The central point is the distinction between two cognitive systems (reflective
     and intuitive) that allegedly drive decision-making processes. This hypothesis,
     initially put forward in the mid 1990s by the psychologists Seymour Epstein and

Steven A. Sloman (see Stanovich and West, 2000: 658–660), has been severely criticized (see Gigerenzer and Regier, 1996; Viale, 2018: 81–98).

29. Generically speaking, a system is robust if it can tolerate disturbances that affect its functionality. In these pages, the following meaning is preferred: the ability of a system to adapt to changes in the environment, since it can take different stable configurations.

30. Specifically, the function π has an inverted S-shape, and it magnifies low probabilities and undervalues high probabilities (Hand, 2014: 192). As far as the v-value function is concerned, its asymmetric S-shape attempts to show that losing a certain value has much more psychological impact than gaining it. This conjecture has not been confirmed by experimental results (Gal and Rucker, 2018).

31. It is worth noting that the model with the parameters initially estimated by Kahneman and Tversky predicts, in general, about 75% of the choices in simple lotteries. The priority heuristic (see Chapter five), which has no adjustable parameters and follows a lexicographic algorithm, predicts 85% (Brandstätter et al., 2006).

32. In criticizing these heuristic labels, Gigerenzer (1996: 594) equates them with the reason that the doctors in Molière's play, *The Imaginary Invalid*, give to explain the somniferous capacity of opium: it contains *virtus dormitiva*.

33. Redundancy should not be confused with resilience. Repeating elements does not prevent a complex system from collapsing if multiple failures occur. Redundancy attempts to prevent its collapse due to the malfunction of a single component or (sub)system.

34. The empirical zeal of economic psychology does not make it a branch of so-called experimental economics, whose best-known author is Vernon L. Smith. He applied the postulate of ecological rationality to markets and other economic institutions, rather than to the study of individual decisions and the prominent role of heuristics. The aim is to test the impact of perfect and adaptive rationalities on the dynamics of simulated economic institutions (V. Smith, 2008: Chapter 2; Heukelom, 2014: 136–139; Mousavi, 2017).

35. In practice, the subjects surveyed or interviewed are often the researchers' own students or fellow citizens. All of them are WEIRD (Western, Educated, Industrialized, Rich, and Democratic) people since so far the bulk of the research has been done in the USA and Western Europe. Perhaps only the ultimatum game (see section 5.1.6.1) has been carried out worldwide. Therefore, there is a lack of information on the reactions of different groups within the same country and, obviously, of those from other societies and cultures. As might be expected, this situation raises misgivings about the universality of the results obtained. Henrich et al. (2010) present a long and intense debate between those who emphasize the differences in behavior among people according to their biographical, social and cultural profile, in which case the conclusions reached would only have a limited scope, and those who argue that such differences, at most, only alter the reading of the experiment, in which case they barely introduce new nuances into the results.

36. There are electroencephalograms, functional magnetic resonance imaging (fMRI), positron emission tomography (PET), and many other techniques. See Levy and Ehrlich (2018: 630) and A. Baddeley et al. (2015: Chapter 2, section 2.2).

3. The decision-making process

Before embarking on the study of economic decisions it is necessary to define the main concepts used, the decision being the most important of them. To make a decision is to choose among the various options open to an individual or group of people. This process involves motivation (including goals), drives the emergence of judgments about the consequences, and takes into consideration the possible restrictions to its execution. The first section of the chapter distinguishes between decision-making and problem-solving processes, while the second describes the main elements involved in decision-making.

3.1   DECISION-MAKING VERSUS PROBLEM-SOLVING

Problem-solving is not the same as decision-making. Problem-solving begins by recognizing that something is not working as it should and must be solved. Faced with a problem, a cognitive process to find a solution is set in motion. This process is more or less systematic, and more or less based on trial and error. Whereas in decision-making processes options are usually known (although not necessarily available or affordable), in problem-solving processes people have to create their options (or resolution procedures). Accumulated knowledge and previous experience could make things easier, although not always (Eysenck and Keane, 2010: 457–498; Skořepa, 2011: 16–17). The predisposition to follow, with more or fewer changes, already known solving methods may end up being inappropriate or even counterproductive. For example, the fact that a folk remedy has alleviated a given illness does not prescribe it as a solution to cure another with apparently similar symptoms. No doubt having solved a certain problem in the past helps to solve it now and in the future, but it can also be a pitfall if it turns out that the analogy is not right. It is also known that taking some time away from a problem makes it easier to rethink it, i.e., to approach it from another perspective. This can be applied from a household breakdown to a complex mathematical equation. This temporary disconnection allows the non-conscious function of the mind to create new plans. However, the role of the unconscious is very difficult to elucidate, although nobody questions its influence. We have all heard of (literary, scientific, artistic, technical, etc.) creators who woke up one day having found the solution to a problem that had been troubling them for days or weeks.

The case is also known of musicians, chess players, etc., who, after years of practice, have developed, without knowing very well how, a skill, a virtuosity that escapes the deliberative mind. If they think too much about what they are doing, their performance decreases. Anyway, people often face a multitude of problems without much planning. They rely too much on intuition. This is an understandable attitude given that many everyday problems are often ill-defined (Rutherford, 1988: 46). This does not imply that people, if they set their minds to it, are not capable of planning resolution operations, assuming that neither laziness nor time availability prevents them from doing so.

Decision-making is a process of choosing that begins by detecting the different options. Perhaps some of them are quickly discarded as impossible or inaccessible. The consequences of the remaining options are evaluated. Finally, the alternative to be chosen emerges. Nonetheless, once such an option has been identified, people can delay the choice.[1] In any case, the decision taken does not *cause* the consequences, since it only allows for their manifestation. As a rule, several factors play a role. All these steps make up a sequence that can take countless forms. Among the multiple types of decisions, some are characterized by involving some kind of economic value. As already explained, sometimes the economic content is exclusive (the purchase of a house as an investment), in others, it is important (the purchase of an apartment to live in) and, finally, there are cases in which the economic factor plays a secondary role (as happens in sharing a multi-owner apartment for holidays). Even more trivial is the decision of going on vacation in the coming summer. People have a given amount of money and time and some idea of the place they would like to go to. The motivation can be very diverse: a convincing advertising campaign, the place is fashionable, one's own hobbies, the enthusiastic comments of an acquaintance, the expectation of impressing the neighbors, etc. These reasons can be combined. People also usually seek information about accommodation options and procedures for traveling there. In the end, the destination chosen is considered the most desired, adapted to circumstances (holidays with friends, with children, etc.), and/or adjusted to restrictions (money, time, permits, etc.). All these processes have been dissected by decision theory to identify the factors that influenced, and the criteria used in, the choice; an analysis aimed to determine regularities, although there is always room for unexpected choices, against all odds. As Skořepa has written:

> ... in human decision-making, we should not expect the perfect, mechanical links between causes and effects ... Instead, we have to content ourselves with decision science giving us at least a *partial* understanding of why people decide the way they do, at least an *occasional* warning against *potential* mistakes in their decision-making, and at least *indicative* guidance as to what *might* push their decision-making in the desired direction. (Skořepa, 2011: 14, italics in the original)

Three important considerations can be mentioned when addressing decision-making processes:

- The judgments supporting the decisions may not be sound, even if they are consistent with the evidence gathered and processed by people.
- There are simple motivations and sophisticated ones. An example of the latter is the attempt to appease one's bad conscience when one is very indignant about circumstance X but does nothing about it. An empty statement at least serves to think well of oneself. It must always be kept in mind, as indicated in the first chapter, that the motivation adduced in a choice is another choice. Moreover, real motivation can be disguised.
- Power relations are an unavoidable element in any decision. People who formally make the decision do not always do so of their own free will. On many occasions, someone with the power to overcome the resistance of others imposes the decision. This can be done by being present in the decision process either directly or indirectly (as when the decision-maker is convinced that, if it is discovered that they have not followed the established guidelines, they will be upset by awkward consequences). The manifestations of power occur at any social level and environment. They can take many forms, but they are always present.[2]

Two further points should finally be added. First, the individual may consider all the options at stake to be equally attractive. This indifference is not necessarily attenuated by increasing the number of alternatives. This stance ("Option X is as good as option Y") should not be confused with not knowing what to choose. Not favoring any option does not always reveal indifference. People may think that they lack enough information about the decision or feel so overwhelmed that they are unable to establish an order of preference (as in the case, indicated in Reiss (2013: 39), of a death row inmate who is left to choose the method of execution). Apart from extreme circumstances, indifference usually reflects disinterest and/or apathy, something that does not necessarily occur in the case of indecision. Remember the tale attributed by some to Jean Buridan, a 14th-century scholastic philosopher: a donkey died of starvation after being unable to decide from which pile of fodder to start eating. Fortunately, humans can stretch their imagination and create stories even to justify choices about which they were initially undecided. They can also leave the decision to others, like someone who turns to chance by flipping a coin (something that the hapless donkey did not even think of). Secondly, the boundaries between problem-solving and decision-making are blurred. Problem-solving includes a creative dimension (or the search for original solutions), but also an operational one (the choice between available procedures). In other words, solving a problem usually involves making one or more decisions. Finally, a distinction should be made between decision and strategy. The latter refers to the set of decisions aimed at achieving a certain future state of affairs considered better than the current one. It is a process permeated with uncertainty and, above all, with rivals who interfere in defense of their interests. It is a dynamic in which there is room for both conflict and cooperation. In these pages, we do not talk about strategy.

Before closing this section, it should be mentioned that three approaches to decision-making have been deployed throughout history (inspired by Gigerenzer et al., 2011: xvii):

- Extended from Aristotle to computer programs, the proposal of following the laws of logic.
- Since the 17th century, the probability theory has included among its goals the establishment of decision criteria in situations of risk and, according to some authors, uncertainty.
- The claim of heuristics as mental shortcuts to speed up decisions with a modest mobilization of resources. By ignoring information, they can be applied in complex and/or uncertain environments. This versatility gives meaning to the principle of less-is-more, i.e., the frugal nature of heuristics is not at odds with their degree of success. However, it all depends on the attributes of the context.

In economics, the expected utility and prospect theories are a combination of the first two approaches. As mentioned above, they share a conception of rationality that, at the same time, is strict (because its definition is surrounded by exigent and protective assumptions) and restricted (its application outside its formal and logical limits raises doubts) (Morroni, 2006: 111–123). In this book, the focus is on heuristics as a procedure for decision-making.

3.2 BASIC CONCEPTS

In a simplified form, a decision process has two stages: the identification and evaluation of options, and the definitive choice. The complexity and time extension can be very different: in a business decision, the first phase can be laborious (many people busy for days or months), while the final choice only requires a brief meeting of a few people; conversely, in purchasing a consumer good, the final choice can take several minutes (trying on pairs of shoes until deciding which one to buy), while no time at all has been needed to decide what kind of shoes and where to buy them. In Figure 3.1, the decision process begins at point t_0, the instant at which a certain need (or the desire to attain a given goal) is perceived, and continues until moment t_T when the choice is made. Next, the period starts, normally of ill-defined duration, in which the

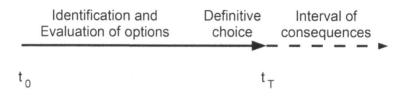

Figure 3.1   Stages of the decision process

consequences manifest themselves. A powerful reason to thoroughly evaluate the consequences is the prior existence of expectations.

The resources invested and the time spent in making a decision have nothing to do with the kind of objects to be chosen from. It all depends on the individual's will and situation. Perhaps many people do carefully evaluate the alternatives to buying a good or service if it has a comparatively high cost (or long-term effects such as a mortgage). However, even in such cases, the decision can be accelerated by many factors: the influence of emotions, the urgency of the moment, purchasing power, etc. All of them affect people differently and change over time.

The specialized literature stresses the components and dimensions of the decision processes. Concerning the components, the following terms should be considered (adaptation of Skořepa, 2011: 19–21):

- The task is the operation of choosing among several options. To carry out a task is to make a decision. To prevent the proliferation and confusion of terms, these pages always refer to the process of choice or, simply, choice.
- The set of options, or alternatives, available, although not necessarily affordable, is called the menu. There are menus with an exhaustive list of options and there are incomplete ones (probably due to uncertainty).
- Action is the choice of a concrete option.
- The alternatives have implications or consequences. Although they can only be experienced once the choice has been made, people have expectations and the capacity to anticipate (pleasant or distressing) feelings associated with the consequences. It should also be noted that outcomes could be certain, predictable, or uncertain. Sometimes, they share the same menu.
- With respect to the number of subjects involved, there are individual decisions and group decisions. Many aspects of daily life are affected by decisions made by collectives: from informal circles of friends to organized groups such as the neighborhood assembly or the executive board of a large company.
- All choices take place within a given natural and, more importantly, social context.

A decision process has the following three dimensions (Skořepa, 2011: 24–29):

- The attributes, characteristics, or features relevant to the different options. Attributes need to be defined as simply as possible, but this does not prevent complexity. For example, foods are differentiated by taste, smell, appearance, texture, and color, each feature with numerous possibilities. The options with different degrees of the same attributes form a single class. Delimiting their boundaries can be somewhat cumbersome; normally there are many attributes involved. Finally, not all people react in the same way to the same traits.
- States of the world or the circumstances within which decisions are made. There are two types of states of the world, neither of which can be subject to choice:
  - Those that originated and evolved for reasons beyond people's control, even though a person may have more or less information about them. An obvious example is the weather at the holiday destination. While the place can be chosen, people cannot prevent bad weather on the days spent there, even though it may ruin the desired leisure. Although weather forecasts can be consulted, far in advance they are unreliable and, in any case, the weather cannot be altered at will. Therefore, the consequences of a choice are not unrelated to the state of the world. It is not always possible to anticipate accurately and act accordingly.
  - Those that are unexpected by-products of past decisions. Not infrequently this has been the case with popular success or fame, a difficult state to achieve when the only motivation is the desire to attain it (Elster, 2007: Chapter 4).
- The considered period: any decision is inscribed within a certain time interval. This time frame can be very long if the consequences are incorporated (see Figure 3.1). For example, on choosing a career, a person can take into account the conditions of daily life during the years of study (atmosphere in the faculty, academic level, etc.), but also the effects beyond the career, i.e., the value that society attaches to the degree, the type of job to which one can aspire, etc. As the span increases, so does the degree of uncertainty (see Chapter 4, section 4.2.2).

Concerning the interaction with the environment, decisions can be divided into parametric (disconnected from other people's decisions) and strategic (or strongly linked to social interaction: I try to anticipate the decisions of others, knowing that others do the same with mine). In both cases, decisions can be individual or come from a group (endowed with a minimum structure). The study of the latter is not a matter for these pages (see, in this respect, Hodgkinson and Healy, 2008; Elster, 2007: Chapter 25; Sofo et al., 2013:

11–14; and Gigerenzer et al., 2022). However, it can be noted that the analysis of decisions by organized groups has at least two dimensions: the singular consequences for the incumbents and the repercussions on the progress of the organization. Their combination gives rise to the typology shown in Table 3.1 (adapted from Joule and Beauvois, 2014: 236). As can be seen, decisions with high internal social effects are the most complicated. Qualities such as the ingenuity or cunning of those involved are key elements when negotiating these issues, even though the style of exercising power, social norms, and legislation also play a large role.

Table 3.1   *Organizational types of decision (a firm)*

Type of decision (example)		Effects on the people	
		Weak	Strong
Influence on organization efficiency	Weak	Irrelevant (Choosing the office decoration)	The collaboration of incumbents is required (Overtime allocation)
	Strong	Top executives decide on their own (Financial decisions)	Clash of interests (Employment regulation file)

From the perspective of these pages, the two key concepts of decision theory are preferences and heuristics. These terms can be defined as follows (refinements in the following chapters):

- Preference is commonly used as the degree of attraction that something arouses, a subjective, in the sense of strictly personal and vital, inclination focused on making comparisons ("I like *A* better than *B*"). Since the evaluation of preferences based on objective criteria is meaningless (Gilboa et al., 2012: 22), economic analysis has considered them as immanent and immutable and has focused its interest on a formal evaluation, i.e., on the fulfillment of certain consistency tests (such as transitivity and so on). Unfortunately, the fact that preferences are a genuine manifestation of subjectivity has been the pretext for neglecting the study of the psychosocial factors that originate and modify them, especially in consumption (Luan et al., 2014: 503). However, the study of the intricate psychosocial processes that underpin them should not be ruled out. Although there are undoubtedly difficult aspects to elucidate, such as the roots of the preference formation process, there are others that do not present major obstacles, such as the analysis of their alterations (as described in Chapter 6).
- Etymologically, heuristics refers to the art of exploring, finding, discovering, or inventing something. It refers to both the sudden occurrence that

allows us to solve a small domestic breakdown and the mental shortcut that allows us to make complex decisions. Although heuristics are consciously applied, the mind's unconscious background is often behind them, either by nurturing confidence in the choice or by awakening ingenious solutions (Gigerenzer, 2014: 30 and 2015: ix). In decision theory, the concept of heuristics collects a set of simple and easy-to-apply algorithms that speed up decisions, from the most ordinary to the most compromising.[3]

Preferences inherently incorporate the intention to choose. However, as noted above, intentions do not necessarily trigger actions. A further complication is that desires can change at any time, even on the fly. The relationship between affordable and available options may also be altered (Skořepa, 2011: 39). Finally, in the case of groups, the existence of some procedure for making the preferences explicit should be assumed, given that its members may have different personal preferences. When the choice is finally made, not everyone has to be equally satisfied, regardless of the method implemented to make the decision.

Another important aspect is to distinguish between preferences and needs. To begin with, it should be stressed that the concept of needs has different meanings. The term comes from debates on the human condition and its evolution. Its adoption by the different social sciences has given rise to multiple particular conceptions. In economics, in contrast to disciplines such as anthropology or sociology, the meaning of needs is simple: the feeling of something (present or expected) lacking, that is, people feel that something is missing, something they cannot do without. This gives rise to paradoxical situations: a person can wish for what they do not need ("I want another drink, but I need to stop drinking"), just as they may need what they do not want ("I need to diet, but I am uncomfortable with the feeling of hunger"). Consequently, the meaning of needs is very restricted, even becoming a simple synonym for desire, as is common in marketing. In these pages, priority is given to a broader meaning: needs are the set of (material and social) requirements essential to enjoy a fully human existence. Needs are both universal (deprivation makes any individual or collective action impossible) and contingent result (needs are expressed in concrete goods and services). Therefore, the concept of needs is placed at a higher level of generality than preferences, which are developed from needs after a long mediation of historical, social, and personal factors. Preferences are the embodiment of needs.

Health and personal autonomy constitute the most basic and universal needs (Doyal and Gough, 1991: 49–75). Without them, humans cannot effectively participate in community affairs by pursuing the goals they deem valuable.[4] On the one hand, lack of health hinders the exercise of many human skills. Its serious loss impedes, or makes impossible, the normal development of a life project. On the other hand, if personal autonomy is understood as the recog-nized and respected capacity to influence the social fabric, people must be able to set goals, think about how to attain them, evaluate the results, and assume responsibility for the consequences. Failure to meet these two needs puts the physical and/or mental integrity of people at risk. That said, there is no doubt that the ways of having access to nutritious food and clean water, adequate shelter from inclement weather, working in a risk-free environment, receiving appropriate health and reproductive care, experiencing a safe childhood, being able to build meaningful relationships of affiliation and social interaction, to have the ability to participate in and enjoy recreational activities, and so on, have been very diverse depending on geographical location, historical moment and social context. Consequently, preferences are no more than specific con-cretions within a huge array of possibilities.

Heuristics are characterized by the following features (according to Todd and Gigerenzer, 2000: 738–739; Gigerenzer and Gaissmaier, 2011: 451; Gigerenzer, 2015: 11; and Keller and Katsikopoulos, 2016):

- They are a mental (un- and consciousness) tool. Heuristics can be quickly applied in decision-making or after a careful process of selection. In this case, people evaluate the one that seems best suited to the situation at hand.
- They reflect the human capacity to make adaptive inferences under the pragmatic principle: "cope satisfactorily".
- They fulfill the less-is-more principle, i.e., less precision is not the price of less effort.
- They focus attention on the cues characterizing the options, especially those with salience. This is integrated into an original mental representation that pushes the choices.[5] Obviously, it entails some risks: the reflections of genuine diamonds are perfectly imitated by simple rhinestone crystals.

The human mind does not use a few general-purpose cognitive tools but rather deploys a wide collection of adaptive plans (Todd and Gigerenzer, 2000: 741, 768). Among these, heuristics feature for being associated with the following type of propositions: the fast and frugal heuristic X is more suitable than A, B, C, … when it comes to making decision Y involving options characterized by cues H within a given environment E. However, it should be pointed out that heuristics only examine and evaluate a few cues. Therefore, inferences are drawn from partial knowledge, which is usually unavoidable due to the difficulty for the human mind of processing large volumes of information and the presence of uncertainty.[6] However, many disciplines rely on sophisticated inference techniques, among which multiple regression stands out. Based on probability and statistical theory, these techniques involve systematic calculations to integrate all available information (including noise). Each unit of information is then weighted and combined with the rest. To the contrary, heuristics are based on the correspondences between the pieces that make up a given reality. They do not try to exhaust the information distilled by the environment, but rather to exploit its structure, that is, its regularities and redundancies. Although reality contains a bunch of dispersed elements, it is supposed that they are not randomly arranged.

There are certain common errors in interpreting the concept of heuristics. The following list brings them together (adapted from Gigerenzer, 2008: 21):

- Their results are always second best. However, in many decisions optimization is not possible, either because of the uncertainty or the complexity (up to computationally intractable levels). Consequently, predictions from heuristic algorithms could be very accurate (see Chapter 5, section 5.1.7).
- They reflect the imperfections of human cognition. False: heuristics are a genuine creation of the mind that adapts people to the social and natural environment.
- They are usually applied in decisions of little importance (or small world). The greater the complexity and uncertainty, the more people are advised.

The algorithm is the last concept to be outlined. As noted above, it denotes a specific procedure of choice (or problem-solving). For example, the proof by nine is an algorithm. It is a quick test to verify whether multiplication or a division is correct. With the spread of calculators, practically nobody uses this criterion anymore (in fact, many young people have not even heard about it). It is worth adding that, if the proof detects that an operation is wrong, it is sure, but if it indicates that the result is correct, there is a small probability that this is not true. It, therefore, shares heuristic features: the diagnosis is usually good, although not infallible. On the other hand, the formula for obtaining the solutions of a second-degree equation of type $ax^2 + bx + c = 0$, with $a, b, c \neq 0$, that is,

$$x_{1,2} = \frac{-b \pm \sqrt{b^2 - 4ac}}{2a}$$

gives the correct answer in all cases. It is a mathematical algorithm. Halfway there are computer algorithms that search for correlations and regularities in huge databases (or big data), whether from natural or socioeconomic phenomena (Christl and Spiekermann, 2016).

The algorithms used in decision theory are very concrete criteria for making a decision. The main job of researchers is to study their advantages and shortcomings. Moreover, these algorithms can either be invented, that is, they have essentially been designed to comply with some desirable properties, or they have been derived from field experiences in which real people make real or simulated decisions. To illustrate the former, let us take the example of choosing between two lotteries under risky conditions (the brackets indicating "prize, probability") (inspired by Brandstätter et al., 2006: 417):

A. (€4000; 0.8; €0, 0.2)
B. (€3000, 1).

It is not difficult to imagine algorithms for choosing between *A* and *B*. Some may focus on outcomes while ignoring probabilities, while others may consist of applying the probability calculus in a rudimentary way. In the first group, individuals may follow rules such as the following:

- Calculate the average winnings of each lottery and choose the highest. In the example suggested, *B* is chosen since €3,000 are the average winnings, an amount higher than that of lottery *A* (€4,000/2).
- Add the results of each lottery and choose the highest one. In this case, *A* shows the highest figure (€4,000).
- Apply the minimax criterion: the lottery with the highest minimum value, i.e., *B* is chosen since its minimum amount (€3,000) is higher than the other minimum (€0).
- First of all, add the results of both lotteries and extract the average, i.e., €4,000 + €3,000 + €0 = €7,000/3 = €2,333.30. Then count the number of values equal to or higher than this average. Finally, the lottery with the highest number of cases is chosen. As can be seen, this complicated algorithm does not lead to any choice in the proposed example.

Among the second type, the following algorithms can be imagined:

- The most probable outcome of each lottery is identified (€4,000 for *A* and €3,000 for *B*) and, without going into further consideration, the largest one is chosen: lottery *A* in this case.
- Find the worst result of each lottery and choose the one with the lowest probability. In the example, the worst result is €0 in lottery *A* and €3,000 in *B*. Therefore, *A* is chosen because €0 is less probable. This is a paradoxical choice, although it derives from the peculiar algorithm used: €0 is a result less probable than €3,000, the maximum and also minimum amount of lottery *B*.
- The rule is established that only probability values above a given threshold will be considered, e.g., ≥ 50% for lotteries of one or more outcomes. Next, the largest quantity is taken. The choice, in this case, falls on *A* (80% exceeds the threshold and corresponds to the highest figure).
- The mathematical expectation criterion leads to the choice of lottery *A*.

All of these algorithms are valid but contrived. Although the design of algorithms has achieved an extraordinary degree of formal sophistication (see Skořepa, 2011: Chapter 6), in these pages the priority is algorithms rooted in psychological field experiments.[7] This condition has at least three implications:

- It means the abandonment of the powerful line of purely formal work in decision analysis.
- The search for prescriptive algorithms loses importance. These algorithms, when applied to a certain class of decision processes, guarantee better results than those attained using any other algorithm. It should be remembered that the identification of prescriptive algorithms requires an algorithm to choose between algorithms (Skořepa, 2011: 23).
- Real life is a patchwork of diverse situations, not always well defined. Moreover, the consequences of decisions only rarely escape divergent interpretations. Faced with these difficulties, it is at least as significant to describe decision-making procedures commonly used by people, as to focus on the consequences.

In economic psychology, there are no universally valid algorithms, and they are not infallible. Some algorithms are more or less advisable depending on the context. What is indisputable is their rationality.

NOTES

1. The decision taken at a given time and place is not necessarily executed. The arrival of new information may cause people to change their minds, as well as unforeseen changes in the decision context. In economic issues, changing decisions on the fly is commonplace.
2. Power could be defined as the ability to get others to do what you want them to do (and not to think about what you do not want them to think about). Power demands to be displayed since it is about the perception of certain (known and imaginative) cues, but it is only credible if it is successfully exerted. Six sources of power have been identified: of threatening or punishing non-compliance, giving or promising rewards in exchange for compliance, based on the belief that they have more information, based on greater experience or knowledge, based on legitimacy, and that based on identification with a given powerful entity (Hogg and Vaughan, 2014: 238; Solomon, 2015: 389).
3. The term heuristic has other meanings more or less close to the one indicated. For example, in the field of computer engineering, it is a procedure for identifying possible solutions to a given problem and, hence, a tool for reducing the space of options in choosing the best one (Groner, 1983: 13–16). In turn, in handbooks of cognitive psychology, such as Eysenck and Keane (2010: 464), emphasis is placed on mental acuity, so the meaning of heuristics is close to insight.
4. To undertake an action, regardless of the motivations and/or results, people must be able to describe it. This requires mastering a (verbal or gestural) language

learned from adults (Steedman, 1989: 207, 212–214). The lack of this contact explains the incomplete development of so-called feral children.

5.   These mental representations are part of the probabilistic mental models. Leaving details to one side, it can be said that these models estimate the probability that an inference is true because the premises (knowledge, beliefs, etc.) are also true. More information in Gigerenzer et al. (1991).

6.   And with an unexpected ally: forgetfulness. As argued in Schooler and Hertwig (2005: 610–611), would it not be a nuisance to remember all the old telephone numbers or the different parking bays in which we sometimes parked? This irrelevant and obsolete information would interfere with remembering what matters here and now.

7.   In this case, lottery *B* would be chosen by most, because of risk aversion when a given sum can be gained (see Chapter 4, section 4.2.1).

4. Elements for the analysis of economic decisions

Economic analysis has been particularly interested, although not exclusively, in decision-making in the consumer realm, although at best with poor psychological and social contents, as explained in Chapter 2. To begin with, in this chapter, a simple model is proposed on the factors that broadly influence economic choices. This implies giving prominence to people's biographical traits and circumstances, as well as their lifestyles. The remainder of the chapter is divided into three sections: the first encompasses the treatment of risk and uncertainty, the second explores the diversity observed in inter-temporal choices, and the third focuses on the psychological dimension of sunk costs and the endowment effect.

Before diving into the chapter, there should be a warning that most of the examples mentioned belong to the sphere of the final consumption of goods and services. However, the text also contains some cases relating to the management of one's own resources (income, savings, investments, etc.). Unfortunately, research on the latter is less developed than on the former.

4.1 PSYCHOLOGICAL AND ECONOMIC COMPONENTS

Economic choices are influenced by two main types of factors:

- A conglomerate formed by preferences, beliefs, emotions, and information stored in the memory (either after a dedicated searching process or not). Choices are driven by the interaction between these elements. It should also not be forgotten that this relation is built upon the characteristics of human perception and the configuration of the social environment.
- Constraints of all kinds (physical, temporal, economic, legal, moral) that reduce the set of affordable options. Some are objective (such as purchasing power) and others have been assimilated by people (such as social norms). It should be added that people's management of their resources, or mental accounting, has received considerable attention in economic psychology, which is why a specific section is devoted to it.

Figure 4.1 is a simple representation of the connection between preferences, beliefs, emotions, and information, given the social (and natural) framework and different types of constraints (inspired by Elster, 1989: Chapter 4 and 2007: Chapter 11; Noguera and Tena, 2013; and Hausman, 2012: 113). This is the basic and generic conceptual framework for explaining economic decisions.

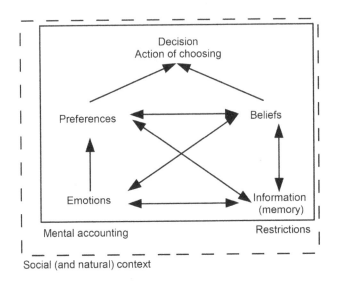

Figure 4.1   Network of factors influencing decisions

The first thing to take into account is that preferences are not central. Economic psychology's quest to unveil the background of decisions has highlighted the role of beliefs and emotions, as well as that of memory. As shown, beliefs can influence choices both directly and indirectly through preferences. The latter is taken for granted, but the former effect may seem surprising: the herding behavior described by the critical mass model would be an example (see section 5.1.6.3).[1] As far as emotions are concerned, they usually act through preferences, although if they have great intensity and urgency they can determine decisions on their own.[2] After having passed through the sieve of perception, the information collected and stored in memory is mixed with previous experiences. The resulting combination plays a fundamental role in the formation of beliefs and preferences, and vice versa, which explains the double arrows connecting these elements. Another mutual influence is established between emotions and information: memories are stored with the emotions that accompanied them, the latter being a key factor in facilitating their retrieval. The following pages contain examples relating to all of these links.

4.1.1 Preferences

To begin with, it is worth remembering that the word preference has at least four different meanings (from Hausman, 2012: 1):

- It denotes the option that a person considers as more pleasant: people saying they prefer to travel by bus than by subway indicates that the use of the former is more satisfactory than the latter. The choice presupposes that both alternatives are equally affordable.
- The comparison between two or more options of the same class, one of which ends up being considered superior. The sentence "I prefer car A to car B" actually expresses the following subjective preeminence: "I consider that A is better than B," a relation that economists write as $A > B$. The preferred brand is more trustworthy, more convenient, and so on. The reasons may be very diverse.
- A mere synonym for order of priority, like the signs that indicate for whom certain seats (in a bus, train, etc.) are reserved. On many roads, there are also lanes for slow vehicles. This primacy does not determine the degree of satisfaction of the users.
- As a simple allusion to a choice: when the waiter asks which dish is preferred from the menu, he only wants to know the customer's choice. He does not care why.

Interestingly, all these meanings are close to the concept of preference as it has been used, at one time or another, in economic discourse. Economic psychology mixes the first two meanings. Indeed, they stress the private and personal character of the evaluation made and the attached justifications (including that of not knowing why what has been chosen was chosen). This rationalization appears before the final choice and, not infrequently, afterward (Hausman, 2012: 6). Thus, people interested in buying a car observe those models they like, and once a specific one has been acquired, they then try to ascertain whether there are more of the same. The purpose is to reinforce the choice made since, if it is a popular car, it seems more suitable: "So many people cannot be wrong."

This conception of preferences considers them to be undoubtedly learned. This fact, however, does not prevent each individual from uniquely manifesting their preferences, always in line with accumulated experiences (including the impact of unforeseen circumstances). People regularly process and reprocess all the contents of their memory, shaping their preferences and, consequently, ending up with a fairly clear idea of their preferences, but much less of how they came to have them.

The last two meanings are close to the conventional view: the analysis of preferences is reduced to the (appropriate) properties of options order. This is a more feasible approach if it is assumed that preferences are given.[3] Moreover, the waiter's disinterest in the customer's motives evokes the point of view of revealed preferences.

Approaching preferences from the perspective of economic psychology means, above all, deploying a series of contributions and conceptual distinctions concerning the process of preference formation (Hausman, 2012: 112–113). The insistence on the psychosocial bases of preferences also includes the analysis of the multiple and subtle ways in which they can be modified, especially in the sphere of consumption (see Chapter 6). These endeavors inevitably erode the theoretical relevance of logical properties (coherence, transitivity, etc.) of preferences. Concerning plain psychology, it should be stressed that it is also interested in preferences, but rarely uses this term. Psychology deals with motivations and desires, but constraints and manipulations play a secondary role.

At first, economic psychology proposes a double distinction to the term preferences (Skořepa, 2011: 31–32):

- According to their degree of persistence, it is possible to distinguish between elementary preferences and final (or total) preferences.
- According to how they are disclosed, the difference between raw preferences and preferences based on inferences is set.

Elementary preferences are the inclinations that characterize people's choices. Therefore, they are spread over time, but this persistence does not mean they are immutable. Concerning final preferences, these are the ones that determine the particular choices at a given time and place. For example, although a person may have certain clothing preferences, the influence of a strong advertising campaign, a momentary offer, the skill of the salesperson, etc., may cause them to end up buying a different model from the one they are used to. It could also happen that the desired garment is out of stock (and this person is not willing to waste more time looking for it in other stores). The differentiation between elementary and final preferences makes it possible to incorporate unexpected and ad hoc changes into the analysis.

Concerning elementary preferences, the following considerations should be kept in mind:

- They are not always very well defined. This leaves room for final preferences to materialize in numerous ways and, more importantly, to be easily reoriented. In this respect, it should not be forgotten that the consumption sphere is overflowing with an enormous variety of items and claims. The huge array of final preferences and the enormous variety of goods and services are mutually reinforcing.

- They are not rigid, that is, they signal at the same time what is liked (or disliked) and also maintain a remarkable ambiguity in the face of various alternatives.
- They can change as the state of the world changes. This is evident in the case of the socioeconomic status shifting. Elementary preferences can also be altered by personal circumstances such as the couple who, having preferred to live with discreet neighbors to preserve their privacy, on having children, come to prefer sociable ones, since they now need to meet a trusted person for babysitting. Another trivial situation may be the following: having a car makes it easier to satisfy the preference for a certain type of show (in sports, music, etc.), given that it allows you to travel. Finally, here we should include the impact of possible unpleasant situations, such as those who come to detest dogs after one has bitten them.

Final preferences reflect the influence of the momentary situation. In consumption decisions, they even alter the perception of relative prices. To illustrate this, let us take the following example (adapted from Vohra and Krishnamurthi, 2012: 9–10):

- We are on holiday, sunbathing on the beach. Suddenly we would like to drink a very cold beer, especially a favorite brand. A friend tells us that he has to fetch something from the car, parked near a luxurious hotel in which, if we agree, he can buy our beer. Since the bottle will be expensive there, he asks us how much we are willing to pay. What is usually the answer?
- With the hotel option discarded as too expensive, the friend tells us that, returning from the car, he made a detour to pass near a kiosk and buy our beer. However, he did not dare since it was the same price as in the hotel. How do you react to this news?

The most common answer to the first question is that people are willing to pay between double and triple the usual price. If the hotel moves within this range, the beer is bought because of the expectation that, in a luxurious place, everything is more expensive. Even so, the price at the kiosk, the same as at the hotel, will be considered abuse. Although we are on holiday, that is, in a period in which the control of expenses is relaxed, we are aware that the hotel and the kiosk are not sale points of the same category. Price comparisons are always linked to the general context: enjoying leisure makes it easier to pay a price for a particular drink in an airport, or on board an airplane, cruise ship, etc., that would not be tolerated in a bar at home. People, therefore, first identify the context, then compare its elements.

Table 4.1   *Combination of preferences*

Preferences		Disclosure process	
		Raw	Inferential
Nature	Elemental	Interiorized tastes	Identifying a novelty
	Final	Sudden appetite	More or less careful examination

According how they arise, it is necessary to distinguish between raw prefer-ences, those closely associated with individual's tastes or desires, and those that emerge as a result of inferences. The former determines choices immedi-ately: people simply confirm that they like the choice and stop thinking about it (Gilboa et al., 2004: 11). Later, suitable stimuli will activate such preferences again. They can also be called visceral preferences, a word that is now stripped of any negative connotation. It only intends to denote what is internal, intimate, or endearing without, in turn, denying that the preferences are learned. The raw preferences refer to people's basic tastes ("I have always loved chocolate"), the origin of which is lost in the process of people's socialization.[4] Therefore, it comes as no surprise that these learned dispositions will end up as part of their own identity. They have a consubstantial character and are inseparable from their holders. Concerning the preferences based on inferences, it can be said that they emerge after a more or less careful inspection of the available options. Sometimes these inferences include benchmarks: A is chosen instead of other options because it is concluded that it contains a given attribute above, or below, a certain threshold. It should be noted that the benchmark may be based on arbitrary assumptions and, hence, susceptible to manipulation (see Ariely et al., 2003). If the reference changes, so does the choice. Whatever it may be, if the choice revealed by inference is pleasant, it is inscribed in the mind.

The division of elemental/final preferences and raw/inference-based prefer-ences can be combined, as in Table 4.1. The mix between raw and elemental corresponds to tastes internalized by people, which are usually resilient. However, there may also be elemental preferences that are temporarily with-held until the object in question has been identified, as indicated by the inferen-tial/elemental combination. For example, when faced with a new presentation of an ingredient, even if it has been explained and seems appealing, it may take a moment to taste it due to a lack of previous experience or, rather, familiarity. The mix of raw/final preferences includes cases of a sudden change of appetite: "I really like X, but I choose Y because I am imitating the other diners." Finally, in an exotic restaurant, the choice of several unknown dishes triggers the for-mulation of inferences (e.g., looking for associations that presumably inform the tastes). If no conclusion is reached, choosing can be done randomly. As can be seen, all four examples come from the world of food, an inexhaustible source of contingent construction and unexpected alterations of preferences.

Another common example of analyzing preferences is the consumption of luxury and high-end products. As is well known, this includes items such as clothing, shoes, leather goods, watches and writing implements, jewelry, automobiles, electronic equipment, houses and furniture, artwork, and so on, to which can be added hotels, resorts, and exclusive restaurants. In almost every type of goods and services there is a top level. This is characterized by the following attributes (Delpal and Jacomet, 2014: 28–30):

- The quality and scarcity of the raw materials used, as well as the particular skills of the workers (craftsmen) who made them.
- Their reputation for indicating status (ostentation) and spreading certain aesthetic (and, by extension, symbolic) values. Both qualities are exploited by manufacturers and sellers to create exquisite stories that feed the advertising initiatives.
- The points of sale are usually located close to each other to benefit from the halo effect which, in this case, reinforces the elitist character of these products.[5]

Luxury and high-end goods or services can only be afforded by upper and affluent middle classes and, occasionally, lower middle classes.[6] These goods reflect the socially recognized status of the purchasers, being more attractive the higher the price. For occasional consumers, they are an indicator of aspiration (see Szmigin and Piacentini, 2015: 190; Trentman, 2016: 439; and Currid-Helkett, 2017: 11–19). Luxury is, therefore, a social marker, especially important for people in the process of enrichment.[7] It is not surprising that lavish consumption, which includes luxury items, large spaces (homes and estates), and personalized services, is defined more in terms of experience than strict possession. In other words, the object is only the vehicle for hedonism which becomes an autonomous raw preference. To paraphrase what was pointed out in Chapter 1, lavish consumption and the enjoyment it provokes are mutually reinforcing. It is a relationship with an evident addictive potential: more than the satisfaction that the object transmits, people end up preferring the status conveyed by such preferences.

It is also necessary to distinguish the experience of luxury goods from the consumption of so-called experience goods and connoisseur goods, although sometimes they overlap. The former are goods or services whose quality is not known until they have been consumed, as occurs with many cultural performances. Once the product has been experienced, people are not necessarily satisfied. They can even be disappointed. Connoisseur goods attract consumers convinced that only initiated people (or, at least, so they claim) can enjoy them. They include artisanal foods and beverages and, especially, everything that is suitable to be collected, such as antique car models, stamps, etc. The association between knowledge and satisfaction gives notoriety to both the initiates and the objects related. However, they neither have to be expensive nor do they reflect a desire for ostentation. In short, preferences can be impregnated with signs of status, as well as hedonism and snobbishness.

The discussion on preferences would not be complete without referring to some widespread ideas which, seen from a psychosocial perspective, deserve reformulation. Three points of the analysis of preferences should be considered:

- the disdain for the concepts of wants and tastes;
- the assumption that choices are evidence of preferences;
- the importance given to the property of transitivity.

First, it should be pointed out that the concept of wants is much more flexible than that of preference (Hausman, 2012: x and 6; Reiss, 2013: 32). It indicates what people wish to do or have, but nothing prevents them from wanting two or more different things at the same time. Conversely, two or more things cannot be preferred simultaneously. By definition, the relation of preference always results in the choice of a given option, which may or not be executed. Moreover, the aforementioned simultaneity should not be confused with indifference, a situation in which the choice may end up being made at random. In addition, it should again not be forgotten that preferring an object does not imply it is wanted (it may be a consolation prize).

Preferences and tastes are close terms: raw preferences can be understood as an expression of tastes. Therefore, raw preferences can determine issues from ordinary consumption to decisions on one's health and future. However, it could be suspected that this synonymy distorts the concept of preferences, given that "there is nothing written about tastes." Everyone has their tastes: some people like white wine and some people prefer red wine. There is a deep and intimate motivation that makes any discussion about it futile. Trying to find out which taste is better is a waste of time. True. Even so, to maintain that preferences are on a higher analytical plane than tastes responds to a double theoretical commitment:

- Preferences are assumed to be permanent and unalterable (an ontological postulate).
- Preferences are considered inscrutable: there is no need to specify them, no need to wonder about the factors that have originated and modified them (a methodological position).

The refusal to connect preferences and tastes on the pretext that the latter are banal is a ploy to shift scrutiny away from the former and, hence, to strengthen the postulates of optimal choice. The message is that axioms do not regulate vulgar appetites, but rather immanent and immutable preferences (Hausman, 2012: 17–19). However, the goal of economic psychology is not to debate tastes, but to unveil the personal factors and social influences that explain them. This task is far from being futile: although personal tastes are merely circumstantial, they are of great value as indicators of the historical and social place of people, as well as of the context in which they are at a given moment.

Regarding the second point, although it is true that in principle choices are evidence of preferences, this does not support the assumption that the former exhaust the latter. On the one hand, choices do not explain why something was chosen. To find out, it is necessary to review the role of the elements in Figure 4.1. This job is as revealing as it is often arduous. On the other hand, the choices made do not necessarily reveal people's preferences (Hausman, 2012: 24–28). For instance, as indicated, choosing nothing does not mean not having any preferences. People may give up if they are unable to establish a ranking due to the huge number of comparisons the choice entails. More usually, choosing not to choose is a good maneuver if the choice could be regretted. It also happens that people know their preference but do not implement it due to a lack of will. Regardless of the barely mentioned circumstances, the divergence between preferences and choices may be caused by the following objective reasons:

- Because of poor quality or inadequate information, as when a friend recommends a movie to us thinking that we will like it (it presumably fits our preferences) but, once seen, it turns out that this is not the case. It can also occur that the lack of knowledge of the entire billboard pushes us to see a film far from our tastes. In general, even though we may like an option, we may choose another one because it has known characteristics.
- Due to environmental pressure: I go to a concert by musician I don't like very much because I abide by the decision made by the group of friends with whom I share my free time.
- For unforeseen reasons that prevent me from enjoying the choice: when I arrive at my favorite restaurant, there is an unexpectedly long queue.
- Due to prior commitments of the individual. This is the case of someone who chooses to drink water rather than wine, even though she prefers the latter, because she has promised her friend to drive her home after the party (Hausman, 2012: 3).

In addition to the above-mentioned reasons, as explained in a later section, there is the impact of all kinds of restrictions.

The last point deals with the principle of transitivity of preferences. As mentioned, over the last century many researchers studied the ordering of preferences. This work is closely associated with the formulation of the axioms

seen in Chapter 2 since its goal is to guarantee the consistency of preferences
required by perfect rationality. In this vein, transitivity is very important. It
takes the following form: if $a \succ b$ and $b \succ c$, then, $a \succ c$, a, b and c being
certain options. Intransitivity occurs when $c \succ a$, an anomaly that is considered
a manifestation of irrationality. Indeed, we could consider the case of a person
who prefers to drink a cup of coffee (C) to a cup of tea (T), a cup of tea to
a herbal infusion (I), and the latter to coffee, that is, $C \succ T \succ I \succ C \succ T \succ \ldots$
Faced with this arrangement of preferences, someone could offer this person
to exchange coffee for tea by paying a small amount of money; then pay to
replace tea with an infusion, and then the infusion with coffee. And so on and
so forth, so that they will be paying until they run out of resources, without
having been able to establish any preference. This is the money pump effect.
However, it is unthinkable that people do not become aware of the trap as they
watch their money dwindle (Chater et al., 2018: 797; Gigerenzer, 2021: 3552).

Intransitivity is not actually an obfuscation of the mind, but rather a very
common situation and usually without remarkable consequences (Thaler and
Tversky, 1992: 82; Skořepa, 2011: 112, 137, 154; Rizzo, 2019). Intransitivity
can occur for three main reasons:

- The impact of exogenous factors such as social norms. Consider the
  following case (Reiss, 2013: 40 and 176): at the time of dessert, the host
  asks the guest to choose between a large apple (A^L) or a small apple (A^S).
  Although the guest likes apples very much, for etiquette reasons, they
  go for the small apple ($A^S \succ A^L$). Immediately, the host remembers that
  they also have an orange (O). The guest finally chooses the large apple.
  Hence, $A^L \succ O \succ A^S$. The appearance of a normally sizable piece of fruit,
  the orange, allows them to justify the final choice of the large apple. The
  intransitivity hides the fear of giving a bad image (the conventions in force
  discourage a guest from appearing to abuse hospitality).
- The limitations of sensory perception: regarding the temperature of bath
  water, a person establishes the following preferences: 25°C ~ 26°C and
  26°C ~ 27°C, although 27°C $\succ$ 25°C. Transitivity is disrupted because
  the individual should also be indifferent between 25°C and 27°C. This is
  known as improper intransitivity and it is explained by the fact that human
  perception is not fine-tuned enough to distinguish a degree of difference in
  temperature (Katsikopoulos and Gigerenzer, 2008: 48).
- Due to preference reversal (Tversky et al., 1990; Thaler and Tversky, 1992:
  81–83). An individual is asked to choose between lottery A which has
  a high probability of winning a modest prize (say, 8/9 of winning €100),
  or lottery B in which more money (€250) can be won but with a low probability (1/9). The first one is the most frequently chosen ($A \succ B$), although
  the second one is the most valued, i.e. the participants ask for higher

compensation, C, to give it up (C_B dominates C_A). Therefore, depending on how the choice is presented, the preference changes. The following intransitivity stands out: $C_A \sim A > B \sim C_B > C_A$, that is, C_A is indifferent to A and preferred to B, which is indifferent to C_B and preferred to C_A. In this case, the reversal implies a cyclical choice due to the different criteria used in valuing lotteries: on playing, the more certain outcome, and, on asking for compensation, the higher value.

There is nothing exceptional about intransitivity. It easily appears on combining just three objects (a, b and c) active in three environments (1, 2 and 3). For example, the objects are companies and the environments are market segments. Suppose that company a sells products in segments 1 and 2, with a clear advantage in the former; firm b also operates in 1 and 2, being more successful in the latter; and, finally, company c covers segments 2 and 3, with more sales in the third one. Let us consider Table 4.2 in which the sign ++ indicates that the corresponding segment is the most favorable for the company, the sign + means that it has reduced commercial performance, and 0 that it does not operate in that segment.

Table 4.2   Intransitivity

Items/segments		Market segments		
		1	2	3
Firms	a	++	0	+
	b	+	++	0
	c	0	+	++
Prevalence		a > b	b > c	c > a

As can be seen, the companies meet the following dominance relationships: $a > b$, $b > c$ but $c > a$.[8] As a general rule, intransitivity is likely to appear when different elements interact in different circumstances, as in the case of species competition in a given ecosystem (Gigerenzer and Goldstein, 1996: 664). The same happens if the relationship between elements suffers the impact of conflicting stimuli, something common in psychology. For example, the relationship "being a friend of" does not have to be transitive (a fact already identified in the first half of the 1950s as reported in Edwards, 1954: 405).

In summary, preferences have the following characteristics:

- They take the form of subjective comparisons of options, without being exhaustive or logically consistent.
- They are not immanent but learned. Preferences are shaped by socialization and learning processes. For example, since eating is much more than

ingesting certain chemicals (Steedman, 1989: 214; Lyman, 1989), food preferences and, by extension, consumption patterns, have to be understood as an extension of people's identity and lifestyle (Hausman, 2012: 119).

- They are easily altered, either subtly or coercively (see Chapter 6).
- They do not necessarily reflect people's selfishness: people show empathy for others, care about the environment, collaborate in all kinds of NGOs, etc.
- Satisfying preferences does not imply achieving a higher level of welfare (Berg, 2014a: 382). In economics, welfare is associated with the satisfaction of current preferences, which implies a plethora of goods. However, the fact that rational people always choose the best for them does not mean that this is also the best for others. For example, the welfare of a sadist means satisfying an antisocial preference.[9] Whatever it may be, people may prefer things that are far from their daily experience (such as preserving endangered species) or that do not materialize at the moment (as is often the case when cooperating for a future goal). Therefore, the relationship between preferences and welfare is more complex than it might seem at first glance (Reiss, 2013: 214–225).

Having reviewed the concept of preferences, it is now time to address the other broad factors that determine economic choices.

4.1.2   Beliefs

Beliefs are ideas, convictions, or particular visions of reality. They are learned from other people or emerged from interpreting lived experiences. They become so strongly rooted in the mind that people think they have always held them. Beliefs include not only worldviews, ideological postulates, or moral principles but also positions and opinions on everyday facts such as, for example, thinking that milk and dairy products are the healthiest foods, that a cactus near a computer screen absorbs radiation, or that there are numbers that bring good or bad luck.[10] It should also be pointed out that groups of people who share a certain belief do not usually have stable and well-defined boundaries.

Every belief is rational, but this does not imply that it is true. While the truth is a feature of the relationship between the world and the belief, the quality of being rational only stresses that an attempt has been made to gather evidence, of whatever kind, to support it. However, these proofs may be insufficient and/ or wrong. Beliefs facilitate the process of decision-making, since collecting more and more information comes at a cost and can excessively delay the final decision, a fact which can be counterproductive. Indeed, beliefs provide reasons, which does not mean that they are the most appropriate ones. An old joke explains that two hikers were walking up a mountain path when, suddenly, a menacing bear appeared. One of them immediately turned around and started to run back down the trail. He was convinced that this was the only way of escaping, despite the load he was carrying. Paradoxically, the other hiker calmly sat down, took off his backpack, and put on a pair of sneakers. When the first one saw him acting like that, he said: "Do you think you can out-run the bear? The second hiker, still sitting, replied: "Not out-run the bear, but out-run you." Beliefs support all kinds of decisions, from the most successful to the most disastrous. Although, as is obvious, beliefs are stored in the memory, some are expressed more often, i.e., they are more accessible, a fact explained by the influence of people's social environment and lifestyle. At the same time, recurring beliefs are also the most selective: people concerned about cleanliness see more dirt everywhere than anybody else (Hogg and Vaughan, 2014: 165).

Some beliefs have been proven to be true, such as the length of a circumference being equal to $2\pi r$, or the Earth orbits the Sun. However, there are beliefs that have been contradicted: not all swans are white, nor do all rivers flow into the sea (the Okavango flows into a desert). Going a step further, there are very ambiguous beliefs: what does it mean to believe in eternal life or the benefits of the free market? It is not surprising that, in common parlance, believing something does not imply full adherence: someone may believe that it will rain tomorrow and suspect at the same time that they may be wrong.

Beliefs, like preferences, are mental representations, not states of the world. They can be formed all at once by an intense lived experience or emerge slowly through the influence of other people, information, etc. (Aronson, 2008: 114). As Figure 4.1 shows, beliefs have a strong influence on choices. This explains why advertising for goods and services strives to create and modulate them and, as far as possible, associate them with basic emotions, such as the fear of losing one's health. An example would be so-called functional foods. These are highly processed products with presumably very nutritious and restorative properties. Their large-scale appearance occurred during the 1990s when the large generation born after World War II reached 40 to 50 years of age, an age when health concerns usually begin. Simultaneously, more and more information about cardiovascular disease was being reported in the media, with the dreaded cholesterol as the main risk factor. Although the food/health link has been known for ages, in recent years the food industry has associated it with the consumption of a certain type of product. This is a stratagem that attempts to boost sales in an almost saturated market, given that the population of developed countries is growing slowly and the share of income devoted to food is tending to shrink. Consequently, the market has been flooded with products derived from milk (yogurts with supplements), cookies and fruit juices (with fiber), drinks (for energy recovery), and a long etcetera. It is emphasized that they provide the ideal daily dose of some basic nutritional components (vitamins and minerals), which would help to keep at bay important health threats. Therefore, these foods and drinks are like drugs or, in food industry jargon, "nutraceuticals": their consumption guarantees health, an attribute that packaging underlines with a bloated dietician discourse. The fact that many foods ensure the adequate daily intake of the different nutritional components is put aside. There is no doubt that a varied and balanced diet has the same effect (and is probably cheaper). While many of these products are easy to consume as they do not require a table or cutlery, or to be cooked (they are perfect for "TV meals"), their greatest quality is that they do not imply a change in the current sedentary and overeating lifestyle, the real cause of the proliferation, for example, of coronary heart disease. Despite the amendments, the campaign to spread the beliefs associated with such products has been an absolute success for the food industry.

Beliefs and social environment are closely connected. Sharing beliefs (conventions, stereotypes, etc.) is a key attribute of any social group. Socialization processes are aimed at making individuals assimilate the beliefs and social norms of the group. People know that their opinions and behavior are observed, and they therefore adopt the beliefs of the group. Nonetheless, although people tend to move in relatively narrow circles, society is composed of many groups able to influence people regardless of their social place. This impact can lead people to detect contradictions and to express discrepancies. It may be that, if control within the collective is strong, differences will not emerge (they are silenced to prevent conflict). However, if the distancing or dissent is great, the group will be abandoned, often at a given personal cost.

The psychologist Salomon Asch (1907–1996) is remembered for his experiments on group conformity, that is, the role of social pressure to implant certain beliefs. In his experiments, people ended up convinced of something false only based on the coincident (and half-baked) opinion of the other participants, despite overwhelming evidence to the contrary. It was enough to show firmness in answering and for all the other people to give the same wrong answer. The individual was oblivious to the connivance between the other participants and the experimenter. Disconcerted but unable to resist social pressure, the target person ends up conceding: "That's how it should be, if you think so" (mentioned in Poundstone, 2010: 268–270 and Aronson, 2008: 19–21).

This pressure can also take coercive forms. In these cases, the fear of possible reprisals for dissent imposes dissimulation: history is full of examples of people who, participating with enthusiasm, at least seemingly, in events organized by political, religious, or military authorities, camouflage their strong rejection behind feigned gestures and proclamations. These public manifestations of adhesion do not respond to any personal conviction. The organizers have certainly made a strong propaganda campaign and think that public opinion is very moldable, although threats and repression are what ensure attendance. Anyway, it should be borne in mind that humans believe above all in believing (a worthy tool of socialization). Since believing is not the same as acting, the level of commitment can be very low.

As is evident, the facts described above do not mean that different groups (from small to large circles) have different beliefs that may change. There are countless examples of the first phenomenon: in Western countries, best friends are invited to have a meal at home, while in Japan they are taken to a restaurant. And what about tips? There are countries in which the practice does not exist, whereas in others not giving is strongly censored. There are even places in which tips are a serious offense. It is also not difficult to find examples of evolving beliefs: decades ago it was called a crime of passion but now it is gender violence, after having been considered domestic violence; a century ago being tanned was seen as an indicator of low social status, whereas today it denotes the opposite (except in China and other Asian countries where, among other reasons, the first meaning still prevails: many people go to the beach while avoiding at all costs getting a tan).

The social dimension of beliefs has an important collateral effect: the tendency to believe that others, in similar circumstances, would think or act the same way. This phenomenon is called false consensus. For example, if a person who has a particular cell phone is asked what proportion of people they guess have a similar device, the answer is usually many or most. One's beliefs (and, by extension, one's behavior and/or lifestyle) are projected onto society as a whole: under similar conditions, the others act the same way, since this is the dominant trend in society (Hogg and Vaughan, 2014: 96). This extrapolation makes it possible to justify our own decisions because our choice is presumably the most common. False consensus also abounds in institutional contexts, in which there is usually a clear hierarchical order: for example, in the executive committee of a company, when asking for the opinion of people present to make a decision, if the leader speaks first, it is common to support their words; if they speak last, the participants will be ambiguous, waiting to know the leader's position. The more the members of the group tend to overestimate the leader's aptitudes, the more the false consensus effect is accentuated (Chabris and Simons, 2015: 144).

A by-product of false consensus is to confer maximum attention on the information ratifying one's own beliefs while ignoring information that contradicts them. This is the confirmatory bias: "The only people who seem sensible to us are those who think as we do," wrote the 17th-century French moralist François de la Rochefoucauld. Then, if it is not feasible to ignore information against one's own beliefs, an attempt is made to discredit it by demanding a burden of proof superior to the evidence backing one's personal opinion. It is hoped that there is no way to accumulate such a volume of proof. People may then end up thinking that:

- If one's own beliefs, and/or actions, are the benchmark for evaluating the credibility of those of others, we do not have to worry too much about understanding them: they are people whose minds do not work very well.
- The whole of society shows the same traits as the fairly homogeneous circle in which people usually move. Although it is comical, it is not uncommon to find someone surprised by the outcome of a political election because they argue: "I do not know anyone who voted for the winning party or candidate!"

In recent years, the Internet has become a powerful tool for false consensus and confirmation bias. The Internet makes it easy to maintain permanent contact with other people who share the same beliefs. This reinforces them, however implausible and in the minority they may be. As is evident, these beliefs can range from harmless hobbies to fanatical attitudes.

Rumors are another element to keep in mind when dealing with beliefs (inspired by Sunstein, 2009: 23; Elster, 2007: Chapter 23 and 2010: 125–136; and Hogg and Vaughan, 2014: 104). Some rumors do not go beyond the neighborhood, while others, due to the Internet, are rapidly spread worldwide. Leaving to one side whether they are true or false, with good intentions or not, the fact is that many believe and spread them. This generates an information cascade: the more people are interested in certain content, the more it spreads. The amount of concerned people grows exponentially. The rumor has rapidly and massively spread just because others have given it credibility.[11] This creates a solid business basis for the companies that promote and control the social networks.

This reaction is understandable given that people can only acquire direct, not necessarily perfect, knowledge of what happens in their immediate environment, especially if they are witnesses. Therefore, if much of what we know comes from indirect sources, how can we refute it? Luckily, people are aware of this fact, so they are prone to give varying degrees of credibility to the information they collect. Unfortunately, this assessment tends to favor the contents that confirm and, hence, reinforce the beliefs. This explains the successful dissemination of falsehoods if, for whatever reason, there is a state of opinion tilted toward these contents (Vosoughi et al., 2018). The credibility of these messages is intensified by the emotions (surprise, fear, indignation) that commonly accompany them. Even so, the fake news makers have to guess the right tone and the appropriate moment to broadcast their captivating contents, depending on whether they only intend to attract attention, or whether the purpose is to defame and harm someone.

Once assimilated, it is not easy to stop believing a rumor. Once a rumor is widespread, refusing to accept it can seem like snobbism while rejecting it can be understood as proof of the weakness of personality. Nonetheless, there are also those who make an effort to deny rumors. There are even websites such as www.snopes.com that analyze their trajectories and discredit them. Probably the best way to discredit false stories is to have them rejected by people who are considered honest and/or trustworthy thanks to their expertise on the topic. Unfortunately, this intervention may come too late. In the meantime, denials by those concerned often only reinforce suspicions (Sunstein 2009: 69).

Another interesting point regarding beliefs is so-called quasi-magical thinking, i.e., the inclination to believe that circumstances beyond one's control can be altered at will (Wilkinson and Klaes, 2012: 130; Hand, 2014: 16; and Hogg and Vaughan, 2014: 99).[12] For example, in some places, to ensure the desired result, children are told that they must blow the dice before throwing them. There are also soccer fans sitting in front of the TV set, who are constantly shouting at the players about what they should do. This behavior is reminiscent of the well-known principle of Walt Disney (1901–1966): "It is enough to crave something very much for it to come true."

Superstitions are the typical example of quasi-magical thoughts. They can take innocent forms, such as the idea of tempting fate ("If you don't study, I'm sure the professor will ask you tomorrow"), or establishing complicated doctrinal corpus and rituals (then approaching magic), some of which have endured for centuries. Beyond the obvious babbling, the propensity of humans to elevate spurious relationships and fortuitous circumstances to the category of causal connections should be highlighted. This is a particularly strong argument if the person who announces it deserves credibility. For instance, it has been observed that people keep their hands in ice water for longer if someone who looks like a health expert explains to them that persistence indicates longevity. There is also the perception that if I leave home without an umbrella when it looks like rain, it will end up raining, whereas if I carry the umbrella all day, it will certainly not rain. In other words, reality always goes against our expectations. This appreciation is motivated by the capacity to better remember what has a greater emotional impact, such as being soaked for not carrying an umbrella or having carried it for nothing for hours.

In 1948, psychologist Bertram R. Forer (1914–2000) gave a questionnaire to his students to define their psychological profiles (mentioned in Motterlini, 2010: 46). Once the information was collected and interpreted, he gave each student their profile. He then asked how accurate the result was. The answer was unanimous: very accurate. The surprise was great when the students discovered that the distributed profile was the same for everyone and elaborated from horoscope clippings from various magazines. This is a classic experience of why the predictions of astrologers, magicians, cartomancers, or clairvoyants are so successful. In reality, all they do is foresee very common circumstances, always stated in a very vague way. The prediction of having, for example, an unspecified setback at work next week is always correct: who does not regularly suffer some kind of annoyance at work? If no detailed fact is mentioned, any anecdote complies with the (alleged) prediction.[13] Additionally, it should be stressed that these charlatans are also masters at exploiting wishful thinking, or the propensity to consider true what people wish to be true. This bias is perhaps the best example of the influence of preferences on beliefs (according to Elster, 2010: 146 and Cialdini, 2016: Chapter 2). Finally, they also do not forget to feed their customers' vanity ("Do you realize that even the stars are watching out for you?").

Quasi-magical thinking is, however, more than a simple anecdote. It includes the refusal to accept the course of certain events, regardless of who is responsible. This is the case of irreversible situations in the face of which people act as if nothing had happened. This is a common situation in the event of strong emotional impact, such as when someone refuses to accept the death of somebody else.

Another very singular belief is to consider a posteriori that unforeseeable events were easy to foresee. After having observed the consequences of an event, people reconstruct the process of what happened, incorporating such results as if they were the expected evolution of the event. No room is left for surprise. This is the so-called hindsight bias: incredibly, nobody noticed it coming, it is argued, since it was obvious that what happened would happen (see Hoffrage et al., 2000; Motterlini, 2010: 121; Angner, 2012: 96; and Aronson, 2008: 8). In essence, people update their previous judgments, probably embedded in uncertainty, according to the information regarding the consequences. This reconstruction has an adaptive value and is shaped by the preferences, emotions, etc. of people. Even so, this bias can take exaggerated forms, as with the "prophets of the day after." For example, some people exclaim "I knew it!" when a player misses the key penalty that decides the match. Quite a few fans, including some opponents, ask themselves: "Why was the least suitable player chosen to take the decisive penalty, whichever way you look at it?" Consequences not only lead us to update previous judgments, but also such results are considered inevitable, and therefore it is absolutely incredible and unjustifiable that no one noticed them. As mentioned, these prophets leave no room for contingency, chance, or fatality, elements that usually bother them. The hindsight bias is rooted in a recurrent phenomenon: after a misfortune, people look for those in charge who were not able to foresee what happened, given that it was quite obvious that it would happen. This is an accusation of negligence or recklessness that is made leaving aside the objective scrutiny of the events that occurred. In other words, it is done by disregarding the need to carry out an accurate investigation of the possible factors that explain what happened. In any case, as is evident, nobody anticipated the consequences, not even such conspicuous prophets (although there are also cases in which the warnings were ignored, as happened with Shiller's admonitions at the turn of the century about the collapse of the U.S. housing market bubble, or were silenced by the argument that they were false alarms).

This bias is common in companies and, by extension, in all types of institutions (Thaler, 2015: 22): whoever holds power, when faced with a failed project or operation, may conclude that this bad result should have been foreseen because it was not so difficult to anticipate. Therefore, subordinates have been negligent. By refusing to acknowledge the influence of uncertainty, managers shift all responsibility onto their attendants: the bad consequences reflect their inability and indolence, and therefore they will pay severely for it.

Self-deception is the resistance to taking into consideration the objective evidence that shakes a certain belief (Elster, 2007: Chapter 7). Self-deceived people know that there is something wrong but either omit to take the necessary steps to obtain more information (as when someone looks in the mirror and sees that he has put on weight, but does not weigh himself because it is only "a few kilos that I will lose whenever I want"), or deny that this fact has any importance ("I know people who have lived many years despite being heavy smokers").

The mechanism of self-deception is as follows: evidence is taken into consideration; the most plausible explanations are rejected because they go against our desires; and, finally, a more acceptable belief is generated. In other words, people tell themselves a story to overshadow worries. It is not usually difficult to imagine an example: despite the evidence that the defeat of my favorite team was caused by the poor physical condition of the players, I continue to think that the referee is to blame.

In the realm of self-deception, abstaining altogether may be easier than dosing. This is the problem with dieting: controlling the diet is a difficult task because people have to keep eating, so there are numerous opportunities to abandon the self-imposed discipline. If the restriction is easy to circumvent (tobacco is sold in many places, there are many gambling halls, and access to alcohol is easy), people can enter a spiral of promise and relapse. A blueprint to emerge from this vicious circle is to impose costs on oneself: this is the case of people who tell everyone that they have stopped smoking, and therefore if they are seen smoking, their credibility will be undermined. To put one's own reputation on trial encourages discipline. However, a relapse can then lead to a severe crisis of self-esteem.

Self-deception denotes weak will. However, on the one hand, people often develop stratagems to overcome it: they can place the alarm clock on the other side of the room (or buy the nice "Clocky," the designer of which received the Ig Nobel Prize in Economics in 2005), run down the street instead of on a treadmill at home because they have to come back, and so on (Ubel, 2008: 99). On the other hand, when people face situations in which they think they lack sufficient self-confidence, the stratagem of self-handicapping emerges. This is the elaboration of an excuse, or pretext, in the expectation that things will go wrong (Motterlini, 2010: 42–44). It is a typical situation to confront challenges: if tomorrow you have an important exam, you will go to sleep late and therefore the failure could be attributed to the fact that you did not get enough sleep. The reason for the bad result would be a circumstantial fact and not the little work dedicated to its preparation. This stratagem mitigates regrets, although it also reflects the fear of not being recognized enough by others. Such excuses increase the chances of explaining failures reasonably well and, above all, of enjoying successes with particular intensity. In short, disguising or sabotaging one's own abilities is a peculiar way to protect our self-esteem in a situation in which our credibility is at risk.

This section cannot be closed without talking about prices, one of the most important vehicles for the transmission of economic beliefs. Prices affect purchase decisions through a triple signal (adapted from Earl, 1995: 78; Solomon, 2015: 84; and Szmigin and Piacentini, 2015: 185–188):

- They delimit the purchasing power available to people. At a glance, prices delimit what people can buy or what is unaffordable for them.
- They convey the perception of quality: more expensive is often perceived as better quality.
- Prices are compared with current or other remembered prices. This evaluation can give rise to a positive claim or a negative regret.

Setting aside the first signal, which is an absolute barrier, it should be highlighted that prices feed beliefs about the quality of goods. This is an attribute encompassing functional aspects to mental associations of all kinds. For example, the prepared foods (or affordable clothing) sector hires well-known chefs (or famous fashion designers) to give their product prestige and, hence, to increase the customers' willingness to pay. However, it should be noted that the relationship between quality and price, although it may be assumed to be direct, is non-specific. There is no reason to presume it is proportional. Although higher quality is often coupled with higher prices, the latter does not always imply higher quality. It is not even a robust belief to assume that higher prices are like a reputation premium, i.e., a guarantee of not being cheated.

The third cue referred to prices is their perception in relative terms. For example, in a context of higher prices for goods of a given class, a significantly low price immediately focuses attention: it becomes a bargain. Conversely, a comparatively high price makes the item an outcast. Low-cost stores, for example, create the sensation of a permanent orgy of discounts. However, supermarkets are the business that best exploits the appeal of markdowns. They discount many different items regularly, but especially products identified as seasonal. The latter is a powerful magnet to attract customers who, once in the supermarket, end up buying all kinds of goods.[14] To the contrary, the perception of generalized price increases dampens consumers' moods. The feeling that everything is becoming more expensive exasperates people. The loss of purchasing power is especially distressing if it affects most of the goods or services a person buys.

Another curious case from the perspective of economic psychology is that of duty-free stores. Located in closed duty-free areas, the absence of taxes on their products attracts many buyers, even though the prices paid are usually higher than those found abroad. The absence of taxes is more than offset by the floor prices. However, this shopping could be like a ritual: travelers, especially for leisure, are buying some indulgences, while others wish to bring gifts to those who have stayed at home. These seem to be the motivations behind purchases of items such as sweets, cosmetics, or liquors. Moreover, acquiring them at the last minute saves having to carry them. It should also not be forgotten that people obtain more satisfaction from receiving a number of small gifts over time than from a one-time gift of the same total value. The reason is quite simple: gifts have the social function of renewing mutual recognition (and affection) again and again. Therefore, gifts reinforce the bond of reciprocity between people (Eibl-Eibesfeldt, 2012: 351).

There is no doubt about the power of sales. Nonetheless, on the one hand, the greatest satisfaction comes from having taken advantage of an unforeseen opportunity ("I was casually passing by when, suddenly, I saw it ... and I didn't let it slip away"). Therefore, stores periodically advertise significant bargains (in force even for a few hours or minutes, wherever the law allows[15]) to attract customers with the prospect (a belief) of obtaining an unexpected bargain (Thaler, 2015: 62). On the other hand, sellers should modulate the sales. Take the case of a certain model of a very popular car. Its high demand means a minimum two-month wait before receiving the vehicle. Meanwhile, manufacturers and dealers have decided to take advantage of the market boom by raising the car's price. According to field surveys, the majority of people criticize this decision: it is an opportunistic and unacceptable price increase. However, if before the boom the sellers were promoting the car by offering a discount, the fact of eliminating it due to demand pressure does not provoke great rejection. Many people accept that, if demand has skyrocketed, the promotion is pointless. The discount has complied with its function and it is reasonable to remove it. Therefore, the elimination of a discount does not provoke as much rejection as a sudden surcharge, which is often considered an abuse.[16] Finally, concerning sales, it should be stressed that individuals may fight to obtain a discount on a particular purchase and, at the same time, be prone to acquiring an expensive good or service, regardless of its price, motivated by the powerful social image it projects. Many people, undoubtedly backed by certain beliefs, see no contradiction in that.

4.1.3   Emotions

Emotions are usually identified as an intense mental state aroused by something directly experienced or remembered, that stirs people. They are usually capable of inducing external physiological changes such as bristling hair, snorting, reddening, crying, laughter, or voice alterations, and internal changes such as pulsations or stomach contraction. They can also alter attitudes: sadness slows down thinking, while euphoria reduces attention to what is being done. The alterations caused by emotions are automatic, even though the individual can modulate their external manifestations at will. Emotions, passions aside as it was indicated, do not unleash actions but reinforce experiences. Moreover, people tend to predict their emotional states, as well as their duration, rather poorly. In any case, the vast majority of emotional episodes are quickly forgotten. As is well known, the sum of bodily and mental changes caused by emotions is called feelings.

The amygdala, a small bundle of neurons located deep in the temporal lobes, plays an important role in emotions. Neither its connections with multiple brain regions, such as the hypothalamus, the corpus striatum and the prefrontal cortex, nor its activity in memory processes, comes as a surprise. Its main task is to collect the different signals that give rise to the conscious experience of emotions. Historically, emotions were associated with imbalances in certain bodily humors, which supposedly drive mood. In common language there are still traces of this conception, as when, to indicate that someone is very angry, people say their "blood is boiling." Darwin considered emotions as reflexes inherited from the most distant ancestors, and therefore they have an evolutionary value. Currently, the complexity of the brain processes involved in emotions has been confirmed and, although a few basic emotions (such as fear, surprise, anger, happiness, sadness, love, and disgust) could be distinguished, there is no doubt that people from different cultures and historical epochs express them in their own way. People have different emotional responses: everyone is neither disgusted nor frightened by the same things. On a social scale, different cultures have created exclusive emotions and specific ways of externalizing them. Societies and social groups laugh or cry differently, according to the forms transmitted from generation to generation. Consequently, emotions are both deeply personal and social (in the framework of evolutionary processes).

Without emotions, human behavior cannot be understood. Any (economic) judgment and decision include an emotional load. Emotions are present in the appraisal of options and the formation of expectations, and therefore they influence all broad factors (see Figure 4.1) shaping decisions. Emotions, with the aforementioned exception of passions, rather than giving rise to concrete decisions (actions), predispose us to undertake them: hatred pushes to destroy, contempt to avoid someone, or compassion to comfort others. At the same time, emotions modulate actions: there are different degrees of indignation in the face of injustice (Hausman, 2012: 124). Whatever the case may be, the impulse of emotions may not materialize. Finally, although emotions tend to have a short life, there may be memories, with the corresponding emotional load, that take a long time to fade.

The role of emotions in the continuity of beliefs cannot be ignored either. For example, they can keep absurd beliefs alive (the fascination with the influence of the stars on one's own life), and they can sustain others of low quality (such as thinking that goodwill demonstrations always drive people to improve their behavior). Emotions can also alter beliefs: smug people hardly recognize a mistake (or having offended someone); if necessary, they look for an excuse not to rectify (or apologize) since, in doing so, the fault would be implicitly recognized. It should also be added that emotional reactions are affected by social norms and vice versa.

To conclude these introductory paragraphs, it should be warned that emotions are inherent in the human condition. They are not (raw) impulses that divert people from a genuine mood state, characterized by being aseptic and neutral. Various emotions come and go, overlap, contradict each other, and so on, but they never disappear. Finally, it is very important to realize that, unlike physical needs, people's emotional requirements are never satiated.

The list of emotions is long (see the more than 150 listed in Watt-Smith, 2016). The first group is those that involve a positive or negative evaluation of the behavior or personality of oneself or others. Look at the following list (closely related to the one presented in Elster, 2007: Chapter 8):

* shame: a negative conception about one's character, the fault committed or the humiliation suffered;
* disdain and hatred, or the consideration that other people are inferior or evil, respectively;
* guilt: the negative evaluation of one's own actions which have been carried out voluntarily;
* anger: this is a forceful negative assessment of another person's opinion or action about oneself;
* petulance or smugness: an arrogant assessment, without a hint of modesty, of one's own reputation;
* attraction is the highly positive or irresistible perception of another person's character;

- pride: the firmly favorable opinion of one's own skills and performance;
- gratitude or positive recognition of another person's action towards oneself;
- admiration: the perception that someone else's achievements are relevant, as well as that their behavior towards a third party has been appropriate.

All these emotions have an unmistakable social aftertaste. In evolutionary terms, they are relatively recent, given that primates only show certain signs of them. These emotions are the basis of social and moral norms.

Another block of emotions gathers the evaluations made about what another person possesses, whether this is aptitudes or objects. These are envy, resentment, sympathy, compassion, or delight. These emotions refer to states of the world.

There are emotions provoked by the idea of good things, or bad things, that have happened or may happen. These are, obviously, joy or sorrow. It should be pointed out that negative events from the past can awaken positive emotions in the present, and vice versa, as when past happiness increases the affliction for the present.

Emotions are also ingredients of beliefs related to present or future events. This is the case for hope, fear, love, or jealousy. If a positive expectation fails ("I didn't win the lottery this year either"), people become disillusioned. Looking at the past, people can feel nostalgia, as well as the sophisticated emotion of melancholy (since it implies a counterfactual judgment: what could have happened if a different decision had been made).

Although the preceding paragraphs were not intended to be exhaustive, more than 25 emotions have been mentioned. This remarkable figure pales when cultural differences are incorporated: all societies have added nuances and combined emotions, which have given rise to unique exponents. Some examples are the Japanese *amae* (or the desire to be embraced by another person in pursuit of relief and security), the *awumbuk* of the Baining tribe of Papua New Guinea, which mixes apathy and a certain liberation, or the Portuguese *saudade*, a combination of melancholy and longing (see the corresponding entries in Watt-Smith, 2016).

Emotions are a constitutive element of decision-making processes since:

- They shape motivations: they express the degree of urgency, modulate the interpretation of new information, and so on.
- They feed expectations: the excitement of winning a large prize pushes people to play lotteries in which this probability is infinitesimal. This phenomenon, according to Brandstätter et al. (2006: 412), was already being detected in the 17th century.
- They affect the evaluation of the consequences.

There is no doubt about the strong influence of general mood on economic decisions. It has been proven that at the beginning of weekends or holidays, especially if the weather is good, people tend to tip more. It is also well known how easy it is to take money from someone who is in a state of euphoria. A typical case is that of the lucky gambler who continues to play aggressively because they are doing so "with the casino's money." As a final example, advertisers strive to place their spots near entertainment TV programs, full of surprises, while refusing to place them near serious programs.

One of the emotions that has deserved more attention in economic affairs is regret, i.e., despondency upon perceiving that a different decision should have been made. Since a choice maker may make a mistake and thus be overwhelmed by unpleasant regret, the anticipation of regret often blocks decision-making (Schwartz, 2016: 152–153). Faced with the possibility of messing up and feeling bad, the choice made is to do nothing. Therefore, it is indirectly recognized that acting involves a cost: if the outcome is not as expected, people regret having made such a decision. However, if the loss comes from having done nothing, regret is usually less intense. Often not deciding, not acting, or leaving things as they are, is the easiest way to go. Abstaining spares people the reprimand for having done what they have done, as well as the censure of others. While it is not difficult to justify not having done anything, escaping from one's own responsibility for action with negative results is usually much more difficult. Regret is a component of one of the most powerful forces in human behavior: loss aversion.

A trivial example of regret's burden is people's reluctance to swap lottery tickets. Although the likelihood that any of the tickets involved will win a prominent prize is minuscule, the outright refusal to exchange suggests anticipation of the crippling remorse that would be suffered if the lottery number given up were to be a winner. It is a refusal that can be complemented by the quasi-magical belief that this exchange increases the probability that the exchanged ticket will win. As a general rule, nothing prevents the expectation of suffering a loss from having an even greater psychological impact than a sure loss. Imagined consequences, regardless of the likelihood of their occurrence, often shape the magnitude of regret.

Let us consider the following situation (Motterlini, 2006: Chapter 6): Mr. *A* had thought of selling his shares in firm *X* and buying shares in *Y*, but finally did not do so; by contrast, investor *B* had an equivalent number of shares in *Y* and sold them to buy shares in *X*. It turns out that, shortly afterward, the shares of *Y* rose sharply. Which of the two people will feel worse, perhaps *A* who did not buy shares in *Y*, or maybe *B* who sold them? From an economic point of view, the result is the same: both *A* and *B* have lost the option to accumulate the same value. However, Mr. *B* probably feels worse: it causes more discomfort to have done something wrong than not to have done something right of equal magnitude. An action that turns out to be inappropriate has a greater subjective burden than an omission with the same potential value. Passing up an attractive opportunity is habitually less traumatic than undertaking an initiative that would have been better left undone.[17] Whatever the case may be, this is a short-term perception. As time goes by, i.e., if viewed in perspective, what was not done despite having had the opportunity, gains importance ("If only I had studied more," "If only I had been more attentive that day," etc.). As popular wisdom holds, young people are concerned about the consequences of what they decide, but older people are especially uncomfortable with what they did not do despite having had the opportunity.

As indicated, expectations are another breeding ground for emotions. Their fulfillment, or not, and the degree to which this manifests itself, unleashes an avalanche of emotions. The possibilities are innumerable. For example, an unexpected success can generate both enthusiasm and the impression that it is undeserved, as happens to the child overwhelmed by the pile of Christmas presents received, considering that their behavior does not justify it. Even so, whoever attains an objective beyond what was proposed usually shows evident satisfaction. If the milestone achieved is against all the odds, the feeling is one of euphoria. However, if the result falls short of the expectation, even if it is positive, people are disappointed. The margin by which an expectation has or has not been achieved is also important. If it is too narrow, success may lose value: only those that are comparatively ample are attributable to one's own capabilities, such as effort, clairvoyance, and so on. Narrow victories or defeats leave too much room for chance. In any case, it is important to remember that one stratagem to limit regret is to restrict expectations. This magnifies unexpected gratification and curbs regret over failures (Medvec et al., 1995 and McGraw et al., 2005). There is no doubt that expectation management modulates loss aversion (Schwartz, 2016: 191).

To conclude, the hedonic treadmill should be briefly discussed (Scitovsky, 1976: Chapter 4, Motterlini, 2010: 88–91; Ariely, 2010: Chapter 6; Wilkinson and Klaes, 2012: 91; de Vries, 2013: 151; Solomon, 2015: 481). It is known that the emotional impact of certain events (winning an award, having a child, moving into a new house, buying a car, etc.) pushes people to exaggerate their importance for their well-being and, by extension, lives. It should be noted that this effect acts both positively and negatively (as when a loved person dies). At first, the impact is intense, but it usually dissipates within a few days or weeks. People adapt to the new reality more quickly than they thought they would be able to. This is backed by an effort of rationalization capable of modulating the perception of the event and, consequently, lightening its impact. Once the fact has been assimilated in such a way that causes, as applicable, neither euphoria nor pain, people's attention returns to the daily routine. In consumption affairs, hedonic adaptation has a particular implication: durable items of continuous use (house, refrigerator, clothes) or cyclical use (automobile, washing machine), end up losing interest. Even the possible narcissistic pleasure they initially brought (as status signals) fades away. This disillusionment is an important motivation behind the periodic purchase of consumer durables (except if they are of very sporadic use): when people no longer find long-used furniture attractive, they are likely stimulated by the expectation of renewing it.

4.1.4 Memory

Memory plays a very important role in the decision-making process. People, by carrying out a scrutiny of the possible consequences, noticing the contextual factors of the decision, taking note of the opinions of other people, and so on, accumulate information, which is added to the stored information stemming from what they have already experienced. Memory can be understood as an endless search for interpretation and retrieval of information. This process gives continuity to one's own life.[18] Additionally, as already noted a few pages above, people love the information that ratifies their opinions, so they give priority to the information which reinforces their convictions and reinterprets that which contradicts them, while they hate to be kept in the dark about required information and they are much less concerned about ignoring something (Nisbett, 2016: 175).

Two basic stages of memory can be distinguished: short-term and long-term memory (Morgado, 2017: 42; A. Baddeley et al., 2015: Chapter 1, section 1.5). Short-term memory stores small amounts of information for limited time intervals. It has a restricted capacity and fades easily, no matter how insignificant is that which interrupts people's attention. For example, the effort to momentarily retain the several digits of a given telephone number fails due to any ridiculous interference.[19] However, the role of this type of memory should not be underestimated: among other functions, short-term memory ensures the ability to hold a conversation and, in general, it is indispensable for the execution of specific tasks since it gathers information about what is happening when it is happening.

An important component of short-term memory is sensory memory. It briefly stores what is perceived by the senses, especially visual stimuli.[20] This mental capability allows humans to see a film as a continuous entity, even though it is made up of static frames separated by minute spaces of time (A. Baddeley et al., 2015: Chapter 1, section 1.5). Perception is a very complex process that goes from the reception of certain physical–chemical signals by certain cells (which make up the senses), to their codification and interpretation by the brain. This process is activated immediately and automatically, being as old as living beings. However, a lizard warming itself in the sun, although it registers the sensation, is incapable of thinking about it. In contrast, the human mind focuses attention (auditory, visual, etc.) to identify the source and undertake a conscious plan to make the most of it or limit the excess, depending on the individual goals and feelings. Finally, it is worth mentioning that the process of perception can show three types of limits: confusion provoked by subtle object arrangements such as the well-known optical illusions; due to lesions in the organs of reception, which are a serious hindrance to everyday life; and as a result of damage at the brain level, the consequences of which are much worse (all of which are explained in detail in Eysenck and Keane, 2010: 154–201).

Short-term memory is a part of the so-called working memory, a mental function that connects what is perceived to what is stored. Working memory manages information to carry out complex processes such as reasoning, learning, problem-solving, or decision-making. This information usually emerges in tasks such as reading, cooking, dressing, and so on. It also plays a prominent role in formulating concrete expectations (receiving compensation or punishment) and detecting prediction errors. The fact that short-term and working memory share mental processes does not imply that they are the same (Morgado, 2017: 98–105 and 2019: 86; A. Baddeley et al., 2015: Chapter 1, section 1.6 and Chapter 4, sections 4.1–4.3): the working memory is more dynamic since it contributes to managing the information necessary for the execution of demanding and complex tasks, which is made easier by a good night's sleep or by not being under stress.

Long-term memory is the system of storing information about personal events, experienced facts, learned knowledge, and so on. It can be intentionally accessed for many years: information essential to recognize things or unforeseen circumstances that strike people can be remembered for a lifetime (Szmigin and Piacentini, 2015: 140; A. Baddeley et al., 2015: Chapter 6 and Chapter 7). It also stores concepts, schemas, procedures, etc. related to learned skills, such as fastening shoes, picking up cutlery, or riding a bicycle. In short, long-term memory is not only the repository of memories, but also ensures the persistence of the ability to perform actions, whether they be narrow skills, such as playing chess or playing an instrument, or broad ones, such as mastery of a particular trade or professional practice carried out over years.

Long-term memory includes so-called semantic memory (or knowledge about world facts such as what is the capital of, historical characters, etc.) and episodic memory (or autobiographical memories such as what happened on that trip, or who was the first love, or the road where a severe fine was received, etc.) (Morgado, 2017: 75–76). Both can be understood as the precipitate of events, and associated narratives, in which personal life has been involved. On the one hand, such content about people, facts, and circumstances of the world, and personal experiences, are learned and endowed with a diverse emotional load. On the other hand, these memories can be suitably expressed in oral or written form, always in a creative way. Indeed, they are flexible and changeable, that is, the long-term memory processes invent details and mix different things when retrieved. That makes this memory much more than a simple storehouse: after selecting and ordering the events, they are stored inextricably mixed with the emotions that accompanied them. This combination is key to their retrieval since emotions act as relevant cues. As just noted, because retrieving is always a process of reconstruction (Gigerenzer, 2007: Chapter 2; Motterlini, 2010: 184; and Aronson, 2008: 148–149), memory is never completely accurate, although it is not usually completely wrong either.[21] However, although the most emotional events are more easily and vividly remembered, all memories weaken with time. This increases the narrative padding, the incorporation of ornamentation, the justification of intentions, and the elimination of unpleasant aspects. Therefore, the recovery of memories is not unrelated to the imagination. This does not detract from the value of memory: the quality of not being a mere storehouse makes it a creative tool. It is capable of recombining fragments and associating disparate ideas to approach problem resolution, or decision-making, differently.

Beyond the results of neuroscience, here barely pointed out, economic psychology emphasizes the following two aspects:

- The information collecting process is not unrelated to the effort of attention. As Simon stressed, people gather more information if it captures their attention for whatever reason. However, the abundance of information, as this author also stated, can lead to a lack of attention. The initial motivation to accumulate information turns into a feeling of suffocation if its volume overwhelms people.
- The fascination with stories can lead people to detect connections in simple coincidences and cause/effect concatenations in correlations,[22] especially if the events are chronologically ordered (as happens in the *Post hoc, ergo propter hoc* fallacy) (Poundstone, 2010: 94). This penchant for stories ranges from innocuous pareidolia, or the recognition of familiar shapes in random arrangements of objects, to the identification of all kinds of plots and conspiracies, a field in which the Internet excels. For this reason, an anecdote is often more persuasive than statistical data. Stories filled with emotions, even if their plots are delirious, remain more rooted in the memory than any objective scientific evidence or proof. Furthermore, if the stories have gaps, it does not take long to fill them in with what is closest at hand, often people's own opinions and prejudices (Chabris and Simons, 2015: 230–251).

If choices are influenced by memories, the consequences of decisions taken also affect the latter. In addition, in the process of being stored in the memory, decisions are simplified and reduced to their basic elements. The impact of consequences and the schematic version of past decisions become the guide for more or less similar future decisions. This is all under the influence of the powerful associative capacity of the mind. However, there are some considerations to bear in mind:

- Repeated experiences reinforce learning, i.e., they leave a greater imprint on the memory. For example, if someone travels very little by plane, it is more difficult to remember what to do at baggage and passport control.
- Memories with strong emotions attached are easier to retrieve. In addition, emotions nurture the impression that what is remembered is more vivid and detailed (Morgado, 2017: 126).
- Memory is selective: people tend to remember what is comforting, while bitterness and contrariness are set aside.
- In dealing with situations that have lasted over time, first impressions and last ones leave more of a trace in the memory. The intermediate phases are usually forgotten. This circumstance explains why some people want to be the last to speak in a meeting if, afterward, the proposal has to be voted on, or the first to present their point of view if the debate is expected to be long and the vote has to be taken many hours later (more details in Aronson, 2008: 95–96). This is a smart stratagem but is usually insufficient to alter the participants' positions and, especially, commitments.
- Remembering and recognizing are different mental processes, the latter being less elaborated (Morgado, 2017: 119). Remembering requires a voluntary effort to retrieve the contents at issue (inattention makes it difficult), while recognizing is the capacity of the mind to automatically identify objects that are not new to people, i.e., things imbued with an irresistible sense of familiarity (more information in the next chapter).

Having reviewed preferences, beliefs, emotions, and memory as the underlying elements of decision-making processes, it is necessary to include environmental factors such as management of the available resources and constraints.

4.1.5   Mental Accounting

Mental accounting refers to the way people manage their resources in their personal lives. This concept, created and disseminated by Thaler in 1985, although Japanese researchers suggested the same idea a few years earlier, encompasses both the criteria for allocating and evaluating expenditure on consumption and those for undertaking saving, investment, and debt decisions.

All of these ordinary financial decisions involve a whole series of cognitive operations of coding, mobilization, and revision, which are of interest to economic psychology.

Mental accounting assumes, first, that people manage several mental accounts of particular scope and duration (devoted to travel, shopping, leisure, clothing and footwear, etc.), and, second, that they can offset each other (Thaler and Loewenstein, 1992: 112; Wilkinson, 2008: 150; Wilkinson and Klaes, 2012: 219–220; and M. Baddeley, 2013: 145–146). Such accounts take the form of a double-entry table in which the columns indicate the different categories of expenditure, and the rows, the weeks (or any other unit of time) until the next income. However, since there is at least one column for savings (i.e., for expenses planned for later), this table mixes short-term allocations with more distant ones. There are also columns reflecting past expenses with lasting financial effects, such as a monthly mortgage or consumer loan payments.

The concept of mental accounting has been criticized for not considering the social and biographical profiles of the people involved and cohabitation formats (Kamleitner et al., 2018). Indeed, Thaler leaves to one side family modalities and their evolution over time. These are two issues addressed by sociology (and of interest for marketing) that are basic to knowing who establishes the priority of expenditure and how the allocation of resources will be established. The structure of cohabitation affects the definition of the accounts and their management since both aspects are associated with the roles played by, and the economic contributions of, its members. There is no doubt that the addition of such sociological issues would improve the analysis of mental accounts. However, this question will not be addressed in these pages either.

The two most debated issues in mental accounting are the substantive scope and the time horizon of the accounts. Regarding the first point, it is common to ask, for instance, whether holiday expenses correspond to a single account ("holidays"), or assemble resources from more than one ("travel," "hotel," "gifts," etc.). Most authors favor narrowly defined accounts: a "cinema" account instead of "weekend entertainment," or "car" rather than "transport." In any case, the scope of mental accounts is flexible: it adjusts to the circumstances and/or interests of people. A person who loves theater very much will have several accounts depending on the festival, the main character, the type of play, etc. For someone who only goes sporadically, theater will be just one element of the "entertainment" account. However, if holidays are exceptional, specific sub-accounts will be opened for traveling, accommodation, and other expenditure. Each type of outlay will be subject to a specific control to prevent the overall figure from displaying excessive deviations. As for the second issue, it seems that the time horizon of the accounts grows with the purchasing power of people: a person with few financial resources lives from day to day, whereas the rest make time projections of increasing scope with income. Be that as it may, mental accounting is a method of self-control: most people manage their expenses quite neatly and check them regularly (Cartwright, 2018: 86–90). As already mentioned, cases of compulsive shopping are rare and do not stand out among other psychotic deviations.

There is also an account conceived for small daily purchases or a petty cash account. These expenses are considered of little relevance, such as simple indulgences, minor unforeseen purchases, etc. This explains why this account is loosely managed. However, people with self-control problems bill all kinds of goods and services to this account. Since these expenditures are insignificant, they end up losing sight of the considerable amount that is accumulating. Fortunately, most are aware that, although from a daily or weekly perspective discretionary spending is small in magnitude, over time the figure can be large. For this reason, people tend to resist commercial promotions that, by expressing the financial obligation in daily terms and/or comparing it to the cost of any modest regular expense (such as a coffee, a public transport ticket, etc.), would have them believe that it is hardly anything at all.

In short, mental allocation is a tool for the management of the available money and, therefore, makes it possible to detect excessive deviations. Any suspicion in this regard will be carefully examined and, if necessary, appropriate measures will be taken to prevent a lack of control. If exogenous factors cause serious problems in one or more accounts, most people opt for severe discipline until the situation recovers.

In financial language, fungibles are economic values that can substitute for each other since they have the same quality. Similarly, in these paragraphs fungibility refers to the mechanism of compensation between mental accounts: overspending in one is compensated for by underspending in another (Wilkinson and Klaes, 2012: 225). These transfers take place within very narrow margins since they make people uncomfortable. At the outset, the preferred option is waiting: if the monthly budget for eating out has been exhausted, people usually decide to wait until the following month to return to a restaurant. If this is not possible (an unavoidable commitment appears), an exception is granted by temporarily moving resources from another account (which is inevitably reduced). Moreover, if it turns out that an allocation repeatedly becomes excessive because the concerned goods or services cost less than expected, the account's allocation will shrink.

The principle of fungibility opens the door to inconsistent behavior. This diagnosis should be contextualized. Indeed, it turns out that to prevent annoying transfers between accounts due to unexpected situations, it is advisable to have liquid funds to cover such deviations and emergencies. As a result, many people keep bank current accounts with considerable balances, despite their poor returns (which may be negative due to fees). Meanwhile, these same people use credit cards which, unless paid off on time, imply high-interest loans.[23] People end up paying interest rates five, ten, or more times higher than the interest received on the bank account. This is an absurd decision from a financial point of view, but understandable from a psychological one: it is the price paid to mitigate the uneasiness coming from possible unforeseen events. Although mental accountancy makes it possible to organize the dispersed economic operations of daily life, it cannot prevent the impact of uncertainty (Chater et al., 2018: 807).

It is worthwhile pausing for a moment to consider the effects of electronic means of payment on mental accounting. Credit cards (and other comparable digital media) open up the possibility of postponing payments long after the act of consumption. Irrespective of whether the expense is paid in one or more installments, from a psychological point of view this implies:

• the perception that purchases are more affordable;
• a lower subjective load of the comparatively larger expenditures, since they are paid blended with others. For example, paying €180 on the spot for a dinner has more psychological impact than including this figure within a total balance of €1,800. Flat rates are no stranger to this fact: although paying separately for each use would in many cases be cheaper, a constant and timely payment has a lesser psychological impact.

The spread of electronic payments has led to an increase in the frequency of purchases. Since the lack of sufficient cash is no longer an impediment to purchasing, there is a possibility of uncontrolled spending. However, this has not happened. Electronic money has only given rise to everyday purchases being less spaced out. Therefore, credit cards are not usually a permanent source of deviations (Trentman, 2016: 424): continued use plunges people into a stream of purchases and payments, generating the impression that purchases are paid for without delay. Nonetheless, credit cards are ideal for justifying impulse purchases that are difficult to justify. Cards reinforce the impulse to buy and skew consumption towards comparatively more expensive goods and services. This leads to deviations even though, as mentioned above, they are usually momentary. If the mere fact of having credit cards triggered people's expenditures, those who have several of them would find themselves in a desperate situation, which is not the case. The uncontrolled shopper exists with or without credit cards. On this point, it should be stressed that the main cause of people's financial bankruptcy is poverty, not the lack of control in the use of electronic means of payment. It is the absence of resources that can lead to card abuse, not the other way around. The underlying reason is often a low-paying job, unemployment, serious health issues, alcohol or gambling problems, and so on.

For many people, savings and debt are complementary plans. Saving is deferred consumption and a bank loan is a quick way to consolidate the social position, obviously to the detriment of future income. The decision to save is explained by the needs of the near future, which are shaped by the stages of personal life (going on holidays, acquiring consumer durables, retirement, etc.). Most savings, therefore, show a cyclical character. Except for affluent people, the primary goal of saving is not to build a fund (pension, investment) or a patrimony (purchase of assets), but to cover future financial needs as they become visible (Wilkinson, 2008: 161). However, if incomes grow rapidly, savings accounts fatten, albeit only temporarily: consumers need time to learn where to spend the extra money they are earning. In addition, history points out that savings behavior depends on global stimuli and circumstances (Trentman, 2016: 417–422). For example, a strong pro-savings campaign comes to naught if consumer credit is cheap.

As a general consideration, it should be borne in mind that decisions to purchase goods and services always incorporate a hedonic component. This fact can also be associated with mental accounting. In this vein, it is worth indicating that satisfaction with what is being consumed is not unrelated to how and when it is paid for. In turn, the discomfort involved in paying reflects how and when consumption has occurred. This explains, for example, the practice of many restaurants of offering fixed-price menus: it facilitates the enjoyment of the meal since, from the outset, customers already know how much it will cost. It is as if the meal has been paid for in advance. All these cases respond to the fact that, from a hedonic point of view, there is practically no one who wants the enjoyment of a consumption act to be harmed by the thought of how much it is going to cost. At the same time, many want to know. This concern reflects the eagerness to control mental accounts.

Finally, the analysis of mental accounting has also addressed to some extent the role of money. Different research studies have confirmed that money is valued in relative terms, that it is treated differently depending on its origin, and that it is affected by the degree of maturity of the decision made. To begin with, assume the following two situations (Motterlini, 2006: 15; Poundstone, 2010: 148):

- A person wants to buy a book that costs €20, but shortly before entering the bookstore, an acquaintance tells them that this book can be purchased for €15 in another bookstore ten minutes away.
- An individual wants to buy a television set that costs €550, but shortly before entering the store, they learn that ten minutes away there is another shop in which it costs €545.

Currently, people indicate that they are more willing to walk to buy a cheaper book than to buy a cheaper TV set. However, the saving (€5) is the same in both cases. Therefore, €5 out of €20 seems a more relevant amount than €5 out of €550. Very often money is valued in relative terms, perhaps a possible manifestation of the so-called psychophysical "law" of Feschner-Weber (Solomon, 2015: 208).

The relative value of money is also affected by the emotions associated with the envisioned purchase. This explains the unbridled rise in an ascending auction when several people bid for the same item, and the extra price that a fan is willing to pay for a ticket to gain entry into the stadium. The emotion linked to this kind of competitive spending relaxes control. The opposite can also happen: year after year, it is easy to observe how the recommendation to buy a study book, even if it involves a modest expense, causes discomfort in more than a few university students. These students will not hesitate to spend a much higher amount on leisure the following weekend, and all those that follow. The subjective value of money is undoubtedly influenced by the emotions that accompany the expenditure that it makes possible.

The origin of the money also affects its subjective evaluation. It has been proven that receiving extra money, assuming full freedom to spend it, pushes people to consume more. If people had to finance such purchases with their ordinary income, they would never make them. This relaxation is common in the case of bonuses and additional payments. An example of this is the double payment in July and December, a local Spanish practice (in many countries the yearly salary is only divided by 12) set by law many years ago to encourage summer spending and Christmas shopping. It is analogous to what happens in April in the United States, when most income tax refunds are received. For years, the commercial sector has been quick to label them as "government pay," while all kinds of promotions proliferate. In short, people seem to have a personal scale that reflects the frivolous/serious origin of the money: a small lottery prize or double paycheck is quite frivolous, while a wage raise is a serious event.

The perception of money also changes according to the state of a decision. Let us take the two following situations, suggested many years ago by Kahneman and Tversky (see Wilkinson and Klaes, 2012: 234):

• Since you have decided to go to a concert you buy the ticket in advance (worth €50) but when you enter the concert hall, you realize that you have lost it. What do you do? Do you go to an ATM to withdraw €50 and buy another ticket, or do you become angry about the loss and go back home without attending the concert?
• You leave home with a €50 bill and, when you try to buy the ticket at the cashier's window, you realize that you have lost the money. What do you

do? Do you go to an ATM to withdraw €50 and buy another ticket, or do you become angry about the loss and go back home without attending the concert?

The answers, although the economic value involved is the same, differ: there are more people prone to going back home when they have lost the ticket bought in advance, than when they have lost the banknote. It seems that the frustrating decision causes more discomfort with a higher degree of maturity or execution.

It has also been proven that the problem of sunk costs diminishes as time goes by. Sunk costs is a term related to the difficulty of recovering the resources devoted to purchasing certain rights to consumption, or invested in a project, and then diverting them to other purposes (more information in section 4.4). This is the case with season tickets for spectacles such as the theater, opera, cinema, etc. At the beginning of the cycle, people take advantage of the rights acquired, but the absences increase as the end of the season approaches. When the memory of the amount paid is fresh, not using the season ticket is perceived as a loss. As the purchase date is left behind, the psychological pressure to take advantage of the rights decreases.

Summing up, mental accounting emphasizes that people try to keep the allocation of income under control (Tomer, 2017: 47–48). Strictly speaking, this takes the form of patterns of behavior according to a certain criterion. Although few people keep a systematic written record of expenditures (except, perhaps, if a large and/or persistent expenditure is foreseen, or if income falls seriously), this does not mean that there are no mental routines for self-control. This is to ensure the availability of resources for the intended purposes and to curb spending for non-priority purposes. This routine is also emotionally satisfying.

4.1.6   Restrictions

Restrictions limit the set of opportunities available to people. Among the external factors that constrain choices, the economic analysis highlights the lack of sufficient purchasing power (surely all passengers would prefer to travel in business class, but most do not have enough money to do so). This constraint is currently associated with purchasing power in absolute terms, although it is also influenced by mental accounting. Furthermore, elements such as time availability (which includes deadlines set by oneself or by third parties), the consequences of previous decisions, the actions of third parties, and so on, can also be constraints. Finally, people internalize conventions, social norms, moral contents, etc., which may also restrict choices, even though it is not difficult to ignore them if necessary. This fact, if known, will not necessarily be censured.

Regarding preferences, it is worth noting that people may desire things that fall outside the attainable set of options, either permanently or temporarily. Some wishes are impossible, such as, for example, spending holidays at an Atlantis resort. Others may be possible (such as going skiing in the middle of August) but objectively inaccessible (the trip to the southern ski resorts is too expensive). In any case, the existence of inference-based preferences complicates the analysis. For example, a person may look favorably on going to study at a university in a certain city, a perfectly affordable option, but end up choosing another one because it has a greater cultural offering, a better climate, or any other reason that makes it more attractive. Additionally, it should be highlighted that restrictions do not alter elementary preferences, but they do change final preferences: the fact that someone has had to choose different shoes than the ones they preferred does not change their elementary preferences. This type of setback usually stops posterior rationalizations.

With the addition of psychological aspects, the relationship between choices and preferences becomes complex. On the one hand, opportunities can shape preferences. Aesop (*c.*620–564 BCE), in one of his well-known fables, explains that a fox, on seeing a grapevine, felt like eating grapes. Although it did not succeed, it did not become very angry because it concluded that the grapes did not seem to be ripe. The fox, therefore, generated a belief to justify a change in preferences. Similarly, people have mental resources to adapt their preferences to the available options. More draconian is the stratagem of burning one's ship, i.e., consciously cutting back on options, in particular, the possibility of backing out. This forces people to work towards the desired goal, even if it is unpleasant (Shefrin and Thaler, 1981). There is also the case in which preferences modify the set of options. As the saying goes, "Who enters the conclave as pope, usually leaves as cardinal." The fields of politics, big business, administration, etc., are a permanent source of examples of disguising goals since it makes them easier to attain. To the contrary, those who ardently manifest their desire to achieve them fail miserably. Enunciating preferences can therefore reduce the options.

Preferences and opportunities are not two opposing realities, but two elements of the decision-making process that maintain an intricate relationship. Except in cases of the most stringent constraints, opportunities can often be altered, even if after a considerable effort. Preferences can also be modified, but this only happens if the opportunity set is clearly and inevitably mutilated. Methodologically, it must be stressed that, when thinking about options and preferences, one must be very alert to how these have been identified. In the field of consumption, for example, any good or service is deployed in a more or less large range of variants. Consequently, it will be necessary to refine the categories used for the debate on opportunities and preferences to be relevant.

It is not true that people are differentiated more by the options available to them than by their preferences (Elster, 2007: Chapter 9). While not everyone can attend the gala session of an opera concert, there are often performances at lower prices, as well as low-cost technical means to listen to opera as many times as it is wanted. Nonetheless, there are people not interested in opera, perhaps because they do not have a trained ear (an aptitude). In reality, as insisted in these pages, neither are preferences unrelated to the inputs received from the social group in which people have been socialized, nor do preferences escape the singularities of their personality. In short, both preferences and opportunities differentiate people. Whether one dimension has more weight than the other will depend on the context.

Before closing this section, it should be noted that constraints also affect beliefs. This would be the case of quasi-magical thinking, characterized by ignoring the physical, economic, and other constraints. Therefore, when facts contradict beliefs, they are either abandoned or, more likely, people are prone to attribute this to not having enough conviction or faith. For example, no matter how much you flap your arms, you will not be able to lift yourself into the air, but you can always explain that the effort made is still insufficient (Hausman, 2012: 36–37).

4.2   RISK AND UNCERTAINTY

Many decisions are characterized by the presence of risk or uncertainty, two circumstances studied in depth in economics. This work has been successful in the case of risk, with models of proven quality, while with uncertainty it has only been possible to make some conceptual advances, because of its intractable nature.

Decision-making is faced with varying degrees of ambiguity:

- There are cases in which the decision is made under certainty, i.e., people choose between perfectly known and completely reliable options. In a restaurant, given the preferences of people, the content of the menu, the rules of etiquette, and the available budget, there is very little room for surprise. Furthermore, if a person regularly has lunch in this restaurant, as soon as they enter it, the waiter starts to prepare the order. Neither the waiter nor the customer expects a surprise.
- There are decisions in which people cannot escape the discretionary power of Fortune. In this case, two different situations can be distinguished (Lavoie, 2014: 73):

- The options have consequences whose values and degrees of predictability can be objectively gauged. Everybody involved knows this. For example, despite not knowing the roulette box in which the ball will stop, all participants in the game know how it works and can estimate the probability (or frequency) of the various outcomes. The stakes are open, but ambiguity can be approximated. This is a risky situation.
- The decision is made blindly: "What will my future be like if I choose to study architecture instead of industrial engineering?" Even under the assumption, not always valid, that the options are known, there is no way to specify the consequences of the choice. They are completely inaccessible and indecipherable. The decision is impregnated with uncertainty, i.e., it is made in a state of mind marked by unavoidable imperfect knowledge.

The following pages will explore the concepts of risk and uncertainty in economic decisions.[24]

4.2.1 Models of Risk

The common meaning of risk refers to a situation in which danger or a loss, or a decision that opens the door to them, is foreseen. Risk is the expectation that something will go wrong; therefore, it is recommended to avoid those situations (Gigerenzer, 2014: 32). Prudence is appealed to, while recklessness is severely discouraged. Some elevate this caution to the category of zero risk, a widespread illusion in today's society. However, for decision analysis, choices under risk are characterized by known outcomes, all of them mutually exclusive and associated with a certain probability. According to Bernoulli, Knight (1964), and many others, a risk situation is that which contains a set of events, and their respective probabilities, perfectly identified. Even though the concrete result is not known, there is no room for unexpected consequences. When rolling a die no one knows what number will come up, but there is no doubt that it will be between 1 and 6 with a probability for each result of 1/6 (assuming, of course, that it is not loaded). An analogous argument can be used for all kinds of games of chance, such as cards, lotteries, or slot machines. Risk, therefore, is understood as a gamble (Randall, 2011: 32). If the sums at stake arc high, the possibility of a large loss gives the choice a varnish of danger, which brings the meaning of risk closer to the popular one. By contrast, the possibility of gaining millions with the purchase of tiny participation, as happens in the big lotteries, eliminates all anxiety and triggers enthusiasm to the point of absurdity. The insignificant probability of winning is eclipsed by the huge potential gain. This is a psychological fact since for the people involved objective calculation no longer exists.

If gambling defines risk, it can be concluded that there are almost no risky economic decisions (Neth et al., 2013: 136; Aikman et al., 2021: 320; and Mousavi and Gigerenzer, 2014). Indeed, economic agents do not usually have the full list of possible outcomes as well as their respective probabilities. Therefore, the principle of mathematical expectation, and the other tools of the theory of probability, cannot be applied. Conversely, on playing the roulette table, it is possible to distribute the tokens among different boxes, estimate the probability of success and, hence, calculate the potential gain. Nonetheless, many economists argue that the cases with all the options identified can be transformed into risk situations, despite ignoring objective probabilities, either because of the experience's character or the fickle nature of human behavior, by applying subjective probabilities. This stratagem was already proposed in the 1930s and enunciated under the assumption that the distribution of such probabilities is highly profiled, a feasible condition if people behave as if they were perfectly rational. Later, it was added that risk analysis could also encompass decisions in which the range of options is intuitively known and preferences are readily available.[25]

The establishment of subjective probability values is a trick to tame uncertainty. These values, rather than reflecting the frequency with which a certain event may occur, reverberate people's beliefs about it. Since assessing options under uncertainty is not possible, it is suggested to make assumptions about the beliefs involved. Unfortunately, the consequences will remain inaccessible. The expectation that subsequent information may alter such beliefs does not change the diagnosis: subjective probabilities are arbitrary quantifications of premonitions, an artifice that aims to reveal with presages what is inscrutable (Gigerenzer, 2014: 26). Consequently, some authors vindicate the role of uncertainty, although it discomforts people. They reject what they consider to be an academic sleight of hand (Neth et al., 2013: 137).

Whereas the technical meaning of probability connotes chance, its common meaning expresses plausibility. It emphasizes, therefore, the reliability of a belief, which makes this conception of probability a poor version of the subjectivist one. For instance, when it is indicated that there is an 85% probability of being mugged in a given neighborhood, the figure is spurious. This value only tries to reinforce the following admonition: the possibility must be taken seriously since it is believed that it is a common occurrence or, in other words, it can happen. Often these assertions are only aimed at creating or reinforcing a certain state of opinion. It is not a serious formulation of a hypothesis.

A more complex method to deal with beliefs and uncertainty was proposed by John Maynard Keynes (1883–1946). He distinguished between the following three situations (according to Lavoie, 1992: 45–50 and 2014: 78–81):

• The data collected allow for objective estimation of risk.

- The probability distribution is known, but incompletely. For example, to understand the price dynamics of a given commodity, people can observe its prices in organized international markets. However, in doing so nothing is known about local and informal markets. This lack of information could be overcome, but perhaps at a prohibitive cost.
- There is no way of knowing the likelihood of an event. Nothing can guide a search in this respect: what is the probability that in September 2061 a pandemic will break out and disrupt world trade?

Since everyone makes subjective estimates to deal with situations of high ambiguity, Keynes, on the one hand, was prone to grant a minimum of credibility to these quantifications and, on the other, he assumed that they are inevitably affected by the state of mind (optimism, anxiety, etc.), or animal spirits, and by the context. Because such beliefs are omnipresent and merited limited confidence, he proposed adequately integrating them into the analysis of probability. He then coined the concept of the weight of an argument. In today's terms, this can be interpreted as the ratio between the relevant information that can be processed when the decision is made, and the amount of information that people would like to have and be able to process. In other words, it is the reliability that the available information deserves, being aware that there is no way of knowing for sure what information is missing. This belief, as happens with subjective probability, can be reinforced or weakened by the arrival of new evidence. Perhaps aware of the weakness of his proposal, Keynes encouraged analysts to continuously track what is happening and to constantly review the relevance of the information gathered. In addition, he cautioned that in the face of uncertainty, the probability distribution estimated from previous similar cases is not a good benchmark. It is also important to consider the degree of confidence that this distribution deserves. Past cases are a poor guide when deviations are perhaps systemic.[26] He also recognized that probabilities and weight of evidence are independent properties that do not necessarily compensate for each other. In short, Keynes was skeptical about subjective probabilities and recommended a careful analysis of the properties of beliefs (formulation, diffusion, collapse) fueled by uncertainty. His proposal reinforced an approach to ambiguity, the latest exponent of which would be the prospect theory, briefly described in Chapter 2.

Leaving to one side the above theoretical considerations, on dealing with risk perception, economic psychology has emphasized the different attitudes of people towards gains or losses. Based on a large number of field experiments, researchers have arrived at the results shown in Table 4.3 (adapted from Angner, 2012: 140). To understand it, imagine the following lottery:

- A person receives €1,000 and the chance of playing a game in which there is a probability of 50% of winning €1,000 more (option *A*) or of pocketing an additional amount of €500 for certain (option *B*).
- A participant receives €2,000 and the option of playing a game in which they can lose €1,000 with a 50% chance (option *C*), or lose €500 for sure (option *D*).

Table 4.3   Aversion and propensity to risk

Attitudes		Probability level	
		High but not sure	Low but not impossible
Results	Profits	Aversion to risk ("Better not to play")	Propensity to risk ("To be able to win, play first")
	Losses	Propensity to risk ("I play to have at least the chance not to lose")	Aversion to risk ("Better not to regret it")

As can be seen, *A* is equivalent to *C* (in both cases the mathematical expectation is €1,500), while *B* is equivalent to *D* (the total sum is €1,500 for certain). However, more than eight out of ten participants choose *B* in the first game (upper left cell of the table), while seven out of ten choose *C* in the second one (lower left cell). In the first lottery, risk aversion predominates: the certainty of outcome *B* prevails over option *A*, which presents a considerable probability of losing the extra money. Conversely, risk appetite dominates when there is the possibility of avoiding certain losses: *C* is the option with a chance of losing nothing. In this kind of case, many prefer to opt for the well-known "double or nothing." Following the table, the upper right cell shows the typical attitude of those who participate in large lotteries: the expectation of winning an extraordinary prize explains why people ignore its very low probability. At the end of the 1960s, Tversky performed the following experiment (with updated figures): in a lottery, people could win €190 with a probability of 8/24, or win €200 with a somewhat lower probability, of 7/24. He observed that, for small frequencies, people tended to disregard the probability (or frequency) and focused on the prize (which is slightly higher). However, for probabilities of winning equal to or greater than 50%, people increasingly opted for €190, i.e., the difference in probability ended up standing out over the prize. Finally, the lower right-hand cell of Table 4.3 contains losses stemming from risk aversion. The most representative case is the loss of something's worth, such as a car, house, etc. This chance justifies taking out insurance: although the probability of losing them is very low, it would be a very distressing experience. The low probability of loss is ignored because of the strong emotional impact it entails. This insensitivity to probability also occurs when people are informed that they may be suffering from a serious illness that the diagnosis does not yet rule out (Slovic et al., 2005: S38).

Continuing with the analysis, it is necessary to explain these other two results:

- The smaller the probability of winning something, the less risk aversion there is. Most people, for example, prefer (€6000, 0.001) to (€3000, 0.002). The prize size stands out over such minuscule odds: since it is unlikely to win anything from one lottery or the other, people choose the one with the biggest pot.
- Although (€3,000, 1) is preferred to (€4,000, 0.8) despite the mathematical expectation of the latter lottery, €3,200, the choice changes if the options are (€3,000, 0.25) and (€4,000, 0.2), with mathematical expectancies of €750 and €800, respectively. With respect to the first lottery, in the second one probabilities have dropped by three-quarters (1 versus 0.25 and 0.8 compared with 0.2). Even so, the preference for (€4,000, 0.2) indicates that the probability of 0.25 is judged to be more similar to 0.2 than 1 is to 0.8.

Table 4.3 does not have a dynamic dimension. For this reason, it does not take into account people who find it difficult to stop gambling, especially if they are losing money. They then tend to take risks beyond what is reasonable. The stream of losses pushes recklessness in an attempt to reverse the situation. Caught in the mire like this, people are prone to make higher and higher bets: it is the growing "double or nothing."

Although considerable effort has been made to include risk in decision models, in real life many economic choices do not respond to the above casuistry. Even assuming that people have time to evaluate them, many decisions have consequences that are inaccessible to scrutiny. It is time to approach uncertainty.

4.2.2   Reflections on Uncertainty

Without pretending to diminish the relevance of Ellsberg's experiment, to speak about uncertainty is to consider issues addressed with imperfect information and, much more importantly, to talk about the future. In Western culture, the future is imagined as situated in front of people (it is opening up) while the past is left behind (the irrevocable facts located at the back). For the Aymara people (spread over the current countries of Bolivia, Peru, Chile, and Argentina), the image is just the opposite: the lived past remains in front of people because it is what they saw, while the future is placed behind people because there is no way of knowing anything about it. The unknown remains outside the field of vision (Klein, 2015: 15). This perspective has an important implication: locating the past before people's eyes is a reminder of how important it is to learn from experience. In contrast, the image currently prevailing in the West encourages discovering the future, and hence, modifying it at convenience, or preparing for it adequately (an objective that in some cases includes avoiding it). If the future unfolds before people, it is argued that it would be foolish not to scrutinize it thoroughly, a necessary condition for making forecasts that lead to an advantageous (economic, for example) position. As a result, there is strong resistance to understanding and assuming the nature of uncertainty (Elster, 1991: 57–58).

Uncertainty encompasses very diverse situations, the differences between them being a matter of degree. Three cases can be distinguished (by appropriately combining ideas from Knight, 1964: 233–234; Fitzgibbons, 2002: 17; Vercelli, 2002: 92–94; Randall, 2011: 34; and Gigerenzer, 2014: 32):

- Gross ignorance about something in particular (such as answering the question: What's the capital of South Dakota?) and the lack of knowledge about the future in the short or medium term. In the first case, there are more or less accessible sources of information that make it possible to overcome, or reduce, the lack of knowledge on the subject. In the second one, forecasts are a continuation of current trends, despite the suspicion that unnoticed factors may alter such expectations. Some people identify elements that they believe may have an impact on the course of events, even though they do not know the details. The future in the short and medium term is, therefore, imprecise. If the state of affairs was remarkably stable, people could classify forecasts according to their feasibility (and degree of confidence). This is a subjective matter that does not escape intuition, emotions, and so on.

- Surprise or unexpected results caused by the decisions of others or by chance, or by an inextricable mixture of both. Whatever it is, people express their astonishment at what has happened, given that no one expected it. This is what Taleb (2007) calls a "black swan" (see also Earl, 1986: 118–123 and Lane et al., 1996: 50–51). Life is full of surprises, such as meeting an old friend by chance after many years. Lotteries are par excellence the field of surprises, some of them incredible: in 1985, a person won the lottery of the state of New Jersey twice, with a gap of four months; more recently, in 2019 and 2020 in the city of Reus (in Catalonia), a person won significant amounts in the Christmas lottery. Although this fact has an infinitesimal probability, it should not be forgotten that there are thousands of lotteries all over the world and hundreds of millions of regular players

(Hand, 2014: 86). There are also social and economic crises that explode by surprise, even though there are always people who gave the appropriate warning, often in the form of admonition. They were probably labeled alarmists and quickly ignored. The upward trajectory of stock prices, for example, seemed unstoppable. Predictions suggested that today's upward trend would continue tomorrow. All models were projecting that the basic forces driving the market would continue unabated. Furthermore, there was no reason to believe that the monetary authorities would stop injecting liquidity into the financial system. Everything seemed to be working perfectly ... until moments before the collapse of the markets (the crash). There was a huge surprise: suddenly, everyone became aware of the monumental (self-)deception. To use an analogy, the dangerous rise in boiler pressure was ignored because it contradicted one's own wishes and/ or interests until, inevitably, it exploded amidst general astonishment and consternation. A given set of bad sensations quickly mixed with vertigo provoked by the scope of fraudulent accounting practices. In brief, the power of surprises combines unpredictability and shock. In some cases, their impact may be limited to temporary turbulence which, despite its intensity, eventually opens the way to new routines (without the previous ones having necessarily disappeared altogether). In other situations, surprises mean the irrevocable end of the known regularity. Financial crises are part of the first type; the slaughter of swine, after months of proper feeding and care, of the second one (seen from the animal's point of view).

- Unknown unknowns or deep ignorance. This is the uncertainty of the long-term time horizon: not only can the distant future not be approximated, but influential intermediate events are now also completely inaccessible. What is ignored is ignored. There is not even the option of applying the scenario technique (Earl, 1995: 124–126). Futurologists are the usual victims of deep uncertainty since any forecasting can only employ available knowledge. Exploring the profound future is doomed to failure: in any intermediate year or decade, relevant events may occur which are impossible to guess at the present moment. These facts could easily and drastically alter the tenuous connection that links the now with the distant future. For example, in the mid 1960s two prestigious futurologists, Herman Kahn (1922–1983) and Anthony J. Wiener (1931–2012), published the book *The Year 2000. A Framework for Speculation on the Next Thirty-Three Years*, in which they predicted the world situation in that year. Despite the volume of information handled and the use of the scenarios technique, the authors assumed that the Soviet bloc would continue to exist (it disappeared at the end of the 1980s), while currently common advances, such as microelectronics (second half of the 1970s) or the cell phone (1990s), were not foreseen. In general, very long-term predictions are often captivating (especially on being sprinkled with technological determinism), but they remain pure and dispensable speculation.

The concept of weight of evidence has been explained above. It is now clear that, in case of deep uncertainty, the extent of what is not known cannot be known. The most important (economic) decisions, whether personal or institutional, are unique and made under this type of uncertainty. The economist George L. S. Shackle (1903–1992) insisted on the first feature: their singular character makes it impossible to apply the analysis of probability (Earl, 1995: 113–120). The second aspect, i.e., total unpredictability, implies the recognition that the whims of the wheel of fortune are inscrutable and unavoidable. Seen in perspective, uncertainty makes it impossible to foresee the course of historical events, which transforms the long-term dynamics into a contingent process (or the fact that reality has unfolded in a certain way, but it could have been otherwise). It is not surprising how disturbing uncertainty (and its concomitant, the volatility of things) is for the human mind. However, people's eagerness to create patterns stemming from lived experiences, combined with the goal of sufficient satisfaction (see Chapter 5, section 5.1.4), leaves room for the emergence of heuristic shortcuts to facilitate decision-making under uncertainty (Lavoie, 1992: 60). Although it may not be possible to tame uncertainty, some recommendations can shed light on it. Namely (inspired by Lavoie, 1992: 56 and 2014: 91; and Gigerenzer, 2015: 31, 67):

• If the social, economic, or political environment looks like it will remain stable, the recent past and present are plausibly the best guide for figuring out the future. Conversely, if there is turbulence, it is better to postpone the decision. This cautious attitude is wise in the short or medium term, but not necessarily in the long term.

• More important than the probability of a given outcome is to assess the degree of stability, or fragility, of a given reality about unforeseen events. In practice, this implies taking measures to reduce the exposure to negative eventualities, for example by accumulating reserves or diversifying assets. This is a necessary, but an insufficient ploy. We should be aware that the future always leaves room for the unexpected. However, reasoning based on the worst-case scenario only leads to paranoia.

• If it is plausible that the decision taken will provoke a severe reaction from others, it is worth maintaining discretion. This is a common practice in major political and business decisions since it reduces the amount of uncertainty attributable to interaction with third parties.

• It is usually advisable to follow the opinion of the majority (the rest of the companies in the sector, for example), since it indicates the future behavior of people. However, this monitoring must be critical to prevent the loss

of potential opportunities. Anyway, it should not be forgotten that many decisions are made according to habits, customs, and social norms.
• Long-term socioeconomic predictions are nothing more than examples of overconfidence of the experts involved.

People know that uncertainty characterizes most decisions, especially those with long-term outcomes, but the mix of routines and emotions prevents decision paralysis. An example is recurring affective predictions, i.e., a mental simulation of the consequences of the choice on the personal or professional situation. Thus, the decision to share my life with my partner is made by closing my eyes and imagining our future life. The decision algorithm consists of anticipating and calibrating my hedonic reaction. Therefore, foresight enters the distant future embedded with strong emotionality. This neutralizes an objective evaluation of expectancy. Even the recommendation to listen to someone who has already lived this kind of experience is rejected since, it is argued, my case is singular. Perhaps there are only two situations in which people pay some attention to uncertainty effects: when surprises blow up previous regularities and when the plausible consequences are substantial (Lavoie, 2014: 94).

4.3   INTER-TEMPORAL PREFERENCES

The human experience of time takes the form of sequences of events. However, this displacement from past to future changes its speed according to context and, above all, age (Klein, 2015: 136–146). The perception of time is very elastic: sometimes things seem to pass quickly, sometimes very slowly. Up to one-and-a-half years old, a child does not distinguish before from after. Around the age of four, children can temporally order the activities of a whole day. At the same time, they become aware of the duration of short intervals of time, such as one minute. Anyway, the present persists: when going on a trip, they ask again and again, "How much further is it?" "When will we get there?" In adolescence, awareness of the greater or lesser duration of a given span is consolidated, even though this feeling changes according to circumstances. As people get older, the feeling that time runs faster and faster increases. This is caused by memory: more events from childhood and youthful years are remembered than from recent times. The reason would be that memories accumulated from approximately 4 to 25 years old are the most persistent since they were the first to be fixed in the mind. Moreover, the routine makes it easier to disregard the near past. The rapid passage of time is a perception that grows as the brain ages, especially from 70 years old, although past and present physical and mental activity can slow it down. Without denying that the psychological experience of time is a very interesting subject, the aim of these pages is much more modest: to describe how people choose between economic options located in a future time within reach. In other words, we aim to describe how inter-temporal choices reflect human preferences concerning time. Among other issues, this analysis provides elements to understand the role of anticipation and expectation.

Time is an inherent dimension of any economic process. Understood as a uniform and imperturbable displacement, that is, *à la Newton*, the time of economic affairs is represented by an arrow that goes from a past that cannot be modified to a future embedded in uncertainty. Whether it be models of productive activity, financial operations, consumption, or any other economic event, the incorporation of the temporal dimension, whether in metric format or logical perspective, is a challenge. The analysis of people's inter-temporal preferences is no exception. Decades of study have given rise to a great diversity of models. However, the novelties provided by field research show that there is still a great deal of work to be done.

4.3.1   Basic Assumptions

Studied at least since the time of John Rae (1796–1872) (Loewenstein, 1992; Frederick et al., 2003), inter-temporal preferences deal with choices with the following features:

- The consequences are known, which does not mean that uncertainty, understood as gross ignorance or surprise, can be completely overlooked. For example, if an acquaintance who is going away for a few days asks us to take care of her dog by paying us €100 when returning, the possibility that she will suffer a fatality and, therefore, we will never receive the money cannot be completely disregarded. This is a very rare eventuality, but not impossible. Implicitly, inter-temporal models often assume that people are confident that there will be no unforeseen changes in the state of the world, even though they cannot entirely rule it out.
- The time horizon of inter-temporal decisions is that of everyday affairs, i.e., the period during which most personal actions and projects are defined, usually between a few weeks and a few years. Although it is possible to imagine choices with values located in the distant future (many years away), the model is not prepared to deal with such uncertainty. Indeed, people are reluctant to seriously consider a time horizon in which their preferences are poorly, if at all, defined. In addition, it should be pointed out that the model ignores the influence of beliefs (with moral values such as concern for future generations) and developed plans (such as that of the farmer who alternates crops to maintain soil fertility). This last point means that the analysis neglects choices linked to long-term objectives.

- The values located in the future can be arranged in the following three ways:
  - Those that materialize at a future point in time, such as receiving monetary compensation for having performed a task or the requirement of paying a fine before a certain date. It is assumed that these future values can be shifted to the present or, if necessary, delayed even further. In addition, once in possession of the future value, they can immediately enjoy it with no additional restrictions (Soman et al., 2005: 353).
  - Future events that last over time, such as enjoying a few days' holiday. The future in sight does not refer to a specific moment, but rather is long-lasting.
  - Sequences of lasting future events but whose order can be altered at will. People can establish the arrangement of the different tasks. All of them are independent of each other, i.e., there are no technical or economic restrictions on the order of execution.

In Figure 4.2, the point t_0 represents the present time. A given future value is located at point t^* and a future duration is defined along the interval (t^{**}, t^{***}). As can be seen, the figure shows the ordinate values of such future amounts (points V^* and V^T). The exact positions of the values projected to the present reflect the perception that people have of them at t_0. As will be detailed below, these projections on the ordinate axis are a key concept of the models on inter-temporal choices.

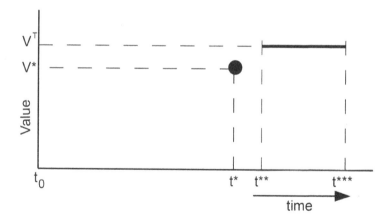

Figure 4.2   Future values and intervals

Concerning future point values, people may react impatiently: "I want the promised money right now," "I'm going to pay the fine and forget about it." However, people may also decide to wait: "I will pay the bill on the last day." Although the preference for the present predominates, some people delay future actions, assuming that this option is feasible: faced with the anxiety of going to the dentist, a person decides to postpone the visit because the toothache is still bearable. The human capacity for anticipation explains this behavior: future consequences provoke enjoyment (or fear) from the moment they are glimpsed. Moreover, although the future is constantly approaching, it is often far enough away that, in the meantime, preferences may change.

Let us consider an experiment in which some people were asked how long they were willing to wait for the following outcomes (from Loewenstein, 2009: 390):

- win €40;
- lose €40;
- lose €1,000;
- receive a strong non-lethal electric shock;
- be kissed by a desired movie star.

The questionnaire proposed five waiting periods: receiving the consequences immediately, after 24 hours, in three days, after one year, and in ten years. Most people chose short waiting periods (up to 24 hours) for winning or losing a little money. They showed a preference for the present. As for losing a great deal of money (€1,000) and the electric shock, participants wanted to postpone it as long as possible. About receiving a very special kiss, the maximum waiting time was three days, in other words, neither being kissed immediately nor after weeks or months. A fleeting and unrepeatable pleasure deserves a reasonable wait. This wait is itself a pleasure: the expectation of the kiss is also enjoyed. This is called hedonistic anticipation (Morgado, 2019: 32).[27]

Many experiments suggest that people normally prefer to postpone unpleasant outcomes. However, if the inconvenience or loss is lessened by experiencing it immediately, many prefer not to postpone it. This is the case of fines: the possible discount if it is promptly paid, convinces even those who would tend to wait until the end of the paying period. Unfortunately, it should be stressed that the exact relationship between the degree of discount and the propensity to pay (the fine in this case) is not known. Conversely, if an unpleasant result can easily be postponed, the temptation to postpone it again and again grows. The example of the dentist mentioned above is a classic one: even though I panic about the dentist, while the visit is far away, my will to go remains firm … until the day before, when I call the dentist's office and postpone it. Even so, the more important and irreversible a negative consequence is, the more interest there is in delaying it: if you have to lose a leg, you look for a remedy that avoids it or, at least, postpones it as long as possible.

Instead of a single future value, there could be several. For example, a person may have to choose between two values far from the present, the one farther from the present having a larger size than the closer one, such as choosing between receiving €1,000 in one year or €800 in 11 months. The preference is shown by the projection of the two figures to the present. There are three possible choices:

- The individual prefers to receive €800 when promised.
- They decide to wait for €1,000 in one year.
- The person chooses at random.

Comparing amounts and waiting times is a common type of experiment in analyzing inter-temporal preferences. The goal is to link the changes in preferences and combinations. In this kind of exercise, there is the interesting variant of obtaining, say, €1,000 after one year or €1,100 after one year and one month. Faced with this dilemma, people tend to prefer to wait: after the inevitable 12 months, a little more money justifies a little more patience. Many field studies confirm that a small extra is actually enough to transmute impatience into waiting. The same happens in a bar in which the coffees of each client are recorded so that, when ten coffees have been consumed, customers are entitled to a free pastry, which can be two if the wait is up to fifteen coffees. Many think that it is worth waiting a little longer if the prize is greater (Wilkinson and Klaes, 2012: 292). However, if it is a question of receiving €1,000 after one year or €1,100 in three years, waiting does not pay off. Then, the question is: how much additional time are people willing to wait for an extra sum? No conclusive answer has been found. It seems that the relationship between extra value and additional waiting time depends on each person's personal situation (income level, age, etc.) and the context (Soman et al., 2005: 358). Since there are innumerable combinations of values spread over time, their influence on choices is still under study.

Inter-temporal preferences may be altered by the anticipation of possible regret. Continuing with the case of the bar, imagine that waiting for the second pastry clashes with the diet. In this case, the customer will not wait. Perhaps they will not even enjoy the first one. Let us take another example: a student is entitled to take an extra exam in a few days to raise a given subject mark. If there are several applicants and only one will receive the highest mark, candidates considering that they have little chance will decline the opportunity, if only so as not to regret having studied for nothing. Even so, if there is a possible grant at stake, the students will try anyway. Inter-temporal decisions are never unrelated to the specific circumstances and expectations of the people involved.[28]

Changing current preferences is the most relevant trait in respect of long-lasting future events. Something that everyone has experienced sometimes: the expectation of happy holidays this year, in a wonderful place (as we have been repeatedly told), turns into a fiasco once there, so that we start wishing that the holiday will end as soon as possible. Once there, i.e., when we are living the expected future interval, our preferences have fully changed. In general, the analysis of these situations requires distinguishing between valuation before and after the future has arrived. Unfortunately, the analysis of inter-temporal decisions involving values spread over a certain future interval is mostly still pending. To begin with, the following two situations can be distinguished:

- Making a decision well in advance and knowing that in the interim there may be unexpected changes of state. This is the situation of people choosing months in advance amongst several holiday destinations. People do not know what is going to happen before and during the holidays.
- People who go out at night to have fun have to choose between finishing early or staying out late, even though the next day they feel the effects of not having had enough sleep. It is a decision that has to be made on the fly, i.e. while enjoying the party.

By pretending to extend the experience that is being lived, it is assumed that the satisfaction obtained up to that moment will not diminish (Ainslie, 2005: 641). Of course, if the expectation fails miserably, that is, the party is frustrating from the very beginning, it is abandoned much earlier than anticipated (sometimes by seeking an alternative entertainment as a consolation prize). However, if this is not the case, people can choose between leaving it at the previously decided moment, and extending the experience. This second option can be explained by the following two reasons:

- The party is very pleasant and hence the preference for the present prevails: the enjoyment offsets the discomfort of the following day, which can always be lessened with larger doses of coffee.
- People choose to extend the experience because of the expectation that somewhat later the party will become better. This expectation is what overcomes the next day's pain of not having had enough sleep. However, if the party remains dull until the end, therefore ruining this second expectation, the frustration will be enormous.

All these cases are very complex because anticipations, successive expectations, the memory of previous experiences, surprises, etc. play a role.

Consequently, there are several factors that complicate the analysis. For example, before going on holiday, people may have some doubts about the chosen destination; then, if the experience is disappointing, their worries will be confirmed (and they will perhaps blame themselves for it). Nonetheless, if this is not the case, the enjoyment will be more intense: it is very satisfying that the initial suspicions were groundless. It should be remembered that any progressive improvement generates a series of increasing stimuli, which have an intense and positive emotional effect. At the same time, experiences with declining values are widely rejected. They necessarily lead to an intensely annoying ending. In short, when inter-temporal decisions involve experiences extended over a given interval, they are prior and living expectations, which can lead to various alterations in preferences. The trace they leave in memory will shape similar future decisions.

The last type of inter-temporal choice is the sequential ordering of successive values (Prelec and Loewenstein, 1997; Angner, 2012: 166; Cartwright, 2018: 168–170). For example, a person has to decide at the current moment, t_0, the order of three tasks to perform from instant t^*, as shown in Figure 4.3. These are compulsory tasks, although independent of each other, so they can be executed in any order.[29] However, their value is not the same: task A has the highest value, i.e., it is considered the most pleasant, while task B is the most painful, and task C has an intermediate position.

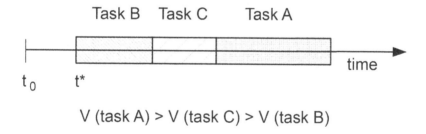

$$V \text{ (task A)} > V \text{ (task C)} > V \text{ (task B)}$$

Figure 4.3   The sequence of growing values

The figure shows a very common situation: a person decides to spend Sunday cleaning and tidying the apartment (a chore they find burdensome) and going to the movies (an activity they like very much). Which do they do first? Studies indicate that people prefer to choose sequences of increasing value. For example, they first opt for cleaning (the unavoidable penalty), and then they go to the movies (leisure). This order makes the cinema a deserved reward. People anticipate that this task order is the most satisfactory. Conversely, leaving the domestic burden to the end denotes a weakness of will and makes the task of cleaning even harder (no reward at the end). Most people undoubtedly prefer to order the execution of tasks from least to most pleasurable. However, the problem of the temporal distance among tasks to be considered part of the same sequence has not yet been answered. What no one disputes is that ordering by increasing values indicates that immediate rewards are not always preferred.

4.3.2   Empirical Results

Field experiments have shown that inter-temporal choices change depending on personal and/or social circumstances (Soman et al., 2005: 351, 354). These investigations usually take the form of questionnaires in which participants have to choose between different monetary values, several temporal displacements, and particular contextual conditions. The results can only be approximated given the hypothetical character of the choices made and concerns about the representativeness of the sample. The huge variety of real situations and people involved in them explains that, although inter-temporal choices have been studied for decades, there are still a small number of robust results. A great deal of work is yet to be done (Wilkinson, 2008: 220). There are, however, valuable findings, most of them related to the case of choices concerning precise values (more information in Soman et al., 2005; Wilkinson, 2008: 207; Loewenstein, 2009: 396; and Urminsky and Zauberman, 2016). Namely:

- In the case of winnings, people prefer immediacy: money should be cashed the sooner the better, preventing unforeseen events from making this difficult or, worse, impossible. Moreover, telling people that they have just received a prize, and not letting them cash it until some time later, only irritates them: What are you waiting for? Nonetheless, if an extra amount is added for waiting, people tend to accept it. Therefore, if the arrival of a shipment is delayed, people are fine with the seller offering a discount (or adding a free extra).
- The preference for the present has economic (waiting delays possible lucrative placements of the value to be received) and psychological reasons (waiting lengthens the enjoyment of buying something or increases the discomfort stemming from a future payment). Whatever the case, it should be stressed that the closer a consequence, the more attention and scrutiny it deserves, whereas if it is (still) distant it seems less relevant. In this vein, it has been conjectured that procrastination, pathological cases aside, could have a strategic character: people believe that, later on, they will have more resources available or will be less busy than now (Soman et al., 2005). However, this argument may be just a pretext.

- People prefer to postpone future losses, especially if they are significant. Immediate losses must be avoided: the fine is paid on the last day allowed. Even so, if accelerating them makes it possible to limit them, people do not let this opportunity slip away. This is the aforementioned case of fines with a discount for early payment. To refine the argument, it is pointed out that the volume of incentives accepted to accelerate losses is usually greater than the size of the extra incentives requested to postpone gains.

Other noteworthy results are as follows (adaptation of Wilkinson and Klaes, 2012: 266–268):

- The preference for the present decreases as the considered time interval moves further into the future. This is the postulate of decreasing impatience: the vast majority of people tend to prefer €1,000 today rather than €1,100 half a year from now and, simultaneously, they are likely to prefer €1,100 in two-and-a-half years rather than €1,000 in two years. The difference in these cases is the same (half a year), but if all the concerned winnings are further away, the preference changes. Moreover, those who continue to prefer €1,000 in two years versus €1,100 in an additional six months, i.e. they continue to be comparatively more impatient, end up abandoning this preference. This happens, for example, if they are offered €1,000 in four years or €1,100 in four-and-a-half years. In the end, everyone accepts being more patient for a somewhat larger amount. Generally speaking, the preference for the closer value diminishes as the amounts between which to choose are spread further and further apart in time.
- If the amount to be cashed at a future date is considered irrelevant, waiting is not worthwhile. However, patience is easier to activate when comparatively larger figures are involved, for a given temporal interval. For example, someone who is indifferent to earning €15 now and €60 in a year, is also indifferent to earning €250 now and €350 a year from now, or €3,000 today and €4,000 in a year. As can be seen, the indifference involves figures progressively closer to each other: the distance is 4, 1.4 and 1.3, respectively. As more money is at stake, the preference for the present is comparatively decreasing.
- As suggested above, the amount required as compensation for postponing a reward is two to four times greater than the sum people are willing to give up to cash it immediately. Delay and promptness are asymmetrical decisions.
- Indicating a postponement with a future calendar date is not the same as indicating it as a delay to the present. Time as duration pushes people to demand more money in exchange for waiting. Framing a choice in terms of duration increases the preference for the present.

- Initial values can psychologically outweigh the stream of future benefits, even if they are greater (according to the usual financial rules) (Loewenstein and Prelec, 2009a). For instance, in recent years, energy-saving models stand out among household appliances such as washing machines, refrigerators, etc. Studies on attitudes towards purchasing this type of device, which involves a larger initial expenditure and a stream of small and persistent future savings (both in comparative terms), show the preference for the present, i.e., cheaper (and less efficient) appliances end up being purchased. Even though it offsets the initial outlay, the small economic advantage spread over time of the most expensive and efficient models is not convincing. The electricity bills are conceived in a fragmented manner and for an indefinite period, without usually having an outstanding value to the available income. This contrasts with the higher initial expense required for these devices. This is why some governments have established direct incentives (subsidies) for the purchase of more energy-efficient appliances, cars, etc.

- Age also plays a role. Young and old people show a comparatively greater preference for the present, the former because of their impatience to discover new things and the latter because they know their years to come are limited. However, all age groups coincide in their lack of concern for the global and long-term consequences of present decisions. Thus, the need to act to curb climate change is often no more than rhetoric: the years of waiting to see the benefits of a commitment pale in comparison to the immediate advantages of non-compliance. Moreover, the scale of the measures to be taken encourages doing nothing, while waiting for others to act as well. As long as they are not a widely accepted moral postulate, actions taken to mitigate climate change will collide with procrastination. Many ask themselves why they should bother to invest in environmentally friendly techniques and moderate their level of consumption. They argue that indisputable evidence of environmental damage and more accurate costing is needed before doing so. However, others reply that by the time the levels of certainty demanded are available, it will already be too late, given the strong inertia of the climate and the irreversible nature of biodiversity loss. In any case, the analysis of inter-temporal choices does not correctly capture this whole debate, due to the important state changes involved and the temporal span at stake.

- Some have wondered whether cultural background, understood in a broad sense, affects the degree of patience. Although much work remains to be done, some partial experience suggests that there is little influence (Du et al., 2002). However, the comparison has been made between urban residents of different countries, although perhaps it would be more relevant to compare the urban and rural populations.

Inter-temporal decisions are also influenced by presentation framing. Saving, for example, can be defined either as a choice between enjoying money now or later or as a partial postponement of current in favor of future consumption. This second way of presenting savings seems more friendly and encouraging. Let us now consider the case of two couples who have decided to buy a car (and also a second, more complex case, in the following paragraph, taken from Loewenstein and Prelec, 2009a: 428–429). At the dealership, the first couple is told that they have to wait two months to receive the car, while the second one is informed that it could be four months. Two months later, the dealer tells the couples that there are some cars to be delivered, but if they wait for two additional months, a new model will come out. This model is along the lines of the one they wanted to buy, but slightly better and at the same price. Which couple is more likely to choose to wait? It is unlikely to be the first. They have been promised a shorter waiting period and, therefore, the new offer seems like losing the opportunity to have the car right away. Loss aversion and the preference for the present work against having a slightly superior car. Concerning the second couple, whose delivery date for the car has not changed, the superior model may even seem like a windfall. In this case, loss aversion is focused on the new model, which encourages them to forget the initial one. Also, they do not feel immediacy as much. In conclusion, people psychologically prepared to wait because of the decision frame will likely show more patience. Indeed, the second couple could already have the car, but they had made up their minds that they had four months of waiting ahead.

Now suppose a more complex case. A person is interested in purchasing a high-priced hi-fi system. The first store tells them that the sophisticated music equipment can be paid for in two installments: the first is due in one week, the second in six months. Specifically, there is a choice between,

A1. A first payment of €1,600 and a second payment of €1,100.
A2. A first payment of €1,150 and a second payment of €1,600.

Before deciding, they go to another store in which buying the same hi-fi equipment involves two payments of €2,000: the first in the same week and the second in six months. However, this person is immediately informed that there is an interesting offer: there is the possibility of choosing between,

B1. A rebate of €400 on the first payment and €900 on the second payment.
B2. A rebate of €850 on the first payout, and €400 on the second one.

It is easy to see that options *A*1 and *B*1 (with a total to be paid of €2,700) and *A*2 and *B*2 (with a sum to be paid of €2,750) are the same. Therefore, whoever chooses *A*1 would have to choose *B*1, just as whoever chooses *A*2 would also have to choose *B*2. However, field experiments indicate that this consistency does not usually occur: when there are two or more payments, people mostly prefer the option with the higher initial figure if the choice involves payments (or losses, as in store *A*), while they choose the higher discount (of the two first suggested) as in store *B*. Specifically, if presented separately, a majority choose *A*1 in shop *A* and *B*2 in *B*. This result highlights the importance of the first figure perceived in installment transactions (typical in consumer durables): it can be either a comparatively higher down payment that makes the transaction more attractive because it supposedly offloads the future burden, or the opposite stratagem involving a substantial upfront discount that operates as an anchor, i.e., the customer thinks they cannot let this offer slip away. Nonetheless, the subject is still under discussion. In any case, this is an example of a framing (and anchoring) effect, or how contextual elements can alter the preferences of people (see Chapter 6).

In short, empirical studies carried out in recent decades have concluded that the emotionality of the moment, habits, beliefs, age, etc., are factors that cause alterations in inter-temporal preferences. Such a variety of personal and social circumstances overwhelms the various models of inter-temporal preferences proposed so far. These models, for the most part, revolve around the concept of the discount rate.

4.3.3   Models of the Discount Rate

The concept of discount rate does not present any formal difficulty, although it raises many theoretical discussions. Let Figure 4.4 have the value V_{t^*} located at future time t^*. This amount will be projected on the vertical axis, which represents the making-decision moment. There are two issues to be considered:

- What is the connection between the value of the discount rate, defined below, and the degree of impatience of people?
- What is the significance of the hypothetical path connecting V_{t^*} and its present value (dashed with segments in the figure)?

Suppose two people are asked what the present value is, i.e., in t_0, of $V_{t^*} = €1,000$ to be cashed in t^*. One of them states $V_0 = €100$, while the other says $V'_0 = €500$ so that $V_0 < V'_0$, as shown in the figure. Since present values are subjective assessments of future ones, the person who considers that the future €1,000 now seem as if they were €100 is less patient than the one who values them at €500. In other words, the person who indicates a lower present value (€100) is less attracted by the future figure (€1,000). In conclusion, the smaller the present value, the greater the preference for the present: "Since I value the future so little, why wait?"

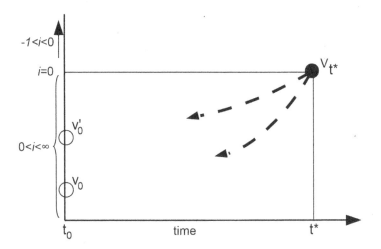

Figure 4.4   The concept of discount rate

The discount rate reflects the relationship between the future value and its subjective perception at present. Formally, the present value (V_o) results from dividing the future one at t^* (V_{t^*}) by the factor $(1 + i)^t$, t being the time units between t_0 and t^*, and i the discount rate, i.e.,

$$V_o = \frac{V_{t^*}}{(1+i)^t}$$

For example, the current projection of $V_{t^*} = €429.19$ in 25 years, is now $V_0 = €100$, if the yearly discount were $i = 6\%$. If the same amount had been discounted at 15%, $V_0 = €13.04$. Therefore, the higher the discount rate, the lower the current valuation of a given value located at a future point, and vice versa. Alternatively, the higher the discount rate, the less patience people have or, also, the greater the preference for the present. As is evident, the operation of discounting is the opposite of capitalizing, which takes the familiar form

$$V_{t^*} = V_o (1+i)^t$$

Thus, $V_0 = €100$ deposited for 25 years at 6%/year, ends up being $V_{t^*} = €429.19$, i.e., $100 \cdot (1 + 0.06)^{25}$.

As explained below, models of inter-temporal choices focus their attention on the value and behavior of the discount rate. A considerable effort has been and is still being made in both subjects. However, a strong assumption underlies the discount rate concept: the range of psychological and contextual factors regarding the current valuation of future magnitudes can be reduced to a specific and instantaneously emerging figure. Unfortunately, several empirical studies have detected that discount rates change according to people and/ or circumstances. Moreover, there is nothing to prevent the hypothesis that a person, even for the same inter-temporal decision, has a range of possible discount rates, one of which is occasionally selected.

It might seem that there is a direct and close relationship between the concept of discount rate and the basic rules of financial mathematics. However, the reality is more complex. The following two points should be highlighted:

- Since the discount rate presumably summarizes the personal and contextual factors that shape the subjective perception of the future, the huge variety of factors, as field experiments have shown, has pushed analysts to suggest more and more mathematical formats for approaching present values. Alongside the canonical algorithm described above, these formats range from simple rules such as $V_{t^*} = V_0 \cdot t$, i.e., €100 today equals €500 in $t = 5$ years (thus, the discount rate is implicit), to very complicated expressions in which the considered discount rate is surrounded by a lot of parameters (Wilkinson, 2008: 202).
- Financial rules apply to profitable transactions subject to general economic conditions and expectations, but inter-temporal preferences are only subjective positionings about the future. If financial markets were perfectly efficient, a given future amount could be rejected if its present value placed at interest would result in a larger capitalization value. In an efficient environment, this divergence would disappear since interest rates and discount rates would coincide. However, the degree of efficiency of financial markets does not support this assumption.

The discount rate reflects an idiosyncratic and contextual disposition. This is a fact that a simple figure and the rules of financial calculus cannot exhaust and fit, respectively. All these assumptions reveal how precarious the knowledge of the psychological mechanisms behind inter-temporal decisions still is.

Before going further, it should be noted that some authors, especially American ones, use the discount factor (δ) instead of the discount rate (i). The relationship between the two concepts is as follows (Angner, 2012: 155):

$$\delta = \frac{1}{1+i}$$

or,

$$i = \frac{1-\delta}{\delta}$$

Thus, when $i = 0$, $\delta = 1$ and, as i grows, δ approaches zero. The rate and the discount factor have to be interpreted in opposite ways: the higher the rate, the smaller the discount factor, and vice versa.

Returning to Figure 4.4, the second of the questions posed must now be addressed: how should the specific trace that ties the future value and its projection on the vertical axis be interpreted? This is not a secondary issue: as detailed below, it can be assumed that the discount rate is either the same figure throughout this path, or it can change. In other words, the preference for the future may remain unchanged or change as time goes by, or as future time t^* approaches. This is a key issue since it reflects important psychological assumptions which give rise to different models of inter-temporal choices. However, before going deeper into the subject, attention focuses on the three zones in which the vertical axis of Figure 4.4 has been divided. Each reflects the possible signs and magnitude of the discount rate. They are interpreted as follows:

- $V_{t^*} < V_0$, under the condition $-1 < i < 0$. In this case, people deeply disdain the present. They are only interested in the future reward. This attitude recalls what St. Teresa of Avila wrote: "I live without living in me, and I expect a life so high, that I die because I do not die." Then, for example, the value $V_{t^*} = €100$, with $t = 6$ years and $i = -0.1$ has a present value of $V_0 = €188.16$. The fact that the present value exceeds the future one shows the enormous importance given to the latter. Any action taken by people is aimed at achieving this desired future, at whatever price, as happens in the business of reselling tickets for very popular sports and musical events; the desire to be there explains the exorbitant prices people pay.

- $V_{t^*} = V_0$, i.e., the future value is not discounted, $i = 0$. The future has the same importance as the present. This is the saying that those who plant trees do so for the enjoyment of their grandchildren and future descendants. Nonetheless, in everyday life, concrete actions projected so far into the future are exceptional. This does not prevent people from feeling that they have a moral commitment to future generations, even if it is absurd to think that this extends for centuries and centuries. For example, it is well known that many American First Nations had the rule of making decisions that would not harm anyone until the seventh succeeding generation.[30] While the null value of the discount rate identifies such beliefs, it should be noted

Table 4.4   *Models on inter-temporal choices*

Types	Key variable
Values and waiting periods integrated	Exponential discounting
	Hyperbolic discounting
Similarity models	Heuristic algorithm

that the inter-temporal tools are insufficient for analyzing decisions with a very long time horizon.

- $0 < V_0 < V_{t^*}$, $0 < i < \infty$. This is the usual situation. People show more or less preference for the present. Thus,
  - As the discount rate approaches zero, the future becomes more important. This is the case for those who save for a major future purchase or retirement. These are two future situations that people perceive perfectly.
  - As the discount rate is progressively larger (it tends to infinity), so is the preference for the present. *Carpe diem*: now enjoy everything you can and do not worry about what the future may bring. As is already known, in extreme cases this principle can lead to profoundly uncontrolled behavior. A first example is a scene in the movie *Rebel without a cause*, in which two drivers challenge each other to drive towards a cliff at high speed, the first who brakes losing the bet. Known as the chicken game, this kind of challenge reflects a profound disregard for the consequences, albeit catastrophic. This senseless recklessness also characterizes arms races. A second example is the case of people addicted to narcotics: the abstinence syndrome pushes them to continue consuming, although it no longer brings any satisfaction and they would like to stop. People's lives are confined to the present since the addiction has suppressed the future.[31]

Continuing with the exposition of the discount rate concept, Table 4.4 shows the classification of the main models proposed so far. It should be noted that:

- Models have been classified according to whether they define a unique variable reflecting values and waiting times, or compare the attributes of inter-temporal options.[32]
- The models integrating values and waiting times are divided into whether or not the discount rate is uniform.
- The proposals for comparing the attributes of inter-temporal options, or similarity models, attempt to detect the heuristic algorithm applied by people when choosing between future options. There are several variants.

The following sections briefly discuss these models. First, it should be warned that their history is paradoxical. At first sight, it is expected that the research should have begun with all kinds of experiments. This is a necessary step to approximate the psychological mechanisms, and the associated discount rates, behind people's choices. Since inter-temporal choices change according to contexts and people, the experimental challenge is colossal, but it would have outlined the complexity of the phenomenon. However, things went very differently. The first proposed model, that of exponential discounting (1937), was created as another expression of the postulates of perfect rationality. Given its difficulties in explaining observed inter-temporal preferences, since the 1960s many other designs have been proposed. Not all of them are equally close to psychological reality.

4.3.3.1 Exponential discounting

For years, the canonical model of inter-temporal decisions was exponential discounting, proposed by Samuelson. It includes two important assumptions (Wilkinson, 2008: 193; Angner, 2012: 115, 158):

- From the outset, people have a preference for the present. Subsequent field studies have confirmed this hypothesis, especially when monetary values are at stake and factors such as the individual's financial situation or consumption preferences are not considered (Read et al., 2018).
- The discount rate does not vary over the time interval spread between the present and future points. The supposition that people are consistent in discounting the future is the model's Achilles heel.

Figure 4.5 is a representation of the exponential model. As just mentioned, its main attribute is that the discount rate is the same along the path linking the future value at t^* and its present value (t_0). In the figure, the lower curve shows a comparatively higher discount rate, the value of which is the same at t_0, t_1, t_2, and t_3.

The expression, in continuous terms of the present value for the exponential model, is

$$V_0 = V_{t^*} \cdot e^{-it}$$

For instance, if V_{t^*} = €5,000, t = 10 years and i = 0.05, the present value is €3,032.65.[33] In the exponential model, the perception of the future does not change at any time, i.e., people always manifest the same impatience over time, whether high or low. Thus, if someone spends their entire monthly salary on parties as soon as they receive it, as long as they always act in the same way, this behavior will be considered rational. By contrast, changing their attitude

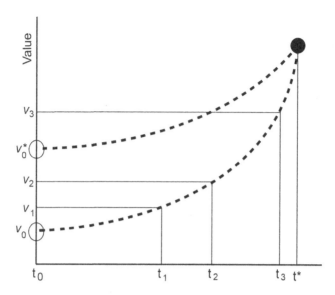

Figure 4.5   Exponential discounting

and starting to foresee expenses and save will be classed as irrational. This is
an absurd diagnosis (Berg et al., 2008). Despite its creator warning that the
model was very simple, neither he nor anyone else ever made any improvement (Lowenstein and Prelec, 1992; Thaler, 2015: 99). Many years had to pass
before some empirical studies detected the phenomenon of preference reversal
or discount reversal effect and, by extension, the problem of self-control.
New models had to be developed to reflect how temptations can make people
impulsive.[34]

4.3.3.2 Hyperbolic discounting

Many authors dedicated to economic psychology agree that the current standard model for inter-temporal choices is the hyperbolic model. Its most basic
version is as follows (Mazur, 1987):

$$V_0 = \frac{V_i^*}{1+it}$$

with *i* being the rate of discount.[35] This expression projects the future values to
the present in a less steep way than the exponential model: for example, recovering the data of Figure 4.4, €429.19 in 25 years with *i* = 0.06 is now worth
€171.67, so the devaluation is less pronounced. This is a predictable result

given that hyperbolic discounting follows the dynamics of simple interest: $V_{t^*} = V_0(1 + it)$. Therefore, the design of the hyperbolic model causes a comparatively smaller devaluation of the farther away values compared to the closer ones. This is the above-mentioned postulate of decreasing impatience.

Before continuing, it should be stressed that, in some cases, decreasing impatience can lead to preference reversal (Thaler and Loewenstein, 1992: 97; Prelec and Loewenstein, 1997). Consider the following illustration: faced with the alternative of receiving €100 or €200 right now, people choose the higher figure; however, if they are immediately informed that the €200 means waiting for, say, a year, they change their preferences in favor of the lower amount (€100); but if they have to choose between €100 in a year or €200 in a year and a month, the higher figure is again the preferred one.

In the hyperbolic model, time preferences change in favor of increasing patience: the farther away a future reward, the lower the discount rate applied by people. This tolerance to waiting is shown in Figure 4.6. At its top, a given value, V^*, has been placed at future points increasingly distant from the present (located at the origin of coordinates). At the bottom, the magnitudes of the discount rates have been plotted when V^* is progressively farther away. For example, the discount rate is i^* at instant t^*. This magnitude increases if the

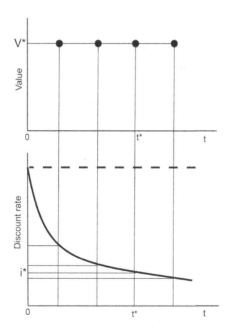

Figure 4.6   Changes in the discount rate due to the waiting period

date is closer to the present and diminishes if it is farther away. The exponential model assumes that temporal distance never alters discount rates. Their value may be different for each person, but they never change, as shown by the straight line at the bottom part of the figure.

As the Weber-Fechner "law" pointed out, the perception of changes at a given magnitude depends on the initial quantity. Therefore, a proportionality emerges which can be described by a hyperbola (Ainslie, 2009: 141; Angner, 2012: 161). Nonetheless, as is clear from observing the most basic expression of the hyperbolic model, any factor that decreases the impact of i causes the denominator to lose weight and, hence, the curve becomes flatter. In brief, any parameter between 0 and 1 that affects i can be interpreted as a decreasing trend towards preference reversal.

As mentioned previously, the hyperbolic model and its variants focus on changes in the discount rate over time. Hence its interest in the study of the procrastination effect, which can be represented as shown in Figure 4.7. Unlike the exponential trajectory, the depicted curve grows progressively steeper due to a change in the individual degree of patience. This gradient reflects an increasing preference for the present, or a greater degree of impatience, as the future approaches: as long as the future is far away, it is well worth waiting for (or keeping the commitment to) the value located at t^*; but as this moment approaches, patience runs out. Indeed, at point t_1, a bend in the curve appears, indicating an alteration of preferences: from being more patient between t_0 and t_1 to being more impatient between t_1 and t^*. Before reaching t_1, people show

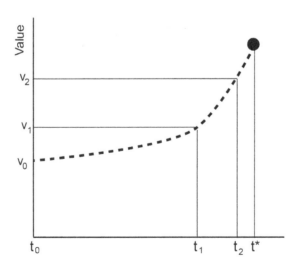

Figure 4.7   *Hyperbolic discounting and procrastination*

greater preference for the future, but then suddenly change their attitude: as the foreseen future is seen as being near, the preference for the present revives.

The hyperbolic model implicitly accepts that people have many occasions to rethink their decisions as the future approaches or, to be more concrete, anxiety pushes people to break the commitment made sometime before. This is the case of the aforementioned proximity of tempting desserts which abruptly breaks the long-standing promise to follow a strict diet. Temptation has won: immediate desires prevail, and future gratification (associated with the diet) can wait. The hyperbolic discounting model aims to capture the common fact of procrastination, or the preference for the present when the future is approaching (Ariely, 2009: 139–166; Motterlini, 2006: 81). This phenomenon, as field research indicates, emerges more readily when commitments involve hassles, especially if prolonged in time, such as making home improvements or following non-urgent health treatments (such as giving up smoking).

Procrastination can be commercially exploited. A famous case is gyms: many of them offer membership through periodic payments (monthly, yearly) renewed by default. It turns out that many members attend comparatively less often. Since access is guaranteed, being a member justifies procrastination: "I will go tomorrow or the next day." Maintaining membership reduces regret since the commitment to go is always alive. However, if such users had paid entrance fees on a pay-as-you-go basis, at the end of the year the gym would have been cheaper for them. From the gym's point of view, members who go very infrequently are good business: guaranteed membership fees but limited use (lower maintenance and staff costs, etc.) (della Vigna and Malmendier, 2006; Motterlini, 2010: 68 and 2014: 138). Something similar can happen with flat rates for telephone services: for many customers, paying for each call would be cheaper. (Wilkinson, 2008: 170; Prelec and Loewenstein, 2009: 508; and Cartwright, 2018: 193–194).

This incoherent behavior reflects a self-control problem (O'Donoghue and Rabin, 2003). People make commitments for the medium and long term, but this does not prevent them from acting short-sightedly when the time of execution approaches. On the one hand, immediacy is preferred: to motivate the use of sun creams, dermatologists know that rather than talking about possible skin cancer in the long term, it is more effective to mention the immediate adverse aesthetic effects, such as skin blemishes, etc. (Thaler and Lowenstein, 1992: 94). On the other hand, people have the intuition that today's preferences may later change, even though they do not know how. Faced with this suspicion, people tend to act in three different ways, the description of which requires just a simple example (see Ho et al., 2006; Wilkinson and Klaes, 2012: 297). Several people are very fond of potato chips, so they often buy bags on going to the supermarket. They have two options: to buy a small bag containing a single portion or to buy a large (or family-size) one. Predictably, the latter has a lower price per unit weight. It is assumed that, if they buy a small bag, this will be consumed without interruption. However, on purchasing a large bag, they can either consume all the chips non-stop, or they can eat only one portion and leave the rest for later. Anyway, people are aware that potato chips are an unhealthy product. Therefore, consuming an entire family-size bag in one go is less advisable than eating it over time. For this reason, some people may consider the option of only purchasing the comparatively expensive small bags. Faced with these dilemmas, field studies have identified the following threefold behavior:

- Some people behave as predicted by the exponential model: they buy the comparatively cheaper large bags and consume them in periodic single portions. Therefore, they show no problem of self-control. They know and weigh all the aspects involved in this consumption process, and optimize the decision.
- Some naive people discount hyperbolically: they buy large bags to save money convinced that they will overcome the temptation to eat all the chips at once. However, once the bag is open, they are unable to stop. This weakness of will can cause them considerable discomfort.
- Some people are sophisticated: they only buy one small bag at a time, despite the comparatively higher price. They do so because they anticipate that they will not be able to stop eating a family-size bag in one go. These people also tend to discount hyperbolically but anticipate a potential problem of self-control.

Although people can anticipate their behavior, the naive attitude pushes them to rush, that is, to do things now that would be better left for later. Conversely, the sophisticated inclination tends to postpone for later what should be done now. Or, in other words, people are capable of developing and applying stratagems to prevent falling prey to impulses. This is the case when erasing the dentist's telephone number from the cell phone to overcome the temptation of postponing the visit. Nonetheless, there also are people who conscientiously buy large potato chips bags to test themselves. They consider that to evaluate their strength of will, the best option is to incite temptation. Whatever the case may be, it should be borne in mind that there are no people who always act according to just one of the above-listed behaviors.

Weakness of will consists of doing B (lighting one more cigarette) when it is believed that A (giving up smoking once and for all) should be done. Both options are perfectly attainable and simultaneously desired, but they are incompatible (Elster, 2010: 139). In such a situation, the final preference $(B > A)$ reverses the elementary one $(A > B)$. Unwillingness can take many forms. One of them is the present non-compliance with the commitment made some time ago, while simultaneously reiterating that later on nothing will stop us from achieving it.[36] In other words, willpower always prevails tomorrow since it will (presumably) be free of today's worries. Tasks not performed today seem lighter and more manageable tomorrow, which justifies procrastination.[37] While some people are particularly adept at putting off decisions over and over again, most know that systematically trying to escape the decisions ends up dragging themselves down. They know (with the apparent exception of quite a few students) that it is better to take a small step every day than to rely on a last-minute big leap. This extra effort will inevitably be made under stress, which increases the likelihood of failure. As a result, people will lose a little more confidence in their own will. Since it is a self-reinforcing cycle, it can lead people to a significant loss of welfare.

A reasonably effective way to combat the lack of willpower is to make public the commitment (Elster, 2007: Chapter 13). An explicit restriction on one's future options invites others to collaborate in your particular fight against a weak will.[38] This request can take the form of a voluntary legal constraint, as in the case of gambling addicts who ask to be barred from gambling halls. However, on the one hand, such commitments may be too rigid: if I have promised to shave my head if my favorite team does not win the league, given that it is almost certain to do so, but its best players suddenly go down with food poisoning, do I have to keep the promise? On the other hand, it should be noted that not everyone experiences a lack of willpower as a setback, even though this perception always emerges in the advanced stages of an addiction process. Succumbing at a given moment to temptation (finishing a nice meal by eating a dessert) after a long period of resistance, is by no means irrational. It can be seen as proof of having achieved the goal. Only the evolution of things will show whether this fact has opened the door to future defections (Schelling, 1992 and 2006b; Loewenstein and Prelec, 2009a: 434). Context matters a great deal in these cases: if there are countless occasions to break commitments (to not play slot machines, to abandon social networks, etc.), people's will faces a colossal challenge.[39]

Instead of claiming its normative character as the exponential model does, the hyperbolic model has evolved into more and more complex variants. This evolution does not satisfy everyone: some authors wondered whether the mechanics of inter-temporal preferences are as convoluted as suggested by these models. This complexity requires broad and deep cognitive skills, something not very credible from a psychological point of view. Moreover, the exponential and hyperbolic models failed to explain a couple of facts. Namely (Stevens, 2016):

- The magnitude effect or the tendency of people to show a decreasing discount rate as the reward size increases, given a waiting time. Between

€30 now and €50 in a year, most people choose the lower immediate figure, but on choosing between €3,000 today and €5,000 in a year, things change. Larger values make people more patient. Although exponential and hyperbolic models open the door to predicting that if the ratios between the values involved and between the delays do not change, the choice does not change either, this is not usually the case.

•   The sign effect or the change in the discount rate depends on gains or losses. As explained above, people discount gains rather than losses, except if losses can be reduced by accelerating the decision.

To develop a novel line of research and, at the same time, explain these two anomalies, several researchers have proposed incorporating heuristics into inter-temporal choices. The following section explains the basis of this approach and its main results, but with the caveat that there is much work still to be done.

4.3.3.3 Comparisons of similarity

The main analytical work of authors such as Leland (1994, 2002), Rubinstein (2003), Vlaev et al. (2011), Scholten et al. (2014), and Marzilli et al. (2015) is not to determine a rate (and, by extension, a function) of discounting but to describe, as far as possible, the psychological drivers of inter-temporal choices. The goal is not to build a theory about the cognitive processes underlying these choices, but simply to study inter-temporal preferences with tools that psychology recognizes as its own. This approach, known as the heuristic of similarity comparisons, assumes that people compare the attributes of the alternatives at stake, i.e., rewards and delays. This research accepts consolidated results such as that, *ceteris paribus*, people show a preference for the present and tend to be more patient in the face of still distant outcomes. The first strand of work is developed in Marzilli et al. (2015) and, with slight modifications, in Scholten and Read (2010). These models are based on the criterion "money earlier or money later": the participants have to choose between a small monetary value (V^s) sooner (t^s) or a larger one (V^l) later (t^l). Then, the analysts take note of how people project different values and delays "small-and-sooner" (*SS*) and "large-and-later" (*LL*) to the present time. This is shown in Figure 4.8.

The *SS-LL* options are presented in random order on a computer screen and the participants indicate their preferences. From the results obtained, parameters of a model including some heuristic elements (such as reference points, comparisons between values and expectations, etc.) are calculated. The ensuing model is very complex since it combines probabilities, functions with certain suitable properties and attribute weightings. Unfortunately, this complexity is unconvincing since it implicitly assumes people have extraordinary

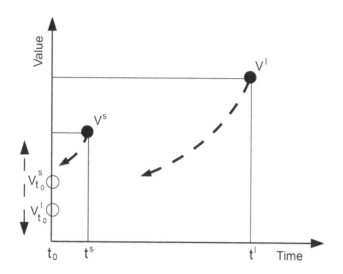

Figure 4.8   A map of values and delays

cognitive capacities and broad time availability. Consequently, it does not seem that this line of research has good psychological foundations.

Other authors propose models that are simpler in form, but no less powerful. To begin with, let us consider again the situation depicted in Figure 4.8, i.e., two options with different values and delays. A heuristic is suggested that performs a double comparison: one concerning the values and the other involving the time lags. The related algorithm is as follows: for example, on comparing the options (€100, 1 month) and (€105, 3 months) the difference between the values of these pairs is small, but the delay is not; people then ignore the monetary figures and choose based on the delay, i.e., the shorter one (€100 in one month) due to the preference for the present. In brief, given two pairs of *SS-LL* options, the choice is determined by the element (magnitude or delay) with the least similarity. Therefore, the inter-temporal choices follow a criterion close to the lexicographic one (detailed in the next chapter). However, if there is a similarity in all dimensions, e.g., choosing between (€100, 30 days) and (€105, 35 days), the choice can be made randomly or according to some other criterion. This method of choice has been observed in many field experiments (see Leland, 2002; Rubinstein, 2003; Stevens, 2016).

Consider the following example from Rubinstein (2003: 1211). People have to choose between the *A* and *B* cases, assuming that today is January 1, 2022:

A1. Be paid €400 on January 1, 2024.
A2. Take €800 on July 1, 2024.

B1. Be paid €425 on January 1, 2024.
B2. Take €430 on July 1, 2024.

Faced with these dilemmas, most people prefer to wait in the first case (*A2* is chosen: doubling the amount of money justifies extending the waiting half a year), but they reject waiting in the second case (*B1* is chosen: receiving a little more money does not compensate for an extra half a year). In case of *A*, people see the difference in the amount of money as more significant than the difference in the delays, while in *B* the opposite is true. This is a simple algorithm that clearly explains the choices. However, some considerations emerge. A first question is: what comparison ratio do people apply? Field experiments indicate that it is usually the simple numerical difference, i.e., $V^l - V^s$ and $t^l - t^s$. The ratios V^s/V^l and t^s/t^l have also been proposed. This is a criterion closer to how judgments about differences in weight, length, noise, etc. are formed according to empirical results obtained in psychology. The second question is: to what extent are such differences considered relevant? It has been suggested that people follow common ratios such as double, triple, etc. This criterion is not unrelated to biographical and contextual factors. In any case, there are still no definitive results.

This inter-temporal choosing procedure can be depicted as a decision tree as shown in Figure 4.9 (Stevens, 2016: 5; Stevens and Soh, 2018: 628, 632–634).

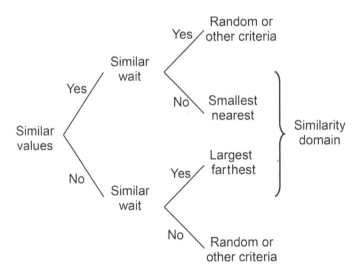

Figure 4.9   Similarity algorithm

First, attention is focused on the amounts at stake. If they are similar, the next step is to check what happens with the delays. If the latter are also similar, the option is chosen at random. However, if one of the delays is significantly shorter (right now, or well before the other), this option is chosen despite its monetary value being smaller (*SS*). If neither the monetary values nor the delays are considered similar, it is chosen at random. People believe there is no reason to discriminate between the alternatives. If the delay is similar, the larger value is chosen even if it is the farthest away (*LL*). The algorithm makes deterministic predictions concerning the cases included in the similarity domain. Even so, the distances involved are particular perceptions of each person. Therefore, when they are not large, choices are less predictable. If people choose at random, each option will be preferred close to 0.5 times. By contrast, if the comparisons are visibly different, people will coincide in their subjective appraisals and, hence, their choices will be more predictable. The main virtue of this algorithm is that it only includes simple comparisons, something that seems nearer to real mental processes.

Table 4.5 contains a hypothetical example of the similarity algorithm operative, as shown in Figure 4.9. It is a mere illustration designed according to the literature and is not based on any field experiment. In the cells, italics denote pairs of options in which choices are made at random, and boldface denotes choices where comparisons are unambiguous.

Table 4.5   Similarity algorithm

Choices		Waiting	
		Similar	Dissimilar
Value	Similar	*(€500, 4 weeks)*	**(€500, 4 weeks)**
		(€550, 5 weeks)	(€550, 6 weeks)
	Dissimilar	(€500, 4 weeks)	*(€500, 4 weeks)*
		(€700, 5 weeks)	*(€700, 6 weeks)*

The attribute comparison models aim to capture how people compare pairs of values and delays, always assuming common cognitive capacities and criteria of easy implementation. Although the analysis is still in progress, there is no doubt that, once the attributes have been detected, people apply simple similarity relations: they determine the psychological distance between the options and take a decision.

4.3.4 Sequences of Increasing Values

None of the models discussed above is concerned with the temporal order in which people prefer to do things. As was noted some pages ago, several research studies have found that people appreciate consecutive improvements or sequences of increasing value. The following experiment illustrates this point (excerpted from Loewenstein and Prelec, 2009b: 446; see also Prelec and Loewenstein, 1997). Some people were asked what they preferred:

A. Dining at a trendy French restaurant [86% favorable responses].
B. Dining at a popular Greek restaurant [14%].

Immediately, those who had chosen option *A* were asked to make the following choice:

1. Dining at the French restaurant on a Friday in one month's time [80%].
2. Dining at the French restaurant on a Friday in two months' time [20%].

Finally, a moment later, these same participants were asked to choose between,

3. Dining at the French restaurant on a Friday one month from now and dining at the Greek restaurant on a Friday in two months [43%].
4. Dining at the Greek restaurant on a Friday in one month and dining at the French restaurant on a Friday in two months [57%].

As can be seen, 80% of those who chose *A* preferred option 1. Only 20% were willing to delay a little further going to the trendy French restaurant. Even so, when the options were mixed, the majority (57%, option 4) chose to postpone going to the French restaurant. This result is the opposite of the previous one! Options 3 and 4 changed the framework: if an improvement sequence is made explicit, people prefer it. Only when going to the French restaurant is an isolated option does immediacy take over.

Consider another case in which participants had to choose among several options about where to eat on the following weekends. There were two sets of alternatives (*A/B*, *C/D*) as shown in Table 4.6 (drawn from Loewenstein and Prelec, 2009b: 449–450; see also Loewenstein, 2009: 402). Between *A* and *B*, the majority preferred *B*. Only a few people were willing to start with the more entertaining option (going to a restaurant). The hedonistic impulse encouraged postponement. The choice between *C* and *D*, options that include going to two restaurants, one of them high class, and located at the end of the sequence, gave rise to much closer numbers. Once the results are known, the following considerations should be made:

•   *C* and *D* are options equal to *A* and *B*, respectively, the only difference being the third event (eating in a Michelin-starred restaurant instead of at home). It seems that this third element should not have much influence: whoever prefers *A* (or *B*) should also prefer *C* (or *D*), but this is not the case. The addition of the third activity has altered the preferences.

- As can be observed, the majority prefer to split the choices: eating twice in a row at home has few supporters and going twice in a row to the restaurant, despite the difference in quality, does not win either. Nonetheless, there is no doubt that restaurants have a strong hedonistic value, especially those listed in the Michelin Guide. Therefore, preferences are prone to sequences of increasing values, although there is some room for an encouraging beginning.

Table 4.6   Sequences of increasing values

Option	This weekend	Next weekend	Two weeks later	%
A	Restaurant	Eating at home	Eating at home	16%
B	Eating at home	Restaurant	Eating at home	84%
C	Restaurant	Eating at home	Michelin Restaurant	54%
D	Eating at home	Restaurant	Michelin Restaurant	46%

Based on these results, the stratagem for successful excursions (city sightseeing, cruises, etc.) is not surprising: they should start with an attractive welcome followed by more normal experiences that, inevitably, lead to a spectacular culmination. They have to capture the tourists' attention from the first minute and end with a high-impact event, such as a gala dinner and after-party with the captain and officers of the cruise ship. Many local festivals also close with fireworks, and promoters of all kinds of shows know that what is in the last moment is key. These experiences are the most vivid memories that participants will easily recall. Their intensity will be transmitted to family and acquaintances, who are potential spectators or customers.

Preferring a temporal arrangement of increasing values is a manifestation of anticipation. By delaying what is most pleasurable, a positive expectation is created which increases the intensity of gratification when it arrives. However, this delay has its limits. This is for two reasons: because the opportunity may be lost (the movie you want to see after cleaning the apartment will not always be on the billboard) and because preferences can change in the meantime (the arrival of new information raises doubts about which film to see, which tarnishes what was supposed to be an entertaining evening). Consequently, cleaning the apartment is not followed by going to the movies three days later, but this evening. It should also be stressed that in a sequence it is not the absolute level of satisfaction that matters, but the relative one: once the home cleaning is finished, people enjoy going to the movies, even if they prefer the theater (but there is no show on at this time).

What is a sequence of increasing values anyway? If the actions are far apart in time, are they still so? Let us take the following experiment (Loewenstein and Prelec, 2009b: 447–448): for the next two Sundays you have decided to go to a city where you lived years ago. The city is far away and you will not have much time once you are there, so either you can visit an aunt who has a bad temper, or you can meet some old friends you have not seen for a long time. You have to choose between the following order of visits:

- Next Sunday you arrange the meeting with friends and, the following one, you will visit the grumpy aunt [an option that, in a field experiment, was chosen by 10% of participants].
- Next Sunday you visit the aunt and, the following one, you will share your time with the former colleagues [90%].

The preference is clear: the sequence of increasing values prevails. However, if the temporal distance of Sundays changes, so do a large part of the responses:

- Friends' meeting next Sunday and 26 weeks later the visit to the aunt [48%].
- Next Sunday the appointment with the aunt and 26 weeks later the one with friends [52%].

The participants in the experiment were also offered the following arrangement:

- After 26 weeks, the friends' visit and a week later the one with the aunt [17%].
- After 26 weeks the aunt's visit and a week later the one with friends [83%].

The results are indisputable: a separation of more than half a year dismantles the perception of sequence. The visits are considered different events. However, if the sequence is re-established (the temporal distance is only one week), the preference for progressive improvement returns, even though the visits have been displaced by more than half a year. Unfortunately, it has not been possible to settle the precise distance that breaks a sequence. While there is no doubt that people can arrange events perfectly according to their degree of pleasure, the temporal distribution that constitutes the same succession of events is not clear. It depends on the person and the occasion (the interval is shorter if going out to eat, and longer if going on a trip).

4.4   SUNK COSTS AND THE ENDOWMENT EFFECT

In studying the multiple facets of economic decisions, analysts have detected a couple of important subjective biases: the imperative to go ahead at any cost or the follow-on bias, and the so-called endowment effect.

As seen in section 4.1.5, the issue of sunk costs is about the difficulties in recovering the resources invested in a project. If the item is not flexible enough, it may not be possible to redirect its use and hence make a profit. A coach can be used for regular, school, or occasional transport. If one of the alternatives fails, the vehicle can be easily reoriented for other services. However, the money spent on the preparation, filming, editing, and promotion of films is only recovered if they reach the screen and obtain a sufficient number of viewers. If the box office falls short of expectations, the investment can be written off as lost.

The concept of sunk costs has a dynamic meaning: it is used when someone is reluctant to abandon projects (personal, business, or institutional) that are heading for (economic) failure. Cost estimates and time required to complete them seemed sound, especially if there was the impression that all was understood and under control.[40] Unfortunately, indisputable indications arise that the project is not progressing as planned. In these cases, most of the promoters persist in going ahead (Angner, 2012: 48–49). This is the fact to be highlighted in this section. The amounts already invested are psychologically valued as a loss, a feeling that is aggravated by the fact that the project is still incomplete.[41] This causes an intense unease that pushes people to continue digging deeper and deeper into the pit that the project has become. This stubbornness makes things worse: it is a guarantee that the initially planned budget will be exceeded. Sometimes it is just a hole in the accounts; other times it leads to the ruin of the sponsor. In any case, the expected private or social profitability, however it is measured, goes down the drain.

This psychological bias is a variant of loss aversion. Continuing to invest in a project that will not meet expectations is absurd. It is justified because it is too late to abandon it. In other words, it is argued that the effort already made is sufficient reason to continue persevering. Even so, the most reasonable thing to do would be to cancel it and divert the resources not yet injected to more promising initiatives. Only future costs and benefits should guide decisions, not the past (Nisbett, 2016: 115–118). However, giving up to prevent the hole from becoming bigger does not usually happen. The reputation of those responsible, i.e., the credibility (personal, professional, political) of those leading the project, is at stake. When the project is finally finished, or else abandoned, the damage could be colossal. Loss aversion will have led to an even greater deviation or loss.

Before launching a major risky project, promoters should ask themselves whether they will have enough willpower to abandon it if it proves too expensive, expectations of results seem to fail, or both at the same time. In many cases, enthusiasm (in the case of people), profit (of a company), or political prestige (of a government), leads to undertaking projects despite the uncertainty of their execution schedule and total cost. There are probably estimations in this regard, but once underway they turn out to be too optimistic. Despite the poor prospects, it is decided to go ahead with the project, pursuing the chimera that things will magically right themselves. As a consequence, financial damage accumulates. It will be difficult to dispense with this burden. This attitude is known as the planning fallacy, a term that could refer to a cognitive error, even though it is an attempt to avoid regret. Although promoters explain that all the eventualities of the project have been foreseen and, hence, its economic viability is guaranteed, the crude reality turns these statements into nothing.

The continuity of initiatives at any cost is common in the both private and public sectors, although in the latter there is more information on extraordinary projects that end up suffering no less extraordinary cost deviations (see the extensive report by Flyvbjerg et al., 2003). They can be transportation infrastructures (highways, bridges, tunnels, airports, canals); big science and high-tech facilities, such as astronomical observatories, spacecraft, frontier laboratories, etc.; all types of military systems; and, finally, unique buildings such as spectacular skyscrapers, sports stadiums, museums and so on. The media report on how these investments have exceeded the initial, apparently careful, forecasts. The Suez Canal, for example, cost around 20 times more than the planned amount. The Sydney Opera House, construction of which began in 1957 and was budgeted at AU\$7 million, ended up costing AU\$102 million (about 15 times more). The building was inaugurated in 1973, ten years later than planned. The case of the rail link between France and the United Kingdom (the so-called Eurotunnel, operational since 1994 and today owned by the company Getlink) is also well known. Almost the entire project was financed by private funds, but such participation lost all its value in the middle of the first decade of this century. The reason was a resounding economic failure: the project suffered a cost deviation of 80%, while the demand was about half that estimated. As a result, until recent years there has been no way to cover the debt service (the sum of interest and principal repayments) of the project.

From the point of view of scientific challenges and/or engineering possibilities, there is no doubt that these megaprojects bring valuable knowledge and experience. They are often at the frontier of what is known and/or considered feasible. However, from an economic point of view, they can end up being a bottomless pit. They were undertaken for reasons of national pride, as happened with the Apollo program after the Sputnik shock, or they were justified by the jobs to be created (usually fewer than expected and only for a short period of time). It is also repeatedly argued that they will be a factor in economic transformation (which is more uncertain than their promoters claim). Unfortunately, it is not uncommon for these projects to have economic problems such as the following:

- Overly optimistic cost and revenue forecasts. Often, governments and associated private interests present self-serving figures to prevent doubts about financial viability and/or social profitability.
- Simultaneous development: the project is launched with a general design, but without all the detailed engineering studies having been carried out. If unforeseen obstacles appear, they are resolved on the fly, which usually generates extra costs.
- Deadlines are exceeded for all sorts of reasons, increasing the burden of the financial costs. Given that more funds have to be borrowed and revenues are deferred, it will eventually be necessary to refinance the debt.
- In the case of multinational projects, there are often problems of definition (each participant wants to bring it closer to its interests) and extra costs for coordination and execution (meeting expenses, transport of components). The case of European programs for the joint production of large military platforms (aircraft, battle tanks, and warships) is well known.

After some time has elapsed and the planned expenses have been far exceeded, the sponsors consider it to be incongruous to cancel it. It is argued that it would be the same as losing the resources invested, although their main concern is the public discredit that doing so would entail. The situation can become paradoxical: at first, political and business leaders appease public anxiety by declaring that it is premature to make a precise estimate of the project cost, especially since it is unprecedented, while insisting on its emblematic character and the benefits it brings to the local, regional or national economy. Years later, other political authorities and managers, faced with criticism of the enormous amount of money already invested and the slow pace of the works, declare that it is too late to stop the project. Despite the obvious magnitude of the economic disaster, those responsible will persist in spending more and more. Only on rare occasions will megaprojects be abandoned. An example was the Waxahachie Superconducting Super Collider (Texas, USA), a large cyclotron, the construction of which was started in the 1980s and, amid strong controversy, canceled in 1993.

The problem of sunk costs occurs in many other areas. For example, in wars, the contender about to be defeated maintains hostilities out of sheer arrogance and to honor the large amount of resources (material and lives) already con-sumed. This attitude can also be observed on a personal level. Let us consider, for example, the case of a person who bought tickets for a show in advance. When the day arrives, however, it is cold and snowing and, in reality, they are not feeling very well either. This person would be better off not leaving home.

Nonetheless, so as not to lose the value of the ticket, it is decided to go to the concert, even though this is not very advisable. However, if the ticket had been a gift, they would probably have stayed at home. Shopping malls also try to exploit this psychological trap: they encourage customers to buy because "it is worth the effort to have come this far" or because "you are here now" (as discussed in Angner, 2012: 35–37). Finally, let us consider the case of a person who, having ascertained that the movie is of poor quality, decides to stay in the theater. They do so driven not by any cognitive error, but to neutralize the regret: leaving would certify that the film is bad, which is a reminder that the ticket should not have been purchased; instead, staying means taking advantage of the acquired right, which acts as a kind of emotional barrier (Chater et al., 2018: 807).

In the same vein as loss aversion, the endowment effect stands out: this is the tendency to overvalue what people own (Thaler, 2015: 17). A person, for example, bought a few bottles of wine at €10 each many years ago. Today, they are priced at €100. They like to open one bottle on the occasion of a special celebration. They would neither sell them at the current price, nor would they buy them. This common attitude does not conform to the principles of economic calculation: if they are not willing to sell the bottles at €100 each, this means that they consider them to have a higher value, so why not buy them at €100? The reasons for asking more for what people have than they would be willing to pay if they had to buy it are not clear. This may reflect a hedonistic attitude ("I have not kept the bottles so long not to enjoy them"), as well as a patrimonial one. This phenomenon is easy to observe in the rural world, where small farmers claim that at no price would they sell a plot of land and, at the same time, lament the high price of farmland. They demand a great deal to dispose of their plots, knowing that they would never buy them at the price they are asking. Perhaps it is in collecting where the endowment effect reaches its maximum degree: what is collected not only entails many hours of work, but it is also an activity that gives identity to the collectors themselves. The high value they place on their collection is not, therefore, surprising. Whatever the case may be, the endowment effect should not be confused with the attempt to profit from the scarcity of a good, such as the resale of tickets for a sold-out show (cf. Angner, 2012: 45; Wilkinson and Klaes, 2012: 211). The endowment effect has no strategic character.

The endowment effect also explains the well-known stratagem of the antique dealers: on trying to sell an old artifact or piece of furniture, people emphasize its rarity and the high sentimental value it has for them, arguments that the professional buyer tries to neutralize by stating that there are many pieces available and asking them why, if it is so valuable, they put it up for sale?

The endowment effect implies a certain conservatism in economic choices: the majority prefers to leave things as they are, i.e., not to change telephone company, electricity provider, bank, restaurant, etc. This explains why utilities have to run aggressive promotions to encourage consumers to switch providers. It also helps explain why people often miss the opportunity to take advantage of the downturn in the housing market to buy a better home. It is not that they cannot find larger and better-located properties at attractive prices; it is that they believe they would receive too little for the one they already have. There is a perception that the sale will be at a loss.

Finally, it has been found that in their personal lives people perform a type of mental amortization based on the frequency and satisfaction obtained in the use of a device. If the experience has been positive, the purchase of a new appliance does not necessarily mean the retirement of the old one. The replacement of appliances, cars, furniture, etc., is influenced by the endowment effect: if the object is offered for sale, people want a good price for it, or if they buy a new one, and trade in the old one, they ask the seller for a good trade-in price (perhaps instead of a discount on the new one). In the case of cars, if there is a great deal of competition between dealers, they tend to overpay for a used car in good condition. This value is recovered by selling a new car to the same customer, who is satisfied with what they receive for the old one.

NOTES

1. This is an important observation: the simple appeal to preferences does not sufficiently explain the quick spread of some bizarre fads, such as the Tamagotchi in the late 1990s, the search for Pokémons a few years ago, and endless etcetera. Factors such as social pressure, social approval seeking, positive reinforcement tricks, and so on, can affect decisions and, by extension, behavior. All these factors are addressed throughout the text.
2. This is the case of passions, a type of emotion capable of unleashing irrepressible actions, leaving aside their (direct and collateral, positive or negative) effects. Thus, for example, while reason wants to decide what is just, anger wants what has already been decided to be considered fair (idea attributed to Seneca). Since passions are not mentioned in the main text, the arrow representing the direct impact of passions on decisions does not appear in the figure.
3. This postulate does not deny the possibility of systematic and exhaustive comparisons. Origin and implementation of preferences are two different things. However, what is inevitable is the assumption of extremely powerful rationality, since the attainment of maximum satisfaction (or utility) is a demanding exercise: it must consider all the alternatives and ensure that choices do not contradict preferences (Hausman, 2012: xii, 3).
4. There is also room for genetic inheritance: preference for sweetness, and discomfort with bitterness are universal (Bowles, 1998: 80; Harris, 1989: 147–150 and Bowles and Gintis, 2013: 167).

5.   The halo effect is defined as the appraisal (whether or not positive) that may emerge when somebody tests something, meets a person, or visits a place for the first time (Motterlini, 2010: 107; Aronson, 2008: 140–141). This first impression often leaves a persistent imprint on the memory (Nisbett, 2016: 71).

6.   With cheap versions and fakes, perfect at first glance, available to almost anyone.

7.   Social emulation, built on small cues, is common among relatively close and stagnant income levels. In contrast, for the upwardly mobile sectors, the full exhibition of their new lifestyle is a priority.

8.   When comparisons are involved and the dominance relationship is nonstochastic, the symbol > can be read as ≻ (see Skořepa, 2011: 141).

9.   Harsanyi solved this problem by adding the moral principle of benevolence among the postulates of rational preferences (Reichlin, 2013: 179).

10.   Numbers are an inexhaustible source of colorful beliefs: in the United States there are many buildings without a floor numbered 13 and, since the number eight is the number of good luck in Chinese culture, the Beijing Olympic Games began at 8 p.m. on August 8 (which is the eighth month) in 2008. Religions also stand out for the same reason: in Israel, for example, buildings have an elevator that, during the Sabbath, to avoid having to press the lift buttons, once you get into it, it automatically stops on each floor, both up and down. The list of peculiar behaviors driven by (quasi-)religious beliefs would be endless.

11.   This diffusion pattern is like the critical mass mechanism explained in the next chapter.

12.   Magical thinking attributes supernatural capacities to certain forces or entities: to alter reality, it is enough to properly request their intercession. Quasi-magical thinking does not conjure such powers, but grants given individual gestures, attitudes, or behaviors the ability to modulate/modify reality at will.

13.   The art of prophecy can become very sophisticated, as exemplified by the still famous Michel de Nostredame (or Nostradamus), a 16th-century apothecary, healer, and occultist who published dozens of pamphlets with all kinds of prophecies. He used cryptic and ambiguous language that, strictly speaking, only he could interpret (justifying it as necessary to prevent censorship and persecution); the ideal recipe for success (Hand, 2014: 21–23).

14.   In addition, hyper- and supermarkets and franchises distribute brochures with prices and photographs of all kinds of articles through mailboxes and portals. At first glance, this seems to be a useless advertising expense, since they usually end up in the wastepaper basket. Field research suggests, however, that people look for potential bargains (Guéguen, 2016: 65): when resources are very limited, as is the case for many immigrants and retirees, these leaflets speed up the search for low prices.

15.   In places where the sales period is highly regulated, there are often queues at the store doors on the first day.

16.   Consequently, the best blueprint is to set maximum prices. Any unscheduled deviations, excluding periodic increases, must always be downward. This lightens the psychological burden of spending. This is what characterizes hotels: rooms show a note with the regulated maximum prices which far exceed those normally charged, even in high season. This is also an example of anchoring (see Chapter 6, section 6.2.3.3).

17.   It should be emphasized that the argument does not imply direct and immediate gains or losses, but the expectation of obtaining them. As explained below,

finding a banknote while walking down the street does not cause satisfaction less than the sorrow felt when it is lost.

18. People do not live in an eternal present, but always connect the present to the past, and anticipate the future (Morgado, 2017: 25 and 27).

19. In 1956, the psychologist George A. Miller (1920–2012) determined that the mind can manage from five to nine items simultaneously (quoted in Earl, 1995: 30). Given that the average number is seven elements, it does not seem insignificant that we talk about the seven wonders of the world, the seven deadly sins, the seven heavens and many other sevens that show the importance of this number since ancient times (see, for example, www.britannica.com/topic/number-symbolism). Moreover, people have developed stratagems to organize information and remember it, such as grouping the digits of a long number into threes or applying mnemonic rules (A. Baddeley et al., 2015: Chapter 3, sections 3.2–3.3).

20. However, humans react faster to an acoustic than to a visible signal (Klein, 2015: 86). For this reason, in athletics races, where every instant of time counts, a starting shot is fired.

21. Therefore, the computer analogy is doubly misleading: neither is the relationship between short-term and long-term memory like that between RAM and hard disk memory, since they are not two memories but specializations of one; nor is long-term memory like the CPU of a computer since it does not retrieve information as it was loaded (Bunge, 2010: Chapter 12).

22. There are correlations among variables that reflect a certain association between them, which can be mistaken for cause–effect relationships, and completely absurd or spurious correlations such as those shown in http://tylervigen.com/spurious-correlations.

23. Citibank was the financial institution that issued the first credit card in 1961. American Express followed soon after. At first, only very affluent people could use them. Credit cards took some 30 years to become widespread. The proliferation of electronic terminals made it easier.

24. An exhaustive inventory of the different conceptions of risk and uncertainty in the economic literature can be found in Morroni (2006: 55–78 and 123–127).

25. There is also the variant of applying insufficient reason: why not allocate equal probabilities to the different plausible outcomes? However, this is an unconvincing stratagem since nothing supports this assumption (Elster, 2010: 68; Gilboa et al., 2012: 19).

26. For example, models of financial operations assume that security prices express the average expectations of traders and that these are consistent, that is, exaggerated and fearful expectations cancel each other out. However, the experts' evaluations are not independent of each other. Consequently, information cascades can emerge and be triggered by spirals of decisions in the same direction, which are difficult to control.

27. Resorts and cruise ships that have recently established couples as regular clients know this perfectly well: a short wait and an ideal ambiance accentuate the intensity of the experience.

28. The same is true for stock market speculators: when prices rise, they do not want to leave the market so as not to regret what they might have gained, but if stock values plummet, they leave the market as soon as possible so as not to regret losing even more (Motterlini, 2014: 96).

29. It is also assumed that their temporal limits do not hinder each other.

30. Given the demographic cycle of the Amerindian population before colonization, this conceivable future is equivalent to a time horizon of about 100 years.
31. This is also the effect of the predestination doctrines. Since these doctrines are very discouraging, their spokespersons often concede that what matters is to look for signs of being among the chosen ones. This criterion ends up giving relevance to all kinds of mundane matters (Elster 2007: Chapter 7).
32. To the best of the author's knowledge, no models have been found for the case of future values spread over an interval.
33. The expression in discrete time is the one shown at the beginning of section 4.3.3. Although it has been presented as the generic formula for the discount rate, it is also the one corresponding to the exponential model.
34. This is a trait observed in people from childhood onwards, although to varying degrees and, apparently, with lifelong effects, as the famous marshmallow experiment concluded (Mischel et al., 1992; Reiss, 2013: 282). In any case, children opt to wait if the reward is higher and the immediate one is hidden from view (Elster, 2007: Chapter 10).
35. Analysts have been tinkering with this basic format by adding more and more parameters to achieve the best possible fit to the observed results coming from a given experiment. See, for example, Chung and Herrenstein (1967); Ainslie (1975, 1992 and 2005: 635–637); Loewenstein and Prelec (1992); Kirby (1997); Laibson (1997); Rachlin (2000, 2006); Loewenstein and Prelec (2009a: 420); and Cheng and González-Vallejo (2014, 2016), as well as Heukelom (2014: 172–174).
36. It should be noted that weak will should not be confused with fickle will: to be incapable of carrying out a certain action is not the same as being inconsistent. Moreover, procrastination can also, as indicated, be the result of strategic behavior or motivated by a hedonistic impulse (see section 4.3.4).
37. We should be aware that such commitments are complex processes. At least the following stages may be distinguished: I do not plan to give up (smoking, over-eating, etc.); I think I should consider quitting someday; I think I have to give up even though I am not yet ready; I start to think about a plan on how to quit; and, finally, I execute the decision.
38. There is at least one start-up that has created a website (www.stickk.com) on which to publish commitments, with penalties for non-compliance (Christl and Spiekermann, 2016: 68). Perhaps this is a risky way to fight against a weak will, given how digital networks capture, analyze and exploit personal data.
39. Addictions end up causing abstinence syndrome. They are not like hobbies: nobody suffers from this syndrome doing crafts (Ubel, 2008: 135). However, slot machines are grouped together in large halls, so there is always one that with great fanfare announces a prize. This provokes the sensation of continuous gains. They are also programmed in such a way that, when spinning the wheels (nowadays virtual images), it always seems that the prize was very close (Gigerenzer, 2014: 133–135). Fostering anxiety is also the goal of social network algorithms: they push people to accumulate *likes*, which indicates that they enjoy social approval (Gigerenzer, 2022: 194–196). The dopamine released by the brain causes a feeling of pleasure that transforms playing (or connecting) into a purpose in itself. However, the initial satisfaction of winning over time leads to attempts merely to disconnect from routine and boredom. See Dow Schüll (2014) for an inventory of the multiple positive reinforcement tricks used to generate a gambling addiction.

40. Few things are as familiar as a washing machine, but in reality, almost no one knows how it works. People only know how to make it work. As suggested many pages back, knowing what happens is not the same as knowing how it happens (Chabris and Simons, 2015: 187–197).
41. Appealing to opportunity costs, that is, to the hypothetical gains that have been forgone, will probably reinforce the sense of loss.

5. Patterns, methods and algorithms for decision-making

Having reviewed the major factors that influence economic decisions, i.e., from preferences to constraints, the next step is to identify the most commonly used criteria for choosing, especially when choices feature inferences about the different options. For example, a teenager buys a pair of sneakers because they are from a prominent fashion brand, so the identification of this brand and the imitation of others are the criteria that determine the choice. However, this decision also includes the broad factors mentioned in the previous chapter: the boy thinks that this footwear gives him a maverick image (a belief), he likes the envy it will arouse in peers (an emotion) and he has sufficient purchasing power (a constraint). Therefore, the choice algorithms described in this chapter are built on the factors presented in the previous one. These algorithms can be clustered into a few general methods of choice which, in turn, can be grouped into the three major patterns used by human beings in decision-making. See Table 5.1 (adapted from Gigerenzer, 2008: 24; Gigerenzer and Brighton, 2009: 130–131; Raab and Gigerenzer, 2015: 2; and Schilirò, 2017).

The table lists the main algorithms applied in economic decision-making. The characteristics they share allow them to be grouped into nine methods and, in turn, into three main patterns or basic ways of approaching choices, some based on inferences. This systematization reflects the current state of knowledge which, however, is expanding day by day. While it is unlikely that research will expand the number of patterns and methods, there is nothing to prevent new algorithms for decision-making from being identified.[1] Consequently, the classification in Table 5.1 is only a tentative and provisional proposal (cf. Payne et al., 1993: 21–24, 26–33 for heuristics).

Before going into the explanation of the elements of the table, it is necessary to advance some considerations regarding its construction:

- The table is merely a description of the most common ways of decision-making in economic affairs. It should be stressed that the table is not drawn from the differentiation between intuitive and deliberative judgments, characteristic of cognitive psychologists who argue for the two mental systems, or types (see Chapter 2, note 28). Although the debates in psychological theory are beyond the scope of this work, the unified theory

Table 5.1   *Patterns, methods and algorithms in economic decision-making*

Patterns	Methods	Algorithms	
Heuristics	Recognition	Imprint	
		Fluency	
		Availability	
	Take-the-best	Inspection of one or more attributes	Conjunctive rule
			Lexicographic rule
			Fast-and-frugal trees
		Priority rule	
	Weighting-and-adding	Many possibilities	
	Equal allocation	Tallying	
		$1/n$	
	Sufficient satisfaction	Adjusting aspiration levels	
	Social	Reciprocity	
		By default	
		Imitating other	
Deliberation		Variants of the exhaustive compensatory calculation	
Defection	Random	Several devices	
	Voluntary	Numerous procedures	

of mind, which considers that the various judgments share the same rules (Kruglanski and Gigerenzer, 2011), seems more promising.

- The patterns are the major types of procedures applied in decision-making processes. It should be noted that defection, although it does not include any inference, has been added to make the table comprehensive. Humans have likely manifested these patterns since very early times. It should be stressed that there are traces of their presence throughout the contingent process of the evolution of the species.
- The appeal to methods is merely instrumental: they bring together algorithms that share basic aspects, which facilitates their systematization.
- Algorithms are the key elements of the table. As already mentioned, they are the specific choosing criteria applied in the decision process. It should be added that a given algorithm can be used in decisions of a very different nature, i.e., financial decisions, purchase of durables, and so on.
- It is very important to keep in mind that nothing has been assumed about the effectiveness of algorithms. It may be that scrutiny will result in a failed choice, while a random one will be a resounding success. No criterion guarantees (more) success, regardless of how it is evaluated. The table's aim is to highlight that there are some decision procedures that require

resources and time, while others make the process cheaper and faster. This does not mean disregarding the quality of the results obtained by applying the different algorithms.

- How people justify the choice is off the table, although some algorithms are better than others at constructing such arguments. As is well known, this rationalization is ubiquitous: it appears both before the choice and, very often, after. Moreover, when a decision is important (and at least two options are available),[2] rationalization becomes part of people's identity.

As shown in Table 5.1, the six major heuristic methods are as follows:

- Recognition: people consider all the options but ignore their attributes. They choose the option that elicits the most intense (or fast) recognition, that is, the feeling of being familiar.
- Algorithms that choose based on attributes, or cues, of the various options in play, all of which are fully recognized. Sometimes, a single reason is enough. At other times, the options are arranged in a ranking because their attributes deserve different subjective evaluations, some even having priority.
- Weighting and adding: the attributes of the options are evaluated with no hierarchy. All options share the same level, although they may receive different weightings. The one that accumulates more value (high or low, as the case may be) is chosen.
- Equal allocation: similar to the previous case, since attributes are also not arranged in a hierarchy, but all options are weighted equally.
- Sufficient satisfaction: people explore the options in no pre-established order until they find one that seems satisfactory enough given their aspirations.
- Social: people decide by the rule of reciprocity or imitating others.

All the heuristic algorithms are abbreviated inference rules, easy and fast to apply, and allow us to deal with even those decisions that are the most difficult due to their complexity and uncertainty. They also open the door to robust, though not infallible, predictions. As reiterated throughout these pages, heuristics reflect the enormous creativity and plasticity of the human mind.

Table 5.1 also includes the deliberative pattern characterized by a slow and systematic reflection on the ongoing decision. People approach the attributes carefully, look for possible antecedents that may enlighten them (Lane et al., 1996: 54), and do not hesitate to use sophisticated computational techniques. A singular feature of this decision pattern is the assumption that all attributes of the options can be balanced against each other, whether or not they are evenly weighted. Undoubtedly, it is a cumbersome and costly method, but its advantages include, on the one hand, its ability to cushion regret if the choice is a failure and, on the other hand, its suitability to provide reasons for the defense of the decision taken before third parties. In these cases, it avoids giving the image of improvisation, of having been careless, of having neglected the issue. Although it is a long procedure, it can be accelerated with the experience accumulated in similar cases. This fact, together with the diversity in terms of the steps followed and the techniques employed, explains a large number of potential algorithms.

Mathematical inference techniques are common in the deliberative pattern. Regression models, complex decision trees, neural networks, etc. can be used. Their capacity to process data according to strict logical-mathematical rules encourages the collection of a huge amount of information. Many experts consider that this opens the door to computing optimal choices. This expectation is, however, bound by the quantitative and qualitative limits of the collected information, and uncertainty is discarded. In this pattern of choice, the idea that accuracy is directly proportional to the volume of accumulated data is deeply rooted. The study of heuristics, under the less-is-more effect, calls this postulate into question. As explained in the following pages, several investigations have shown that careful inferences, and thus robust predictions, can be made by investing limited resources and time in information acquisition. In short, optimization-oriented techniques would be remarkably effective in simple and well-defined, so-called small-world decisions, while complex decisions under uncertainty, undoubtedly the most common in economic life, would be fertile ground for heuristics.

The table closes with the algorithms applied in the case of defection, i.e., when people voluntarily give up their capacity to choose. The decision can be made using a device that generates random values or it can be left to the discretion of another person or a proprietary, and usually secret, algorithm. For example, random results are obtained by tossing a coin or a die (not rigged). When the choice is made by a third party, there are two main possibilities: once the decision to be made is known, one or several people choose what they consider appropriate, or an algorithm is used, designed to process huge volumes of data related to the current decisions, people involved and their circumstances. In both cases, it is assumed that the suggested choice will be accepted. In this pattern, two issues should be elucidated: how people choose the entity making the decision and what the detailed nature of the algorithm being applied is. Unfortunately, the current state of research only provides sketches of answers to these questions.

The next sections of the chapter describe the algorithms mentioned in Table 5.1, especially the heuristics ones. The literature on this subject is enormous, but economists have mostly ignored it. The following pages are the first step to correcting this deficiency.

5.1   HEURISTICS

Heuristics are stratagems to speed up the decision process and reduce its cost. For this purpose, the systematic search for information, either from the environment or obtained by diving into memory, is left aside. Heuristics are mental shortcuts that sacrifice the challenging goal of absolute accuracy to speed up the decision. However, heuristics are neither fickle nor frivolous, nor systematically result in poor or counterproductive, even detrimental, decisions. Their effectiveness depends on the appropriateness to the context, with people being smart enough to, if necessary, try again with another heuristic. Therefore, their implementation is a filtering and trial and error operation based on experience in other similar cases and learning.

The list of algorithms, and the heuristics that embrace them, is only one step towards the development of a model, maybe a future theory of the psychological basis of economic decisions. In this vein, one of the most important goals of the analysis is to describe the internal components of the heuristics and, hence, the rules underlying the algorithms. Specifically, the ecological rationality program proposes a model characterized by combining heuristics with some evolved sensory and cognitive capabilities. To this end, the mind is considered as a modular system or, better, as a toolbox that facilitates the adaptation of people to the context. In brief, the mind is understood as an adaptive toolbox (Todd and Gigerenzer, 2012: 8–12). This box is like that of a mechanic: once the engine failure has been identified, the worker decides on the task to be performed and looks for the most appropriate tools to complete it. It often works, but not always (Gigerenzer, 2007: Chapters 3 and 4; Gigerenzer, 2008; Skořepa, 2011: 46). Continuing with the analogy, people have multiple heuristics at their disposal to articulate inferences that accompany decisions, choosing the one that seems most appropriate given the circumstances. At this point, it is not surprising that different people choose different heuristics, since not everyone experiences a given situation in the same way, nor does everyone have the same insight.

As just mentioned, heuristics take advantage of certain sensory and cognitive capabilities resulting from evolution, such as language,[3] the visual tracking of objects in flight,[4] the ability to imitate the behavior of others,[5] the immediate understanding of the frequencies with which repeated phenomena occur, the fabulous capacity of the mind to recognize faces, and so on. All these capacities are rooted in the genetic substrate. However, although these capacities are indispensable for adaptation, they are not sufficient. For instance, the simple fact of being able to follow an approaching person does not reveal their intentions. To identify them, expressions, gestures, messages, etc. must be surveyed. Therefore, memory also plays a relevant role in heuristics (Gigerenzer,

2007: Chapter 4). Nonetheless, the adaptive value of heuristics does not make them evolving entities. Sensory and cognitive capacities evolve, but heuristics are only a creation of the mind that uses them. This implementation follows certain rules, which are common to all heuristics. Therefore, these rules constitute the building blocks of heuristics. Three rules should be taken into account (Gigerenzer, 2001: 43–47 and 2015: 113):

- the search rule: indicates how to proceed in the inspection of the options;
- the stopping rule: advises that the search is finished;
- the decision rule: establishes how the decision is made.

Each heuristic and, by extension, an algorithm, is a unique combination of these rules, just as the elements of the periodic table are differentiated by atomic composition.

5.1.1   The Recognition Heuristics

The ease with which the mind generates the feeling of familiarity with all kinds of objects, even if previous contacts have been quite brief, is surprising. This sensation does not require large storage of information about it. Difficulty in locating an object in the memory does not prevent the impression from arising that it is known. Problems in describing the object in detail do not matter. Its mere presence (a sensory input) is enough to immediately trigger its recognition. For example, everybody has seen a familiar face, even if it takes a long time to remember who they are and where they were seen. This memory search may even fail without the feeling of familiarity disappearing. Under normal conditions, when seeing a logo, an acronym, hearing a certain musical melody, perceiving a certain smell, etc., it is quite possible that people instantly identify the object referred to (Schwartz, 2016: 56). It is enough to see a brand for a fraction of a second to identify the product and evoke its characteristics. However, this does not prevent people from not being able to name many brands of a given type of goods or services, if they are unexpectedly asked about them. Recognition-based heuristics rely on the mind's extraordinary capacity for retaining images, silhouettes, names, faces, etc. If this contact is accompanied by emotions, its imprint on memory is greater.

Recognition comes to consciousness faster than memories, a fact that highlights the adaptive value of this capacity. There is no doubt that, for species, the immediate identification of what may be beneficial (the chemical trail left by potential prey) or harmful (an upsetting vibration in the surroundings) is key to their survival. More specifically, many bird species also consider their parents to be the first creatures they see moving when they hatch. This image is deeply imprinted in the animal's mind.

Two recognition-based algorithms should be distinguished: the imprint and the fluency algorithms.[6] The availability heuristic can also be added, a variant in which the memory is scanned to identify the object being referred to. These algorithms ignore option cues: the pure act of recognition is rightly valid. This sensation is perfectly capable of sustaining inferences about the involved objects, even if their characteristics are not directly and completely accessible to people (Gigerenzer and Gaissmaier, 2011: 460–461). This is expressed by the sentence, "If I recognize the brand, it is of better quality," i.e., the attribute of quality is inferred from the simple act of familiarity (Gigerenzer, 2007: Chapter 7).

5.1.1.1 Imprint

When faced with two or more options, the imprint algorithm gives more value to the one that sounds familiar, a sense that instantaneously emerges, and which is the option chosen. For example, if I have to guess which of two cities in a given country has more inhabitants, I choose the one that I recognize. As a general rule, people can exhibit three degrees of knowledge (according to Goldstein and Gigerenzer, 2002: 77):

- They know nothing at all about the relevant objects. People have never heard of them. These objects are unknown since there has never been any contact with them.
- There was at least a contact some time ago. Even if it was not enough to know its characteristics, it may trigger the feeling that this object is familiar.
- It is enough to see the object for it to be recognized and the memory has no problem in providing, if necessary, more information. At the very least, its basic features are known. Nonetheless, a complete description may not be possible.

In the first case, people choose at random which city has the highest value for a given criterion (number of inhabitants, for example) in the considered pairs. This guarantees a correctness degree of 0.5. In the third case, people are always right since they know for sure which city has more inhabitants. In these situations, the recognition algorithm plays no role. It only operates when ignorance is partial and systematic. In these cases, if the elements and attributes of the class of concerned objects maintain close relationships, the degree of success of the recognition algorithm can be very high (see below).

It should be pointed out that knowledge of one or more attributes of objects of a given class does not prevent people from having trouble inferring their value concerning other cues. For example, a person may know for sure that a city has an airport because they stopped over once, but may have no idea of the number of inhabitants.

Giving more value to the option that triggers a sense of familiarity is common in all kinds of everyday inferences (Mousavi et al., 2017: 284). Let us consider the following two examples:

- A stock market investor only buys shares of companies that have made the headlines in the media and/or have been mentioned by people they know (Ortmann et al., 2008). The algorithm assumes that there is a positive cor-relation between stock returns and these references, which are the basis for recognition. The investor may be aware that this association is not always true, but also suspects that a large number of investors tend to follow this criterion.
- People tend to buy brands they recognize as soon as they see them. Experimental results show that consumers frequently apply this algorithm. If on seeing a given brand, it does not arouse any impression, then they conclude that the brand does not deserve to be purchased. This mental shortcut identifies the option to choose and also evaluates its reliability (Gigerenzer, 2015: 121). As a result, the use of the recognition algorithm is self-reinforcing. It will continue to be applied until a volume of significant information discourages it.

The world of consumer goods and services is the paradise of the recognition algorithm. Companies devote an enormous amount of resources to making their brands ingrained in people's memories. From this perspective, adver-tising and promotional campaigns are nothing more than an attempt to buy consumers' neural space (Gigerenzer, 2007: Chapter 7). Herein lies the importance of the brand being present everywhere: in successful films or series (so-called product placement, see Cialdini, 2016: Chapter 9 and Aronson, 2008: 68–70), in the form of advertising panels, on all kinds of merchandising objects, in the media, and so on. The more often it is seen, the more it sticks in the memory. There are undoubted success stories: if you ask what Figure 5.1, which is nothing more than a silhouette, suggests, practically everyone easily guesses the type of product and its brand name.

Another example of the exploitation of recognition is an Italian fashion company, well-known for displaying hard-hitting and controversial advertise-ments, usually only with the firm's logo. This ploy has made the brand one of the most easily recognized in the world. In politics, it is also common to repeat the same message over and over again, so that it becomes familiar and therefore credible. It does not matter whether or not it is true. As the Nazi prop-agandist Paul Joseph Goebbels (1897–1945) said: "If you tell a lie big enough and keep repeating it, people will eventually come to believe it." Repetition,

Figure 5.1   An example of imprint

however, is a stratagem that requires a previous predisposition of the audience. Moreover, the reiteration must not be burdensome, since it usually generates a negative impression (Hogg and Vaughan, 2014: 198–200).

Regarding the imprint algorithm, the three rules of the heuristic procedures have a very simple formulation:

- the search rule: options are examined without any sequential order or hierarchy;
- the stopping rule: when an option is simply familiar, the inspection task is finished;
- the decisions rule: choose the familiar option.

The third rule may be refined. For example, a person only chooses brands that they recognize, but then buys the model with the second highest price. The algorithm narrows down the set of eligible objects but does not determine the final choice. This is a perfectly plausible procedure in the case of durable items, such as cell phones, hi-fi equipment, etc. The algorithm associates recognition with quality but, assuming that the most expensive model is so because it incorporates some trivial novelty, i.e., without any functional reason to justify it, the next model in the price ranking is the one that is purchased. This model is usually the one that was perceived as being of the highest quality some time ago (Kurz-Milcke and Gigerenzer, 2007: 50). Perhaps this is not a decision rule for a professional buyer, but it can be attractive for an amateur.

Recognition heuristics is not blind. On asking which of the two Ukrainian cities has more inhabitants, Chornobyl, which everyone knows, and Lengrav, most choose the latter even though they have never heard of it (in fact it is a fictional name). The reason is that the recognition of the former is based on notoriety unrelated to the number of inhabitants (Gigerenzer, 2007: Chapter 7). Something similar happens in the choice between the Vatican State and the Republic of San Marino. Everyone is familiar with the former, but many also know that its fame comes not from the number of people who live in it, but from who lives in it. Therefore, most choose the second option. Let us now consider the case of a man with partial experience in picking mushrooms. He recognizes the type of forest undergrowth in which mushrooms are most likely to be found, but this does not mean that he will apply the algorithm to select the ones he will pick. Since there are very toxic mushrooms, he will only pick those that he knows for sure are harmless. Although there is a strong correlation between the type of forest undergrowth and the presence of mushrooms, there is no correlation between their abundance and their edibility. Nonetheless, in a specialized restaurant, given the confidence in the know-how of those in charge, people eat all the mushrooms on the plate even if they do not recognize any of them. None of these examples invalidates the effectiveness of the algorithm. They are just a reminder of how it depends on the characteristics of the decision context.

As has been said, the imprint algorithm works very well when the degree of knowledge is partial and the correlations between the attributes of the concerned objects are high (Goldstein and Gigerenzer, 2002: 76–77). These two conditions are easy to meet given that people's experience is inevitably fragmentary[7] and the components of any context are not usually randomly arranged. Therefore, the effectiveness of the algorithm is not sporadic. Still, in attempting to evaluate the latter, there is a possible third element to take into account: the mediator.

The imprint algorithm accesses the unobservable criteria through a mediator. Sometimes, as has been suggested so far, there are information hints lodged in the memory capable of triggering the feeling that something is known. At other times, people more or less intuitively rely on a variable that seems to be associated with the unknown criterion. This variable is the basis of the familiarity sensation. For example, continuing with the case of the population of cities, people might decide which are the most populated based on how often they believe they have been talked about on television during a certain period. People assume that the references in the news reflect the city's importance which, in turn, would be a solid clue about its population, i.e., the fact that it is often mentioned is a guarantee of having a large population. In this case, the recognition algorithm is extended through a double connection (adaptation of Goldstein and Gigerenzer, 2002: 78; Schooler and Hertwig, 2005: 612; Marewski et al., 2010b: 290ss; and Gigerenzer and Goldstein, 2011b):

- The belief regarding the number of media appearances is an intermediate variable to access the unknown criterion (the population). Therefore, it is assumed that there is a strong link, called ecological correlation, between such a presence, the belief it sustains, and the criterion in question. Experience supports this presumption.

- The assumption is that the more times a city's presence is observed in the media, the more plausible it is that its name will be assimilated and, hence, recognized. The number of appearances is a key factor in triggering familiarity. This is the surrogate correlation.

The recognition of cities is generally more related to the number of times they are mentioned in the media than to their population. However, the most populated cities appear in the media proportionally more than the rest. Therefore, although familiarity is largely explained by media coverage, recognition is usually a good guide to identifying the most populous city since the media talk about them comparatively more often. People frequently make inferences from what they have more or less recently heard in their social circle and in the sources of information they access, probably without being aware of it. Many inferences are based on what the mind has relatively recently registered. Is then the constant and insistent advertising of the most recognized brands ("the best brands," according to many consumers) a surprise?

When evaluating the contextual effectiveness of the algorithm, the experimental work, assuming dual choices, uses the following two concepts (more information in Pachur et al., 2012):

- recognition validity (α) or the probability of a correct answer when only one of the elements of a given pair is recognized;
- the probability (β) of making a correct inference when the two objects are recognized.

Recognition validity measures the ecological rationality of the algorithm. Its calculation is simple:

$$\alpha = \frac{C}{C+F}$$

C being the number of correct inferences and F the number of false ones. Logically, the term α has to be calculated for all pairs that can be formed between the various objects of the concerned class. For example, a group of people had to infer from a set of Swiss cities which ones were the most populated (Gigerenzer and Goldstein, 2011b: 104). All possible two-by-two combinations were considered. The number of cases in which they claimed to have recognized at least one of the cities, i.e., one or both of them were familiar, was then noted. Obviously, in these cases, the choice was not random. After counting the number of correct answers, the value of α was 0.86, a figure that indicates a high degree of success. In a subsequent exercise, people were presented with pairs of cities in which they had to determine the city closest to the geographic center of the country. The validity of the recognition was $\alpha = 0.51$, a value near random. As expected, while the recognition of a city's name is largely correlated with its population, it is not related to its geographic position.

The term β is analogously defined, $\beta = C/(C+F)$, but only considering the pairs in which both options are recognized. However, this does not always mean choosing the right option.

According to several experiments, the proportion of correct judgments obtained by applying the imprint algorithm, $f(n)$, is given by the following formula (Goldstein and Gigerenzer, 2002: 78),

$$f(n) = 2\alpha \left(\frac{n}{N} \right) \left(\frac{N-n}{N-1} \right) + \frac{1}{2} \left(\frac{N-n}{N} \right) \left(\frac{N-n-1}{N-1} \right) + \beta \left(\frac{n}{N} \right) \left(\frac{n-1}{N-1} \right)$$

N being the number of objects of a certain class arranged in pairs randomly displayed, and in which people have to choose the object with the highest value according to a given criterion. In addition, n denotes the subset of the recognized objects and $N - n$ that of the unrecognized ones. Consequently, the summands of $f(n)$ represent the three possible stages of recognition:

- The first one deals with the case where only one of the options is recognized, $N \geq n$. It accounts for the correct inferences in applying the recognition algorithm. The ratio is multiplied by α.
- The second one shows the situation $n = 0$, that is, all the elements of the successive pairs are unknown. The subject answers and guesses randomly. Therefore, the probability of success is $1/2$.
- The third one indicates when both options are recognized, $n = N$. This is the proportion of correct inferences using the knowledge that goes beyond simple recognition.

To conclude the description of the pure imprint algorithm, it is worth noting that it fulfills the less-is-more effect. A classic example is guessing the players or teams that are likely to win a certain tournament (the Wimbledon Tennis Championship, the Football World Cup, etc.). The surprise is that people who only recognize half of the participants can achieve a level of accuracy of around 70% in predicting the winner. Of course, this figure indicates that the algorithm is not infallible, but it is a score that exceeds that of experts who have much more information about the concerned objects (Serwe and Fring, 2006).[8] This confirms the paradox that knowing too much can be an obstacle to successful forecasting. Some studies have detected this effect with two, three or four alternatives (see Goldstein and Gigerenzer, 2002: 79; Gigerenzer and Gaissmaier, 2011).

5.1.1.2 Fluency and availability

The heuristic of fluency consists of choosing the option that is first identified, even if all of them are eventually recognized (Gigerenzer and Gaissmaier, 2011: 462). This heuristic is based on the mind's agility to identify a given object, assuming that people are capable of discriminating the reaction times of their minds.[9] Otherwise, people choose at random. For example, the presence of fluency has been detected in the very short-term evolution of stock market values (better if the company and the identifying code are easy to pronounce, as indicated by Alter and Oppenheimer, 2006) and in the perception of the purchasing power of coins and banknotes (Alter and Oppenheimer, 2008).

The three rules characterizing the fluency algorithm have a simple formulation:

- the search rule: the options are inspected in any order;
- the stopping rule: the first one that is familiar stops the search;
- the decision rule: this option is chosen.

The fluency heuristic exploits the gradual recognition according to the information stored in the memory. It infers the existence of a direct link between the value of the option and the speed at which the recognition emerged (Mousavi et al., 2017: 285). The fluency algorithm does not waste a second in examining the specific attributes of the alternatives. However, since people have particular personalities and experiences, the same option will be felt at different speeds. This process is not unrelated to the context and frequency of exposure to stimuli. For example, if a name is repeatedly heard, its appearance in the memory is accelerated, which gives it a halo of relevance. Then,

- The tendency to forget harms fluency efficiency, as does time pressure.
- The faster the options decay, the lower the performance of the algorithm. If the brands of a certain class of consumer goods follow each another in rapid succession, the mind has difficulty retaining them. This is a context unfavorable for the algorithm.

The fluency algorithm also manifests the less-is-more principle: since only the retrieval time from memory matters; any additional element could be a distortion. If extra information is added to the identification process, it can spoil the algorithm's effectiveness.

The algorithm of fluency is distinguished from the imprint one by the greater role it gives to memory. At the same time, it brings it closer to the availability heuristic, as Table 5.1 shows. Disclosed by Kahneman and his followers, the availability heuristic is a cognitive bias caused by the explicit search in the memory for the referred object until it is fully identified.[10] Therefore, this heuristic relies on information stored in the memory and involves classes of events instead of choices between two or more options. Leaving aside the serious criticisms that this alleged bias has received, basically due to the absence of a minimal psychological mechanism to explain it (see Sedlmeier et al., 1998), in these pages the availability heuristic will be simply understood as the propensity of people to consider as more plausible that which is easier to remember at a given time. This propensity depends directly on its emotional charge and/or its temporal proximity. If people are asked about the number of victims caused by airplane crashes (or terrorist attacks, earthquakes, etc.), the answers show higher values if one has recently occurred (and was widely covered by the media). As any memory dressed in a compelling narrative captivates people, they tend to attach more importance to the content than to its frequency (or reliability, as the case may be). Each aircraft accident concentrates a high number of victims, but air transport causes fewer victims per km/passenger than traffic accidents (more dispersed and with a low number of victims at a time). As a result, traffic accidents often go unnoticed, except for drivers who witness one. They then slow down because what they have just seen reminds them that accidents are commonplace. It is better to be cautious, but a few miles later, this is forgotten. Although the availability fades as time goes by, as long as the memory is vivid, there is the possibility of making hasty decisions. This is especially the case if a certain social psychosis has been triggered. At this point, emotionally charged narratives are a powerful factor of (self-)persuasion. Their strength lies in their ability to displace scrutiny of received and stored information, whether for good or for bad.

5.1.2   The Take-the-Best Heuristics

Many heuristics check the attributes of the options to make inferences. Depending on the number of cues involved and the treatment they receive, two methods of choice can be outlined: the take-the-best and the weighting-and-adding heuristics, as shown in Table 5.1. This section presents the take-the-best algorithms, i.e., those that determine the choice according to the value of the options' cues, either by considering only one attribute or by applying a specific selection process based on many of them (Katsikopoulos, 2014).

When only a single signal is considered, it is assumed to be closely associated with the target variable that is not directly observable. For example, female peacocks are impressed by the male with the showiest tail, an attribute that would reflect its vitality; in the case of male deer it is the size of the antlers that stands out; in certain frogs the power at which they croak, and so on. The mating seasons of many animal species are a series of exhibitions of a single cue. Turning to the realm of human experience, common phrases such as "Health is priceless" or "True friendship is a treasure" provide a reason so absolute that there is no room left for any other cue. Nothing compares to, and nothing compensates for its loss. In consumption, advertising often emphasizes *the* reason why people ought to buy a certain article. No other possible arguments matter (Gigerenzer, 2007: Chapter 8). Also in business management, many decisions are made for a single (good) reason. For example, a company that provides professional services to other firms has decided to take steps to win back former clients. As is obvious, it is essential to determine which clients can be considered definitively lost, thus avoiding wasting resources on them. A possible method to do that is, first, to try to gather as much information as possible about the former clients (or a representative sample); second, to apply statistical techniques to evaluate the impact of the different variables; and, finally, to use the result obtained to make forecasts about the possible comeback as clients. The rapid and frugal alternative is to set a certain period (some months) that, according to the experience of managers, supports the belief that the former client will not come back (Wübben and Wangenheim, 2008; Artinger et al., 2014). Also known as the hiatus heuristic, it has a high predictive capacity although it focuses on a single reason.

In other cases, several attributes are considered from the beginning. In general, the decision is made after evaluating the different attributes of the options arranged in a ranking.[11] The values of the cues are inspected according to a hierarchy, except for the conjunctive rule that is sequential (see below). Cues can be both quantitative and qualitative variables (Gigerenzer et al., 2008: 231). It should be remembered that the arrangement of attributes in a ranking as an algorithm of choice of goods and services was detected by economists many years ago: it is about the conjunctive and, above all, lexicographic algorithm. The latter consists of people, according to their preferences and the elements that accompany them (discussed in Chapter 4, section 4.1), ranking the different attributes of the options available, choosing the option that survives a process of elimination in which the cues have to exceed previously set reference values.

The word lexicographic alludes to the rigid arrangement of the letters of the alphabet (A, B, C, ... Z) following, in this case, a very ancient convention (Goldstein and Gigerenzer, 2002: 82). Arranging the different attributes of the options in a hierarchical order of validity is also observed in nature: in the mating season, males compete by displaying some traits in a certain order. First, they observe and compare their size; if there is no clear winner, they evaluate who bellows the loudest; if this is not decisive either, they chase each other trying to drive the rival away; finally, if necessary, they will fight until there is a clear winner. The order of items is also key in Indo-Arabic numbers. To find out which number with the same digits is higher (or lower), just move from left to right: if two digits are the same, look at the digit immediately to the right and so on until a tiebreaker is reached. The digits follow a lexicographical (decimal) order: the position indicates their magnitude. In contrast, Roman numerals do not have a lexicographical arrangement: neither the letter nor its position allows people to guess which number is greater. For example, which of the numbers MDCCCLXXX or MCMXI is greater? It is impossible to tell at first glance (the former is 1,880, while the latter is 1,911).

Finally, within the group of take-the-best heuristics, the priority algorithm should be mentioned. This is an algorithm to drive choices in simple lotteries. Despite its limited scope, it is worth mentioning because, since the formulation of expected utility theory, if not before, this type of lottery has been the empirical basis for supporting decision theories. This historical background justifies its presence on these pages.

5.1.2.1 Inspection of attributes

Recognition heuristics support inferences in which people have partial knowledge of the options. If all options are known, inferences can be based on their attributes, the value of which is assigned from information retrieved from memory, or explicitly collected on purpose. Once the options have been contrasted, starting from their attributes, it is possible to choose the most relevant one concerning the issue posed.

To begin with, let us consider the experience of inferring which of the four cities (*a*, *b*, *c*, and *d*) has more inhabitants (inspired by Gigerenzer and Goldstein, 1996). Cities are presented in pairs. The participants' task is to retrieve from memory information about certain cues that are presumably related to the number of inhabitants. For example, the concerned attributes are as follows: the city has an international airport, houses the headquarters of a large company, has at least one first division soccer team, has an important art museum, and has a university. Table 5.2 shows, for a given participant, the inspection hierarchy and their hypothetical degree of knowledge of the attributes. A positive sign indicates that the person has reliable information about this cue.

Table 5.2   Inferences with the take-the-best heuristics

Lexicographic algorithm			Items (cities)			
			a	b	c	d
		Level of knowledge	+	+	+	−
Information stored in the memory	Cues	1. Soccer team	+	−	?	?
		2. Airport	?	+	−	?
		3. University	−	+	?	?
		4. Big firm HQ	?	−	−	?
		5. Art museum	?	?	−	?

A negative sign means that the person believes that this city does not satisfy the corresponding attribute, and a question mark indicates that she has no idea. As is obvious, if from the outset an object is not recognized (as in the case of city *d*), all its attributes are necessarily unknown. The algorithm cannot be applied in these cases. The choice only takes place between the recognized cities *a*, *b* and *c*, which will be compared in pairs, i.e., (*a*, *b*), (*a*, *c*) and (*b*, *c*).

The mechanics of the algorithm is as follows:

- If the participant has to infer which city of the pair (*a*, *b*) presumably has more inhabitants, the chosen option is *a* because the first and most important attribute of this city (it has at least one top-level soccer club) outperforms *b*. Having obtained a clear winner, it is not necessary to move to other cues.
- In the pair (*a*, *c*), no attribute allows us to determine the more populated city. The choice is random because no positive values are contrasting with negative ones.
- In the choice between *b* and *c*, the algorithm goes down to the second attribute since the first one is not decisive. Remembering with certainty that *b* has an international airport, it is chosen. If this attribute had given rise to an ambiguous result, we would have moved on to the next one. It is only chosen at random if at the end of the procedure, according to the established order, there is no clear winner.

In the simplest case of binary choices, the lexicographic algorithm has the following three rules (Martignon and Hoffrage, 2002: 34; Gigerenzer, 2015: 124):

- the search rule: inspect the signals of the recognized options following the order from the most to the least important;
- the stopping rule: the search stops at the first cue that discriminates between the options;
- the decision rule: the option with the largest cue value is chosen. The choice is made randomly if the evaluation process is closed without a winning option.

The operation of the algorithm includes two more points:

- Cues are inspected singularly and unconditionally, i.e., they are evaluated in isolation (their possible interdependencies are ignored) and their values do not have to meet any thresholds (but see below).
- The ordering and degree of knowledge of the attributes are idiosyncratic to each person, i.e., they reflect their preferences and beliefs. From the

algorithm's point of view, these are exogenous data related to the particular personal and social story of each person.

Although there is still much to study, according to Gigerenzer and Gaissmaier (2011: 465) the take-the-best heuristic seems appropriate for contexts of moderate to large redundancy, variability in the weight of the signals, and small sets of options (for the comparative analysis of its effectiveness, see section 5.1.8).

As noted above, the lexicographic algorithm is common in consumer decisions. In these processes, choices are often driven by raw preferences. Nonetheless, if the decision depends on an inference characterized by ordering and ranking of the attributes, three variants could be distinguished:

- The conjunctive rule: the consumer only considers the option (be it a product or a brand) for which the attributes exceed certain thresholds. The inspection is sequential and does not follow any particular order. Although there is no exhaustive hierarchy, the options are evaluated against the previously established minimum levels.
- The lexicographic algorithm: the attributes are arranged by level of importance and the options are discarded until only one remains, that is, the one whose attributes meet, one after the other, all the requirements (Kurz-Milcke and Gigerenzer, 2007: 49). This implies that the choice process considers less and less relevant attributes.
- The elimination-by-aspects rule, very similar to the previous one.

Attribute-based selection is common in the case of durable goods (clothing, household appliances, automobiles, furniture, etc.) and relevant services such as schooling, telephony, electricity supply, or leisure. These consumption decisions share two important aspects: on the one hand, their price per unit and/or the attached financial liabilities (periodic bills or credit payments) are relevant to income and, on the other hand, they have multiple attributes (functional, status, aesthetic, etc.) that can be more or less objectively identified.

The mentioned variants can be illustrated with the case of a person who wants to buy a house (example inspired by Szmigin and Piacentini, 2015: 216–228; see also Lavoie, 2014: 105–108 and Solomon, 2015: 78). Apparently they have found four houses for sale which are valued according to the six attributes listed in any order in Table 5.3.

The attributes taken into account are specific to the person making the decision. Their preferences, mixed with beliefs and constraints, indicate their lifestyle, aspirations, current mood, etc. This explains why the central body of the table contains objective values (such as price or square meters of garden) and subjective valuations (such as the four levels showing the person's opinion about the type of residents in the neighborhood). It should be noted that possi-

Table 5.3　　Initial data (attributes and values)

Attributes/options	House 1	House 2	House 3	House 4
Price (thousand euros)	250	200	280	180
Distance to school (meters)	500	400	200	400
Garden size (sq. m.)	110	130	150	150
Neighborhood (four levels)	A	B	D	C
Building renovation cost (thousand euros)	40	30	40	10
Number of rooms	6	5	5	4

Table 5.4　　Initial data (indicators)

Attributes/options	House 1	House 2	House 3	House 4
Price	2	3	1	4
Distance to school	1	2	3	2
Garden size	1	2	3	3
Neighborhood	4	3	1	2
Building renovation cost	3	2	3	1
Number of rooms	3	2	2	1

ble houses close to a market or with several bathrooms have not been considered because these attributes do not merit the buyer's attention.

To speed up the analysis, Table 5.4 is used instead of Table 5.3. In this table, the previous information has been fully replaced by indicators. If looked at closely, nothing has changed: the figures are arbitrary, but they respect the order in which the options were presented and the order in which the attributes were rated. These scores are also consistent: a more expensive house receives fewer points (since it goes against the interests of the buyer), while the score increases with the number of rooms. House 4, for example, has four points for the "price" cue, which means that it is cheaper than house 3.

The conjunctive algorithm establishes that the attributes have to meet a minimum value that was set by the buyer. These thresholds eliminate attributes and, hence, a certain order of priorities is drawn up. In Table 5.5 these minimum values, or thresholds, are shown in the last column. As is obvious, these thresholds hide concrete values, such as the maximum willingness-to-pay for the renovation or the preferred distance to the school.

As can be seen, the score for the price of house 3 clashes with the minimum level set at three. Because the threshold is not met, the letter N (No) appears in the corresponding cell. If values are equal to or exceed the related threshold, the letter Y (Yes) is written. Only house 2 meets all the required levels. Therefore, this is the house that is bought. The remainder have at least one

Table 5.5   Conjunctive rule

Attributes/options	House 1	House 2	House 3	House 4	Threshold
Price	N	Y	N	Y	3
Distance to school	N	Y	Y	Y	2
Garden size	N	Y	Y	Y	2
Neighborhood	Y	Y	N	N	3
Building renovation cost	Y	Y	Y	N	2
Number of rooms	Y	Y	Y	Y	1
Total	NO	YES	NO	NO	

Table 5.6   Lexicographic rule

Attributes/options	House 1	House 2	House 3	House 4	Ranking
Price	N	N	N	Y	1
Neighborhood					2
Number of rooms					3
Building renovation cost					4
Distance to school					5
Garden size					6

attribute that does not reach the level desired by the buyer. The criterion also could have been to choose the option that exceeds the thresholds the most times, without necessarily satisfying all of them. In any case, the definition of the attributes and their subjective valuation, and the thresholds, are specific to each person.

The lexicographic algorithm establishes a strict hierarchy of attributes, as shown in Table 5.6.

Now, the order of the attributes has changed, except for the price, which is often the most relevant. Since there are priorities, the order becomes a hierarchy. The attributes draw up a ranking. House 4, which is the cheapest (it has the highest index), is the one chosen. The attribute at the top of the hierarchy is unrivaled, as no other house costs the same. Therefore, there is no need to move on to the next attribute. End of the algorithm.

It is no coincidence that price is the main attribute. This may not be the case for low-value items. However, on purchasing a home, a car, a holiday destination, or a major appliance, price is likely to play the leading role. The other attributes are secondary, but paradoxically it will be the last one in the ranking that, after successive ties, determines the choice (see below).

Let us now take the more complete example presented in Table 5.7. A person finds five car models attractive (due to the influence of socio-biographical,

Table 5.7   Another example of the lexicographic rule

Attributes/options	Car A	Car B	Car C	Car D	Car E	Requisites
Price	€18 500	€17 900	€19 000	€18 900	€20 400	< €20 000
Number of doors	5	5	5	3		5
Fuel consumption	4.8	4.5	6.5			< 6 l/100 km
Acceleration	8.7	9.1				< 10 s
Color	Yes	Yes				Metallic blue
Equipment		Yes				Automatic headlights
...		...				...

economic, etc. factors). They will choose the one that satisfies the most attributes, ordered from most to least important: the maximum price of the car is €20,000, it must have five doors, it has to consume less than 6 liters/100 km, it has to accelerate from 0 to 100 km/h in less than 10 seconds, it has to be available in a metallic blue color, it has to include lights that turn on automatically, and so on. When the sixth attribute is reached, all the cars have already been discarded, except model *B*. No more attributes need to be added since there is a winner: model *B* will be purchased. It should be stressed that acceleration and color do not eliminate any car, so the algorithm moves on to the next attribute.

Tversky proposed the elimination-by-aspects rule. This is a variant very close to the lexicographic algorithm. Let us consider Table 5.8, which shows two final columns: one with the ranking and another with the minimum points that the attributes must meet. In this example, house 4 is chosen since it is the only one remaining after the fourth criterion in the ranking (the "building renovation cost"). The other options are eliminated because they have not passed one or more of the previous cut-off points. In contrast to the lexicographic algorithm, some thresholds shape the ranking. Specifically, all the options that exceed the threshold in a given attribute pass to the next tie-breaker round, even if there is one option that stands out. This is what happens in Table 5.7. In the example of the house, while in Table 5.6 the attribute "price" is sufficient to determine the house to be chosen, in Table 5.8 two options pass the requirement, and therefore the algorithm moves to the next ranking position.

In applying the lexicographic algorithm, the following considerations should be taken into account:

• It is assumed that people identify the attributes they consider relevant and that they can arrange them hierarchically. Sellers need to know in detail how each consumer defines and ranks the different attributes. Indeed, if there are *n* attributes, they can be ordered in *n*! different ways: the *a*, *b* and *c* attributes can be arranged as (*a*, *b*, *c*), (*a*, *c*, *b*), (*b*, *a*, *c*), (*b*, *c*, *a*), (*c*, *b*, *a*)

Table 5.8   Elimination-by-aspects rule

Attributes/options	House 1	House 2	House 3	House 4	Ranking	Cut-off points
Price	N	Y	N	Y	1	3
Neighborhood		Y		Y	2	2
Number of rooms		Y		Y	3	1
Building renovation cost		N		Y	4	1
Distance to school					5	2
Garden size					6	1

and (c, a, b). Therefore, if the number of attributes is large, the problem has an intractable size.

- The algorithm does not specify how attributes have been selected and ranked. Consumers select and rank the cues according to budget, other people's opinions, beliefs, aspirations, advertising persuasion, etc. (Kurz-Milcke and Gigerenzer, 2007). These are data prior and exogenous to the application of the algorithm.
- In the automobile example, it was indicated that the number of attributes could be higher than six. In reality, the number of attributes is likely to be smaller (about four). On increasing the number of options and attributes, the use of the algorithm becomes challenging. Some studies indicate that, in making decisions, people accumulate information from three to nine attributes, with a progressively smaller number as options increase.
- The algorithm is applied much more rapidly than has been explained on these pages. No one takes paper and pencil and writes tables like the ones shown. People simply have a ranking of a few attributes in mind and, as they go through the options, they quickly discard the ones that do not meet their requirements. All in just a few minutes. As is well known, sellers (of cars, furniture, etc.) facilitate the process by showing the models that, according to what the buyers say, are closest to their particular set of attributes.
- The choice is always determined by the least important attribute, i.e., a car is bought for the chrome plating, which is a very secondary attribute compared to the price, engine power, or fuel consumption. Details matter a lot. Regardless of what the advertising highlights, be it functional attributes and/or emotions, manufacturers and sellers cannot neglect the details. Their presence differentiates products and positively draws the attention of customers. As a result, many purchases are often determined by futile aspects. Car dealers, appliance salesmen, etc. know the importance of the gadgets incorporated into the product. Therefore, manufacturers and sellers strive to add details to their entire product range. Obviously, their quality

will be different depending on the model. Some of them will have very exclusive details.

- If the ranking of the attributes changes, the option chosen changes as well. As said before, the hierarchical order is specific to each person, and also to their circumstances. This explains why it is important for the salesperson to know the customer's priorities. For this reason, their initial question is always: "What are your thoughts?" The answer makes it possible to build the right argument, which ends up focusing on the details. Sometimes, even the previous ranking is (partially) modified.
- The algorithm is not suitable for choosing between options with important qualitative aspects or imbued with uncertainty. It requires attributes of simple metrics and being easy to rank.

Before closing this section, it should be pointed out that the lexicographic algorithm can be applied far beyond the sphere of consumption. This is the case of the so-called Δ-inference, a lexicographic rule applied in staff selection and promotion processes (see Luan et al., 2019: 1739–1740).

5.1.2.2 Fast-and-frugal trees

A variant of the lexicographic algorithm is fast-and-frugal trees, a classification method of interest in all kinds of scientific and technical disciplines, including economic and business management decisions. The algorithm consists of successive levels arranged hierarchically, i.e., from highest to lowest relevance. As a rule, in each level, there are a very limited number of options, and the one that meets a certain evaluation criterion is chosen. This method of decision-making has been known since ancient times. However, following the contributions of mathematicians and engineers in the last two centuries, nowadays very complex decision trees can be deployed, whose resolution requires sophisticated algorithms implemented by powerful computing systems (Martignon et al., 2012: 366). Fast-and-frugal trees are a return to the design of simple and therefore transparent and robust decision trees. This algorithm is undoubtedly appropriate when decisions have to be made quickly and/or the search for additional information is very expensive (Luan et al., 2011; Katsikopoulos et al., 2020: 14–23 and 61–67; Gigerenzer et al., 2022: 175–176; Gigerenzer, 2022: 45–46).

To describe the fast-and-frugal tree algorithm, a common example is to determine the priority for hospitalization of patients whose diagnostic tests indicate the possibility of a cardiovascular problem. Patients are categorized according to the following sequence: if an electrocardiogram shows abnormalities, it is considered likely that the person has a coronary disease, so a referral is made to the appropriate medical care. However, if the test is negative, it does not mean that the person is free of such a health problem. Therefore, people are then asked if they have chest pain. If the answer is no, the risk is considered to be low. If yes, a final question about any other symptoms is posed to determine the level of risk (Martignon et al., 2012: 364; Aikman et al., 2021: 322; Katsikopoulos et al., 2020: 29–38). With a limited number of simple dichotomous questions, set one after the other,[12] the different possibilities that may affect the objects under consideration are discarded.

Regarding fast-and-frugal trees, the three rules of the heuristics have a very simple formulation:

- The search rule: determine a few cues and arrange them in a ranking. In each level, there are (as a rule) dichotomous options, one of which does not meet the aspiration level of the relevant cue.
- The stopping rule: it activates when a particular object meets the cue of a certain level and, therefore, it exits the tree. Otherwise, continue to the lower cue level.
- The decisions rule: the object is classified when it meets the aspiration level of a given cue. In the last and least important level, all objects are categorized and exit the tree.

There is not yet a large repertoire of applications of fast-and-frugal trees in economics and business management. Aikman et al. (2021: 323–342) propose a case designed to evaluate the eventuality of bankruptcy of large financial institutions. Four indicators or cues are established, and arranged according to a precise ranking, giving rise to the fast-and-frugal tree reproduced in Figure 5.2 (adapted from Aikman et al., 2021: 338).

This fast-and-frugal tree is proposed as an algorithm that complements the indicators and statistical analyses commonly applied to assess the risk of bank default, as required by various international regulations. Thus, data was collected for 116 banks from 25 countries up to the end of 2005 and 2006. Since the study was conducted after the 2008–2009 crisis, the authors knew that 42 banks had serious problems (some disappeared) and 74 did not. With such data, 11 indicators are calculated from which four are chosen. Namely (Aikman et al., 2021: 333–335):

- In order of importance, the first cue is the balance-sheet leverage ratio which measures the solvency of the bank. According to the data collected up to 2006 for the sample of banks, this cue is set at 4.1% so that, if the leverage ratio is below this figure, a serious risk of default (red flag) must be assumed, regardless of the score that financial institutions may have in other cues.
- Market-based capital, whose threshold is set at 16.8% according to the data collected. Consequently, a cue below this figure indicates that the bank has

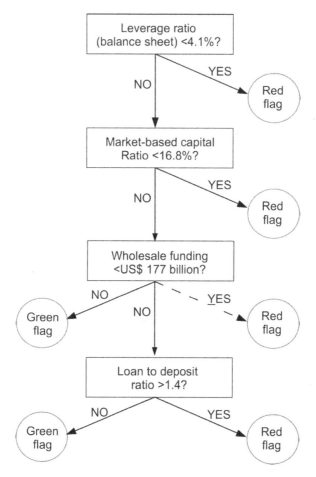

Figure 5.2   An example of fast-and-frugal tree applied to an economic decision

very risky assets. This is an indicator of economic weakness even if the leverage ratio is acceptable.

- The third cue, the wholesale funding, attempts to assess the bank's illiquidity risk. Also according to the sample, if this cue is above US$177 billion, the bank does not appear to be in a delicate situation. However, the authors warn that some experts may require this cue to be more restrictive, so that, at the indicated threshold, banks deserve a red flag (exit indicated by an arrow pointing to the right).[13]

- The loan-to-deposit ratio closes the fast-and-frugal tree. The value is set at 1.4 times, with a green flag for those who exceed it and a red flag for those who do not.

The algorithm was correct in 82% of cases of failed financial institutions, while there was a 50% occurrence of false positives, i.e., the fast-and-frugal tree predicted a default that was did not happen. Without the third cue, the level of accuracy among defaulted banks improved, but false alarms also increased (Aikman et al., 2021: 339). In addition, the paper insists that the order of the cues is based on economic intuition (probably rooted in the insight granted by the experience as a financial regulator of some co-authors), and suggests a method to determine the order of the cues. Finally, the degree of success of the algorithm in forecasting bank failures is compared with other regression-based models. Despite its simplicity, the level of accuracy of the fast-and-frugal tree is similar (Aikman et al., 2021: 340–342).

The authors insist that the proposed analysis is not aimed at replacing the much more complex models applied by regulators, although they stress that fast-and-frugal trees are easy to apply, transparent and robust (its high predictive capacity could easily be verified since the evolution of the banks after the crisis was known). In any case, the authors acknowledge that the proposal is still provisional and, of course, subject to discussion for improvement.

5.1.2.3 The priority heuristics

The priority rule is a multistage algorithm to be used in very simple lotteries. This fact differentiates it from other heuristics: the priority rule is identified by the type of problems to which it is applied (Fiedler, 2010). Specifically, the algorithm addresses lotteries with two options, such as

$$(x, p; y, 1 - p),$$

x, y being monetary values and p the probability of the x value. The players know these figures and are perfectly aware that the outcomes are mutually exclusive. The priority algorithm indicates the order in which people inspect and evaluate the suggested lotteries. For example, a group of students was asked to indicate which of the following lotteries, arranged two by two, they would be most willing to play (Brandstätter et al., 2006: 412):

- (€500, 0.5; €0, 0.5) or (€2,500, 0.1; €0, 0.9) [88% chose the former];
- (€220, 0.9; €0, 0.1) or (€500, 0.4; €0, 0.6) [80%];
- (€5,000, 0.5; €0, 0.5) or (€25,000, 0.1; €0, 0.9) [73%];
- (€2,200, 0.9; €0, 0.1) or (€5,000, 0.4; €0, 0.6) [83%].

In the first lottery, the pair with the smallest positive win (€500 < €2,500) and also with the lowest probability of minimum gain (€0) (0.5 < 0.9) was chosen. In contrast, in the second two lotteries, the one with the lowest probability of winning nothing was chosen (0.1 < 0.6). Therefore, it seems that participants gave more importance to the probability of minimum gain (€0, 0.1), than to maximum (€500, 0.4). In the third dilemma, the first case reappeared: the pair with the smallest gain was chosen, but also with the lowest probability of not winning anything. Finally, in the last pair of lotteries, the choice was similar to the second case: the choice of the first pair again gave rise to the suspicion that probability guided the students. Putting together the results of these four lotteries, an average of 81% chose the option with the lowest probability of minimal gains.

These, and many other similar experiences, suggest that the choice is made after a minimum inspection of the lottery elements. Everything indicates that attention is first focused on the value of the minimum gain; then, on the probability of the minimum gain, and, finally, on the maximum gain (highlighting the surest one). Therefore, the choice amongst simple lotteries follows an orderly evaluation; hence the name priority rule. The sequence shows that the probability of maximum winnings is not among the reasons considered.

The priority heuristic is detailed in the following four phases (adaptation of Mousavi et al., 2017: 290–291 and Brandstätter et al., 2006: 413):

- Simple lotteries with non-negative outcomes (or winnings) contain the elements of a maximum win (M), a minimum win (m) and a minimum win probability (p_m) with $p_M + p_m = 1$.[14] As is obvious, the sequential consideration of these three elements can only be made in six ways: (M, m, p_m), (M, p_m, m), (p_m, M, m), (p_m, m, M), (m, M, p_m) and (m, p_m, M). One of them is the one that individuals apply, that is, the priority heuristic.
- To specify the sequence applied in choosing lotteries, multiple field experiments have been carried out. They show that p_m is not the first element taken into consideration, which eliminates two of the suggested cases. It has also been found that risk aversion in the domain of profits pushes people to focus at the outset on m, the worst outcome. Therefore, the two sequences to be analyzed are (m, M, p_m) and (m, p_m, M). Since their first element is the same, the research has addressed the second and third components. The conclusion has been that p_m merits more attention than M. Therefore, the priority heuristic is (m, p_m, M): first, people detect the worst outcome; second, they are interested in its probability; and, finally, they look for the maximum gain.
- Once the order of inspection has been identified, the stopping rule should be set. At this point, the heuristic of sufficient satisfaction comes into play. Although this heuristic is described in section 5.1.5, for now, it is enough

to indicate that for two simple lotteries, A and B, people start by comparing the minimum gains, $\Delta m = |m_A - m_B|$, and, by empirical evidence, the search is stopped if $\Delta m \geq 0.1 \cdot M$, being $M = \max\{M_A, M_B\}$, i.e., the maximum gain has to be at least up to ten times greater than the difference between the minima. However, if $\Delta m < 0.1 \cdot M$, people decide to consider the relationship between the probabilities of minimum gains. Empirically it has been found that, if $\Delta p_m = |p_{mA} - p_{mB}| \geq 0.1$, the inspection stops. If not, it is necessary to move on to the comparison of the last element, i.e., the maximum gains.

- The more attractive lottery, for either winnings or probability, is the one finally chosen; more specifically, the higher (minimum or maximum) gains and the smaller probability of minimal gains.

This casuistry was observed experimentally in dual monetary lotteries. Since such lotteries had never been studied from a psychological perspective, a new heuristic was detected. Analysts called it the priority heuristic. In substantive terms, this heuristic combines elements from three different sources: the initial focus is on outcomes rather than probability; next, it mimics the take-the-best heuristic; and finally, it incorporates the level of aspiration (the hypothetical 1/10th magnitude thresholds). The goal is to avoid the minimum results. This is what the algorithm ultimately emphasizes. The priority heuristic is simple because it only applies one or a few reasons, even though it examines the entire lottery. Moreover, the probabilities are treated linearly and the aspiration level is present in all intermediate steps.

As an illustration of the described procedure, let us look at the choice in the following two lotteries, which are considered separately (adapted from Brandstätter et al., 2006: 412):

$L1$. (€200, 0.5; €0, 0.5) or win €100 for certain;
$L2$. (€2,000, 0.5; €0, 0.5) or win €100 for certain.

The choice in each pair starts by comparing their minimum gains: in $L1$ and $L2$, they are €0 and €100, respectively.[15] The difference in absolute terms between them is the same: €100. As for the probabilities of these results, the distance between them is also identical in both lotteries: 0.5. The difference between them is the maximum gains: $L1$ with €200 and €100 and $L2$ with €2,000 and €100, respectively. Therefore, in the case of $L1$, since the larger gain only doubles the difference between the minimum gains, the choice favors the safe €100. By contrast, €100 $\geq$ 0.1·€200 stopped the algorithm: the greater gain is not sufficiently attractive to the option of a safe gain. And, what happens in $L2$? Field experiments indicate that the majority prefer to gamble. The reason for this is the large gap between the maximum potential profit (€2,000) and the difference between the minimums (€100), i.e., €100 < 0.1·€2,000. If following the process, the criterion of the probability difference in absolute terms of the minimum gains, 0.5 > 0.1, is applied; the rule stops because it is higher than 10%. The lottery with the largest number is chosen because its probability is not comparatively small enough than the sure option. Risk propensity has emerged. However, if this lottery were

*L*3. (€500, 0.5; €0, 0.5) or gain €100 for certain

the distance between €500 and €100 is not convincing. It is a case analogous to *L*1. Indeed, the hypothetical rule mentioned above is confirmed: people stop the inspection when the figures at stake are ten or more times apart. In this circumstance, the attractiveness of the certain (or larger) gain fails to prevail. Now suppose

*L*4. (€20,000, 0.05; €0, 0.95) or €100 for certain.

In this case, Δm = €100 < $0.1 \cdot M$ = €2,000 and Δp_m = 0.05 < 10%, so most people are drawn to the higher gain (€20,000). Its low probability does not matter. As mentioned, people show this behavior by playing large lotteries. Finally, consider the lottery

*L*5. (€100, 0.5; €0, 0.5) or (€100, 0.95; €0, 0.05).

In this lottery, there is no difference in the minimum winnings, €0, which are smaller than the maximum gains, €100. It is necessary to look at the probabilities of the minimum winnings, 0.5 and 0.05, which maintain a distance of more than 10%. Upon inspection, people tend to choose the second option (€100, 0.95; €0, 0.05) to be the most attractive: maximum profit value (€100) and lower probability of minimum profit (0.05).

All these empirical results are related to the widely used base 10 numbering system, although it is not universal. These thresholds, therefore, have a historical and cultural nature. Studies on this subject, still in progress, are trying to refine this result, as well as elucidate the relationship between the size of these thresholds and the social and biographical characteristics of people.

In short, the priority heuristic has the following three rules (Brandstätter et al., 2006: 413):

- The priority rule: the examination of the lottery elements begins with the minimum gains, then the probabilities of the minimum gains, and, finally, the maximum gains.
- The stopping rule: the inspection stops when the difference between the minimum gains is equal to or greater than 1/10 of the maximum gains at stake; otherwise, it is checked whether the probabilities of minimum winnings are separated by more than 10%. If so, the search is stopped. If the

distance is equal to or less than 10%, the higher result stops the algorithm definitively.

• The decision rule: wherever the inspection stops, the most attractive lottery is chosen, i.e., the one with the largest gains (minimum or maximum) and the smallest probability of minimum winnings.

The algorithm drives the choice between dual lotteries involving gains. If people must decide between losses, it is sufficient to replace the word "gains" with "losses" in the three steps of the heuristic. Its extension to lotteries with more than two (non-negative) outcomes has also been studied. In this case, a small alteration of the priority rule emerges: minimum gain, minimum probability of gains, maximum gain, and maximum probability of gain. This fourth reason differentiates them from dual lotteries.

To close this section, it should be highlighted that the priority heuristic solves the Allais paradox discussed in Chapter 2, section 2.1 (see Brandstätter et al., 2006: 414, and Katsikopoulos and Gigerenzer, 2008: 41–42). In the choice between 1(*a*) and 1(*b*), the maximum gain is €762,000, and therefore the aspirational level for gains is €76,200. The difference between the minimum winnings, i.e., €152,000 minus €0, exceeds this level. The inspection is stopped. Therefore, the lottery with the most attractive minimum gains is 1(*a*), and therefore the priority heuristic makes a correct prediction. When the choice is between 2(*a*) and 2(*b*), the minimum gains are equal (€0). People then continue the inspection: the difference between the minimum gain probabilities is $0.9 - 0.89 = 0.01$, which is less than the 10% aspiration level. The choice is therefore decided by the maximum gain, i.e., 2(*b*). This prediction is also correct. The paradox detected by Allais no longer stands.

5.1.3 The Weighting-and-Adding Algorithms

The weighting-and-adding heuristics bring together algorithms that, once a relatively small number of attributes of the options have been identified, proceed to their direct comparison. Although no hierarchies are established among the attributes, they can be weighted according to many different schemes (Payne et al., 1993: 24). These heuristics open the door to the establishment of substitution relationships between options since their cues are assumed to be comparable and compensable with each other. However, this supposition clashes with the degree of dissimilarity between the attributes. If all of them belong to the same class, the application of this algorithm raises no doubts. By contrast, if there is incommensurability, the comparison may be forced, even absurd. It should also be added that this type of algorithm is appropriate for choices with negligible consequences and an absence of uncertainty. It is not difficult to imagine everyday examples: a person wants to buy a cake; on arriving at the usual bakery, they observe in the shop window what kind of cakes are on sale today. Neither is the price comparatively significant nor is there any room for surprises (this person knows the product and the offer will not change until the next day, a time horizon outside the choice process). The consumer realizes that today there is a choice between cream and chocolate cakes. Both seem attractive to them, but they wonder whether the cake with a great quantity of cream is nicer than the chocolate one. A question then arises: how many units of cream compensate for the loss of one unit of chocolate? In this way, a cream/chocolate substitution ratio can be established, which will only be valid for the specific day, place, and consumer.[16] As observed, in this example the compensation relationships (attributes involved and quantities included) are rooted in raw preferences. If the choice had included a cake with a new flavor, this person might have made some inferences about it. These are examples of small world choices, using Savage's terminology.

The role of the compensatory algorithm, as a tool for inferring the preferred option, can be further explored by revisiting Table 5.4, concerning a person who wants to buy a house. There are four options to be compared, with each based on six attributes (those that the buyer has considered most relevant). Let us consider Table 5.9, in which, in addition to the indices of each attribute/house, the last column has been added showing the weighting that the person gives to each attribute. In this case, the number of rooms and the social environment have more weight than the other attributes. This does not mean that the house with the most rooms will be chosen. Weighting reflects the importance of the attributes, but none of them is usually strong enough to prevail on its own. Obviously, each of the possible weighting schemes may be considered as a singular algorithm.

Table 5.9   Initial data for an example of the comparison algorithm

Attributes/options	House 1	House 2	House 3	House 4	Weighting
Price	2	3	1	4	3
Distance to school	1	2	3	2	2
Garden size	1	2	3	3	1
Neighborhood	4	3	1	2	4
Building renovation cost	3	2	3	1	1.5
Number of rooms	3	2	2	1	4

After applying this compensatory algorithm scheme, house 1 is chosen, as shown in Table 5.10. For each house, the person directly multiplied each attribute by its specific weighting. Then, they added up each column. The largest figure is that of house 1 (41.5 points), which narrowly wins over house 2. If each attribute weighed the same, the sum by columns would reveal a tie at 14 points between houses 1 and 2. Therefore, it would be necessary to choose at random (or, perhaps, to add a new attribute).[17] The key point of the compensatory algorithm is that it places all attributes on the same level: "proximity to school" does not rank higher than "renovation effort" and so on. There is no hierarchy; at most there are only different weightings. However, it is difficult to understand what it means to say the "number of rooms" weighs the same, double, or whatever, as "proximity to the school." These are two attributes of different classes and, consequently, it is arbitrary to establish a direct comparison between them. In fact, beyond very simple cases, there are few choices in which direct compensatory rules can be applied. For example, how much does a larger freezer compensate for a much more energy-consuming refrigerator? Or how much more sophisticated does a meal have to be to share it with people we do not like? Or what is the exact commuting time that justifies taking a higher-paying job?

Table 5.10   Applying a weighting algorithm

Attributes/options	House 1	House 2	House 3	House 4
Price	$2·3 = 6$	9	3	12
Distance to school	$1·2 = 2$	4	6	4
Garden size	$1·1 = 1$	2	3	3
Neighborhood	$4·4 = 16$	12	4	8
Building renovation cost	$3·1.5 = 4.5$	3	4.5	1.5
Number of rooms	$3·4 = 12$	8	8	4
Total	41.5	38	28.5	32.5

The algorithm can also be used to make predictions. This is what rational calculation methods do, i.e., the usual mathematical and statistical techniques: they establish relationships between variables (attributes) based on weighting the available data. However, even in the simplest cases, the weighting values used are of paramount importance in determining the option to be chosen. Inspired by Luan et al. (2014: 501–502) let us consider the example in Table 5.11. This table shows the changes in the ranking of countries according to the medal valuation rule used.

Determining which country has the best athletes, based on medals won, is more intricate than it seems at first glance. The result is far from indisputable since the algorithms applied to evaluate the medal list give rise to different country rankings. Consider, for example, the following five valuation criteria:[18]

A.   The total number of medals is linearly added, or unit weighted. This criterion was applied by the *New York Times* newspaper for an obvious reason.

Table 5.11   Medal ranking in the 2008 Beijing Olympic Games

Country/medals	Type of medal			Ranking according to the applied criterion				
	Gold	Silver	Bronze	A	B	C	D	E
Australia	14	15	17	5 (46)	5 (132)	5 (89)	5 (365)	6
China	51	21	28	2 (100)	1 (346)	1 (223)	2 (823)	1
France	7	16	17	7 (40)	8 (100)	7 (70)	7 (310)	8
Germany	16	10	15	6 (41)	6 (125)	6 (83)	6 (329)	5
Italy	8	10	10	9 (28)	9 (80)	9 (54)	9 (222)	9
Russia	23	21	28	3 (72)	3 (206)	3 (139)	3 (571)	3
South Korea	13	10	8	8 (31)	7 (193)	8 (67)	8 (253)	7
Ukraine	7	5	15	10 (27)	10 (65)	10 (46)	10 (208)	10
United Kingdom	19	13	15	4 (47)	4 (149)	4 (98)	4 (380)	4
United States	36	38	36	1 (110)	2 (330)	2 (220)	1 (880)	2

B.   Five points are assigned for a gold medal, three for a silver medal, and one for a bronze medal, a weighting criterion set at the 1908 London Olympic Games.
C.   In the same way, as with the previous case, the weighting is three points for a gold medal, two for a silver medal, and one for a bronze medal.
D.   The gold medal receives nine points, eight for silver, and seven for bronze. A criterion similar to the two previous ones, but with higher absolute magnitudes, is detrimental to the gold medals.
E.   A lexicographic rule is established: only gold medals are counted, with silver and, if necessary, bronze medals breaking any ties. This was the criterion used by the Chinese press, also for obvious reasons.

Four countries (Italy, United Kingdom, Russia, and Ukraine) maintain the same position in all five algorithms, although others could be imagined to alter it. The other six countries change their positions according to the criteria. An infinite number of other possible algorithms could be designed, each giving rise to slightly different rankings and differences between countries. Any inference about the overall quality of the athletes will therefore be disputed: the result depends on the attributes selected, the type of background information that supports them, and the computational criteria. How many times does a ranking of quality, efficiency, etc. obtained from certain data and weightings, and applied to all kinds of objects such as schools, films, artists, etc., raise doubts and controversy? The ridiculous origin (a weekly that had to increase sales by any means) and the nonsense behind the quality lists of universities, is a well-known example (see Morson and Schapiro, 2017: 65–118). In all these cases, the concerned parties strive to develop gaming-the-ranking stratagems.

The weighting-and-adding algorithm has the following rules:

- The searching rule: arrange the options and their attributes in any order and assign certain weights (positives, zero, or negatives).
- The stopping rule: apply the corresponding weighting to each attribute of the options and then add them together.
- The decision rule: choose the option with the largest value.

This algorithm applied to small world situations usually makes good predictions. In this context, attributes may be neither qualitative (beauty, merits, etc.) nor multifaceted. They may also be poorly correlated with each other, and thus the establishment of linear relationships between attributes emerges as a reasonable assumption.[19]

Beyond the above comments, it should be emphasized that not all non-hierarchical heuristics are compensatory, as shown in the following subsection.

5.1.4   Equal Allocation

The weighting-and-adding algorithms assume that the options, although not arranged in a ranking, can have different weights. However, there is also the possibility that all options are treated equally. The tallying and $1/n$ algorithms are characterized by allocating the same weight to the attributes (or options).

5.1.4.1 Tallying

The tallying heuristic chooses the option that has the highest number of favorable signals, without further considerations (Gigerenzer and Gaissmaier, 2011: 469; Gigerenzer, 2015: 132). The algorithm merely counts cues (hence all of them are weighted equally), and therefore it never chooses an option where there are no cues. If there are contradictory signals, it counts those in each direction and, then, infers the option to be chosen. An example of the application of the tallying algorithm is the way skiers evaluate the possibility of snow avalanches (McCammon and Hägeli 2004). Before setting off, they look for cues as to whether the situation is avalanche-friendly: Have there been any avalanches recently? Has it rained recently? Does the slope of the mountain facilitate avalanches? And so on. It seems that skiers examine up to seven cues. If all are in favor of avalanches, the decision is to stay home. If there are none or a low enough number of cues favoring the possibility of avalanches, it is likely to be inferred that there is no danger for the next few hours. Parents apply a similar procedure when a child says they are not feeling well: observe the symptoms. If the simple inspection advises visiting the physician, the doctor will make a diagnosis using the same procedure, i.e., a series of questions to the patient and a visual inspection. This is all there is in most visits to the doctor. Only when the initial treatment does not seem to work and/or the diagnosis suggests something important may be hidden, will the doctor advise special tests to obtain more detailed information (Kattah et al., 2009). Tallying is also the first algorithm to be applied when a machine is not working properly or when a preliminary analysis has to be made about the financial situation of a company. There is no doubt that hunter-gatherer tribes followed this same algorithm when deciding on the hunting path: they looked for signs on the ground to confirm whether there was prey in the vicinity and in which direction it was moving. As with the recognition heuristic, the tallying heuristic is ubiquitous: attention is focused on the value of a few, presumably revealing cues, which are inspected in any order. In general, the experience transmitted by others and that directly lived, as well as accumulated knowledge, are the key factors in identifying the relevant cues, determining their value, and deciding what to do. Although the rigor of the scrutiny performed by an amateur or an expert will be very different, what should now be emphasized is the ease and immediacy with which this algorithm can be applied.

The components of the tallying algorithm are as follows:

- The searching rule: identify cues and arrange them in any order.
- The stopping rule: end the search when there are many signals that favor one of the options.
- The decision rule: choose the alternative with the most favorable cues.

Two important considerations must be made regarding the implementation of the tallying algorithm:

- As just indicated, the search should be stopped if r signals out of a total of R ($1 < r \leq R$) suggest one of the options. The number r is optional: occasional circumstances can lead people to alter (up or down) the favorable number of cues for action. If they consider that the algorithm does not discriminate enough between options, two possibilities open up: to choose randomly or to apply the precautionary principle (in the absence of sufficient evidence, even momentarily, the best option is to refrain).
- The tallying heuristic does not ignore any relevant signal, although it is never likely to perform an exhaustive search. It is only interested in the basic attributes according to the accumulated knowledge and experience. The set of evidence considered depends on the context in which the decision is made. It should be pointed out that the class of the decision must be precisely defined: fishing in the river is not the same as fishing in the sea.

Field experiments have confirmed that the algorithm has a strong predictive capability. For example, it can predict which school will suffer more dropouts according to the proportion of students of different social profiles and the scores they have obtained in some previous aptitude tests. No further information needs to be collected. In any case, the predictive ability of the algorithm is still under analysis, as well as its contextual rationality.

5.1.4.2   The 1/*n* rule

The 1/*n* algorithm establishes that the available resources must be equally distributed among all the options. This may be the time devoted to the children by a couple, the allocation of funds between stocks, the weighting of the votes of assembly members, or the criterion for the distribution of the profits obtained by a group of people. This algorithm considers that the *n* alternatives have to be treated equally, without necessarily giving further reasons.

The application of the 1/*n* algorithm as a portfolio diversification criterion has received much attention. Before addressing this subject, it is worth emphasizing the role of recognition heuristics in this type of decision: the vast majority of investors prefer to buy stocks of companies they recognize. Amateur investors are likely to recognize only a few companies, usually domestic ones, while financial experts know about many more. Moreover, experts often appreciate that a company is widely known, and therefore most fund managers end up buying stocks of the same companies. Experiments conducted years ago have shown that the application of the recognition heuristic yields excellent economic returns (Borges et al., 1999). However, it is not enough to identify the firms whose shares to buy; it is also necessary to establish criteria for incorporating them in the portfolio (Durbach et al., 2020) and for distributing the available funds. Under this last point, investors can apply the 1/*n* rule. As expected, the turnover resulting from this algorithm has been repeatedly compared with the other criteria, especially the median-variance method proposed by Harry Max Markowitz. This exercise is encouraged by the fact that this economist, in his personal life, instead of using the optimal criterion he had designed and for which he was awarded the Nobel Prize in Economics in 1990, admitted to adopting the simple criterion of equally dividing the money among the stocks under consideration (Gigerenzer, 2007: Chapter 2; Gigerenzer, 2008: 22–23 and Gigerenzer, 2014: 93). And he was right: several studies have confirmed that the 1/*n* algorithm outperforms more complex criteria, except in situations that are not very operational. Thus, in DeMiguel et al. (2009), 14 criteria are compared for optimal fund allocation in portfolios subject to risk, plus the 1/*n* heuristic. Specifically, they define seven portfolios with the most extended monthly data from 1963 to 2004. After the calculations, no optimal model consistently outperforms the 1/*n* rule. Moreover, its financial performance is comparatively higher the shorter the employed data series. The analysis concludes that only if it were possible to handle data stretched over several centuries would the other algorithms prevail without discussion. The reason is that their use requires a huge volume of information, but there are no figures for this time range (Neth et al., 2013: 138–139).

Without going into technical details, if there are n assets, the Markowitz model assigns a weight to each of them. This portion within the portfolio comes from a calculation based on the assumption that the future probability distribution of the risk matches the behavior of (the sample of) the observed stock.[20] The estimation of weights also requires the calculation of the mean and variance of all assets. However, for n assets, there are $(n^2 + 3n)/2$ parameters to be estimated (for example, 65 for $n = 10$). Therefore, the larger the portfolio, the greater the computational requirements. In contrast, the $1/n$ algorithm ignores all historical information and assigns the portfolio weights equally. Since the future is inevitably unknown, it does not bother to make calculations with the information accumulated from past periods. Under uncertainty, the plan that was optimal in the past does not necessarily have to be optimal in the future (Luan et al., 2019: 1738–1739). For this reason, the $1/n$ rule is only interested in ongoing information. This is how current investors' expectations of stock performance are incorporated. As a result, the algorithm avoids sensitivity of forecasts to changes in the initial conditions and, hence, being trapped in the trade-off between bias and variance.

The bias/variance trade-off belongs to the large family of precision and effort trade-offs. Let us consider a true value μ of a given population to be estimated from m randomly drawn samples. It is assumed that the population does not change and there is no doubt that the samples are random. On attempting to predict μ the following three sources of error appear (adaptation of Gigerenzer, 2021: 3557):

- The bias or the difference between the mean of the estimated values and the actual target value, i.e., $\bar{x} - \mu$. The bias indicates the fit between the model and reality.
- The variance or root mean square difference between estimates from different samples and the mean of the estimated values: $\frac{1}{m}\Sigma(x_m - \bar{x})^2$. The variance indicates the sensitivity of the model predictions to the data samples.
- The random error that has zero mean and no correlation with the bias.

The total systematic error of a prediction is expressed as follows (see Gigerenzer and Gaissmaier, 2011: 458; Brighton and Gigerenzer, 2012; and Mousavi et al., 2017: 288):

Prediction error = (bias)^2 + variance + random error

The samples can give rise to predictions of μ that are all close to each other (small variance) but with a systematic bias. It can also occur that the predictions have a very small or no bias, but high variance, i.e., dispersed estimated values that compensate for each other (quite a lot). It turns out that, under uncertainty, there is no reason to expect predictions with both small bias and variance. Therefore, since the variance decreases with larger samples, but increases with the number of free parameters to be estimated, a simple model such as $1/n$, although it may be quite biased, can make comparatively better predictions than complex ones, because the impact of the variance has been canceled out. This trade-off is shown in Figure 5.3.

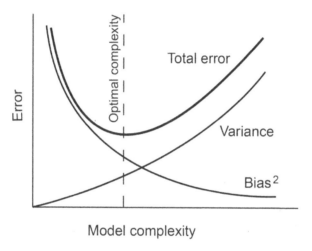

Figure 5.3   Total error in predictions

Models with many free parameters, after intensive calculations on large samples, achieve good fits. However, a comparatively small bias does not guarantee accuracy when predictions are made from different samples. Complex investment models require a great deal of data from the past, which inevitably mixes useful with spurious information. In making predictions, it is difficult to distinguish which is which. In contrast, the $1/n$ heuristic leaves out all prior information, which implies misspecification of the model and hence comparatively more bias, although it is immune to wrong or inappropriate data, and exhibits low variance even when small samples are used. In short, combining moderate bias and low variance is a cautious approach based on the conviction that there is no reason to believe that a more sophisticated criterion will ensure better forecasts in an uncertain environment.[21]

Finally, the components of the $1/n$ algorithm are as follows:

- the searching rule: consider only recognized options;
- the stopping rule: make sure that all options have been considered;
- the decision rule: the available resources are equally allocated.

Before ending this section, it can be highlighted that the $1/n$ algorithm also satisfies an important social norm: to divide equally what is obtained by cooperating. The ultimatum game, mentioned below, can be understood as a social version of this algorithm.

5.1.5   The Satisficing Heuristics

Simon argued that human rationality can only be understood if its limits and the nature of the decision context are taken into account. He thought that people can only store knowledge and evaluate the elements involved in decisions to a limited extent. This postulate was called bounded rationality: the socioeconomic environment is too complex and uncertain for the human mind to manage all possible options and foresee their consequences (see Simon, 1959: 277, 1987a and 2000; Payne et al., 1993: 26; Selten, 1998 and 1999; Harstad and Selten, 2013; and Altman, 2017a). The postulate does not claim that humans are irrational, i.e., they repeatedly make the same mistakes or, worse, they consciously act against their physical and/or psychological integrity. Simon only stated that the past, present, and future reality is never fully known, if only because of the mind's difficulty in processing massive amounts of information. Concerning the context, he considered that it is important not to forget that it is contingent and changeable. In brief, cognition and context form an inextricable whole, just as scissors are only useful if they have two cutting blades. A very wise analogy from Simon: if our attention is focused on the blade representing the mind, the heuristics inevitably reflect the weakness of human cognition, since they do not comply with the requirements of strict rationality; and, if our attention is centered on the other blade (the context), people are mere particles reacting to the stimuli of the environment in a completely predictable way (Gigerenzer, 2008). Simon understood rationality as an emergent property of the confluence between these two "blades."[22] This approach combines cognitive aspects, social influences, and the unpredictability of the world (Todd and Gigerenzer, 2000: 730). Therefore, as already suggested in the first pages of this book, for Simon and his followers, humans are neither perfectly rational nor hopelessly irrational. Human rationality is complex, unique, adaptive, and paradoxical. It may be genuinely creative, but at the same time, it is highly impressionable. While it is often predictable, it is not infrequently surprising.

People make decisions by applying the algorithm they think is the most appropriate given the context. Therefore, people are involved in a learning process under the influence of the good and bad consequences of previous decisions. Simon then concluded that, if the optimum is an illusion, when making decisions people accommodate the *satisficing* option, a neologism that arises from the combination of satisfying and sufficing. Although there are occasions on which it is feasible to make decisions oriented towards the optimum, in large world conditions the goal of sufficiently satisfactory results prevails, whether they are gains or limited losses (Rutherford, 1988: 51; Simon, 1987b).

The searching rule of the sufficient satisfaction algorithm consists of running through the options one after the other without any predefined order. This inspection stops when an option reaches a certain level of aspiration. As long as the options already evaluated are rejected, those still pending are ignored. The first of the options that is sufficiently satisfactory is chosen. This threshold is singular to each person. It is explained by people's lifestyles and expectations (personal, professional, financial, etc.). Relevant changes in daily personal life, socioeconomic status, work situation, etc. mean aspiration changes. Meanwhile, if Ω_t is the aspiration level at time t, the algorithm prompts to choose the first option with a value at least equal to Ω_t. However, if none is found to satisfy it, people can lower the goals until an option can be chosen (Mousavi et al., 2017: 286). It is also necessary to warn that the aspiration levels may be subject to certain substantive or temporal conditions (Gigerenzer, 2020: 1374).[23]

As seen, the *satisficing* heuristic has a dual nature: it is an algorithm for making decisions, but it also reflects a particular conception of rationality. The two interpretations complement each other (Todd and Gigerenzer, 2000: 731).

5.1.6   Social Heuristics

Among heuristics, the social ones stand out. They are a set of algorithms that deal with decisions strongly influenced by interaction with other people. Sometimes they consist of responses to the previous actions of others, and sometimes they attempt to anticipate the reactions of others to our previous actions towards them. In both cases, the behavior of the others is closely observed. Although this attention effort and the dynamics of interaction may be very exhausting and intricate, respectively, these facts do not deter humans from constantly making inferences about each other's (re)actions (Gigerenzer,

2007: Chapter 11). Three social heuristics will be emphasized here (Gigerenzer and Gaissmeier, 2011: 471–473; Sofo et al., 2013: 4–6):

- Reciprocity is the basis of conditional cooperation. Cooperation consists of adding one's own effort to that of the community to favor a common objective. This behavior has distinguished the human species since primitive times. This social proclivity has facilitated the survival and expansion of human groups by reducing internal tensions and strengthening them in the face of threats coming from the natural environment and, especially, from possible rival groups.
- The heuristic of the default choice, that is, the tendency to choose the suggested option. That is all it comprises. It is a social heuristic since the proposal is undoubtedly the initiative of someone else, whose reasons do not necessarily coincide with those of the decision-maker. Although it could be very interesting to investigate such motives, this issue goes beyond the description of the algorithm.
- Imitation of others, especially if the objective is to be quickly accepted within a group. In the economic world, imitation of those who have been successful is a common recommendation. Thousands of students in economics and business management are taught every day to take note of the most fruitful decisions (Artinger et al., 2014).[24] It should be added that, together with language and learning, imitation is one of the three key processes of cultural transmission.

The three heuristics are common when a decision with strong social implications has to be made, but good information is not available (Gigerenzer, 2015: 136). This is a very frequent situation given the complexity of the social environment: people have to interpret and anticipate the behavior of others in a complex web of mutual influences. Moreover, the minds of others cannot be directly read. It is therefore inevitable to support decisions with heuristics. These social shortcuts ultimately expand those that evolution has been deploying to adapt living beings to the natural environment. However, the sophistication of social heuristics exceeds the requirements to thrive in natural ecosystems. Finally, it should be stressed that the analysis of social heuristics leaves aside moral valuations, i.e., it is only focused on their effectiveness in attaining social adaptation (Gigerenzer and Gaissmeier, 2011: 471, 473).

5.1.6.1 Reciprocity
A distinctive element of the human species is its strong inclination to cooperate (Bowles and Gintis, 2013: 93–110). Cooperation ranges from actions in favor of the continuity of the group as a whole to the preservation of the welfare of specific people. When necessary, some people have not hesitated even to

assume a personal cost to contribute to the improvement of the fate of their fellows. These are actions that are welcomed by the majority and a source of satisfaction for the protagonists.

Cooperation in human societies has become a social norm that members internalize from birth (Fehr et al., 2002). It is associated with trust and equanimity, being a moral value in its own right (Elster, 2007: Chapter 21). Human groups have never understood cooperation as an annoying constraint to individual development, even though the readiness to cooperate weakens in the face of strangers and, above all, if there are doubts about the willingness of others to cooperate (see below). It also weakens under the influence of certain ideological stances that promote self-interest and strive to legitimize inequalities (aversion to which is widespread, although not innate).

The term cooperation ranges from simple collaboration (or mutualism) to altruism (Bowles and Gintis, 2013: 1–2). Collaboration means the coordinated execution of a given task, which presupposes a minimum distribution of responsibilities and a certain degree of mutual trust. Specific functions are assigned to people according to criteria such as age, gender, experience, knowledge, skills, and so on. Mutuality is indispensable for the functioning of society as a whole.[25] One example is the social acceptance of money, a quality that is only lost in situations of enormous socioeconomic and political crisis. The psychologist Stanley Milgram (1933–1984) illustrated the importance of collaboration by leaving many franked letters scattered in the streets of a city. More than half of them managed to reach their destination, which means that many citizens picked them up and put them in a mailbox. A few years ago the experiment was repeated but without stamps on the envelopes, and 20% of the letters reached their destination. The expression "being a good citizen" summarizes the strength of mutualism.

Altruism is a sign of empathy, as when people show the way to a stranger who does not know the city, without expecting anything in return.[26] However, providing this information comes at no cost (only a small part of one's time). Therefore, this degree of generosity is hardly considered an example of altruism. The term usually refers to providing help to someone at a significant cost (Fehr and Fischbacher, 2005; Hogg and Vaughan, 2014: 503). This would be the case for development workers in a poor country or those who rescue immigrants on the high seas. Undoubtedly, these actions carry penalties and risks. Even so, this strong prosocial behavior is often applied selectively: those who have been victims of an unforeseen misfortune (an earthquake, for example) deserve more attention than those whose hardship is the result of reprehensible behavior (such as excessive alcohol consumption).

Cooperation is not uncommon among animal species. Canids, for example, organize to hunt, while in social insects (ants, bees, etc.), cooperation is the rule. In these cases, cooperation involves creatures with a strict kinship relationship, although it has been observed that some ant species create supercolonies, i.e., societies formed by descendants of hundreds or thousands of queens. Whatever the case, all members are recognized by the same chemical signal. In contrast, human cooperation can include people with no biological links to each other, such as strangers never met before (Silk, 2005; Silk and House, 2011; Hare, 2017).

Tribal hunter-gatherer societies were made up of groups of up to 150 people, all belonging to the same lineage (inaugurated by a mythical ancestor), endowed with certain behavioral norms (which gave them identity), and active in a given territory. As they were almost all related, it was easy to form a network of mutual help, always respecting certain manifestations of individuality and spaces of privacy. The origins of this form of social organization date back to the first hominids. Even so, these collectives regularly displayed stable relationships with neighboring groups, with which they exchanged experiences, goods, people (to form couples), etc. A network of friendly relations was built up and, after sporadic clashes, rebuilt. Only in the face of strangers was a certain initial reserve advisable. It was not rejection, but caution to avoid suffering a hostile reaction. However, once the initial surprise was overcome, people's inclination to communicate and establish links with other people made it easier for the newcomer to be received peacefully and eventually accepted into the group (Eibl-Eibesfeldt, 2012: 181, 289 and 623). This behavior is distinctly human, although the admission of strangers has also been observed among bonobos. Therefore, social proximity is not clouded by the diversity of origins of its members: strong bonds can be created even without sharing the same genetic base or enjoying a previous family relationship. The human species is powerfully predisposed, on the one hand, to develop group identities and shows, on the other hand, an enormous capacity for integration, qualities that give it a parochial look (Bowles and Gintis, 2013: 37).

Human groups have always shamed, ostracized or punished free-riders. To preserve cooperation, they are warned that no one will help them in case of need. They are also threatened with retaliation. The effectiveness of these admonitions depends on the size of the group. In a village or small town, a simple warning may be enough to motivate potential offenders to change their attitude. Within short social distances, the fear of gaining a bad reputation is dissuasive. However, in societies with enormous population masses, a high degree of mutual ignorance and an extreme social division of labor, it has to be people with influence and authority who revalidate customary norms and establish legal norms to warn and, if necessary, penalize non-cooperators. Still, this is not enough: like never before in history, in today's societies of millions of anonymous people, cooperation requires huge doses of trust (Eibl-Eibesfeldt, 2012: 315; Thaler, 2015: 146).[27] In any case, people tend to cooperate with those who cooperate and defect along with those who defect.

Cooperation is conditional. Therefore, if free-riders manage to escape from potential retaliation, the willingness to continue cooperating quickly weakens. The idea is rapidly spread that the only way to penalize free-riders is to stop cooperating too. The uncontrollable growth and consolidation of free-riders lead to the collapse of the cooperation network.

However, it is not only free-riders who are frowned upon. Those who make an excessive contribution also arouse suspicion, especially if they aim to make their contribution public and notorious. There are two main reasons for this suspicion: the first is that it places in a bad position those who cannot match, for whatever reason, this contribution, and the second is that many consider that behind this eagerness to cooperate lies a strategic behavior, i.e., the pursuit of some specific advantage.

The importance of cooperation does not impede the manifestation of competitive impulses. Without being exhaustive, there are at least four different cases:

- The aim is to reaffirm one's own capacities on undertaking, immediately or later, a given action. This expression of self-esteem is not necessarily intended to displace, or to be directed against someone. It may arise from the rejection of a certain state of affairs.
- In a negotiation or a struggle, each party defends its interests. If opportunities, resources, time or space are available in lesser amounts than required, the race for a better personal/group position can be relentless.
- In situations of alarm or danger, many choose to save their skin, without further delay and consideration for the fate of others. Urgency is often at odds with waiting for collaborative actions.
- Competitive craving likely takes its most extreme form when it comes to groups. The psychologist Philip Zimbardo and many others have corroborated through experiments how important identity is in human groups, even if it is based on spurious traits (Motterlini, 2010: 105). Being part of a group is pleasant because people are recognized and recognize themselves. This is such a strong feeling that it can easily fuel intergroup rivalry. For example, to attain maximum performance it is often sufficient to encourage emulation among workers organized in purpose-built teams. Not infrequently, intergroup antagonism quickly degenerates into hostility, which opens the door to cruelty that, in the case of the human species, seems to know no bounds. Surprisingly, the fiercest animosity suddenly disappears if the groups, previously at odds, have to face a common problem (a rival, for example).

Among these cases, negotiations stand out. As is well known, a negotiation is a tug-of-war process in which two or more parties, while recognizing the differences in interests and/or values that separate them, also claim to be willing to agree. Parties consider that failure may have comparatively worse consequences. In negotiations, contextual elements are very important, whether informal or institutionalized, whether public or secret.[28] However, negotiations are not always strictly competitive, i.e., they take the form of a zero-sum game (the winner's gain is entirely at the expense of the loser). Although the analysis of negotiation processes goes beyond the scope of these pages, it is opportune to introduce the following minimum typology (reworked from Raiffa, 1982: Chapter 1):

- There are negotiation processes in which the parties, despite antagonism, recognize that they can reach a satisfactory agreement, however difficult it may be. Because of mutual distrust, an initial tentative phase of mutual observation is probably indispensable. Nonetheless, the parties are confident that agreements will be honored, and therefore the process also serves to dispel possible malicious intentions. Even so, the negotiation will almost certainly not arouse any enthusiasm to cooperate beyond what is strictly necessary to implement the agreed solution. In short, the degree of confrontation is as high as the perception that compromise is desirable.
- There are negotiations in which the parties always act strategically, with no lack of bad faith, betrayal or exploitation of power differentials. This is the case in negotiations with kidnappers or racketeers and, as the aforementioned author stresses, it also characterizes the assertions, often a confused mixture of arrogance and prejudice, of "dilettante diplomats." In other words, there is a high degree of confrontation mixed with the fact that at least one of the parties is unwilling to settle for an agreement.
- The third case mixes not very divergent interests with parties that are hardly prone to compromise. This is common in workplaces when the people involved have a margin to distribute, after negotiation, different tasks (who is in charge, with what schedule, etc.). Raiffa proposes the example of university departments and laboratories, although it can be extended to any environment featuring a flexible assignment of tasks. In these cases, no one wants to be taken for a sucker. Therefore, the defense of self-esteem prevails. Even so, repetitive negotiation between the parties leaves room for agreement, despite the difficulties.
- There are situations in which the degree of antagonism is low and agreement is fervently desired. Negotiation is imbued with a willingness to cooperate: this is the case of a couple in love negotiating how to spend their free time, or of partners of a successful business discussing the next investments. In these situations, the parties' goal is to preserve mutual trust. This type of negotiation does not show any hint of competitiveness.

Manifestations of self-esteem, moments of rivalry and tensions in the negotiation processes (in the first three cases just mentioned), however acute they may be, should not be confused with the persistent and fierce defense of one's own interests. It does not seem that selfishness, either in its rational form (the agent carefully chooses the decisions whose consequences are most favorable to them) or in its hedonistic form (focused on immediate and exclusive reward), is the dominant feature of human behavior. Nonetheless, when social relations usually involve strangers, the calculation of what can be gained readily appears (Eibl-Eibesfeldt, 2012: 623). It is not surprising that the postulate that human actions are based (for some, exclusively) on cost/benefit individual calculations has been widely accepted in modern times (and, as evidenced in Frank et al. (1993) and Etzioni (2015), it is especially widespread among students of economics and management). Still, it is an oversimplification to explain people's (economic) behavior based on a single principle, in this case an alleged innate selfishness.[29] People are capable of adopting a huge and changing range of attitudes towards others. They tend to adapt their behavior depending on the situation, which they usually identify without any problem. The propensity for conditional cooperation and the periodic emergence of competitive impulses form an intricate network of social interactions that cannot fit into a single behavioral principle.[30] As a conclusion, it can be said that a minimum of selfishness is required to live and a minimum of reciprocity is necessary to live together. Or, to put it from the perspective of social systems, a minimum of competition is indispensable for them to change, although without a minimum of cooperation, they cannot survive.[31]

In recent decades, the human inclination to cooperate has often been a challenged postulate. Among the many reasons, first and foremost is Adam Smith's principle of the invisible hand. In recent decades, this postulate has been understood as if it were the basis of social organization. However, this reading distorts and impoverishes this author's thinking, as has been made clear in Chapter 2, section 2.1. Secondly, Garrett Hardin explained the tragedy of the commons, or how people are unable to stop the degradation of a shared natural resource. This hypothesis was disproved by the research of Elinor Ostrom (1990): if the resource is part of the group's identity, the possible selfish impulse is usually overcome. Only when disagreements are extreme could the common resource be destroyed, unless third parties can prevent the destruction (Hogg and Vaughan, 2014: 411–415). Finally, the non-cooperative outcome of the prisoner's dilemma was understood, as Mancur Olson did, as an illustration of the weakness of cooperation in the face of free-riders. However, if the parties involved know each other and/or they will interact in the future, the most frequent situation, cooperation will predominate (Bowles and Gintis, 2013: 6, 21).

Reciprocity, or the establishment of the tit-for-tat rule, is probably the social heuristic par excellence: cooperation is always the initial choice, but defection is repaid immediately and with the same coin. Starting by collaborating is a vote of confidence in others. Later on, the rule is to imitate the last observed behavior (Fehr et al., 2002; Seabright, 2005; Wilkinson, 2008: 342; Eibl-Eibesfeldt, 2012: 351–357; and Nowak and Highfield, 2012).[32] Reciprocity is a social algorithm that mixes initial gentleness, punitive readiness (non-cooperation is punished) and forgiveness (if cooperation is restored, everyone joins in). This mix reflects the importance of mutual trust, but also its weakness in the face of manipulation. Therefore, to a large extent, reciprocity is the pursuit of trust and reliability.

The previous paragraph leads us to think that reciprocity, and its absence, require direct contact between people. However, since reciprocity is an internalized social norm, this condition is not necessary: *A* cooperates (or avoids doing so) with *B* because *B* has done so (or not) with *C*, which *A* knows and praises (or disapproves). At this point, there is no doubt that cultures (defined simply as the system of social meanings and habits shared by a community) have fostered a sense of responsibility towards third parties. An extreme example is Dersu Uzala, the nomadic taiga hunter featured in Akira Kurosawa's legendary film based on a true event. Leaving a hut, he leaves firewood, matches, salt and rice in it, in anticipation of someone (of whom he probably knows nothing) arriving at the shelter in desperation, thus preventing them from falling victim to the region's harsh weather. The social norm of leaving public spaces clean (lawns, benches for sitting, etc.) would be another more everyday example.

The heuristic of reciprocity takes on different degrees of intensity depending on the context. There is no doubt that, within the family nucleus, strong emotional ties incline people to satisfy the needs of their members without apparent limits and without demanding material compensation. Nonetheless, beyond this circle the chain of mutual aid, or consecutive exchange of favors, is strongly manifested: I am buying a round of drinks today because, in a group of friends, sooner or later, everyone buys drinks for everyone else. What if someone ducks out? They will end up being kicked out of the group (Samuelson, 2005; Silk and House, 2011). This common situation highlights the permanent tension in reciprocity issues and, more generally, between cooperating and not cooperating. At this point, an important experiment is the game of public goods (Bowles and Gintis, 2013: 22–24; Thaler, 2015: 144–145). The standard version brings together about ten people who are strangers to each other. To start with, they all receive, for example, five one-euro coins. Each person then has to decide how much they want to contribute to a common fund. The amount chosen must be placed in an anonymous envelope. Once everyone has released their envelope, the person in charge opens all of them and doubles the total placed amount. This value is divided equally among the participants. And so on.

From the point of view of a selfish rational agent, the best option is to put nothing in the envelope. However, if everyone acts the same, no one wins anything. Several such rounds and the game becomes meaningless. However, if only a few participants put (more) coins in the envelope, the difference between the money collected by those who do not contribute and those who do will grow; collaboration by some increases the sum retained by the former, while that of the latter is comparatively reduced. As the contributions are anonymous, no one has to thank anyone and no one can blame anyone for anything. The best option is for everyone to contribute the five coins and the ones they progressively accumulate.

Experiences with this game show subtle results: at the beginning, most contribute about half of the funds received, less than in an ideally cooperative environment, but much more than expected from fully selfish people. However, after several rounds, the contribution will drop at the slightest suspicion that someone is contributing less than the rest. Even so, if there is a way to penalize offenders, cooperation is easily regained (Fehr and Gätchter, 2000). There is no doubt that participants observe each other. It has also been concluded that the cooperative attitude is more evident if players share a given socioeconomic profile, or if third parties are observing them, or if they have to continue interacting in the future.

Another experiment, probably the most famous in economic psychology, is the ultimatum game. Conducted since 1977 by Werner Güth and collaborators, they did not publish this experiment until 1982 (Poundstone, 2010: 112). The game gathers two people at a table, one of whom receives a certain amount of money, for example €100. This person then has to make the other a sharing proposal, both knowing that if the offer is rejected they leave with nothing.

Offering the other participant €1 is a very rational option: they would have to accept it because it is better than nothing. Still, everyone knows that this will not happen. Faced with an offer considered unfair, the other player (who, probably offended, will think: "Do you take me for an idiot?") will opt for retaliation, that is, they will reject the proposal. Numerous experiences worldwide (according to Henrich et al., 2010: 5–7 and Cartwright, 2018: 385–387) indicate that there are few offers below 30%. Those below 20% are almost always rejected. Not surprisingly, more than half of the players usually offer half the money. Most of the rest are between 40% and 50%. There are very few offers above 50% that are not always accepted (see also M. Baddeley, 2013: 82–83 and Thaler, 2015: 142). These results do not change as the quantities involved increase. However, given the limits of experiment budgets, it is not known what would happen if the gamble involved thousands of euros. There are hints that the participant who receives the offer is likely to accept, even if it is proportionally very small (Thaler, 1992: 28; Cameron, 1999).

The almost certain possibility that unequal offers will be rejected makes it advisable to act strategically, i.e., to opt for the decision that avoids retaliation (Angner, 2012: 198). This decision is also often underpinned by moral considerations ("Offers should be fair"). This explains why, when several pairs are involved, if it is established that the money from the unaccepted offers will be shared equally among all participants, the rejection rate does not drop. The retaliated-against participants are not surprised: they admit that the decision contains more ingredients than a mere strategic calculation.[33] Otherwise, if the game is repeated by switching roles of the participants, even in a random order, the bids are quickly concentrated as half and half.

The game also shows the effect of vested rights on equity (Elster, 1991: 117). Thus, if the roles of offeror and acceptor are allocated not randomly, but according to some principle of authority, more unequal splits are tolerated. More dramatic results are obtained when offers are made randomly by a computer: people, who know this, accept them all, no matter how low they are (Blount, 1995). The presence of power or chance makes a difference.[34]

Another variant is when participants play with money they have brought from home. For example, a sum of €100 to which both players have contributed equally. In such cases, any proposal that is not strictly half and half is very likely to be rejected. This is a blunt reaction: it is only acceptable to recover at least €50 (Thaler, 2015: 266).

In the variant known as the dictator game, the other player has to accept the offer made whether they like it or not. In this case, the average offer is lower, but there are still many offers that are (almost) fair. Moreover, equitable offers are more numerous when there are people watching. This circumstance demonstrates the importance of one's own reputation: the participants want to give a good image; they want to show strong social preferences (Poundstone, 2010: 118, Bowles and Gintis, 2013: 44). This attitude is so powerful that it can even occur when no one is looking.

5.1.6.2   The default choice

If there is an initial suggested option, this algorithm opts to choose it. No effort is made. There is no interest in attributes. The algorithm is one of two ways of choosing not to choose: doing so by consent. The other is to choose nothing.

Acceptance by default is explained by reasons such as lack of attention or interest, the urgency to choose, belief that there are no better alternatives within reach, blind trust in the proposal, etc. This heuristic assumes that the person making the default offer knows what is in their best interest and that they formulate the proposal with honest intentions.

The default options are as old as certain social mores. For example, the law in the United States in principle establishes that all people keep their birth surname, but if desired it can be changed upon marriage. Almost no man adopts his wife's surname, but about 80% of women change to their husband's, either exclusively or attached to their maiden name. One reason for doing so is to prevent bureaucratic problems caused by the fact that the parents have different surnames and the children carry only the father's surname. Another case has been that of piercing the earlobes of female babies. In some countries, this option was imposed for years by default (parents were not asked about the issue).

The default choice can be risky. It is reported that in some cities, especially the United States, if a cab fare is paid by card, the customer has to choose between the tipping percentages shown by the system. Although the figures are quite high, very few opt for the option of not adding a tip. In general, the economic world is full of default conditions: they are common, more or less explicitly, in many contracts and agreements. Even though these compromises should merit careful attention (see the deliberative pattern below), people do not have the necessary knowledge, time, negotiating skills, and so on, for this.

As is well known, the data contained in computer networks are subjected to the scrutiny of all kinds of algorithms. Many companies try to predict the lifestyle of internet users and, hence, their choices for all kinds of things (Christl and Spiekermann, 2016). This information is sold to commercial firms and governments. Among the multiple uses that can be made of all this information, improving the effectiveness of the default choices suggested to consumers stands out: big data analytics allows vendors to attach appropriate custom narratives to the default choices.

5.1.6.3 Imitating others

Both animals and humans run away when they see others escaping. It is worth imitating them since the cost of a possible false alarm is less than the cost of being caught and eaten, or being badly injured. Beyond emergencies, in everyday social, political and economic life, people systematically scrutinize the decisions of others and their outcomes. If the latter are satisfactory, why not copy them? For example, although many firms' managers have sophisticated tools for setting prices, empirical studies indicate that, in a context of limited information, the basic criterion is to observe and adjust one's own prices to those of competitors. This approach does not dwell on possible differences in quality and tries not to weaken the image (reputation) of the brand (Rusetski, 2014). Something similar happens when companies decide where to locate their facilities (Berg, 2014b).

The heuristic of imitating others predominates in situations where social interaction takes a strategic form: people's decisions depend closely on the expectations they have about what others will decide. Thomas C. Schelling, already mentioned in Chapter 2, section 2.2, was a pioneer in modeling interdependent behavior. He was not interested in highly regulated interactions, such as those of parlor games, characterized by explicit, unambiguous and exhaustive rules, but in the interactions of everyday life. In this domain, social norms and individual actions are combined, the latter induced by what we believe others will do and, in turn, others decide what to do based on what they believe we will do. The cross-influences between people cause a mutual pulling effect, either through direct observation of behavior or motivated by beliefs about what others will presumably do. All this can lead to an explosive momentum if people end up persuaded that a large majority will act in the same way. The critical mass model developed by Schelling (2006a: 91–110), with contributions from Simon (1954) and Granovetter (1978), attempts to represent the phenomenon.

Technically, the expectation about the behavior of others must exceed a given threshold from which the process feeds back: at the beginning, it is barely self-sustaining; then it starts to grow, first at an accelerated rate and later in a progressively decreasing way; finally, it stops. This dynamic is analogous to a nuclear chain reaction: a certain concentration of a particular isotope is indispensable for the fission to start, then grow explosively on its own and, as the fuel runs out, slow down. Something similar happens with a public event such as a concert, exhibition, conference, etc., where the attendance ends up being massive (the hall is crowded) because everyone, at a given moment, was convinced that everybody would go. However, this gregarious impulse contains two exceptions: the minority of people who will attend regardless of the presumed level of attendance (they probably think it is interesting), and those who, precisely because everyone is expected to go, do not go (a snobbish behavior).

Figure 5.4 presents the basic elements of the critical mass model: there are some people who will participate in any case (the certain attendees, A), some of whom will try to convince others and, together with the promotional effort of the organizers, will spread the belief that the event will be a resounding success. If this expectation holds, the total number of participants is N. Nonetheless, it should be taken into account that there are some people with a snobbish attitude towards the event (B), so the actual number of attendees is slightly lower than the potential number.

The shape of the curve indicates the path of the number of attendees: first, the curve is flat, i.e., the belief that there will be a high number of participants is not strong enough. Above a certain threshold (U) the number of attendees skyrockets as the expectation has reached a point that drags many others along. Eventually, attendance grows at a progressively slower rate until the irreducible group of non-participants is met. The model assumes that people act not because they have the same preferences, share the same beliefs or hold the same information, but by mere imitation of others. Obviously, not all successful events respond to the critical mass mechanism. It may simply happen that participants come under threat, because of the weight of social norms, etc.

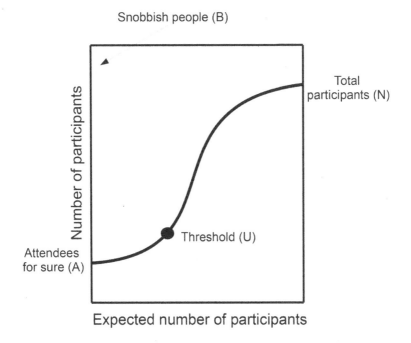

Figure 5.4   *Critical mass model*

The critical mass model, despite its simplicity, describes numerous decisions.[35] In the United States, an experiment consisted of participants downloading their favorite music from the Internet. Some people were previously informed of the download ranking, while others were not. It should be stressed that even the fictitious rankings led people to choose the music tracks they included. This (presumed) popularity made them very popular, regardless of any other considerations (Sunstein, 2009: 47–48). The belief that something will be popular makes it so.[36] It is not uncommon to find people who claim not to have much predilection for a product, or an event, but who buy it, or go, if it seems that many others will. In these cases, if expectation fails, astonishment often overcomes anger. This readiness is also exploited by the commercial stratagem that consists of paying (or giving small gifts to) tens or hundreds of people to queue for hours in front of stores selling a particular new item (software, novel, etc.).

This attracts the attention of pedestrians and, above all, of the media, which spread it all over the world. Marketers expect the display of the (presumed) popularity of the product to attract many other customers: Why are you waiting to buy it? Are you aware that everybody else is doing it too?

As a general conclusion, the algorithm of imitating others facilitates group acceptance. Therefore, it has a strong socialization value. Its search rule is to observe the decisions made by others in a given class of situations (e.g., how to dress). This search can be stopped when the specific choice that best characterizes the group (the right brand of clothing) is identified. The decision rule is to act in the same way, without rushing, but also without delaying.

The critical mass model only describes the self-reinforcing mechanism involved in all social imitation, even in weak modalities. It assumes that imitating the behavior of others is very convenient, although this implies ignoring the cost of this heuristic: it leaves aside other possible alternatives, which remain unexplored or barely known. If the context changes, surprisingly perhaps the people who rejected imitation will end up succeeding. Indeed, the imitation algorithm is ideal as long as things remain stable, but it may lead to inferior outcomes if the context changes. In this case, it might have been better to decide based on one's own experience and knowledge.

5.1.7 Bias in Probability and Randomness

Having reviewed the main heuristics and their algorithms, there are a couple of issues that deserve special attention: people's difficulties in understanding probability and randomness, and the type of experiments that compare the contextual effectiveness of the different heuristics and other choice criteria. The first issue is discussed in the following paragraphs; the second, in subsection 5.1.8.

Among the numerous cognitive errors identified by the heuristics and biases program, a good handful refer to the problems of the human mind to correctly grasp situations with a strong presence of probability and randomness. These were some of the first errors detected by the researchers working on this program. Several decades later, these biases are widely known. However, over the years, more and more voices disagree with such findings.

To begin with, let us take the following question: "Imagine a young man with long hair, fond of reading and writing poetry, and reputed to lead a bohemian life: which is he more likely to be, a violinist or a waiter?" Needless to say, the most common answer is violinist, since people think that the young man has the attributes of an artist. However, in any neighborhood, city or country, there are many more young people working as waiters than as violinists. This error seems to point to the availability heuristic: the answer is based on a cliché, the first argument to emerge from memory. However, if the question were simply:

"Which is a young man more likely to be, a violinist or a waiter?", everyone would have given the correct answer. Faced with this error, analysts of the heuristics and biases program concluded that the human mind has serious difficulties in understanding the notion of probability. However, it is clear that this diagnosis is premature: although the error is unquestionable, it lacks significance. This is a simple linguistic trap: people stumble over the word probable. The common meaning of this concept has no mathematical connotation, but denotes what is plausible or credible. Therefore, people apply the pertinence rule: the description matches that of an artist. The divergence between common and technical language explains why people misinterpret the experiment. Although this refutes the cognitive bias hypothesis, it does not eliminate the observed difficulty people have in correctly interpreting probability (and chance). Fortunately, this problem disappears with minimal training, since it is not caused by a faulty design of the brain circuits, but simply by the mind's tendency to use frequencies.

Before going into the probability issue, a few remarks on clichés could be addressed. As is well known, the human mind is prone to create categories. This facilitates understanding of the world, but it is vulnerable to the trap of clichés, especially if the message is wrapped in appropriate narrative. From this perspective, the above example is also a warning of the susceptibility of judgment to narratives.

Thinking in categories makes it much easier to identify roles and power differentials, which facilitates adaptation to the social environment and provides some ability to anticipate many events. However, the use of this cognitive device implies losing sight of the complexity of people and the nuances of their circumstances. In other words, it can turn categories into stereotypes, or generalizations that grossly oversimplify people's identities. Stereotypes highlight one or more attributes that (presumably) identify the unique and persistent attitudes of human groups (Hogg and Vaughan, 2014: 50–56). Stereotypes are learned without people realizing it, just as fish do not know that they live in a wet environment (according to Aronson's 2008: 324–328 witty analogy). If they become widely shared, stereotypes encourage prejudices that stigmatize and discriminate against entire human groups, such as the following case of subtle sexist prejudice: if a boy is unable to solve a math problem, the teacher attributes it to a particular problem of the student; but if it is a girl who does not know how to solve it, it is a gender fault (shown in Angner, 2012: 93 and sourced from http://xkcd.com/385/).

If prejudices are hostile and aggressive, they can fuel serious social conflicts. Once unleashed, they are difficult to curb, although they never resist the slightest critical approach. They arise at best from extrapolations of isolated cases, certainly not representative, in which information gaps have been filled with more or less nonsensical beliefs, leaving aside proven information. In short, clichés facilitate adaptation to the social environment, but at the risk of oversimplifying it.

The probabilistic fact known as regression to the mean also confuses: it happens that extreme values of variables associated with real events are necessarily followed by less exceptional ones. In other words, sometimes there are better results, sometimes worse (Hand, 2014: 19). Periods of excellent performance of a player (or company profits) are always followed by others with more normal values, a trend which does not mean that the player (or the firm) is in trouble. A student who usually scores between nine and ten out of ten points, at any given time may score eight points, or maybe seven, but rarely 11 points (technically impossible) or three points (an exceptional circumstance that deserves to be explained). Under normal conditions, the results of a good student will oscillate in the top band of the score range and, when not so good a student, in the low band. The fact that a variable undergoes small variations in the vicinity of its average does not mean anything. Kahneman (2011: Chapter 17) illustrates regression to the mean with a noteworthy example: it turns out that highly intelligent women tend to pair up with comparatively less intelligent men. Why? What does it mean? This assessment is spurious. It reflects only a trivial fact: the correlation between spouses' IQs is always less than perfect. The smaller the sample of women, the larger in comparative terms the social circle in which they have found a partner. Then, since IQs have the same distribution in both sexes, it is mathematically inevitable that highly intelligent women will be paired with men who are less intelligent on average. The same is true for highly intelligent men. Also under normal conditions, socioeconomic variables oscillate constantly within a reasonable range. Although this does not indicate any relevant cause, the mind is often committed to looking for it.[37]

Entering into the subject of probability perception, two issues have deserved much attention as a result of several experiments (Gigerenzer and Hoffrage, 1995; Sedlmeier and Gigerenzer, 2001; Martignon et al., 2003; and Gigerenzer, 2015: 24–27):

- Why are frequencies easier to understand than the same information expressed in probabilities?
- Why do probabilities continue to be used without specifying the reference class?

Regarding the first point, imagine that after three mammography campaigns in a given city, the following conclusions were reached:

- Ten out of every 1,000 women had breast cancer.
- Of the ten women with cancer, nine reported a positive test.
- Of the 990 women without cancer, 89 reported a positive test.

Therefore, the test was correct in nine out of ten sick women and in 901 of the 990 who do not have cancer. Consequently, the test failed in one case out of ten sick women (it indicated that they did not have cancer: false negative) and also failed in 89 women who did not develop the disease (i.e., they were false positive). These same results can be expressed as follows:

- The probability of a woman developing breast cancer is 1%.
- If a woman has breast cancer, the probability that the test will be positive is 90%.
- If a woman does not have breast cancer, the probability of obtaining a positive test is 9%.

This second way of exposing the results, that is, in terms of probabilities, is common on applying Bayes' theorem. According to this theorem, the probability that a woman who has tested positive for cancer actually has cancer is obtained from the expression:

$$\frac{0.01 \cdot 0.9}{0.01 \cdot 0.9 + 0.99 \cdot 0.09} = 9.2\%$$

This ratio calculates the probability that the test will be successful (which occurs in 90% of the 1% of cases) and divides it by the sum of this same value and the probability that the test will fail, which happens in 9% of the remaining 99% of women. The result has a double reading: although the test increases the probability of detecting the disease (from 1% to 9.2%), this improvement is far from absolute certainty (there is a 90.8% chance of not being sick).

As noted, the probability-based approach is difficult to assimilate. Conversely, if the results are expressed in frequencies, as on the right-hand side of Figure 5.5, it is easy to conclude that a woman with a positive test may be among the nine people out of 98 (9 + 89) with possible cancer, i.e., 9.2%

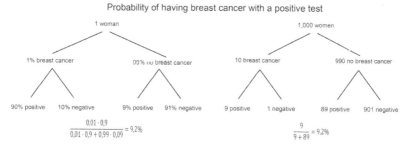

Figure 5.5　　Probabilities versus frequencies

of the presumed cases detected have cancer. Therefore, the vast majority of women with a positive test do not have the disease. The approximate frequency of having breast cancer with a positive test is one in 11 cases.

The result is obviously the same, but the frequency tree makes it easier to understand the impact of evidence that is not perfect, i.e., if the test were always correct, whether or not there is disease, the problem would disappear. Using frequencies it is easy to understand that a positive test does not mean that having the disease is almost certain. Quite the contrary.

It has been known for decades that information expressed in frequencies ("I find snails every fifth time I go out to pick them"), is grasped more quickly than information presented in probabilities ("I find snails 20% of the time I go out to pick them"). To explain this, it is hypothesized that everyday experiences since childhood refer to things that are or are not: no one is 82% dead, just as a woman is never 17.37% pregnant. Evolution has thus created a frequentist mind (Gigerenzer and Hoffrage, 1995: 689) and, consequently, the explanation in probabilistic terms is, from the outset, more confusing: stating that 37 women out of a group of 213 are pregnant preserves the dichotomy of being pregnant or not (37 yes, 176 no), but simply pointing out that there are 17.37% of pregnancies opens the possibility of believing that all are pregnant to that extent, which is absurd. The expression in terms of probability, which superficially underlines the reference group, requires a greater effort of attention. Understanding the percentage values requires a certain amount of training that is not necessary to grasp the same issue expressed in frequencies (Koehler, 1996; Gigerenzer and Edwards, 2003).

Regarding the second issue raised, i.e., the confusion caused by the use of probabilities without specifying the reference class, consider an example concerning the efficacy of mammograms in the prevention of breast cancer. Data are shown in Table 5.12 (adapted from Gigerenzer, 2015: 15–17).

Table 5.12   Mammograms in women aged ≥ 50 years

Participants in mammography campaigns over 10 years		Out of every thousand women without a mammography	Out of every thousand women who had a mammography
Benefits	Women dead from breast cancer	5	4
	Women dead from cancer	21	21
Damage	Women without cancer who experienced false positives	n/a	100
	Women with non-progressive cancer who have undergone unnecessary therapies	n/a	5

The table shows that four out of every 1,000 women aged 50 years or older who passed the tests died from breast cancer in the ten years considered. As can be seen, this is one death less than if the mammography had not been performed. Therefore, the reduction due to the test has been 1‰ for breast cancer and zero for cancers in general. However, this information is often poorly disseminated, which fuels alarmism and leads to useless interventions. To begin with, it can be explained that these tests save many lives each year without indicating the specific magnitude. Moreover, the reduction in relative terms can be highlighted while the absolute values are ignored: instead of indicating that the reduction dropped from 5‰ to 4‰, it is stated that it is 20% (in reality, it is 0.1%). Thirdly, both the proportion represented by breast cancers within the cancers suffered by women and the evolution of this figure are overlooked. Finally, it should be noted that the interpretation of the data may be correct but poorly explained: for example, if the time range of the tests is reduced to two instead of ten years, many may believe that repeat mammograms decisively increase survival. These are four ways of explaining a piece of information that only confuses.

Beyond the table, another common criterion is the survival rate over a given number of years, a figure that, strictly speaking, does not indicate a reduction in mortality. For example, the five-year survival rate is defined as the number of cancer patients alive five years after diagnosis, divided by the total number of patients with that diagnosis. Unfortunately, even if the test advances the detection of the disease, it does not necessarily contribute to extending life, since everything depends on the incubation period of such a cancer.[38]

Another conundrum is the understanding of random phenomena. A first exponent is the gambler's fallacy. Widely studied and debated in economic psychology, it is the belief that the longer a series of identical outcomes has been going on, the more likely it is that a different one will be obtained. For example, after a series of consecutive red numbers in roulette, it is believed that the probability of the ball landing in a black box increases. Or it is believed that, after several tosses of a coin with a heads result, one or more tails are to be expected to offset the series, given that each coin result appears about half of the times. It is also easy to see that, for a while, many people avoid buying the number that has just won a lottery. They consider that the fact that it won the lottery decreases its possibility of winning again, although they are independent draws. Or, finally, there is the case of the couple who, after having two daughters, decide to have a third child because they believe that the probability of it being a boy has increased. Although sooner or later the result will change, this will not be caused by the degree of uniformity of the previous ones. There is no compensation mechanism, but rather a random process in which the different results are grouped into clusters of varying size (Hand, 2014: 49–50).

Let us now consider the following exercise: a coin is tossed ten times in three series obtaining HHTHTTTHTHT, THHHHTHTTH, and THHHHHHHHH with H = heads and T = tails. Then, are all three series random? The most common answer is to doubt whether the last one is random (or, also, whether it is less so than the former). Known as the "law" of small numbers, this (alleged) cognitive fallacy is one of the heuristics and biases program's favorites (Motterlini, 2010: 59; Wilkinson and Klaes, 2012, 121; Hand, 2014: 196). It is argued that people are incapable of realizing that, for a short series of coin flips, the heads and tails composition can be anything. The configuration of the human mind would thus be inadequate to understand randomness correctly. This conclusion is, again, premature (Farmer et al., 2017: 74): people's everyday experience contains only short series, often of varied composition, and therefore the (near) uniformity of results is perceived as something exceptional (a small number of cases out of the total number of possible combinations). Therefore, considering that a (remarkably) homogeneous short series is non-random is not a cognitive bias, but rather an indication of a well-functioning mind since this conclusion derives from inferences built from everyday experience. The problem lies not in the design of the mind, but the simple fact that everyday experience is not sufficient to assess the full scope of the situation at hand. Therefore, some learning is necessary to become aware of the enormous diversity of short series and their unique properties compared to long series. Fortunately, this is a simple learning process. There is no cognitive bias.

Let us take a closer look at this interesting issue (inspired by Hahn and Warren, 2009, and Hahn, 2014: 230–231). Table 5.13 contains all the outcomes that can be obtained by tossing a coin in series of length $n = 4$. What, therefore, is the probability of certain sets of three outcomes, $k = 3$? For instance, looking closely at the table with the 16 possible combinations of heads and tails, the local outcome HHT appears more often than the group HHH. Although the probability of the two groups is the same (4/16), people will notice that HHT appears in four series, that is, in columns 2, 3, 6 and 14, marked with *, while

Table 5.13   Results obtained on tossing a coin in series of four

1	2	3	4	5	6	7	8	9	10	11	12	13	14	15	16
H	H	H	H	T	H	H	T	H	H	T	T	T	T	T	T
H	H	H	T	H	H	T	T	T	T	T	H	T	H	H	T
H	H	T	H	H	T	T	H	H	T	T	T	H	H	T	T
H	T	H	H	H	T	H	H	T	T	H	T	T	T	H	T
#	#,*	*		#	*								*		

Notes: # means there is at least one HHH group. * means there is an HHT group.

the HHH group appears three times, in columns 1, 2 and 5, marked with #. This is because series 1 contains two HHH clusters even though, having ignored the position within the series, people do not distinguish between them. Therefore, the frequency of the HHH cluster is 3/16 = 0.19, while that of HHT is of 4/16 = 0.25. Consequently, a more homogeneous sequence appears less frequently than a more varied one. According to daily experience, the intuition that HHT is more likely than HHH is not completely unfocused. Obviously, the longer the series and the shorter the clustering, the more intense this effect will be.

Everyday life moves in limited environments, where sophisticated statistical tools can hardly be applied. This common experience is, in turn, a fertile ground for the proliferation of heuristic shortcuts (Farmer et al., 2017: 64, and Gigerenzer, 2018). If I go to the market to buy a certain piece of meat and the first two butcher's stalls I visit do not have it, I will ask the others. There is no reason to give up after these first refusals: it was just a coincidence. This conclusion is not affected by the number of butchers in the market (always a limited number). Selecting a sample and estimating the likelihood of finding the desired product is meaningless. The population consists of a manageable number of elements, and therefore experience and intuition are the best tools for making effective decisions. In this domain the statistical methods have a limited application. Coming back to the last example, people know that when a coin is repeatedly tossed four times, the group HHH appears fewer times than HHT. This intuition does not meet the requirements of statistical theory, but the hypothesis suggesting that something is flawed in the human mind does not follow from it. The question is whether everyday decision-making requires the application of rational statistical postulates which, as should be remembered, were unknown for most of mankind's evolution.

The above analysis can be generalized: if k is the length of a set of results and n is a larger sequence, then,

- If $k = n$, assuming that one series is more probable than another is a fallacy. For example, if $k = n = 3$, the series HHT is not more probable than HHH. The eight possible outcomes, i.e., HHH, HHT, HTH, THH, HTT, THT, TTH and TTT, are all equally probable. Misinterpreting this result is a mental bias, although it can be easily corrected.
- If $n > k$, the intuition that more homogeneous results appear less frequently than non-homogeneous ones is correct, as shown above. There is no bias, but rather a contextually rational intuition. Anyone who has witnessed several flips of a coin, with $\infty > n > k$, will observe that clusters with mixed heads and tails are more common than (quite) homogeneous ones. When faced with (fairly) homogeneous series, people express surprise.

Another alleged mental bias is the hot hand effect or the belief that after a series of consecutive baskets, two or three are enough, basketball players are more likely to hit the next shot. This conviction, shared by players, coaches, fans, and the general public, stems from the conventional wisdom that shots are under the control of the players (while the opposite gambler's fallacy deals with random outcomes). The hot hand belief was also quickly labeled as a fallacy (Gilovich et al., 1985). This conclusion was reached after analyzing NBA players' performance data and results coming from a controlled free throw experiment. It was observed that, after small clusters of the same result (basket or miss), the next shot changed. The series of alternating basket and miss led to the conclusion that people misunderstand random sequences. There was no hot hand effect: players do not dominate the game at will since their moments of fortune (or repeated failure) were just random. However, this conclusion is surprising: after thousands and thousands of games, did no one ever realize that the belief in streaks did not favor teams at all?

The work of Gilovich and colleagues received two criticisms. On the one hand, the mathematical treatment of the data was unsatisfactory, as was highlighted by Miller and Sanjurjo (2018), demonstrating that the probability of hitting consecutively, i.e., being on a streak, is lower than the probability of scoring by simply shooting at the basket. On the other hand, several authors insisted that the hot hand is mainly a psychological issue: if a player scores momentarily above their average, it is convenient to pass them the ball to take advantage of their enthusiasm (or not to pass the ball if the player is on a bad streak). It is necessary to facilitate (prevent) players continuing to hit (miss), since the conviction of being on a roll predisposes them to excel in the game (or else to retire). Trying to take advantage of this psychological effect is an adaptive stratagem: a player's performance in a game (a variable very different from their performance over time), makes it easier for coaches and players to know who to pass the ball to (Wilke and Clark Barrett, 2009; Bocskocsky et al., 2014; Gigerenzer, 2015: 173–175; Raab and Gigerenzer, 2015: 3–4). However, if a player is on a good run, the opposing players will mark them more closely, which will easily put an end to the hot hand effect. For this reason, the phenomenon was analyzed in volleyball because there is no physical contact between players. As expected, the randomness of the streaks was ratified, although in this game they went unnoticed, and thus no beliefs emerged in this regard. In short, the hot hand effect cannot be seen as a fallacy. It is simply a heuristic that is effective when there is a strong correlation between the streak episodes and the overall average number of hits, the latter figure being unknown.

5.1.8   Comparing the Quality of Inferences

Numerous studies are devoted to comparing the predictive capacity of heuristics with each other, as well as with other more sophisticated inference methods, often of a statistical character, such as linear regression, among others (see, for example, Payne et al., 1988; Martignon and Hoffrage, 2002; Marewski et al., 2010b: 288–290; and Buckmann and Şimşek, 2016). In this section, a classic experiment is reviewed in some detail on the contextual validity of the take-the-best algorithm, which is also compared with the quality of inferences from other algorithms (Gigerenzer and Goldstein, 1996: 654–660). There are many similar works, and therefore the present section is only the first approach. Whoever is highly interested in heuristic inference, its virtues and its limitations, must master the design and evaluation of this type of experiment.

To illustrate the degree of certainty of attribute-based inferences, a simulation was performed with nine binary attributes (having a first division soccer team, being a state capital, having been part of the former East Germany, having strong industrial activity, showing or not showing a single letter on car license plates, having a high-speed train station, organizing large trade fairs, being the capital of the federation and having a university) of $n = 83$ German cities with more than 100,000 inhabitants (from 1993 census data). According to Gigerenzer and Goldstein (1996), a + sign was assigned when the city in question met an attribute and a − sign when it did not. In total, there were $9 \times 83 = 747$ attribute values. With this information, the performance of the take-the-best algorithm was tested by inferring which of the two paired cities had more inhabitants. In total, there were 3,403 non-repeating pairs.[39] Since there were nine attributes, the total number of possible city pairs exceeded 30,000.

The first step was to verify that the different cues had different contextual validity, i.e., the relative frequency with which an attribute correctly predicts the target variable (having more inhabitants). For example, in all pairs in which one of the cities had a premier league soccer team but the other did not, 87% of the time this attribute also corresponded to the city with more inhabitants. In the experiment, the frequency with which an attribute predicted a larger population ranged from absolute certainty (the case of Berlin being the capital and the most populated city) to others in which the coincidence barely exceeded that of the random response (in 51% of the pairs with a city forming part of the former East Germany, it had more inhabitants).

High contextual validity is useful in making predictions, but it is insufficient. It is also necessary for the cues to show a high discrimination ratio, d_i.

This is the relative frequency with which attributes distinguish between objects of any given pair, i.e.,

$$d_i = \frac{2x_i y_i}{1 - \frac{1}{n}}$$

x_i and y_i being the relative frequencies of the positive and negative values of the attributes, respectively, and n the number of items. For example, within the set of $n = 83$ cities, the attribute of being the capital of a federated state includes 15 cities, that is, $x = 15/83$, and 68 cities that are not, $y = 68/83$, so $d = 0.3$. The highest value is $d = 0.51$ for the cue "having a university" and the lowest is $d = 0.02$ for being "capital of the federation." This means that the attribute "having a university" is quite frequent in the sample and it is, therefore, a solid basis for making inferences.

The second step was to simulate partial knowledge, which can take the following two forms:

- The degree of recognition of the objects involved, that is 83 cities. The simulation considered from knowing nothing about any to recognizing them all, which means a total of 84 categories: 0, 1, 2, ... 81, 82 and 83 cities.
- The level of recognition of the attributes associated with these cities. In the simulation, six levels were assumed: 0%, 10%, 20%, 50%, 75% and 100%.

The combination of these two sources of partial knowledge resulted in $6 \times 84 = 504$ different types of people. Then, for each of these types, 500 hypothetical people were simulated, the difference in whom of the number of cities and attributes they recognized was random. Given the 3,403 two-by-two combinations of cities, the product $3,403 \times 84 \times 6 \times 500$ yielded a total of 857.556 million simulated tests.

To achieve a realistic implementation of the recognition heuristic, across all possible city pairs, simulated people had to recognize a higher number of cities than those they did not recognize. This ratio was established from a test answered by 26 students at the University of Chicago: in all possible comparisons, they recognized the city with the larger population 80% of the time. Therefore, simulations were run with pairs of cities (for each level of recognition) in which the recognized ones outperformed the unknown ones in about 80% of cases. The result was the curves in Figure 5.6 (adaptation of Gigerenzer and Goldstein, 1996: 656).

The figure shows on the vertical axis the proportion of correct inferences of the take-the-best algorithm for each number of recognized cities, shown on the abscissa axis (from 0 to 83 cases). It also indicates the degree of knowledge

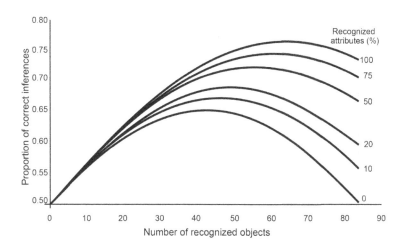

Figure 5.6   Correct inferences about the population of German city-pairs applying the take-the-best algorithm

of the attributes (the six levels mentioned above). Each curve contains 6 × 84 points indicating the average proportion of correct inferences made by the 500 simulated people, i.e., 3,403 inferences each. Among the results shown in Figure 5.6, the following are noteworthy:

- When the number of recognized cities is zero, whatever the level of knowledge of the attributes, the choice of the largest city in each pair is made randomly. Therefore, the proportion of correct inferences is 0.5. The six curves representing the degrees of knowledge of the attributes converge on this value.
- The lower curve represents a null degree of attribute recognition, i.e., the case corresponding to the recognition algorithm. Surprisingly, the simulated people achieve correct inferences 2/3 of the time when they recognize about half of the total number of cities. This proportion drops as more cities become familiar. Thus, the level of correctness of the recognition algorithm is very remarkable, while the less-is-more effect is obvious.
- For the remaining degrees of recognition of the attributes, the take-the-best algorithm comes into action. The proportion of correct inferences increases progressively, reaching a maximum of 77% for the curve corresponding to simulated people who recognize all attributes of 60–70 cities.
- In all degrees of recognition of the attributes, the proportion of correct inferences decreases for higher numbers of recognized cities. Therefore, the take-the-best heuristic also shows the less-is-more effect: knowing

more about more cities does not prevent a worsening level of accuracy. Even so, it is observed that the less-is-more effect takes a progressively less pronounced form (shorter downward sections) and narrower intervals for the number of recognized cities.

The simulation aimed to compare the predictive performance of the take-the-best algorithm against other inference methods, some of which involve complex computations (Gigerenzer and Goldstein, 1996: 656–660; Gigerenzer and Brighton, 2009). Specifically, the comparison concerned the algorithms of simple and weighted tallying and three regression models. In all cases, these algorithms were implemented considering all attributes of the German cities, including the degree of recognition. All these data were handled according to their rules. Leaving aside the details, in the case of the tallying algorithms, the positive values of all attributes were summed up. Then, in each of the possible pairs, the city with the highest value was chosen. If there was a tie, it was chosen at random. For example, with the data in Table 5.2 above, from pair (a, b), b is chosen because it has 3 points, while a has only 2. The peculiarity of the weighted tallying algorithm is that the positive value of each attribute is multiplied by its contextual validity. Coming back to Table 5.2, assuming that the recognition contextual validity is 0.8 and that the validity of the cues decreases (0.9, 0.8, 0.7, 0.6 and 0.5), in pair (a, b) b will be chosen because it has $2.3 = 1 - 0.8 + 1 - 0.8 + 1 - 0.8 + 1 - 0.7$ points, versus $1.7 = 1 - 0.8 + 1 - 0.9$ for option a. Negative values of the attributes were ignored. Only positive evidence was considered.

The linear models were applied as follows:

- The unit-weight linear model is similar to the tallying algorithm. The difference is that it assigns the value 1 when the city has the attribute, a, -1 when it does not, and 0 when it is unknown. The decision criterion is the resulting sum. Thus, in the pair (a, b) in Table 5.2, the choice is random since a has $1 = 2 - 1$ points and b has $1 = 3 - 2$ points.
- The weighted linear model evaluates the attributes in the same way as the previous algorithm, but it multiplies them by their contextual validity. Returning again to the pair (a, b) in Table 5.2, the choice falls on a ($1 = 0.8 = 0.8 + 0.9 + 0 - 0.7 + 0 + 0 + 0$) rather than b ($0.8 = 0.8 - 0.9 + 0.8 + 0.7 - 0.6 + 0$). In Gigerenzer and Goldstein (1996: 657), it is recalled that this algorithm has often been suggested as the optimal one for implementing preference-based choices.
- The multiple regression integrates all the information on the nine considered attributes plus the degree of recognition (equal to 0.8), to calculate $6 \times 84 \times 500$ sets of regression coefficients, one for each simulated person. Concerning the cities and attributes that a simulated person did not recog-

nize, a cue value equal to the average of those corresponding to the cities they did recognize was applied. It should be added that this algorithm, unlike all the others, includes the population of the cities in its calculations. Each simulated individual estimates the population of the cities of the pairs according to the weights obtained in the regressions.

The results appear in Figure 5.7, which also comes from Gigerenzer and Goldstein (1996: 559). The figure shows four trajectories: the upper solid trace corresponds to the proportion of correct inferences of the take-the-best algorithm when the person knows 100% of the attributes. This trajectory is also that of the tallying algorithms. The dashed curve, which largely overlaps the previous one, shows the degree of correctness of the multiple regression. As can be seen, the success ratio is slightly higher when the number of recognized cities is below half. Finally, the lower dashed curve with a sigmoid shape indicates the degree of accuracy of the two linear models. As expected, when the number of recognized cities is zero or total, all the algorithms considered, except the recognition algorithm (lower continuous curve), coincide.

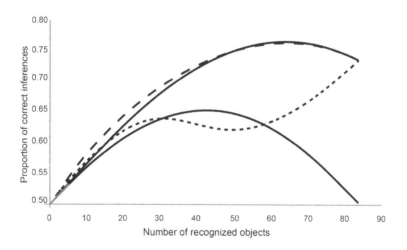

Figure 5.7   *The comparison of algorithms*

Three general results are noteworthy:

- If no city is recognized, all algorithms converge at the randomness level (0.5).

- If the knowledge about the objects and their attributes is total, heuristics achieve many correct inferences equal to that of the most sophisticated algorithms, although at a much lower cost in terms of resources and time.
- The simple regressions, which do not exploit the principle of recognition which has a high correlation with the target variable (the population), are very imprecise. Fortunately, this principle is implicit in the tallying algorithms.

Additionally, in an attempt to show their flexibility, the authors proposed variants of the minimalist and take-the-last algorithms (Gigerenzer and Goldstein, 2011a: 79–80). The former, given a dual choice, applies the recognition heuristic and, only on the assumption that both choices are recognized, the various attributes are randomly sorted (without replacement). For instance, among (*a*, *b*) in Table 5.2, the five cues would be scrolled through in any order: if the attention is focused on the first one, *a* is chosen; if it falls on the fifth one, since it does not discriminate, it is necessary to move to another cue; if attribute three is considered, *b* is chosen. This is an algorithm that follows intuition: although all the brands are familiar, given that very little is known about their attributes, the one with a prominent cue is chosen, by intuiting that this indicates a superior value. It is like buying photographic equipment when, beyond identifying a few brands, people do not know anything about the characteristics of the devices. Therefore, they end up choosing the model that presents an attribute that points in the direction of supposedly being better. The inability to evaluate attributes can result in very poor choices. In the take-the-last algorithm, once the objects have been recognized, people retain the value of the last attribute considered and, if it does not discriminate, move back to the previous value and so on. For example, the consumer knows how to evaluate the attributes of the photographic equipment and chooses the first model in which one stands out, after inspecting all the attributes from the last one considered.

It is common practice to compare the accuracy of predictions made by all types of algorithms. Heuristic algorithms, once contextual adequacy is ensured, are usually equally or more accurate than more sophisticated ones. Handling a high volume of information, if possible, does not ensure more robust predictions.

5.2   DELIBERATION AND COMPENSATORY CALCULATIONS

On September 19, 1772, Benjamin Franklin, then settled in London, replied to a letter that, a few days earlier, had been sent to him by the scientist Joseph Priestley. The latter asked him for advice on how to choose between two alternatives: to accept a job as a librarian offered by a British lord or to reject it.

Franklin responded not by telling him what to do, but by proposing a method for making a choice. In essence, he suggested making an exhaustive list of pros and cons of the proposed job, drawn up without any haste (over several days, if necessary). Priestley then had to assign a value to each element on the list and proceed to eliminate items (one or more) from both sides of the list whose total weight was the same. Nothing was to stop this deletion process, since its goal was to identify the column (either the pros or the cons) that, in the end, still contained any item. This column, whose elements had not been fully eliminated, indicated the decision to be made, i.e., whether to accept or reject the job offer. In short, Franklin proposed applying a weighting and adding algorithm framed in a deliberative pattern (Gigerenzer et al., 1999: 76; Todd and Gigerenzer, 2012: 12–14). In the absence of further specification, Franklin presumably applied this procedure in his everyday life (Aronson, 2008: 120).

Priestley had to compare the attributes of the job he was doing with those of the new one he had been offered. Some were quite similar, others hardly commensurable. This heterogeneity did not stop Franklin from placing them all on the same plane and weighting them (not necessarily equally). Thus, the trait of enjoying a higher salary could be contrasted with the discomfort of having to live far from the city, while access to a large library could offset the affliction of losing old friendships. Nonetheless, if the recommendation is interpreted strictly, Priestley's main challenge was to inventory, regardless of heterogeneity, as many attributes as possible. Making an exhaustive list was a cumbersome task. Luckily, the ensuing weighting and linear combination of the elements was straightforward. Still, what probably troubled Priestley most was the unique and predictably irreversible character of the decision. Not only did it change his personal life, but trying to override it would probably be a process fraught with difficulties and uncertainty (Earl, 1995: 103): Will it be possible to get the old job back? Will it be possible to find a similar one? Everyone faces decisions like Priestley's, i.e., singular decisions that change the state of (one's) world and, even if there is the possibility of going back, leave their mark forever. This profound impact perhaps explains Franklin's response: aware of the consequences of the decision, he proposed a method that would consider and weigh all its pros and cons. After a thorough evaluation of the information, this algorithm would determine whether the offer was worthwhile. Franklin was smart enough to know that this calculation might not lead to the best choice, but he also knew how important it is to know how to handle the psychological impact of such decisions, especially if things did not go as expected.

The algorithm of systematically weighting and comparing the cues of the different options was already discussed some pages ago. This explanation is fully valid, but now some important requirements are added to accommodate it to the deliberative pattern of decision-making. Namely:

- An exhaustive and detailed collection of attributes is made. However, while some are easy to identify, others can only be partially and/or imperfectly known. Their comprehensive management will require the incorporation of quite a few assumptions.
- This deliberative effort is supposed to cancel the influence of emotions and expectations. Still, it is difficult to achieve this.
- Even if he decides to change jobs, Franklin's friend will not be able to avoid surprises that alter the state of the world (such as the sudden death of his aristocratic protector). Just as it may also happen that a visit by a lord's powerful friend boosts Priestley's career even further. In brief, the algorithm, however meticulous it may be, cannot foresee all the innumerable fortuitous circumstances that may occur. Uncertainty undermines the efficiency of the algorithm.

The deliberative effort can bypass neither contingency (the lord's friend's visit is an unexpected opportunity to be seized by the mere fact of being in the right place at the right time) nor chance (a myriad of unforeseen events) (Earl, 1986: 179–182, 205).

At this point, three other important aspects of deliberative decision-making should be emphasized:

- With this pattern, people strive to incorporate the maximum number of attributes and options for close inspection. As is evident, the number of two-by-two comparisons increases rapidly as the number of cues increases. In an experiment in which people were asked to choose, given their purchasing power, between four car models according to certain attributes (acceleration, equipment, fuel consumption, etc.), it was concluded that with up to four features per vehicle, or 16 elements in total, people were able to consider them in detail (with about three minutes to do so). However, on the one hand, as the number of attributes increased, the deliberative performance dropped rapidly. At 12 per car, 48 elements in total, people were completely overwhelmed. The same was true if, on the other hand, they were distracted in such a way that they found it difficult to concentrate on the task. In this situation, they chose by intuition, leading to the suspicion that they only retained the attributes they were most interested in. Interestingly, the results of the intuitive choice (a heuristic) were similar to those of a deliberative process (Dijksterhuis et al., 2006; Motterlini, 2014: 105). Thinking too much about the next move also increases the chance of being wrong in many board games. With experience, players develop a collection of mental patterns to understand the game state based on a few meaningful cues and, hence, make a rapid and insightful decision. This expertise is housed in the unconscious part of the mind and is key to success. Ultimately, with any "large world" choice, we must be aware that the profusion of elements facilitates the appearance of cumbersome trade-offs, after having borne important direct and opportunity costs of accumulating information (Elster, 2010: 37–38).

• This type of mental effort is not necessarily linked to major personal decisions. For example, a job proposal, the choice of a career, institutionalizing a relationship, or having a child, are decisions that do not require attentive exploration of the consequences. At the same time, nothing prevents the deliberative pattern from being applied to the possible purchase of a common good or service, especially if it has a comparatively high cost and long-term effects. This would be the case, for example, of the purchase of a house with a mortgage.

• The procedural boundaries of deliberative reflection are not precise. Although this exhaustive and demanding method involves several stages, described below, the rigor and systematics with which they are applied can vary greatly. In any case, there is no such thing as a perfect deliberative process, i.e., one that allows people to understand the decision perfectly, inexorably leading to the optimal choice. It should be pointed out that the presence of aspects that are difficult to elucidate and/or impossible to foresee does not invalidate the deliberative effort, but does limit its effectiveness. As de la Rochefoucauld warned: "To know things well, we must know their details and, as these are almost infinite, our knowledge is always superficial and imperfect." Whereas the effort required for deliberative decision-making can take many forms, none of them meets the demanding conditions of perfect rationality (Earl, 1995: 68). This decision pattern is not the applied version of the postulates of perfect rationality: the advocates of deliberative effort were around long before this theory. Deliberation is often presented as a roadmap for making better decisions than would be made without applying its algorithms, though always avoiding the use of the label 'optimal decisions' (see Hammond et al., 2002).

The deliberative process involves numerous steps, all aimed at ensuring a detailed diagnosis of the choice in progress (adaptation of Hammond et al., 2002; Raiffa et al., 2002: 14–52; and Spetzler et al., 2016):

1. Clarify the content of the decision process.
2. Specify the objectives.
3. Imagine alternative possibilities.
4. Explore, understand and weigh consequences.
5. Clarify dilemmas and opportunity costs.

6.   Manage uncertainty.
7.   Assess risks and willingness to assume them.
8.   Do not lose sight of the connections between successive decisions.

A correct formulation of the decision to be made influences the final choice. This involves the analysis of the decision context, the specification of the options, and, finally, the outline of the consequences. It is essential to prevent careless (is the available information credible?), incomplete (are there elements that are ignored?), and imprecise formulations (or confusing information). It is argued that clarifying the terms of the decisions to be made is also a way of creating new opportunities. In reality, the aim is to reduce decisions to their key elements, which makes it easier to focus on them appropriately. Nonetheless, isolating the key aspects is a necessary but not sufficient condition for carefully and effectively managing the decision processes.

Specifying the content and number of objectives helps the decision process enter into a positive feedback loop: it helps to determine the information to seek and, if necessary, to evaluate it with third parties. Making a list of objectives can be a great help. It is also recommended that people do not forget to ask themselves what others would have done in their place or review situations they have already experienced, or ask others about similar cases.

The setting of objectives is not the same as knowing what alternatives exist. Normally, decisions involve fairly narrow sets of options. Regardless of their size, since it is not possible to choose outside the set of available options, imagining new alternatives implies approaching the decision from another point of view. In any case, in a deliberative algorithm, it is advisable never to choose an alternative that has not been thoroughly examined. For example, it is considered highly inadvisable to choose the default option. As already indicated, this is an alternative that someone else, more or less disguising their interests, has proposed. People immersed in a deliberative process must always avoid this trap, looking for imaginative ways to achieve their goals.

Deliberation requires assessing the merits of each option, i.e., its specific consequences, which should be described and understood as well as possible. This does not make the choice obvious but may prevent surprises. Much of the deliberative effort is devoted to analyzing the implications of the different options, although it is not feasible to fully guess the consequences before making the choice (Hammond et al., 2002: 105). For instance, it is possible to rent a car of the brand a person wants to buy or test it with a provisional license plate. However, this has a cost and does not eliminate surprises with the specific one purchased. In general, consequences can also be weighed against the worst case or the best one.

The more objectives and/or options there are, the more trade-offs are likely to exist: if one option is better than another about some attributes, but worse concerning others, since no option is superior, which one should be chosen? As this problem currently hinders the decision process, it is advisable to eliminate options to reduce the number of trade-offs, if feasible. Another trick is to quantify the attributes and, hence, the options, even though, as a rule, only an ordinal arrangement is possible instead of quantification. Something similar happens when it comes to assessing opportunity costs (Schwartz, 2016: 126): it is often unclear how to specify them, i.e., what benchmark to set.[40]

Major decisions are made embedded in uncertainty. Although it cannot be eliminated, people can try to accommodate the uncertainty by assigning probabilities to the consequences. This stratagem turns the choice into a matter of calculated risk. Even so, subjective probabilities neither dispel uncertainty, as noted above, nor does it disappear by deploying decision trees, gathering more information, asking more experts, and so on. Additionally, the delay in making a decision may have a cost, such as, for example, the loss of one or more of the options. Nevertheless, the accumulated experience should not be underestimated, although in personal and professional life major decisions are often singular. Inevitably, the irreducible nature of uncertainty gives any non-trivial decision the air of a gamble. As for risk, things are different since there are numerous methods for assessing it. However, their application does not exclude the interference of people's particular degree of tolerance of it. As is well known, when faced with risk, it is advisable to seek more information and diversify one's options. It is also feasible to share risks and take out insurance. Be that as it may, analysts in favor of the deliberative method propose reinforcing it with the use of sophisticated data processing techniques such as statistical regression, factor analysis, neural networks, etc. The goal is to unveil the underlying structure of the available information to obtain new evidence. This tactic clashes with the bias/variance problem discussed above.

There are almost no isolated decisions. The vast majority are influenced by those of the past and, in turn, have an impact on those to be made in the future. There is a continuum of decisions: current decisions are based on an irrevocable past, while future ones are difficult to foresee. The interconnections between successive decisions can become very complex. It is neither easy to think backward from the future nor is it free of surprises. If a couple, for example, decide to move to a residential area far from the city center where they work, they will have undoubted benefits, but also related costs. They may have a more spacious house and the neighborhood may be very quiet, but the daily commute will be long (because of the distance and traffic jams) and expensive (because of tolls and parking). This can be detrimental to personal and family life. There is no doubt that a decision made today influences tomorrow's decisions: Will the school for the children be a local one, or will they have to travel to the city? Who will then be in charge of transport? And so on. In the same way, tomorrow's decisions (is it better for children to play in the street or the garden?) affect today's decisions (what should the garden be like? Is a swimming pool necessary?). The elements and their interconnections can be enormously complex.

The literature that spreads the virtues of the deliberation pattern considers the reduction of cognitive errors in decision-making as one of its strengths. Consequently, these authors appreciate the approach to heuristics and biases (see, for example, Bazerman, 1988). This explains why they regard heuristics as an unreliable cognitive tool, although they do not despise it. In essence, proponents of the deliberative pattern conceive of decision-making as a sophisticated blend of science and art that relies on the systematic search for information and the maintenance of consistency throughout the process. These two qualities are regarded as necessary and sufficient to make good choices (see Hammond et al., 2002: xii, 4, 14, 70). As was to be expected, this vision is undoubtedly successful among managers and executives of business and public administration, including consulting experts. The reason is easy to understand: its implementation avoids appearing to improvise and preserves creativity, two assets highly appreciated by higher-ranking people in professional domains. A balanced combination of rigor and originality is a key condition for an upward career path. Nonetheless, the exhaustive application of a deliberative procedure is too cumbersome. In the case of many everyday decisions, this paraphernalia is even absurd. That is why popular wisdom is in favor of not rushing ("Count to ten before deciding") instead of long deliberative sessions. There is a feeling that procrastination can mean missing opportunities. As for decisions with far-reaching personal implications, people, overwhelmed by the magnitude of the task, end up making choices guided by intuition (i.e., heuristics) and affective predictions (mentioned in Chapter 4, section 4.2.2). Still, there is no doubt that different adaptations (or algorithms) of systematic and detailed reflection are very much present in everyday life. Thus, people often meditate on whether or not to file a lawsuit or debate what to wear to the important social event to which they have been invited.

5.3   TRANSFERRING THE POWER TO DECIDE

Table 5.1 on the inventory of decision-making patterns, methods, and algorithms also includes cases in which people give up deciding for themselves. There are the following two situations:

- Random choice: people choose the option indicated by a device that generates results by chance, such as tossing a coin (in case of a dual choice), a die, spinning a wheel that moves freely, etc. Each of these mechanisms can be considered a variant of the random choice algorithm.

- Voluntarily and explicitly transferring the capacity to choose to another person or entity. Strictly speaking, this assignment cannot constrain the free will of the person who chooses instead of the transferor. In doing so, the latter assumes the preferences, expectations, information, beliefs, etc. of the former. Something similar happens when the choice is mediated by a mathematical algorithm: the transferor indirectly accepts the positions of the software owner. Since people do not ask strangers for advice (they would probably be perplexed), the person who chooses instead of the main subject is previously chosen based on all sorts of reasons and interests.[41] Moreover, loss aversion is often a powerful reason for leaving the decision in the hands of someone else (Tomer, 2017: 45).

Chance has always determined more than a few decisions (see Elster, 1991: 56). There are playful ones, such as drawing lots for a gift among the members of a club, but there are also more serious ones, such as drawing lots for social housing or breaking a tie in a vote. Leaving a decision to chance is a procedure that does not usually generate conflict, although it does not prevent disappointment. Chance is also used to establish the order of things, as when a coin decides which side of the stadium teams will play on, or the pairings in a tournament. In Greek and Roman antiquity, the wheel of fortune was even used to assign public posts (Elster, 1991: 70). Beyond history, this algorithm can be applied to both parametric and strategic decisions (Elster, 1991: 69):

- Parametric decisions are those that do not deserve special attention, which is why randomness is used. It may be a choice between two cans of the same soft drink, or in a clinical trial to decide which group of patients will receive the new treatment and which just a placebo.
- In those considered strategic, randomness is the last option. In the face of complexity and uncertainty, the decision is made randomly. Perhaps in these cases, there is the possibility of applying a given heuristic so that the agent must first choose between this and randomness.

Randomized devices are rarely used in individual decisions. It is admitted that they were used even less often. On the one hand, if the choice was a success, most prefer to attribute it to their skills: even those who have won the first prize in a lottery (a purely coincidental event) believe that they had foreseen it. On the other hand, if it was a failure, how to rationalize it? The person will be accused of being frivolous and reckless for having relied on chance. Moreover, it should not be forgotten that there are random decisions that are not random: if a hiker does not know which of two paths leads to a certain destination, taking the one that shows cues of having been the most used is not a random choice (Elster, 1991: 65). It results from an inference, probably belonging to tallying heuristics. For example, observing ocean currents and tracking seabirds, among other cues, was a heuristic successfully employed by Polynesian navigators in their expansion across the Pacific Ocean throughout the first millennium AD (Finney and Low, 2008).

In the future, and partly already happening, the use of third parties in decision-making may take a form never seen before: recommendations on what to choose will come from algorithms linked to commercial interests. As is well known, a simple app is enough to connect people to a complex digital network. It permanently collects huge amounts of personal data (on location, physical condition, card purchases, contacts, planned agenda, etc.), which is combined with information from cameras and sensors installed everywhere (on computers, telephones, streets, cars, cell phones, homes, etc.). There are even data provided voluntarily by users. Once submitted to the relentless scrutiny of algorithms and artificial intelligence systems that look for all kinds of correlations and regularities, although not causes, people and their lifestyles are strictly classified (Gigerenzer, 2022: 122–123). This information is then likely to be sold to personalized advertising companies and, especially in the present case, to firms that promote individual assistance software (apps) for all kinds of issues. This intrusion into personal life has been described as "Big Other", rather than "Big Brother," because of the predominance of private for-profit companies (Christl and Spiekermann, 2016: 129). The advice its users receive ranges from choosing restaurants to possible medical treatments, not to mention the assessments of people recently met through a web search. However, algorithms and deep neural networks, although unrivaled in processing huge amounts of data and images, in well-defined situations, i.e., with known and stable rules, as in the game of chess, their performance outperforms humans, they never actually have a concept of the objects and the relationships between them, so they fail in the face of uncertainty (ill-defined problems and changing rules) and cannot capture the richness of human personality, even assuming that data are correct, which is usually not the case (Gigerenzer, 2022: 38, 104–108). Despite these constraints, digital widgets and the linked software may end up being the most frequently used procedure in making many daily (personal and professional) decisions. It will then be the interests of the data and algorithm owners that will guide the choices.

NOTES

1.   Only individual decisions have been considered. The table does not make explicit the singularities of group decisions. Although the algorithms are fully valid since, after all, groups are made up of individuals, collective decisions also require some mechanism for settlement and compliance. These aspects are not addressed in these pages.
2.   This is the usual situation since one of the alternatives is always to leave things as they are. Additionally, major decisions are normally sequential rather than

simultaneous. For example, almost no one ever receives two job offers at the same time (which adds up to three options with the possibility of not accepting either of them). Incidentally, this leaves little room for a maximizing algorithm (Poundstone, 2010: 213).

3. The capacity for language has evolved by natural selection, although knowing which words refer to which objects is a cultural learning process.

4. The ability of people to catch flying objects, such as a ball, has a clear evolutionary background since it is also displayed by birds and many insects.

5. It has great implications: attentive observation of the behavior of others is a prerequisite for cooperation since it establishes their reputation (or the respect they deserve). All this encourages imitation.

6. In the literature, the terms recognition heuristic and algorithm are used interchangeably. In these pages, the recognition algorithm has been called the imprint.

7. Although people may have a fairly exhaustive knowledge of many different things, such as soccer league results, celebrity adventures, hiking trails, manga authors, and so on, nobody ever knows everything. This circumstance is not unrelated to the social circles in which people develop their lives. Applying the imprint algorithm will be inevitable sooner rather than later.

8. High returns have also been found for portfolios comprising recognized stocks, although the results are not conclusive (Gigerenzer and Gaissmaier, 2011: 461).

9. For instance, if the recognition is based on visual input, the retina captures the light rays instantaneously, although the images take about 65 ms (milliseconds) to settle. The interpretation by the visual area of the brain adds another 200 ms and its arrival at consciousness requires a further 100 ms; in total, about 400 ms. With training, this lapse can be reduced by half. The heuristic of fluency, although not instantaneous, does not take long to obtain a result.

10. A variant is the exercise in which people must identify an object that has been previously presented to them from a list. This tests the ability of people to retain information in the memory.

11. Establishing a ranking causes one of the attributes to prevail in the end (Goldstein and Gigerenzer, 2002; Gigerenzer and Goldstein, 2011a; and Gigerenzer and Gaissmaier, 2011: 463).

12. There is no compensation between attributes: an acceptable value in one or more attributes does not compensate for the deficiencies of one or more others. Therefore, the algorithm has a lexicographic character.

13. In Artinger et al. (2022: 615) this fast-and-frugal tree has been published without this third cue. Unfortunately, this simplification overshadows the interesting debate on the virtues and limits of the algorithm, as it appears in the original paper. Moreover, this discussion highlights that much research is still pending in economics and management to determine the extent of the use of fast-and-frugal trees.

14. As recently indicated, the maximum gain probability (p_M) has no relevant role in the algorithm.

15. The option to gain €100 is the minimum and maximum winnings at the same time. It is certain.

16. If this person had ruled out cakes without chocolate, i.e., the other ingredients do not matter in the absence of chocolate, they would have established a hierarchy of attributes. Therefore, this person would be applying a lexicographic algorithm.

17. If one attribute had an outsized weight, for example, 40 points for the neighborhood, the choice would have been closer to the one-good-reason heuristic. With

the above figures, house 4 would have been chosen. In any case, this is a surprising case because the inclusion of the rest of the attributes in the choice process does not make sense.

18.   Although it is more difficult to read the ranking obtained, it was preferred to arrange the countries in alphabetical order. This rule dispels any suspicion of preference for a particular algorithm and the associated ranking.

19.   A quantity is called linear if its total measure is the sum of its parts: the income of a family is the sum of the income of its members, but capital at compound interest does not grow linearly.

20.   No one, and no algorithm, has been able to accurately calculate the degree of risk (Thaler, 2015: 230–236 and 2016). Since it is not possible to obtain robust and reliable information about risk in an environment embedded in uncertainty, risk distribution is incorporated into models as a heroic assumption.

21.   Obviously, the worst models are those with numerous parameters estimated from small sample sizes. Surprisingly, they are not rare in economic research.

22.   Simon's eagerness to design computer models of decision-making led him to draw an analogy between cognition and computation (Gigerenzer, 2020: 1368), as well as to insist more on procedure than on results. However, in his enormous and varied work, psychology always occupied a secondary place (see Rubinstein, 1998: 21 and Mirowski, 2002: 460–472).

23.   It should be noted that Simon provided slightly different definitions of bounded rationality and *satisficing* terms throughout his career. In turn, the two research programs in economic psychology have interpreted these concepts differently. Much more information is in Artinger et al. (2022: 599–612).

24.   Interestingly, learning from failures is much less incentivized, although it would probably be equally or more illustrative. However, it is not easy to obtain information about them and talking about them is often embarrassing. Moreover, cases in which similar actions led to failure, as well as others of success based on very different decisions, are not usually cited either. In short, exemplary firm stories ignore many details, as well as earlier or later not-so-brilliant moments.

25.   And of all kinds of groups. As Elster (2010: 466) points out, if every player on a soccer team is paid based on their goals, the team will stop scoring. Its best result will be nil–nil. To reinforce coordination and teamwork, bonuses must be established for all players. Mutualism is not a simple thing, even if it is the lowest degree of cooperation.

26.   This predisposition denies the thesis that any manifestation of altruism is strategic, i.e., the result of a mere selfish calculation (or expectation that the favor will be returned). Some are, although certainly not all: how often do the media report examples of philanthropy by wealthy donors who, for example, are running in the next election?

27.   This diagnosis, however, is not new: centuries ago, Ibn Khaldun (1332–1406) was also concerned about how social cohesion (*asabiyyah*) could degrade in urban societies.

28.   With the addition of a wide range of stratagems such as threats, setting tight deadlines, linking the agreement to its ratification by third parties, etc.

29.   The profit motivation is perhaps the most common way of exemplifying the preeminence of human selfishness. This is an ideological postulate which, to the extent that it drives many economic decisions, some try to turn it into a psychological trait. For instance, the extremely competitive environment in which the front office agents of fund management firms work is generalized to society as

a whole. They can earn thousands of euros (or be fired) in an instant. However, their main motivation is not greed, but success as a sign of incredible vision and ability, skills that everybody recognizes. The main consequence of their success is an unrestrained lifestyle and an inflated arrogance (Luyendijk, 2015). In this vein, the myopic individualism can also be mentioned of those who, being rich and relying on the independence this gives, believe that people can disengage themselves from the complex mutualistic web that constitutes any society, understood as a system whose functional maintenance requires strong doses of coordination.

30. In this respect, the surprise of a biographer on discovering the affable character with their relatives and kindness with their friends of a politician, businessman, etc., remembered for their lack of scruples and pity towards their rivals, is ridiculous. Nobody should forget that people can exhibit very different behaviors.

31. Therefore, the relevant dichotomy is not between uncontrolled competition or hierarchically regulated cooperation, but between the degree of regulation of competition and the level of autonomy of cooperation.

32. It should not be forgotten that reciprocity also applies to punishment, such as the law of talion ("an eye for an eye, a tooth for a tooth") which appeared in the Code of Hammurabi, dated 1792 BC. This is a brutal criterion, but at least it prevents disproportionate responses.

33. The assumption that preventing retaliation reflects pure selfishness is an even more far-fetched and implausible explanation.

34. What if the bids depended on a random mechanism activated by the game organizer? What if it was the player making the offer who was in control?

35. M. Baddeley (2010) reviews the economic and sociological literature on herding in human affairs.

36. This popularity can be maintained even when hardly anyone remembers its origin. Undoubtedly, the most famous painting in the world is the *Mona Lisa*. The painting did not receive special attention until August 1911 when it was stolen from the Louvre. The theft quickly became a media event that boosted the painting's fame. Since then, it has been a must-see for anyone who visits the museum, as long as they manage to find a place in the crowd that always gathers in front of it (Ariely and Kreisler, 2017: 176).

37. This bias is widely exploited in the commercial domain. For example, after a player has a bad match, the media promote all kinds of speculation about it. Although looking for relevant causes in random circumstances is absurd, it attracts people's attention and, hence, promotes sales.

38. If the disease is detected at 67 years of age and this person dies at 70, while in another person it is detected at 63 years and they also die at 70, in this second case the five-year survival rate is positive, but this has not meant a longer life.

39. That is, $\binom{83}{2} = \frac{83!}{2!(83-2)!} = \frac{83 \cdot 82}{2}$.

40. There is an old joke which clarifies this point. A son tells his father that on leaving school he missed the bus home. He ran after the bus to catch it but did not make it. Although he is exhausted, he is satisfied with the euro he saved by not paying the bus fare. The father replies: "If you had run after a cab, you would have saved €25!"

41. It should be stressed that the decision-maker is neither an arbiter nor a mediator, as there is no negotiation process.

6. Decision-making in the consumption of goods and services

This chapter briefly explores the processes of choosing consumer goods and services using materials from the previous two chapters. First, a simple model is proposed that combines the broad factors influencing economic decisions (as in Chapter 4) and the heuristic algorithms (as in Chapter 5) commonly applied in consumer decisions. Second, a classification of methods to manipulate people's purchasing decisions and, by extension, economic decisions is proposed. Although both points contain elements still at a seminal stage and others already fully consolidated, the results achieved provide a glimpse of how the microeconomic theory of consumption could be renewed.

6.1   PREFERENCES AND HEURISTICS

Inferences are a basic mental process and, therefore, can be applied in a wide domain of cases. In everyday life, inferences in decision-making are often based on heuristic algorithms. These decisions are also influenced by preferences, which are a singular manifestation of appetence, along with beliefs, emotions, etc. This chapter aims to emphasize that heuristics and preferences (and related factors) are combined in consumption decisions in a flexible sequential arrangement and with varying degrees of intensity. One of these elements can act exclusively: if I like chocolate, I will always choose the option that contains it. It is an idiosyncratic and unquestionable choice. Still, when I go to buy a cell phone I am mainly interested in the features of the models of familiar brands. It does not matter that I do not understand some attributes too well, as they are taken into account because they pave the way to identifying the model as good enough to be purchased. This is all within my budgetary constraints. In general, the routine purchase of a modestly priced good is not the same as the unique purchase of a product that is comparatively expensive relative to income. There is also an important difference between the choice of a new or a well-known brand. The same goes for the purchase of a product that projects a powerful image of oneself or of another that is invisible to outsiders. And so on. The type of algorithm used and the weight of preferences (and beliefs, etc.) change for each type of consumption decision. Nonetheless, an in-depth analysis of all these cases would require a text specifically dedicated to consumption, which is beyond the scope of these pages.

Figure 6.1 shows a general scheme of the combination between heuristics and preferences (and associated elements) in choosing consumer goods and services (inspired by Marewski et al., 2010b: 288; Hauser, 2014; Szmigin and Piacentini, 2015: 81, 94; Gigerenzer, 2015: 128; and Mousavi et al., 2017).[1]

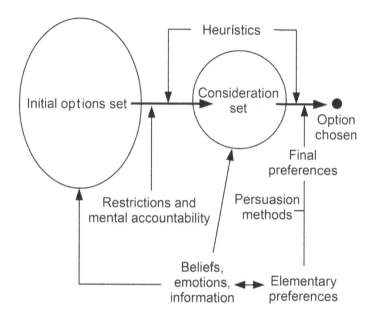

Figure 6.1   A map of factors influencing consumption choices

To begin with, let there be a hypothetical initial set of brands and variants of goods and services of a given class. It is a large set, although it does not contain all the existing options, only those that can be purchased at the current points of sale. This set is not unrelated to elementary preferences, as well as beliefs, emotions, and information available to people. For example, if a person is vegetarian (a belief), they will ignore many of the food products on sale. If it is a choice with a strong emotional impact, such as the purchase of a clothing accessory (because of the social image it projects), only certain aesthetic evocations will be considered. Next, due to economic constraints, especially the price and the budget defined by mental accounting, the initial set of options will be reduced to a smaller one, also called the consideration set (see Yee et al., 2007 and Hauser, 2014). Heuristic algorithms will play an important role in this process. For instance, once the affordable TV set models have been identified, the consumer's tentative selection includes only recognized brands. As the figure shows, within this set, the specific choice takes place, i.e., the expression of the final preference. Of course, this process is not immune to the influence of other heuristics ("I saw this same model at the home of ..."), certain preferences (and associated factors), and, above all, the persuasion techniques described in the following section. Logically, all this bundle of effects takes place within a given socioeconomic context and biographical background, always in constant mutability (Earl, 1995: 70).

In consumption, the heuristics can be applied to both the initial set and the consideration set. Any of the algorithms listed in Table 5.1 can be used in the consumption process. However, certain heuristics would be the most relevant, namely:

- the broad-spectrum algorithm of sufficient satisfaction;
- the focused algorithms, such as the recognition algorithms (to be concrete, imprint, and fluency), the lexicographic rule, and the social heuristic of imitation.

The possibility that other algorithms may be used is not denied.[2] Given the state of development of the suggested model, it is wiser to consider any list open.

The application of the above heuristics in consumer decisions may have single features. For example, Simon's postulate that people look for a product or service that is sufficiently satisfactory was enunciated without taking into account the role of brands and persuasion techniques. If these are incorporated, their presence simplifies the task of knowing whether people are sufficiently satisfied with the purchase, since recognition presumes trust. Moreover, brands (and sales ploys) can even modify elementary preferences, as in the well-known experiment in which a high-quality wine in a bottle with a poor aesthetic and shabby label has very little success, whereas the opposite happens with a low-quality wine, although with an appellation that connotes a strong pedigree.[3]

The role of recognition heuristics in consumption cycles is unquestionable: they quickly narrow down the initial set and, on many occasions, directly point to the purchase option. Its powerful influence is amplified by the emotional associations that brands carry with them. Although the differences the branding creates may be thought to be apparent, they are sufficiently noticeable to distinguish a particular brand from others on supermarket shelves.[4] Therefore,

- The recognition algorithm reveals final preferences: in regular purchases, this routine is interpreted as preference. The choice process follows a very simple rule: identification connotes trust and enhances final preferences. In a figurative sense, it can be said that people enjoy the product as soon as they see the brand. This is another example of the halo effect. The story that accompanies the brand completes the picture.
- The recognition algorithms contribute to loyalty, even if at first glance this seems difficult because it is based on trivial cues (that characterize the class of goods and services). Even so, this loyalty is hardly ever absolute: regular customers do not hesitate to switch brands, often only temporarily, if an attribute attracts their attention ("Let's not miss the opportunity to taste it").

People know that advertisements are unreliable, but the advertised brands are nevertheless the most purchased ones. In other words, advertising slogans and persuasive messages act as a magnet, even if they are not convincing in themselves. This explains why a generic advertising message (e.g., "Start a healthy lifestyle") is now accompanied by information on the calorie content of the concerned food. However, as noted, routine and familiarity end up being indistinguishable.[5] Inertia prevails in many everyday purchases: a certain brand is bought because it is the one that is always bought, a circumstance that connotes trust and convenience (and it is also available in the places in which purchases are made).[6] Recognized brands are considered the most appropriate and vice versa. However, an alternative brand of soft drink, breakfast cereal, or any other everyday product, properly presented and promoted, pushes many customers to break their habit without hesitation: "It's worth taking advantage of the offer," they think. This change is only temporary, as the initial seller also takes action to win back lost customers (Szmigin and Piacentini, 2015: 358, 367–368). The result is an indefinite continuum of promotions, especially using novelty (see below).

Advertising is a creative effort to make brands easily recognizable. On the one hand, advertising agencies design campaigns that combine branding and captivating narratives. Mixed with emotions, the goal is to drive consumption. These messages also indicate the moment of consumption, and with whom and why to share it. All this leaves an imprint on the mind that allows immediate brand recognition. Advertising, on the other hand, also underlines to exhaustion what kind of goods and services are consumed in different lifestyles, while creating new ones, often with the enthusiastic complicity of certain pop sociology and the media. Some brands feed snobbery as well as those that adopt biographical and/or cultural evocations, giving rise to groups of consumers who are passionate about them. Although the weight of these customers in total sales is negligible, their existence contributes to the brand becoming legendary. In general, people hold several social and biographical attributes, to which it is possible to add new ones as a way of introducing new products and services (cf. Solomon, 2015: 293). Promotions are more persuasive if they include a celebrity portrayed as sympathetic, endearing, attractive, committed to noble causes, etc.[7] The resulting image projects a halo that is also a commercial creation. However, the space for the mind is limited and contested, and therefore effective advertising campaigns require persistence and reach. Once this path has been embarked upon, it can no longer be abandoned: if it were, the market share of the brand would probably begin a slow but steady decline, buried by other claims. From the point of view of commercial distribution, it is also necessary for the brand to be accessible, i.e., to have many and varied points of sale, and to maintain its presence in the media, on the Internet, in the streets, etc. All this is to prevent the brand from losing latency in the minds of consumers.

When faced with a novelty (a new brand or variant), algorithms such as lexicographic and imitation heuristics are likely to be particularly active. If the product lacks similar precedents, as with the first computers or cell phones, people are interested in the functional features of the product and want to prevent surprises, and therefore a good shortcut is to buy the model owned by people they know (Earl, 1995: 77).

The concept of novelty deserves clarification. It is known that there can be either radical or partial novelty. In the first case, firms highlight unique attributes to captivate the minority of connoisseurs willing to buy the product, despite its comparatively high price. However, in the consumption domain, even with the most common goods and services, the periodically appearing novelties stand out. The goal of such partial novelties is to attract, even momentarily, new buyers without losing the usual ones. Therefore, any new variant is wrapped in messages that reiterate the already known attributes of the brand while adding, at the same time, new features, however superficial (perhaps only an aesthetic or naive narrative).[8] To capture the attention of consumers, the novelty attributes should not be identical, but nor should they deviate too far from already known models. Otherwise, there is a risk that the novelty will be described as fake and boring or as strange, eccentric, or unpredictable. Too little stimulus means no stimulus and too much is negatively evaluated.[9] An excess of novelty usually leads to failure: any new version has to share attributes, i.e. be partly the same as existing ones. The extremely original only appeals to a minority.

Among social heuristics, the imitation algorithm is commonly applied in the choice of goods and services that, for a given time and place, are indicators of the status, and concomitant lifestyle, of their consumers. This is easily detect-able in brands of clothing, footwear, etc. These items facilitate acceptance within groups, whether related to social categories, beliefs, age or gender. Although not mentioned above, the appeal to reciprocity is another social heuristic that can be detected behind certain promotional campaigns, such as periodic discounts and loyalty programs (customer cards). Although they are displayed as a reward for regular customers, they attempt to establish subtle links between vendors and customers. This bond fosters loyalty.

Brand loyalty plays a complex role in final preferences. It can be expressed as follows: loyalty deters customers from ceasing to buy a given brand but also makes it more difficult to regain them once lost. Loyalty delays the departure of buyers but, at the same time, it amplifies distrust once lost. Therefore, loyalty adds nonlinearity to the relationship between people and brands. This is what Figure 6.2 attempts to show (the lower part is directly inspired by the considerations set out in Hirschman, 1970: Chapter 7 and the upper part is the author's own elaboration).

The figure combines three variables, price (p), quantity (q), and quality (Q). The objective is to show how the influence of the loyalty factor alters the relationship between these variables. The figure is not dynamic, and therefore the points S^* and S^{**} are states of the world, and the arrows joining them represent decisions and consequences. The analysis starts from S^*, that is, a state of the world in which a quantity q^* of a good or service is sold at a price p^* and with a quality Q^*. At a given moment the quality starts to deteriorate, which initiates a shift to the state of the world S^{**}. Note that the loss of quality is indicated by higher ordinate values, i.e., $Q^* > Q^{**}$. In the beginning, due to customer loyalty, the drop in sales is very small, and thus the company's managers do not change the prices.

Let us take the example of a restaurant with remarkable prestige. A loss of quality, for whatever reason, does not cause mass desertion of its demanding clientele, since it is considered a temporary problem. This is the loyalty effect: trust is maintained. However, if the quality does not recover, the loss of cus-tomers will accelerate and, hence, there will be a sudden drop in the quantity sold, even if the company, as shown in the figure, reduces prices. Suppose that, placed in the state of the world S^{**}, with lower prices, quantities, and quality level, the managers try to regain the lost prestige and customers. In the framework of the figure, this means moving towards the state of world S^*. They decide, for example, to keep prices low, while quality increases. Unfortunately, quantity is slow to respond. It takes a great deal of promotion and quality improvement to increase the level of sales and, finally, to raise the price and restore the profitability of the business. In the example of the restaurant, the effort to regain credibility clashes with the distrust of those who, completely disappointed, decide not to return. This is a logical attitude given

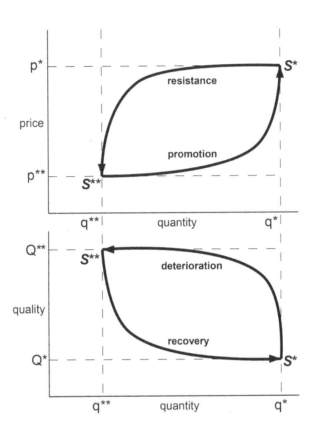

Figure 6.2   The loyalty effect

their patience and even the explicit warnings they gave when they realized that quality was declining. In short, loyalty extends tolerance to comparatively higher prices and/or drops in quality. However, if trust is definitely lost, customer recovery will not be easy (their loyalty was betrayed). Loyalty slows both customer defection and customer recovery.

In this section a simple but hopefully seminal model has been proposed. The analysis of consumption decisions and their connection with heuristics can certainly be more complex, as it can be extended to the following three dimensions:

• The identification of more heuristics applied in consumption and, above all, the study of their frequency of use by consumption situations and type of consumers.

- The effects of the uniqueness and salience of cues, as well as the impact of their periodic renewal.
- The evaluation of the influence of memory. Under this point, it was found that people tend to remember the choice, the place, and the time, but not why they chose what they chose.

Every day and everywhere consumers are faced with thousands of brands and countless consumption occasions. This is fertile ground for an enormous diversity of combinations of heuristics and preferences (and beliefs, emotions, and information). This territory has hardly been explored by microeconomic theory.

6.2   MANIPULATING CONSUMER CHOICES

If throughout the text we have insisted on the non-immanent character of preferences, now it is time to delve into their mutable nature, i.e., the fact that they do not satisfy the axiom of independence (see Chapter 2). As discussed, elementary preferences can change for ever and ever, often because of the consequences of a previous choice or a major change in people's economic situation. At the same time, context and specific circumstances can alter final preferences. Their great vulnerability explains why there are numerous persuasion techniques to conveniently manipulate them (Hausman, 2012: 134). This section aims to classify and describe these stratagems of persuasion and cognitive easing.

6.2.1   Modifying Preferences

A single influence can change final preferences. This alteration does not usually go beyond the short term, although in some cases it may eventually crystallize. In principle, these modifications can be classified as follows:

- The final preferences have to adapt to all kinds of restrictions or the appearance of unexpected advantages.
- A direct experience of a personal nature awakens curiosity, then a fondness, and finally consolidates a given preference. Thus, a person begins to appreciate crime novels because an acquaintance spoke about them with enthusiasm some time ago, or they begin to appreciate classical music because a daughter learns to play the piano.
- Changes in beliefs (including expectations). In this case, people obtain new information about an object, circumstance, or the intentions and/or actions of other people, facts that push them to revise beliefs and, hence, prefer-

ences and choices. This is how some food products became fashionable: in recent years, avocados and almond milk.

- Changes in preferences driven by promotion and advertising techniques. Unlike the previous case, and despite the fuzzy boundaries, the alteration is the result of an elaborate effort involving commercial interests.

In the following pages, attention will focus on the fourth point. As is well known, consumer decisions are taken in an environment infested with persuasive claims to drive people to buy certain products or brands. These techniques can be classified according to different criteria. One possibility is their degree of intrusion into the daily affairs, or specific moments of life, of people. Accordingly, the following three types can be identified:

- Sales techniques that appeal directly to people in an attempt to tap into their sense of reciprocity and/or their search for consistency. These techniques often have a bad image because of their sometimes aggressive character and their tendency to slide into abuse.
- Messages in which brands are more or less explicitly associated with a given lifestyle: consuming those brands means experiencing it or aspiring to it. To ignore them is to undermine one's own social identity. Therefore, advertising focuses on associating brands with consumption opportunities and lifestyle habits.
- Methods that aim to create a favorable cognitive context that encourages particular purchasing decisions and, by extension, any economic decision. This is the area in which economic psychology has probably made its most outstanding contributions. The section on cognitive easing describes how the creation of an appropriate sensory and cognitive background alters choices.

Table 6.1 details these methods (compiled by the author from Joule and Beauvois 2014; Guéguen, 2016 and 2018; and Hogg and Vaughan, 2014: 210–214). These persuasion techniques can be applied separately or in combination.[10] For example, whoever insists we must buy something also appeals to the social status and the exclusivity of the offer.

Before going into the subject, it should be pointed out that, in addition to people who are particularly susceptible to manipulation, there are also circumstances that favor it. Those who want to take advantage of these methods look for people with the right profile, but they also try to create the right conditions. Thus, it is necessary to differentiate between the cue that induces the potential customer to enter a given store (for instance, an irresistible offer on shoes) and the act of buying a non-discounted pair (because there are no more shoes in the customer's size). The initial signal is a commercial gimmick, while the latter is the result of a careful persuasion process (Joule and Beauvois, 2014: 63).

Table 6.1   Methods to modify preferences

Appealing directly to people	Coercive	Intimidation
		Captive markets
	Reciprocity exploitation	The foot-in-the-door
		Low balling
		The door-in-the-face
		A foot-in-the-memory
		Better something than nothing
Cognitive easing	Priming	
	Framing effect	Mode of presentation
		Space and time configuration
		Association of ideas
		Appeal to scarcity
		Familiarity
	Anchoring	

Many, but not all people, fall into such psychological traps. Some realize but tolerate it for whatever reason.

6.2.2   Appealing Directly to People

Addressing people directly is a stratagem that exploits people's readiness to accept reciprocity. It is about people responding appropriately to kind offers. This relationship does not presuppose anything about the value of what is exchanged (Cialdini, 2007: 31–32). However, as the table indicates, there are also coercive forms that take advantage of the difference in power to intimidate or directly impose the choice. Captivating stories and elaborate staging are also used to guide choices.

Threats, coercion, reprisals, etc. aim for the submission of individuals without their consent. The forms may be brutal or sophisticated, but the conveyed message leaves no room for doubt. Even so, imposing obedience is often counterproductive in the long run, especially if it affects many people. To some extent, this explains the use of the "good cop/bad cop" technique. Common in arrests, the victim is first threatened and/or harmed followed by an unexpected relief. The detainee believes that they have narrowly escaped the worst and they are therefore prone to collaborate. In these cases, there is a large power differential between those involved, but the stratagem works even when this is not the case. In the social and economic world, it is not uncommon for requests to be rudely and bluntly rejected, followed by the appearance of a more reasonable and polite person who agrees to consider them, even though by then the petitioner has probably lowered their demands or even given up altogether.

Coercive selling techniques also include the creation of captive markets. In these markets, customers either have no alternative sources of supply or are forced to ignore them by the employment of serious warnings. This is the case, for example, of the electricity or gas company warning subscribers that they must contract a specific firm for the modification of installations, to prevent their facilities from being declared out of date, despite current regulations giving customers freedom of choice. Probably the most successful variant is not based on coercion, but on taking advantage of the lack of universal technical standards. This happens when printers require ink refills of the same brand, when razors only work with specific razor blades, or when electronic devices have functionally linked components. Thus, video game consoles are sold at comparatively low prices, while the opposite is true for software. The reason is that manufacturers choose to subsidize the hardware, as this is a prerequisite for creating a captive customer base. However, a technological background is not always necessary: cruise companies offer cabins at very competitive prices, which attracts passengers who will then have to pay comparatively high prices for goods and services sold on board, with no possibility, obviously, of shopping elsewhere.

Techniques that exploit reciprocity have a fairly common pattern: first, salespeople try to get the target people to accept a certain reciprocal commitment and then reveal their true intentions. Sellers expect people not to withdraw. If necessary, they appeal to people's reputations, i.e., sellers urge people to be consistent with the initial decision to freely consider the offer. This escalation of commitments occurs everywhere (Joule and Beauvois, 2014: 27).

To guide consumption decisions, one of the methods that abuses the appeal to reciprocity is the so-called "foot-in-the-door".[11] To begin with, the salesperson tries to break the personal distance with ritual phrases such as "How are you?", "Everything all right?", etc. In some cases, they may also appeal to an altruistic cause, perhaps accompanied by a banal obligation (such as wearing a pin from now on). In any case, acceptance is always accompanied by flattery: the target person is described as noble, altruistic, intelligent, and so on. The goal is to create a climate of trust to motivate certain behavior. Once the respondent has shown their willingness to listen or to collaborate, the likelihood of leaving the conversation is small. The time for the seller to show their real intentions has arrived: the sale of a good or service, or the monetary contribution to a cause. These stratagems do not usually work when there is no explicit response to the first request, as when the petitioner simply leaves papers on the lap of passengers in the subway or on the bus.

This persuasion tactic, typical of door-to-door salespeople, exploits people's desire to be polite to others. Getting the person to accept a wider involvement also depends on the appearance of vendors and the gestures they make. Nonetheless, the presumed climate of familiarity will not be created if the staging is not well constructed and the storyline is not well scripted. Otherwise, the person being approached will become angry and the potential sale (or contribution) will be lost. The attempt at persuasion should not be too obvious (Aronson, 2008: 83–84). Moreover, this sales technique should be applied to people who are little known or unknown. If the first encounter is to be followed by others, field experiments indicate that it is not recommended to let more than one or two days pass between them since the commitment rapidly fades.

The attempt to exploit people's inclination to reciprocate has sophisticated variants. One example is trips for retirees subsidized by commercial companies. After a sightseeing tour, they are directed to a place where vendors try to sell all sorts of things, often at a good price but of very poor quality. Another example is the organization of informal meetings where potential customers receive free samples and/or explanations about the virtues of the product. This deferential treatment encourages people to buy, especially if those attending the presentation know each other. Social norms dictate that people should be polite and reciprocate. In this practice, a well-known brand of plastic food packaging stood out years ago (Cialdini, 2007: 167). Manufacturers of cosmetics, natural foods, etc., are also masters at organizing talks or tastings. More simply, even promotions that invite people to try a product in the aisles of a supermarket seek to take advantage of reciprocity.

Another sales method starts with a very attractive offer to catch the attention of the potential customer and then, little by little, the real cost of the good or service is revealed. The initial price increases with the addition of add-ons and improvements (with perhaps some small gifts attached), the cost of which was not included in the first price. In this case, there is an art to preventing the buyer from pulling out, as the seller adds more and more extras. The goal of this crescendo is to diffuse the psychological weight of the expense. The irresistible initial offer was just the bait to set in motion a sales process of an increasing amount. The low-balling stratagem is also applied by those who ask "Can you help me?", before indicating what kind of favor is involved. If the answer is affirmative, it is difficult for people to back out of the commitment, even if it is a painful task. It is also the case of the neighbor to whom a tool is lent, a decision that creates a precedent. Later, it will be difficult to say no.

Low balling is a very common technique in the sale of furniture, household appliances, automobiles, etc., in which the items and prices indicated do not include the accessories, the best finishes, transportation, assembly, etc. Sometimes, this sales method takes more aggressive forms, such as advertising offers through flyers suggesting that there are a limited number of units. The fact is that, once people have made the effort to go to the point of sale (and time

and resources have been consumed), they may find that the stock is exhausted
and they have to buy a more expensive version.

The "door-in-the-face" is the stratagem of asking for something exorbitant
and then substantially lowering it so that people end up accepting the second
request. The purpose of the initial offer was actually to establish a benchmark
(or anchor, as explained below) to make it easier to accept the ensuing offer.
The same person must make both offers, as well as not too much time elapsing
between them. This stratagem is typical of negotiations of all kinds: each
party sticks to presumably insurmountable red lines to get the other party to
also make major concessions. The message is that the huge effort involved
in lowering one's own demands requires the other party to also make a large
concession. Each party puts pressure on the other to accept their benchmark
and thus eventually reach an advantageous agreement.

Another persuasive method, which can be called "a foot-in-the-memory",
is to encourage people to remember times when, for example, they committed
an infraction, or behaved badly, etc. This is intended to shame people and,
hence, to encourage a change of attitude in the future. This will probably imply
the purchase of something or the contribution of an amount of money. It is
a technique that requires the respondent to recall their past decisions and take
responsibility for them.

The "better something than nothing" method aims to make people believe
that every contribution, even the smallest, is very welcome. The money col-
lector insists that every contribution, no matter how small, is needed. Who can
resist giving something, even if it is a pittance? It is not a matter of obtaining
large contributions, but of getting everyone to make them.

Finally, it is worth mentioning techniques that exploit reciprocity without
the need to establish direct contact with the potential customer. An example
is the practice of some restaurants of delivering the check with chocolates or
candies. This kindness is intended to show a good image of the restaurant,
but also to increase tips (Guéguen, 2018: 28). In general, any sign of appreciation, up to moderate flattery of the customer, is a good technique to exploit
reciprocity.

6.2.3   Cognitive Easing

The other major method for changing preferences is cognitive easing
(Poundstone, 2010: 93; Guéguen 2016: 45–46). It consists of generating
perceptions (through images, sounds, smells) and meanings (narratives) that,
by evoking emotions, trigger appropriate reactions. It encompasses different
tricks whose action very often goes unnoticed by buyers (Cialdini, 2016:
Chapter 9). They are deliberate, but not intrusive, as they subtly alter the
decision context. They do not achieve their purpose either always or every-

where. However, their influence on final preferences cannot be ignored. First, the priming techniques will be described and, second, the framing effect and anchoring will be studied. These are probably the persuasion methods most analyzed by economic psychology.

6.2.3.1 Priming

Priming techniques appeal to the senses to create an environment, or atmosphere, suitable for driving decisions in a certain direction, without resorting to verbal communication, although they may incorporate gestures (Guéguen, 2016: 198).

Priming and deception are different things. Thus, advertisements for apartments for sale or rent, vacation destinations, etc. usually omit what detracts from the attractiveness of the offer. It is also not difficult to find items for sale or services with very competitive prices that do not mention possible conditions, restrictions, etc. Often the deception is by omission, as it causes less rejection than direct misrepresentation. Social norms and consumer protection regulations can curb such practices. By contrast, priming does not include misleading messages, but only effective gimmicks to divert attention appropriately.

The importance of sensory perception in the buying and selling of objects has always been known: buyers want to see, touch, and try things out to check their physical condition, their suitability, etc. However, if only the five customary senses, i.e. sight, touch, taste, hearing, and smell, are considered,[12] it should be noted that their systematic study for commercial purposes began only a century ago. The degree of knowledge attained is not the same in all cases. For instance, the role of sound has only been fully explored after the sharp decline in the cost of recording and reproducing. The potential of smell is far from exhausted. To illustrate the influence of priming, consider the following examples (extracted from Wilkinson and Klaes, 2012: 109–114; Szmigin and Piacentini, 2015; and Guéguen, 2016 and 2018):

- Blue and, to a lesser extent, green bottles (cool colors) have been found to connote freshness, while yellow and red (warm colors) reinforce the opposite perception (often creating the idea of a strong energetic intake). The combination of yellow and black is also known to be a dangerous cue for animals and an attractive contrast for humans.
- In the 1930s, advertisers of a well-known cola brand noticed that the reddish color of the drink matched Santa's red clothes. This coincidence led them to associate the beverage with Christmas, family meals, and time spent with friends. Of course, this association is not valid for all cultural contexts.

- Some studies have shown that the consumption of drinks increases with the volume of the sound and with tempos equal to or higher than 121 beats per minute (*vivace* and above). This is typical of pubs, discos, etc., where there is an atmosphere of overexcitement that stimulates drinking. It is also encouraged by the fact that conversation is more difficult. In contrast, a discreet volume and tempos from 52 to about 95 beats per minute (from *adagio* to *moderato*), which includes the rhythm of the heartbeat at rest (65–75 beats per minute), facilitates paying attention to what is being done. This musical ambiance is typical of shopping malls since it slows the pace and thus increases the likelihood of purchasing. It is also used in many radio and television commercials.

- There is no doubt that music gives identity to spaces: a fine wine and spirits establishment does not play heavy metal music, but classical music that connotes distinction and sophistication. Sometimes, music reinforces social patterns of behavior. Thus, romantic love songs in a flower shop increase purchases, especially by men. It seems that this reinforces the meaning of giving flowers set by the current canons of male behavior. For women, this type of gift has a more conventional meaning.

- The role of music in telephone waiting is very interesting. It has been repeatedly confirmed that the type of music influences the patience of individuals. It seems that the music of Andean flutes, and any music that is evocative and relaxing, encourages people to wait longer. However, a piece of rhythmic and familiar music gives a less serious air to the situation and makes people hang up sooner. In any case, playing a repetitive verbal message is counterproductive.

- Blinks are another case of sound use. They are just a shout, the beginning of a melody, etc. of about two seconds' duration. They are common on radio stations as a prelude to reinforce attention to an advertisement or announcement.

- Smell plays a key role in restaurants, cleaning supply stores, and newly purchased cars, among others. For example, it has been observed that wafting the smell of lemons through restaurants increases the average expenditure and the time spent at the table. Some stores even put ember-scented atomizers in the air conditioning ducts. There are also air fresheners to give the characteristic smell, often imitating leather, of new cars, public spaces, etc. An appropriate scent, accompanied by sounds of nature, is typical of stores selling natural or organic products. To close this list of examples, the scent of vanilla is especially powerful when selling women's clothing, while that of Damask rose would be so in the case of men's clothing.

- The physical attractiveness of others also influences peoples's decisions. Simple experiments indicate that, if donations are asked for on the street, the amounts collected vary according to the dress (style and color of clothing) of the person making the request. Also, waitresses wearing red receive more tips from men, but not waiters (from either men or women) (Hogg and Vaughan, 2014: 540; Guéguen, 2016: 282–284).

- In the same vein, sexual references should be mentioned as an advertising magnet. However, there is a danger that models with impossibly perfect shapes overshadow the product itself. Physical attractiveness, or the suggested lifestyle, used as an aspirational referent, can end up displacing the brand. Furthermore, this claim does not work for all types of products (Cialdini, 2016: Chapter 5).

Priming works when the stimuli are congruent and not dissonant with existing cultural patterns.

Priming also exploits the possibilities of touch. Without going too deeply into the subject, it should be pointed out that the evaluation of the quality of a service mixes, leaving aside the price factor, material aspects (such as the organoleptic characteristics of the food served in a restaurant), the skill of the staff serving customers (presentation, experience, and knowledge) and the quality of the social interactions between employees and customers (sympathy, kindness, etc.). This last aspect is now emphasized (Guéguen, 2016: 250–273, 295). For example, waiters' recommendations are more likely to be accepted if they are accompanied by brief and friendly physical contact. Imitation of gestures (running the hand through the hair, scratching, etc.) or repeating phrases (affirmations) of the customer also creates an atmosphere of empathy. In one restaurant, an experiment was conducted in which the waiter systematically repeated the customer's order while, in another situation, he simply said "OK." In both cases, the customer could verify that the annotation was correct. The results were that repetition increases the frequency and volume of tips. This stratagem is known as the "chameleon effect": whoever imitates us is perceived as closer or friendlier. Moreover, it is known that broad smiles directed at customers increase tips, especially if they are waitresses and the customers are men. Looks also matter: looking into the eyes in a non-inquisitive way (having a frank look) boosts the favorable opinion that the person observed has of the person looking. However, you should smile, gesture, and move in the right way, avoiding appearing forced or false. Gestures aimed to create an atmosphere of familiarity and mutual trust should appear spontaneous.

Before closing this section, it is worth clarifying that priming does not include subliminal images. In 1957, one James Vicary claimed to have inserted images for three-thousandths of a second into a film shown in a New Jersey movie theater. Such images contained references to specific brands of soft drinks and snacks sold in the theater, the consumption of which skyrocketed. It was all, however, a sham: in 1962 he admitted that the experiment had never been conducted. Through this hoax, he just wanted to give notoriety to his

advertising agency, which was at a low ebb. However, the inclusion of subliminal ads was quickly banned. Later experiments have indicated that this kind
of image seems to increase the desire of the targeted people to drink or eat,
although neither in a generalized way nor of the suggested brand (Morgado,
2017: 73). Indeed, to trigger a desire and to drive the choice precisely are
two very different things (Guéguen, 2016: 39–44). Since the effectiveness of
a stimulus requires it to reach consciousness, the subliminal technique has no
commercial interest. This explains why viewing a video with subliminal messages has less effect on the behavior of people who want, for example, to lose
weight than viewing another in which they believe this type of message to be
hidden, even if this is not the case.

6.2.3.2 Framing

Among the methods for modifying preferences, the framing effect is one of
the most studied by economic psychology. It deals with how the way in which
a given decision is presented can alter it (Cartwright, 2018: 45). Sometimes,
the framing effect can cause reversal preference: A > B if the decision is
presented in a certain way, or B > A if it is presented differently (Wilkinson
and Klaes, 2012: 79). This is what happens in the following conversation
between three monks, one of them the abbot (mentioned in Motterlini, 2010:
55–56 and Nisbett, 2016: 41). One of the monks asks the abbot if it is okay to
smoke while praying, and quickly receives the following answer, "Of course
not, it is almost sacrilegious." Then, the other monk asks the abbot if it is okay
to pray while smoking. He replies, "Of course it is. God hears us at all times."
The framing effect is unquestionable in this case. Smoking connotes rest, so
praying could be considered an ideal complement. However, since praying is
regarded as a higher-order action than smoking, the answer to the first question
is negative: smoking is distracting. Both cases, however, involve the same
actions. Whatever the case, people cannot detach from the frames, which may
alter their preferences and decisions.

Since the 1970s, numerous studies have confirmed the framing effect
over and over again. However, over the years its interpretation has changed.
Whereas at first it was considered a cognitive bias, the frames surrounding
a message are now understood as a tool that, manipulations aside, facilitates
communication (Gigerenzer, 2018). The preferred example of the first interpretation is the case of a severe epidemic that wipes out a given population
(Motterlini, 2010: 51–52; Angner, 2012: 124–129; and Kahneman, 2011:
Chapter 34). It seems that urgent measures must be taken to protect the 600
people living in the infected area. After analyzing the situation, the experts
propose two types of actions, A and B, to curb the disease. It should be added
that, depending on how they are implemented, each type of action leads to

two different results (1 and 2). In the case of A, the following two possible outcomes would be obtained:

A1. A total of 200 people are saved for certain.
A2. There is a one in three chance of saving 600 people and a two in three chance of saving no one.

In the case of B, the actions would result in:

B1. There is no doubt that 400 human lives are lost for certain.
B2. There are two chances out of three that 600 people will die and one out of three that no one will die.

Faced with these dilemmas in a simple questionnaire, most people choose A1 in case A and B2 in case B, even though the four results are exactly the same. The pattern of responses seems to be explained by the weight of emotions: the prospect of directly saving 200 people seems more acceptable than that of saving 1/3 of 600 people. By contrast, option B2 is preferred to B1 because, faced with the negative prospect of losing human lives, people consider it worth the gamble. In case A (presented in positive terms), risk aversion prevails, while in B (expressed in negative terms) risk propensity predominates. Therefore, the perception of the decision, and hence the choice, would not be unrelated to the way it is presented. However, this experiment has been heavily criticized for being sloppily designed. Thus, the alleged framing effect almost disappears if the wording of A1 becomes "200 people's lives are saved for certain and 400 die" and that of B1, "The loss of 400 human lives for certain and the survival of 200." Although this criticism invalidates the presumed bias, it is nonetheless a warning about the influence of the way the information is presented. The people who create and/or disseminate a piece of information may try to promote a particular interpretation and assessment (positive or negative). The suggested inference may either facilitate a correct understanding of the message or confuse and manipulate the receiver. In either case, frames contain non-explicit information ready to be decoded. This type of cue also affects many algorithms.

There are many schemes to appropriately alter the context of a decision. One possible classification distinguishes between the following five types of framing: how the decision is made, the spatial and temporal configuration of the situation, the creation of a certain association of ideas, the appeal to scarcity, and the recourse to familiarity.

To begin with, the importance of the way a choice is presented can be illustrated by the following example. Two people, X and Z, have both bought new cars. In terms of gasoline consumption, the old and new vehicles have the following ratios:

- *X* had a car that did 10 km/l, but the new one can do 13 km/l.
- *Z* had a car that did 25 km/l while the new one does 35 km/l.

The question to be answered is: Which driver saves more fuel after a year in which, for instance, they have driven 10,000 km? The answer usually given to this question is *Z* since they drive many more kilometers per liter. This seems to be the case, but it is not. The related calculations prove that this answer is not true:

- Driver *X*: (10,000/10 − 10,000/13) = 1,000 liters − 769.23 liters = 230.77 liters less after 10,000 km.
- Driver *Z*: (10,000/25 − 10,000/35) = 400 liters − 285.71 liters = 114.29 liters less.

Therefore, driver *X*, who also consumes the most, saves the most. The kilometers per liter frame is misleading, but the criterion of liters per 100 km is not:

- *X* has switched from a car that needed 10 liters to travel 100 km to a car that needs 7.69 liters to run for 100 km.
- *Z* has changed from a car that consumed 4 liters per 100 km to a car that consumes 2.86 liters per 100 km.

At a glance, driver *X* saves more fuel: 2.31 liters versus 1.14 liters per 100 km for *Z*. In this frame, the gasoline consumption is (rounded figures):

- Driver *X*: (10,000/100)·10 − (10,000/100)·7.69 = 231 liters less.
- Driver *Z*: (10,000/100)·4 − (10,000/100)·2.86 = 114 liters less.

The result is the same, but it is easier to obtain an accurate picture if the reference is set in liters per 100 km. Many years ago, in several countries, the kilometers per liter consumption frame was banned as misleading.

Framing can influence even very simple situations. A simple experiment involves placing a full glass and an empty one in the middle of a table. Participants are then asked to do something as simple as emptying half of one glass into the other and then placing the half-full glass near a corner of the table (Gigerenzer, 2008: Chapter 6). Most, it is evident, take the initially full glass and transfer half of the liquid to the other. Later, the first glass is placed at the end of the table, not realizing that the glass in which they have just poured the water is also half full. Although objectively a half-full glass and a half-empty glass are the same, psychologically this is not the case due to the influence of the frame.

A more frequent case is that of a person who has a serious illness that requires surgery. Before making a decision, they want to know whether or not the operation will increase survival. Studies indicate that physicians often frame their answers to drive patients to a certain decision. Thus, to communicate the desirability of an operation, since few patients survive if they do not undergo surgery, the vast majority of doctors choose to frame this option in a positive way ("Ninety-five percent of patients are alive five years after the operation. If many survive without surgery, physicians suggest that patients do not require an operation. In this case, if necessary, doctors can add: "Five years after refusing the operation, only 5% of the patients have died." The frame is adjusted to convey the correct decision of the patients.

There is no doubt that the patients' goal is to make an informed decision, i.e., to know whether or not the intervention increases survival relative to the option of not having surgery (benchmark). There is also no doubt that physicians will frame their messages so that intelligent patients will understand them without making all the information explicit. Some experiments indicate that if the benchmark is low (few survive without surgery), patients focus their attention on the survival rate of the operation. Conversely, if the outcome is that most survive after surgery, attention is focused on mortality. Doctors then choose in each case the ideal framework for communicating the benefits of the operation (Gigerenzer, 2018).

Consumption is an economic area where framing is ubiquitous. For example, food packaging reports in large print that it is 90% fat-free, but almost no one indicates in large print that the fat content is 10%. This is a subtle way of presenting a key product attribute that exploits individuals' beliefs about food and health: "Less fat is healthier."

People find addition and multiplication easier than subtraction and division. That is why it is common to advertise offers indicating "three for the price of two" instead of displaying labels indicating a one-third discount. Moreover, since frequencies are easier to grasp than percentages, the worst option is to signal that there is a 33.33% discount (Wilkinson and Klaes, 2012: 468).

Consider now the following two situations. In the first one, a suitable modification of the number of options alters the choices. This is a very usual stratagem in the commercial domain. Let us take a magazine that offers the following forms of annual subscription (Ariely, 2009: 1–6):

- Access in electronic format costs €60.
- Receiving it on paper costs €130.
- To be able to consult it in both electronic and paper versions costs €130.

Experimental results reveal that a large majority prefer the first option when there is only a choice between the first and the second. Nonetheless, if the third option is added a significant number of people switch to it. It seems as if the extra that the third option contains (the possibility, in fact irrelevant, of consulting it in both formats) justifies the higher cost.

In the second case, after having spent a significant amount of money in a stationery store, the customer is entitled to choose between the following three options (Motterlini, 2006: Chapter 2):

(a)   receive a €10 voucher or a gift of a metal ballpoint pen;
(b)   receive a €10 voucher or any plastic ballpoint pen;
(c)   receive a €10 voucher, or a metal or plastic pen free of charge.

The exercise must be well understood: one day the stationery store offers promotion (*a*), another day (*b*), and finally (*c*). Field experiments reveal that when making a choice in case (*a*) the customer does not have a clear preference (they think, "Which has greater value?"). On the day when the choice is (*b*), most opt for the voucher (it seems obvious that a plastic pen has no value). In case (*c*), the obvious difference between pens inclines many customers towards the metal one. From the hesitation in case (*a*), it seems that simply broadening the range of options (any plastic pen) is not enough to make them choose this option. It is also necessary to include an easily comparable feature to influence the choice: the plastic pen contrasts with the metal pen in case (*c*), so that many people choose the latter. Regardless of the bonus, the details of the decision context matter.

The organization and arrangement of elements within a space and time include multiple stratagems. Here is a small illustration:

• Decoration matters (Guéguen, 2016: 52–53): in a restaurant, a small decorative boat was placed above the tables, along with other seafaring motifs decorating the room. In this setting, 65% of customers chose fish dishes (compared to 32.5% who chose meat) while, in the same venue without seafood decoration, 67.5% chose meat and 35% fish. It is also well known that a décor with wood paneling and furniture gives a feeling of warmth, as opposed to the coldness evoked by marble and minimalist décor.
• Manufacturers pay supermarkets and department stores to place their products at eye level and to the right of where consumers are standing. Often, the basic consumer products, such as bread, milk, pharmaceuticals, etc., are even placed at the back of the store, forcing customers to walk between the shelves. These spatial stratagems increase sales.
• It has been repeatedly observed that the amount of food eaten is influenced by the size of the plate, bag, or container (visual reference). This fact is incentivized by lower prices per unit weight or capacity. Thus, outlets selling popcorn, cola products, etc., in cinemas, theaters, etc., encourage consumption through large-capacity containers (Motterlini,

2014: 147–148). Similarly, the size of the purchase in a supermarket also depends on the capacity of carts, to which could be added the position of the products on the shelf and many other not innocuous details (Ubel, 2008: Chapter 6).

- In drug marketing, it is known that customers prefer large pills, even though tiny pills are associated with high levels of concentration and, hence, efficacy. A branded red pill is also seen as better than a generic white pill. And so forth. There is the curious perception that the smaller and lighter an electronic gadget is, the higher its quality. Small size is associated with miniaturization, which connotes careful design and technological advancement.

- Years ago, in an experiment consisting of showing a poster with the word "VOMIT" to a group of people, most of them showed a disgusted reaction. If the word was "BANANA" they showed neither surprise nor discomfort. The fascinating fact was that, when they were shown a poster with both words, many refused the offer of a banana (Kahneman, 2011: Chapter 4). This was a visceral reaction motivated by simply looking at words written on a piece of paper! As is well known, disgust associated with food is a very basic emotion and is easily aroused. That is why, even though what triggers disgust may be different for each person, supermarkets put some distance between sensitive products, such as pet food and groceries. The rejection, however, goes beyond the alleged danger of contamination. For example, any contact with things that can bring bad luck is avoided: a house in which there was a murder is usually difficult to sell, except if the buyer does not know.

- Some studies point out that the quality of good or bad depends on the placement: a higher position denotes vigor, being upright, while a lower one is associated with slouching, with depression. Positive messages are more quickly identified if they are at the top of a screen. The same occurs with the negatives if they are at the bottom. Playing with space is also what many airports do: to access the boarding gate, travelers are forced to pass through the duty-free store, often taking a winding route rather than following a direct path. The aim is to encourage shopping by the mere fact of passing between the shelves.

- One famous experiment was that of a beverage machine installed in the hallway of a university (Poundstone, 2010: 278). The drinks were paid for according to what people could afford. Some days, a large image of beautiful flowers was prominently displayed on the top of the machine. On other days, the image was that of big eyes with an inquisitive gaze. It turned out that, on average, fewer coins were left on days when flowers appeared. The presence of eyes increased the amount paid. The contribution went up as increasingly direct and threatening looks were shown. However, participants reported that the images had not influenced their willingness to pay for their consumption.

The third framing technique is to trigger the association of ideas. It takes advantage of people's penchant for coherence, which pushes them to construct narratives, even if they may be false. These stories establish all kinds of connections (positive or negative) based on accumulated beliefs, aroused emotions and information received. It is not surprising that advertisements are the result of a careful choice of colors, musical settings, etc., all linked to the goal of associating brands with certain values (the product is modern, safe, elitist, etc.). In adverts for cosmetics and parapharmaceuticals, for example, the actors are often dressed in white coats, which denotes rigor and confidence. In addition, in recent years, companies claiming to have learning methods that boost children's IQ have popped up in some countries. Their commercial names are Mozart, Einstein, and so on (Chabris and Simons, 2015: 287; Nisbett 2016: 39). Other examples of the associative capacity of the mind are as follows:

* It was asked how many victims might be caused by a hurricane named Caligula. What if it was named Josephine? Although the name has no relationship with the event, hurricane Caligula was considered deadlier than Josephine (example taken from Nisbett, 2016: 38).
* Between 1960 and 1975, just under 55,000 American soldiers died in the Vietnam War, but in the same period, there were more than 100,000 suicides in the United States. Also in this country, between 1987 and 1996, there were 15,000 more deaths from suicide than from AIDS. When these data are explained, many are surprised: the widespread echo of the ravages of war and HIV arouses emotions that distort the true picture (Motterlini, 2010: 136).

A peculiar method linked to the association of ideas concerns freedom (of choice). This is a powerful argument to get people to do what is sought (Guéguen, 2016: 84). For example, if someone tries to attract donations, the phrase, "You are free to give," increases the donation rate and its average value. On the Internet, a very common ploy is to suggest "You are free to click here," instead of proposing "Click here." Appealing to freedom is persuasive because it arouses the feeling of having chosen without influence. It is also possible to appeal to the presumed freedom with which others have decided, to motivate someone to choose the same option. There are also advertisements for teenagers in which it is emphasized that parents do not like this option (Ubel, 2008: Chapter 10).

The fourth framing method is the appeal to scarcity (Cialdini, 2007: 232–237 and 2016: 414). As is well known, very scarce or rare things usually deserve a high valuation. This scarcity need not be absolute but can be measured in waiting time and discomfort before receiving it. These two latter forms are the most common. From a general point of view, it is known that the (re)productive capacity of all kinds of goods is a more basic feature of the economic system than scarcity. Even so, momentary drops in supply (a bad harvest, lack of a key input, speculative hoarding, etc.) or sudden increases in demand can occur in markets, leading to situations of relative shortage that momentarily push up prices. Without denying the interest in studying these circumstances, what is highlighted here is the use of scarcity as a priming stratagem: an old sales method is to trigger restlessness in customers, urging them to consume by stressing that there are strong quantitative and/or time limits. A well-known case is the creation of limited editions by major brands (Szmigin and Piacentini, 2015: 16). The appeal to scarcity, however, goes far beyond consumer goods. For example, Bernard L. Madoff (1938–2021), one of the creators of the largest financial pyramid scheme known so far, and which collapsed in 2008, explained to clients the high profitability of his investment fund by alluding to the seizure of very scarce and still little-known investment opportunities. This information allowed him, or so he explained, to ignore the prevailing opinion and anticipate the anticipation of other investors (M. Baddeley, 2013: 28, 59).

Many supermarkets, for example, offer discount coupons with expiry dates, or set offers for very short time intervals. These commercial stratagems create anxiety because not taking advantage of them is a missed opportunity. This explains messages such as "Call now!", "Buy right away!" and other slogans that allude to loss aversion. There is also the case of shops that set a short deadline with very high discounts on a first-come, first-served rule, as well as radio stations that give freebies to the first callers. Another variant is to offer discounts to those who have accumulated a certain number of purchases, which are duly registered. For example, airlines have created frequent flyer cards to obtain discounts for future flights. All these tricks encourage customers to accelerate purchases and remain loyal to the supplier of the good or service.

The last type of framing stratagem is the search for familiarity through authenticity and quality. This is the objective of appellations of origin. It is also the objective of advertising foods based on traditional or homemade recipes, which evoke local and endearing know-how. Several experiments have shown that the same dish presented with an indication of the preparation technique (steamed, grilled, etc.) is much less successful than if it is advertised as "Made according to grandma's style." This is surprising because this second claim contains less information than the first one. To arouse consumers' interest, manufacturers associate their brands with things that are familiar, such as places (soap from Marseilles, beer from a certain monastery, water from spa *X*), traditions (very common in food), and so on. Familiarity, or recognition, is very effective in displacing the accurate evaluation of the attributes of goods and services (Guéguen, 2016: 77, see also Chapter 5, section 5.1.1).

6.2.3.3 Anchoring

Anchoring refers to the first piece of explicit information that, after being perfectly perceived by people, decisively influences their decision. An anchor is a cue that powerfully drives the judgments that accompany choices. The most common example is perhaps the technique of ending prices with 95 or 99. If in a supermarket, for example, there are products with prices such as €12.99 or €199, when people are asked about them many say that these prices are a bit more than €12 or €100. Even though they are very close to €13 (and €200) people infer prices based on the first figure that, after a cursory inspection, they think they have seen (Poundstone, 2010: 179). As we know, this commercial trick is often reinforced by writing the decimal digits, if applicable, in a smaller size font. Related to this, there is an old exercise that consists of quickly showing a group of people the following multiplication (Angner, 2012: 52):

$$1 \times 2 \times 3 \times 4 \times 5 \times 6 \times 7 \times 8$$

and then immediately,

$$8 \times 7 \times 6 \times 5 \times 4 \times 3 \times 2 \times 1$$

When people are asked which result is larger, most make an intuitive extrapolation based on the first figures observed. As a result, the second multiplication is estimated to be much larger than the first: in an experiment with university students, the mean of the first result was 512 and that of the second, 2,250, with 40,320 being the correct value. What is noteworthy, however, is not the accuracy of the mental calculation, but the fact that the result derived from the series beginning with 8 far exceeded the one beginning with 1.

Daily life is full of anchors, the most sophisticated ones going unnoticed. This can be illustrated by the experiment designed by Kahneman many years ago. Participants had to spin a wheel that, after turning freely, stopped at a certain number between 1 and 100. Then, they were asked about the number of states on the African continent. Surprisingly, depending on whether the random number was higher or lower, the number of states indicated by the participants was also higher or lower. An arbitrary anchor, unconnected to the subject, guided the estimates. Moreover, no one admitted that the number obtained by turning the wheel had influenced their answer. The anchoring effect, therefore, acts whether the proposed information seems plausible or unrelated to the issue (Motterlini, 2010: 29; Angner, 2012. 53). It is also a robust effect, given that it can emerge as a benchmark in several circumstances due to the powerful associative capacity of the mind. In general, anchors can be of two types:

- By behavioral inertia: when entering an urban area, putting up two consecutive traffic signs compelling people to slow from 90 km/h to 30 km/h shocks drivers who were until then accustomed to driving at 90 km/h (the anchor). This surprise can lead to accidents. The wise option is to establish a progressive deceleration rate (from 90 km/h to 60 km/h and then to 30 km/h). Drivers need time to adapt to the new limits. The established habit is thus a kind of anchor.
- The anchors of commercial activity. They are usually details or suggestions that, without customers necessarily being aware of them, alter their assessment of the prices of goods and services. For instance, some repair garages deliver repaired cars clean and shiny, connoting that a good job was done. There are also price claims: the aim of the anchors is not to make customers accept the listed price, but to drive the perception of the value of the items on sale.

As can be seen, anchors are reference points (of prices, quality, etc.). A store in which a garment placed in a prominent and highly visible site is worth €100 automatically converts all the others marked at €50 into bargains, regardless of any other consideration (Motterlini, 2008: Chapter 3). This is the so-called price contrast effect, which can take the following two forms:

- When consumers have no experience of the item they wish to purchase (e.g., cameras or fountain pens), they tend to opt for the comparatively cheaper version (Wilkinson and Klaes, 2012: 80).
- When there is usually a large variety of models, as in the case of shoes, bags, jackets, etc., the consumer feels uncomfortable (Which piece to choose? What about the price?) and therefore the presence of articles with a (presumed) discount becomes irresistible.

For example, two groups of students were invited to attend a poetry recital (as reported in Poundstone, 2010: 189–190 and Wilkinson and Klaes, 2012: 80). Some had to pay a modest €2 entrance fee, while others were paid the same amount to attend. Only a derisory 2% of the first group said they wanted to go to the recital, while as many as 59% of the second one claimed they would go. Even so, shortly before the recital, it was explained to students that they would neither pay nor receive any money. As a result, the attendance rose to 35% for the former group, while it dropped to 5% for the latter. This behavior highlights the anchoring effect of the economic values initially presented to the students.

The anchor described below is particularly sophisticated. A supermarket put an item on sale. In the first version, a banner was placed on the shelf indicating the offer and, in addition, setting a maximum number of units per customer (ten, for example). In the second version, the banner was the same and was located in the same position. However, it did not set any limit on the number of units that could be purchased. The result was that, in the second case, most customers only picked two or three units while, in the first version, buyers took seven or eight, i.e., they were close to the maximum number suggested. Therefore, the limiting message (the anchor) encouraged the purchase. It is hard to imagine a more subtle ploy to increase sales. As noted above, the establishment of temporary restrictions on access or discounts also has similar effects (Inman et al., 1997).

Let us look at the experience of a point of sale where the prices of biscuits and cookies were not visible. When one of the salesmen indicated to a customer the price of a biscuit (say €2), the other salesman asked for his help. The customer was then forced to wait a moment. When the salesman returned, he told the customer that the price also included a couple of cookies. In another situation, at the outset, the customer was informed that the biscuit plus cookies cost €2. In the first situation, the sales rate exceeded 70% while, in the second, it was 40% (Guéguen, 2016: 80). Whether or not the cookies looked like a gift made the difference. It should be added that consumers do not have enough information to distrust the unexpected offer. In any case, the effectiveness of anchors is not measured by the degree of acceptance of the proposed value, but by how consumers bring their price expectations closer to the anchor.

Price and other attributes of products are especially powerful anchors in luxury and high-end goods and services. In this sector, anchoring is a ubiquitous stratagem (Poundstone, 2010: 155–157). Shop windows currently display items at stratospheric prices, for example, tens of thousands of euros for a bag or a wristwatch. These articles also appear in magazines, newspapers, or websites, always worn by movie stars, successful singers, fashion models, or other celebrities of the moment. They are also common on the fashion catwalks. These extremely expensive and unique items are anchors. They are shown to draw attention and attract customers motivated by exclusivity and/or elitism, not to be sold. Inside the store, the items found have lower prices, although they can only be afforded by people with high purchasing power. The spectacular prices that are displayed in the windows give prestige to the store and, by extension, to the buyers. Therefore, these anchor prices are an essential ingredient of the status experience that so captivates this type of customer. They are also a key part of the story they quickly tell to friends and acquaintances: "I bought it at *X*, where you would have been surprised at the price of some items."

To close this section, it is necessary to address how the concept of 'gratis' may be used as a significant anchor. Although it has become pervasive in recent years, especially in digital products (Bomsel, 2007), offering products free of charge has a long tradition (Cialdini, 2007: 27). For example, many discos allowed girls to enter for free (or at a very low price), an advantage that boys did not enjoy. Similarly, there have always been places where children can go in gratis, as well as casinos and show halls where attendees may have certain amounts of free drink or food (the incentive of a 'free lunch').

To heavily subsidize products from manufacturers or suppliers is only economically viable if the following conditions are met:

- The cost of production and delivery is negligible. The first copy of a piece of music, a film, or a computer program often requires the participation of numerous people, the purchase of materials and the use of important facilities. However, while this step is expensive (and takes the form of a sunk cost), replication and use of successive digital copies has an irrelevant cost. The same fact was already true a few years ago when the medium was electromagnetic, although total digitization and Internet access have lowered the cost of replication and dissemination of copies to the infinitesimal. In addition, memory devices are becoming cheaper and cheaper per unit of storage. As for data transmission lines, the investment and maintenance costs, once divided by their huge capacity, have such a minuscule economic impact per megabyte transmitted/received that it is difficult to quantify.
- There are no institutional barriers, especially legal ones, that successfully block the dissemination of and access to free products. In the case of software and audiovisual goods, copyright has a significant cost, since it affects each copy (it is a fixed royalty, regardless of the number of copies). The conflict between the companies providing digital artifacts and/or services and the audiovisual sector has been inevitable. It is a repetition of the dispute a century ago, between radio manufacturers and broadcasters, and artists and representatives. The latter wanted to make the broadcasters pay high royalties (per radio set purchased), which was unacceptable to the former. Today, companies that make money selling phones and digital players expect content to be very cheap, while Internet service providers hope that advertising revenues, proportional to the number of people connected, will more than compensate for free access. After a long tug-of-war, the audiovisual sector has reinvented itself (record labels have diversified into the permanent organization of concerts) and content distributed by streaming is paid for (especially if people want to avoid advertising).
- Within the group of potential users, there are those whose anxiety (or naivety) pushes them to pay to access add-ons or improved versions of

the free good. On this point, from the beginning, the digital sector has been betting on versioning. This practice was, strictly speaking, already implemented by movie theaters decades ago: tickets for premieres were more expensive, and the price also changed depending on the day and time. Many successful books also end up being published in paperback format.

The value of free goods is the reaction they trigger in people. Since the demand for free items is always greater than for those with a positive price, even if modest, free offers are a necessary condition to rapidly generate a critical mass of customers. The attention gained is then expected to cause a cascade of information: the number of customers will grow exponentially (perhaps reaching the entire planet). Indeed, being free of charge drives preferences (it is an irresistible cue) and enhances the social algorithm of imitation. Companies benefit by using a gratis product in the following ways:

- As a commercial promotion, it opens the door to premium versions. Although the basic version is free, upgrades and add-ons must be paid for. However, these prices need to be fine-tuned, as they are compared to what is free of charge.
- It eliminates much of the concern for product differentiation: if the price is zero, managers know the other attributes seem less important.
- In the case of audiovisual goods, such as apps, virtual games, music, or movies, being free of charge discourages complaints from users, who are unlikely to regret having accepted a poor quality free good.
- Offering goods or services for free may be part of anti-competitive practice, but it will be difficult to gain credibility for this suspicion.

The anchor of being free of charge is powerful, even though it may reduce the prestige of goods or services. It should not be forgotten that people tend to undervalue what costs nothing, despite how much they enjoy receiving all kinds of freebies. This explains how badly people take it when goods or services that used to be free, such as access to the toilets at a train station or an administrative procedure, become chargeable. Even so, if it is a rule that has been in force for a long time or if it is so widespread that it cannot be avoided, people eventually accept it. Examples are the tourist who realizes that in some countries restaurants charge for cutlery, or the traveler who cannot find a low-cost airline that does not charge an additional fee for choosing a seat, checking in luggage, or paying by credit card.

NOTES

1.   As is obvious, all other decision patterns and methods can also be applied to consumer choices. In these pages, however, only the role of heuristics is studied.

2.   For example, in the case of digital products, default choice abounds, whereas, in the purchase of Persian rugs, a certain degree of deliberation can be expected.

3.   Typography, colors, images, slogans, etc. are signals that appeal to people's beliefs about the product. For example, packages of cookies, yogurts, and fruit juices carry colorful pictures of the fruit, even though their actual content is small (unlike sugar, flour, dairy products, etc.). These images suggest that the product is natural and healthy, and a substitute for fruit. In addition, recognition is easier if the product name and brand name match, as is the case with Velcro and aspirin. In the case of Formica, even the company name coincided. This assimilation has not always been possible: the firm that pioneered photocopies called them *xerocopies*, a word that later manufacturers managed to unseat.

4.   Different brands in the same product class try to attract customers belonging to a given status and lifestyle, even if their boundaries are blurred. For products of different categories, buyers also come from different social groups.

5.   The origin of the routine is diverse: perhaps it was a product bought by the parents or seen at friends' or acquaintances' homes; perhaps the brand appeared in magazine advertisements or was repeated over and over again on the radio; perhaps the person simply tried all the variants available in the nearest supermarket and went on to buy one of them; and so on.

6.   It includes routine shopping and leisure shopping, i.e., purchases from doing the shopping and purchases from going shopping, respectively. In the latter, consumers have time and will continue to search until they find what is sufficiently satisfactory. These conditions make forecasting particularly difficult (Szmigin and Piacentini, 2015: 101; Trentman, 2016: 93).

7.   Celebrities are people recognized everywhere with awe and enthusiasm. This may be due to their wealth, their success in sport, their reputation as an artist, or their projection as a careerist who lives in and from the media. Their mere presence in the media is key to achieving fame.

8.   Cosmetics are the ultimate in this field. The producers of creams, oils, etc., seem to have no limits when it comes to adding, to the same standard chemical base, all kinds of new components whose effects are, according to the narrative, extraordinary. All this is surrounded by bombastic scientific jargon and by the glamour of the brand's association with cities such as Paris, London, Rome, and New York.

9.   In Scitovsky (1976: Chapter 3), people's attitude to novelties is detailed.

10.   Among the stratagems of appealing directly to people, the table does not include the demonstration effect: a decision is made expecting others will imitate it. However, the table does include the term "a foot-in-the-memory," a translation of "le-pied-dans-la-memoire" (Joule and Beauvois, 2014: 168) whose meaning is explained in the text.

11.   More information in Cialdini (2007: 41–51, 98–99); Joule and Beauvois (2014: 100–172); and Guéguen (2016: 97–102, 204–228 and 2018).

12.   This list, originally given by Aristotle, is very incomplete. For example, the sense of balance, spatial orientation, different internal senses, and many more are missing.

7. Summing up

The best way to close this book is to recall John Maurice Clark's opening sentence. Can anything more be added? More impressive than its degree of accuracy is the century that has elapsed since it was enunciated. This is very enlightening. Economic theory and, more specifically, the study of economic decision-making, has for decades lived in the comfort zone of the axioms of boundless rationality. These postulates were labeled either as normative or protected by the as-if clause. Both prevent analyzing how people make decisions in real life. Protected by the shield of alleged abstract and universal principles, economic theory has built a discourse conveniently detached from psychological and social factors. Moreover, this theoretical body claims its aptitude to guarantee, according to its followers, the best possible outcome in any decision (Mousavi and Gigerenzer, 2014: 4). This quality, however, is only valid within the narrow logical-formal limits of the model. In the meantime, the systematic study of the countless economic decisions that people make every day in their personal and professional lives has been postponed again and again. There is no doubt that this analysis has always been, and continues to be, an arduous and time-consuming task, especially due to the difficulty of elucidating the processes of judgment formation and the enormous diversity of contexts, not infrequently imbued with uncertainty. Even so, there is no excuse, especially when disciplines such as psychology, neuroscience, human ethology, sociology, etc. have not ceased to provide results of proven quality.

At present, economic psychology is one of the most active fields of economics. As explained in these pages, it is a discipline that lacks a systematic and unified theoretical corpus. Two major research programs coexist: the more widespread one focuses on discovering more and more biases of the human mind which, by pure reflex, perpetuates the benchmark of perfect rationality. The other proposes to study human rationality in context and displays enviable praxeological rigor. This second program has inspired this book, together with materials from other sources. It is a research program that projects a more realistic and, incidentally, a friendlier conception of human rationality, assuming, without making it explicit, the systemic character of the socio-economic world. On the one hand, it stresses that people are an idiosyncratic combination of unique socialization and personality processes and, on the other hand, it insists that the different variables that shape contexts are never disconnected from each other. Therefore, background and linkages are the key terms of this approach. Consequently, this perspective is receptive to findings from psychology (cognitive, social), without neglecting the contributions from other human sciences. Differences and nuances aside, this attitude is also shared by the main researchers of the heuristics and biases program. Hence, both programs abandon Pareto's postulate, still very present, which separates these domains of scientific knowledge. From a historical perspective, this split has led to poor results.

Although this book is only an introduction, some of the listed results from economic psychology are of sufficient relevance to be incorporated into microeconomic models and, as far as possible, macroeconomic models. Namely:

- The theory of economic decisions, which has given total prominence to preferences, should incorporate beliefs, emotions, and memories.
- A distinction should be made between situations in which risk aversion prevails and those in which risk propensity stands out. Unfortunately, the latter has been less studied. Although losses do not seem to have a greater impact than gains, the strong aversion to loss shown by people should be emphasized.
- Although the preference for immediate reward has been known for decades, except under specific conditions and in the face of sequences of increasing values, it is necessary to delve deeper into the degree of impatience of people and their relationship with different circumstances. At the same time, the design of models should not ignore the role of hedonic anticipation.
- Heuristics are observed regularities in people's behavior, even though their specific implementation may change according to the context and from one person to another. Heuristics are contextually robust procedures for predicting human decisions, although previous experiences and people's insight should also be taken into account. In any case, the incorporation of heuristics into economic decision models should be generalized.
- Cooperation and reciprocity are human attitudes at least as powerful as the competitive one aimed at the preservation of one's own interests. People cooperate with those who cooperate and try to penalize free-riders. However, the proliferation of the latter pushes everyone to abandon cooperation. This may lead to the emergence of self interest as an alternative method for implementing all kinds of initiatives, although with no coordination they are likely to fail and the devoted resources will be wasted.
- In consumption decisions, familiarity and interpersonal comparisons are omnipresent. This highlights the importance of recognition and imitation heuristics, respectively. It would also be desirable for models to incorporate techniques capable of modifying final preferences, especially cogni-

tive easing, framing, and anchoring. Marketing is an excellent source of information in this regard.

It is not easy to find in the economic literature references to the results of economic psychology, especially those discussed in this book. To provide economic models with a greater degree of realism, it would be necessary to expand the presence of these results. Even so, it should not be forgotten that there is still much work to be done in economic psychology. This diagnosis is reiterated several times in this summary, the aim of which was to provide a map of the discipline. Research in economic psychology requires imagination and dedication since it has to overcome many obstacles, while avoiding the temptation to deploy more and more models, as Ptolemy's cosmology did, i.e., to increase complexity in response to the proliferation of anomalies. In economic psychology, adding more and more parameters in pursuit of maximum fit, given that supposedly every bit of information matters, is particularly misguided: it implicitly assumes that people have extraordinary cognitive abilities. Since decision-making processes are inevitably complex, it is inferred that models must also be complex. However, the analysis should not forget that the human mind excels, not for its computational capacity, but in its plasticity and creativity. As we know, people adapt to very different situations and strive to identify causes and establish all kinds of associations. Consequently, the analysis of rationality in the real world must insist on originality and rigor in the design of experiments. These are two indispensable conditions for matching algorithms and contexts precisely. It is not easy, but the reward is robust predictions. *Sapere aude.*

References

Aikman, D., Galesic, M., Gigerenzer, G., Kapadia, S., Katsikopoulos, K. V., Kothiyal, A., Murphy, E. & Neumann, T. (2021). Taking uncertainty seriously: simplicity versus complexity in financial regulation. *Industrial and Corporate Change*, 30(2), 317–345.

Ainslie, G. (1975). Specious reward: a behavioral theory of impulsiveness and impulse control. *Psychological Bulletin*, 82(4), 463–496.

Ainslie, G. (1992). Hyperbolic discounting. In G. Loewenstein & J. Elster (Eds.), *Choice over time* (pp. 57–92). Russell Sage Foundation.

Ainslie, G. (2005). Précis of "*breakdown of will*". *Behavioral and Brain Sciences*, 28, 635–673.

Ainslie, G. (2009). Recursive self-prediction in self-control and its failure. In T. Grüne-Yanoff & S. O. Hansson (Eds.), *Preference change. Approaches from philosophy, economics and psychology* (pp. 139–158). Springer.

Akerlof, G. A. (1970). The market for "lemons": quality uncertainty and the market mechanism. *The Quarterly Journal of Economics*, 84(3), 488–500.

Akerlof, G. A. & Shiller, R. J. (2009). *Animal spirits: how human psychology drives the economy, and why it matters for global capitalism*. Princeton University Press.

Alter, A. L. & Oppenheimer, D. M. (2006). Predicting short-term stock fluctuation by using process fluency. *Proceedings of the National Academy of Sciences of the United States of America*, 103(24), 9369–9372. http://doi.org/10.1073/pnas.0601071103

Alter, A. L. & Oppenheimer, D. M. (2008). Easy on the mind, easy on the wallet: the roles of familiarity and processing fluency in valuation judgements. *Psychonomic Bulletin and Review*, 15(4), 985–990.

Altman, M. (2017a). A bounded rationality assessment of the new behavioral economics. In R. Frantz, S.-H. Chen, K. Dopfer, F. Heukelom & S. Mousavi (Eds.), *Routledge handbook of behavioral economics* (pp. 179–193). Routledge.

Altman, M. (2017b). Introduction to smart decision-making. In M. Altman (Ed.), *Handbook of behavioural economics and smart decision-making. Rational decision-making within the bounds of reason* (pp. 1–8). Edward Elgar Publishing.

Angner, E. (2012). *A course in behavioral economics*. Palgrave Macmillan.

Ariely, D. (2009). *Predictably irrational. The hidden forces that shape our decisions* (revised and expanded edition). Harper.

Ariely, D. (2010). *The upside of irrationality. The unexpected benefits of defying logic at work and at home*. HarperCollins.

Ariely, D. (2012). *The (honest) truth about dishonesty. How we lie to everyone, especially ourselves*. HarperCollins.

Ariely, D. & Kreisler, J. (2017). *Dollars and sense. How we misthink money and how to spend smarter*. Harper Collins.

Ariely, D., Loewenstein, G. & Prelec, D. (2003). "Coherent arbitrariness": stable demand curves without stable preferences. *The Quarterly Journal of Economics*, 118(1), 73–105.

Arkes, H. R., Gigerenzer, G. & Hertwig, R. (2016). How bad is incoherence? *Decision*, 3(1), 20–39.

Arnsperger, Ch. & van Parijs, Ph. (2000). *Éthique économiques et sociale*. Éditions La Découverte & Syros.

Aronson, E. (2008). *The social animal* (10th ed.). Worth Publishers.

Artinger, F. M., Petersen, M., Gigerenzer, G. & Weibler, J. (2014). Heuristics as adaptive decision strategies in management. *Journal of Organizational Behavior*, 36(S1), S33–S52.

Artinger, F. M., Gigerenzer, G. & Jacobs, P. (2022). Satisficing: integrating two traditions. *Journal of Economic Literature*, (60)2, 598–635.

Backhouse, R. & Fontaine, Ph. (2010). Toward a history of social sciences. In R. Backhouse & Ph. Fontaine (Eds.), *Toward a history of the social sciences since 1945* (pp. 184–232). Cambridge University Press.

Baddeley, A., Eysenck, M. W. & Anderson, M. C. (2015). *Memory* (2nd ed.). Taylor and Francis.

Baddeley, M. (2010). *Herding, social influence and economic decision-making: socio-psychological and neuroscientific analyses*. Philosophical Transactions of the Royal Society Biological Sciences. http://royalsocietypublishing.org/doi/full/10.1098/rstb.2009.0169

Baddeley, M. (2013). *Behavioural economics and finance*. Routledge.

Barbé, Ll. (2006). *Francis Ysidro Edgeworth. Crònica familiar* (Ciència i tècnica, 31). Universitat Autònoma de Barcelona.

Bazerman, M. (1998). *Judgement in managerial decision making*. John Wiley and Sons.

Berg, N. (2003). Normative behavioral economics. *The Journal of Socio-Economics*, 32, 411–427.

Berg, N. (2014a). The consistency and ecological rationality approaches to normative bounded rationality. *Journal of Economic Methodology*, 21(4), 375–395.

Berg, N. (2014b). Success from satisficing and imitation: entrepreneurs' location choice and implications of heuristics for local economic development. *Journal of Business Research* 67(8), 1700–1709.

Berg, N. & Gigerenzer, G. (2010). As-if behavioral economics: neoclassical economics in disguise? *History of Economic Ideas*, 18(1), 133–165.

Berg, N., Eckel, C. C. & Johnson, C. A. (2008). *Inconsistency pays? Time-inconsistent subjects and EU violators earn more*. http://ssrn.com/abstract=1692437

Blount, S. (1995). When social outcomes aren't fair: the effect of causal attributions on preferences. *Organizational Behavior and Human Decision Processes*, 63(2), 131–144.

Bocskocsky, A., Ezekowitz, J. & Stein, C. (2014). *Heat check: new evidence on the hot hand in basketball*. http://papers.ssrn.com/sol3/papers.cfm?abstract_id=2481494

Bomsel, O. (2007). *Gratuit! Du déploiement de l'économie numérique*. Éditions Gallimard.

Borges, B., Goldstein, D. G., Ortmann, A. & Gigerenzer, G. (1999). Can ignorance beat the stock market? In G. Gigerenzer, P. M. Todd & the ABC Research Group (Eds.), *Simple heuristics that make us smart* (pp. 59–72). Oxford University Press.

Bovens, L. (2009). The ethics of nudge. In T. Grüne-Yanoff & S. O. Hansson (Eds.), *Preference change. Approaches from philosophy, economics and psychology* (pp. 207–219). Springer.

Bowles, S. (1998). Endogenous references: the cultural consequences of markets and other economic institutions. *Journal of Economic Literature*, XXXVI, 75–111.

Bowles, S. & Gintis, H. (2013). *A cooperative species. Human reciprocity and its evolution*. Princeton University Press.

Brandstätter, E., Gigerenzer, G. & Hertwig, R. (2006). The priority heuristic: making choices without trade-offs. *Psychological Review*, 113(2), 409–432.

Brighton, H. & Gigerenzer, G. (2012). How heuristics handle uncertainty. In P. M. Todd, G. Gigenrenzer & ABC Research Group (Eds.), *Ecological rationality. Intelligence in the world* (pp. 33–60). Oxford University Press.

Brown, A. & Maydeu-Olivares, A. (2011). Item response modelling of forced-choice questionnaires. *Educational and Psychological Measurement*, 71(3), 460–503.

Brown, A. & Maydeu-Olivares, A. (2012). Fitting a Thurstonian IRT model to forced-choice data using Mplus. *Behavioral Research Methods*, 44, 1135–1147.

Bruni, L. & Sugden, R. (2007). The road not taken: how psychology was removed from economics, and how it might be brought back. *The Economic Journal*, 117, 146–173.

Buckmann, M. & Şimşek, Ö. (2016). Decision heuristics for comparison: how good are they? *Proceedings of Machine Learning Research*, 58, 1–11.

Bunge, M. (2010). *Matter and mind*. Springer.

Bürkner, P.-Ch., Schulte, N. & Holling, H. (2019). On the statistical and practical limitations of Thurstonian IRT models. *Educational and Psychological Measurement*, 79(5), 827–854.

Cameron, L. (1999). Raising the stakes in the ultimatum game: experimental evidence from Indonesia. *Economic Inquiry*, 37(1), 47–59.

Cartwright, E. (2018). *Behavioral economics* (3rd ed.). Routledge.

Chabris, C. & Simons, D. (2015). *Le gorille invisible. Quand nos intuitions nous jouent des tours*. Éditions Le Pommier.

Chater, N., Felin, T. & Todd, P. M. (2018). Mind, rationality, and cognition: an interdisciplinary debate. *Psychonomic Bulletin and Review*, 25, 793–826.

Cheng, J. & González-Vallejo, C. (2014). Hyperbolic discounting: value and time processes of substance abusers and non-clinical people in inter-temporal choice. *PLoS ONE* 9(11): e111378. https://doi.org/10.1371/journal.pone.0111378

Cheng, J. & González-Vallejo, C. (2016). Attribute-wise vs. alternative-wise mechanism in inter-temporal choice: testing the proportional difference, trade-off, and hyperbolic models. *Decision*, 3(3). http://dx.doi.org/10.1037/dec0000046

Chetty, R. (2015). *Behavioral economics and public policy: a pragmatic perspective* (Working Paper 20928). NBER. http://www.nber.org/papers/w20928

Christl, W. & Spiekermann, S. (2016). *Networks of control. A report on corporate surveillance, digital tracking, big data & privacy*. Facultas Verlags- un Buchhandels AG.

Chung, S.-H. & Herrnstein, R. J. (1967). Choice and delay of reinforcement. *Journal of the Experimental Analysis of Behavior*, 10(1), 67–74.

Cialdini, R. B. (2007). *Influence. The psychology of persuasion* (3rd ed.). Harper Collins.

Cialdini, R. B. (2016). *Pre-suasion. A revolutionary way to influence and persuade*. Penguin.

Cobb, M. (2020). *The idea of the brain. A history*. Profile Books.

Cremaschi, S. (1998). Homo oeconomicus. In H. D. Kurz & N. Salvadori (Eds.), *The Elgar companion to classical economics* (Vol. I A–K, pp. 377–381). Edward Elgar Publishing.

Currid-Halkett, E. (2017). *The sum of small things. A theory of the aspirational class*. Princeton University Press.

Curtin, R. (2017). George Katona: a founder of behavioural economics. In R. Frantz, S.-H. Chen, K. Dopfer, F. Heukelom & S. Mousavi (Eds.), *Routledge handbook of behavioral economics* (pp. 18–35). Routledge.
de Vries, B. J. M. (2013). *Sustainability science*. Cambridge University Press.
della Vigna, A. & Malmendier, U. (2006). Paying not to go to the gym. *The American Economic Review*, 96(3), 694–719.
Delpal, F. & Jacomet, D. (2014). *Économie du luxe*. Dunod.
DeMiguel, V., Garlappi, L. & Uppal, R. (2009). Optimal versus naive diversification: how inefficient is the 1/*N* portfolio strategy? *The Review of Financial Studies*, 22(5), 1915–1953.
Dijksterhuis, A., Bos, M. W., Nordgren, L. F. & van Baaren, R. B. (2006). On making the right choice: the deliberation-without-attention effect. *Science*, 311, 1005–1007.
Dmitriev, V. K. (1968). *Éssais économiques. Esquisse de synthèse organique de la théorie de la valeur-travail et de la théorie de l'utilité marginale* (1st ed. 1904). Éditions du CNRS.
Dow Schüll, N. (2014). *Addiction by design. Machine gambling in Las Vegas*. Princeton University Press.
Doyal, L. & Gough, I. (1991). *A theory of human need*. The Macmillan Press.
Du, W., Green, L. & Myerson, J. (2002). Cross-cultural comparisons of discounting delayed and probabilistic rewards. *The Psychological Record*, 52, 479–492.
Durbach, I. N., Algorta, S., Kabongo Kantu, D., Katsikopoulos, K. & Şimşek, Ö. (2020). Fast and frugal heuristics for portfolio decisions with positive interactions. *Decision Support Systems*, 138, art. 113399.
Earl, P. E. (1986). *Lifestyle economics. Consumer behavior in a turbulent world*. Wheatsheaf books.
Earl, P. E. (1990). Economics and psychology: a survey. *The Economic Journal*, C (402), 718–755.
Earl, P. E. (1995). *Microeconomics for business and marketing. Lectures, cases and worked essays*. Edward Elgar Publishing.
Earl, P. E. (2017). The evolution of behavioural economics. In R. Frantz, S.-H. Chen, K. Dopfer, F. Heukelom & S. Mousavi (Eds.), *Routledge handbook of behavioral economics* (pp. 5–17). Routledge.
Edwards, W. (1954). The theory of decision making. *Psychological Bulletin*, 51(4), 380–417.
Eibl-Eibesfeldt, I. (2012). *Human ethology*. Aldine Transaction.
Ekeland, I. & Elster, J. (2011). *Théorie économique et rationalité*. Vuibert.
Eklund, A., Nichols, T., Andersson, M. & Knutsson, H. (2015). *Empirically investigating the statistical of SPM, FSL and AFNI for single subject fMRI analysis*. http://doi .10.1109/ISBI.2015.7164132
Elster, J. (1989). *Nuts and bolts for the social sciences*. Cambridge University Press.
Elster, J. (1991). *Domar la suerte. La aleatoriedad en decisiones individuales y sociales* (Pensamiento contemporáneo, 14). Paidós/ICE UAB.
Elster, J. (2007). *Explaining social behavior. More nuts and bolts for the social sciences*. Cambridge University Press.
Elster, J. (2010). *L'irrationalité. Traité critique de l'homme économique II*. Éditions du Seuil.
Etzioni, A. (2015). The moral effects of economic teaching. *Sociological Forum*, 30(1), 228–233.
Eysenck, M. W. & Keane, M. T. (2010). *Cognitive psychology. A student's handbook*. Psychology Press.

Farmer, G. D., Warren, P. A. & Hahn, U. (2017). Who "believes" in the gambler's fallacy and why? *Journal of Experimental Psychology: General*, 146(1), 63–76.

Fehr, E. & Fischbacher, U. (2005). The economics of strong reciprocity. In H. Gintis, S. Bowles, R. Boyd & E. Fehr (Eds.), *Moral sentiments and material interests. The foundations of cooperation in economics* (pp. 277–302). The MIT Press.

Fehr, E. & Gätchter, S. (2000). Cooperation and punishment in public goods experiments. *American Economic Review*, 90(4), 980–994.

Fehr, E., Fischbacher, U. & Gächter, S. (2002). Strong reciprocity, human cooperation and the enforcement of social norms. *Human Nature*, 13, 1–25.

Fiedler, K. (2010). How to study cognitive decisions algorithms: the case of the priority heuristic. *Judgement and Decision Making*, 5(1), 21–32.

Fine, B. & Milonakis, D. (2009). *From economics imperialism to freakonomics. The shifting boundaries between economics and other social sciences*. Routledge.

Finney, B. & Low, S. (2008). Navigation. In H. K. Howe (Ed.), *Vaka moana. Voyages of the ancestors. The discovery and settlement of the Pacific* (pp. 154–197). David Baterman & Auckland War Memorial Museum.

Fitzgibbons, A. (2002). The microeconomics foundations of Keynesian economics. In S. C. Dow & J. Hillard (Eds.), *Keynes, uncertainty and the global economy* (pp. 6–18). Edward Elgar Publishing.

Flyvbjerg, B., Bruzelius, N. & Rothengatter, W. (2003). *Megaprojects and risk. An anatomy of ambition*. Cambridge University Press.

Foer, F. (2017). *World without mind. The existential threat of big tech*. Penguin.

Frank, R. H., Gilovich, T. & Regan, D. T. (1993). Does studying economics inhibit cooperation? *Journal of Economic Perspectives*, 7(2), 159–171.

Frederick, S., Loewenstein, G. & O'Donoghue, T. (2003). Time discounting and time preference: a critical review. In G. Loewenstein, D. Read & R. F. Baumeister (Eds.), *Economic and psychological perspectives on inter-temporal choice* (pp. 13–86). Russell Sage Foundation.

Gal, D. & Rucker, D. D. (2018). The loss of loss aversion: will it loom larger than its gain? *Journal of Consumer Psychology*, 28(3), 1–20.

Georgescu-Roegen, N. (1977). Utilidad. In *Enciclopedia internacional de las ciencias sociales* (Vol. 10: 562–586). Aguilar.

Gigerenzer, G. (1991). How to make cognitive illusions disappear: beyond "heuristics and biases". In W. Stroebe & M. Hewstone (Eds.), *European review of social psychology* (Vol. 2, pp. 83–115). Wiley.

Gigerenzer, G. (1996). On narrow norms and vague heuristics: a reply to Kahneman and Tversky (1996). *Psychological Review*, 103(3), 592–596.

Gigerenzer, G. (2001). The adaptive toolbox. In G. Gigerenzer & R. Selten (Eds.), *Bounded rationality. The adaptive toolbox* (pp. 37–50). The MIT Press.

Gigerenzer, G. (2002). *Calculated risks. How to know when numbers deceive you*. Simon and Schuster.

Gigerenzer, G. (2007). *Gut feelings: short cuts to better decision making*. Penguin.

Gigerenzer, G. (2008). Why heuristics work. *Perspectives on Psychological Science*, 3(1), 20–29.

Gigerenzer, G. (2014). *Risk savvy. How to make good decisions*. Penguin.

Gigerenzer, G. (2015). *Simply rational. Decision making in the real world*. Oxford University Press.

Gigerenzer, G. (2018). The bias bias in behavioral economics. *Review of Behavioral Economics*, 5, 303–336.

Gigerenzer, G. (2020). How to explain behavior? *Topics in Cognitive Science*, 12(4), 1363–1381.

Gigerenzer, G. (2021). Axiomatic rationality and ecological rationality. *Synthese*, 198, 3547–3564.

Gigerenzer, G. (2022). *How to stay smart in a smart world. Why human intelligence still beats algorithms*. Allen Lane.

Gigerenzer, G. & Brighton, H. (2009). Homo heuristicus: why biased minds make better inferences. *Topics in Cognitive Science*, 1, 107–143.

Gigerenzer, G. & Edwards, A. (2003). Simple tools for understanding risks: from innumeracy to insight. *The British Medical Journal*, 327, 741–744.

Gigerenzer, G. & Gaissmaier, W. (2011). Heuristic decision making. *Annual Review of Psychology*, 62, 451–482.

Gigerenzer, G. & Goldstein, D. G. (1996). Reasoning the fast and frugal way: models of bounded rationality. *Psychological Review*, 103(4), 650–669.

Gigerenzer, G. & Goldstein, D. G. (2011a). Betting on one good reason. The take the best heuristic. In G. Gigerenzer, P. M. Todd & the ABC Research Group (Eds.), *Simple heuristics that make us smart* (pp. 75–95). Oxford University Press.

Gigerenzer, G. & Goldstein, D. G. (2011b). The recognition heuristic. A decade of research. *Judgement and Decision Making*, 6(1), 100–121.

Gigerenzer, G. & Hoffrage, U. (1995). How to improve Bayesian reasoning without instruction: frequency formats. *Psychological Review*, 102 (4), 684–704.

Gigerenzer, G. & Regier, T. (1996). How do we tell an association from a rule? Comment on Sloman (1996). *Psychological Bulletin*, 119 (1), 23–26.

Gigerenzer, G., Hoffrage, U. & Kleinbölting, H. (1991). Probabilistic mental models: a Brunswikian theory of confidence. *Psychological Review*, 98(4), 506–528.

Gigerenzer, G., Hoffrage, U. & Goldstein, D. (2008). Fast and frugal heuristics are plausible models of cognition: reply to Dougherty, Franco-Watkins, and Thomas (2008). *Psychological Review*, 115(1), 230–239.

Gigerenzer, G., Hertwig, R. & Pachur, T. (2011). Introduction. In G. Gigerenzer, R. Hertwig & T. Pachur (Eds.), *Heuristics. The foundations of adaptive behavior* (pp. xvii–xiv). Oxford University Press.

Gigerenzer, G., Reb, J. & Luan, S. (2022). Smart heuristics for individuals, teams, and organizations. *Annual Review of Organizational Psychology and Organizational Behavior*, 9, 171–198.

Gilboa, I., Postlewaite, A. & Schmeidler, D. (2004). *Rationality of belief or: why Bayesianism is neither necessary nor sufficient for rationality* (Yale University Cowles Foundation Discussion Paper No. 1484 & Penn Institute for Economic Research (PIER) Working Paper No. 04-011). http://ssrn.com/abstract=523502

Gilboa, I. Postlewaite, A. & Schmeidler, D. (2012). Rationality of belief or: why Savage's axioms are neither necessary nor sufficient for rationality. *Synthese*, 1(187), 11–31.

Gilovich, T., Vallone, R. & Tversky, A. (1985). The hot hand in basketball: on the misperception of random sequences. *Cognitive Psychology*, 17, 295–314.

Goetzmann, W. N. (2017). *Money changes everything. How finance made civilization possible*. Princeton University Press.

Goldstein, D. G. & Gigerenzer, G. (2002). Models of ecological rationality: the recognition heuristic. *Psychological Review*, 109(1), 75–90.

Grall, B. (2003). *Économie des forces et production d'utilités. L'émergence du calcul économique chez les ingénieurs des ponts et chaussées (1831–1891)*. Presses Universitaires de Rennes.

Granovetter, M. (1978). Threshold models of collective behavior. *American Journal of Sociology*, 83(6), 1420–1443.

Groner, M. (1983). Approaches to heuristics: a historical review. In R. Groner, M. Groner & W. F. Bishop (Eds.), *Methods of heuristics* (pp. 1–18). Lawrence Erlbaum Associates. Digital version published by Routledge in 2009.

Guéguen, N. (2016). *Psychologie du consommateur. Pour mieux comprendre comment on vous influence*. Dunod.

Guéguen, N. (2018). *Manipuler et séduire. Petit traité de psychologie comportementale*. Belin.

Hahn, U. (2014). Experiential limitation in judgement and decision. *Topics in Cognitive Science*, 6, 229–244.

Hahn, U. & Warren, P. A. (2009). Perceptions of randomness. Why three heads are better than four. *Psychological Review*, 116(2), 454–461.

Halpern, D. (2015). *Inside the nudge unit. How small changes can make a big difference*. WH Allen.

Hammond, J. S., Keeney, R. L. & Raiffa, H. (2002). *Smart choices. A practical guide to making better life decisions*. Broadway Books.

Hand, D. J. (2014). *The improbability principle. Why coincidences, miracles, and rare events happen every day*. Scientific American / Farrar, Straus and Giroux.

Hare, B. (2017). Survival of the friendliest: *homo sapiens* evolved via selection for prosociality. *The Annual Review of Psychology*, 68, 24.1–24.32.

Harris, M. (1989). *Our kind: who we are, where we came from, where we are going*. Harper & Row.

Harstad, R. M. & Selten, R. (2013). Bounded-rationality models: tasks to become intellectually competitive. *Journal of Economic Literature*, 51(2), 496–511.

Hauser, J. R. (2014). Consideration-set heuristics. *Journal of Business Research*, 67(8), 1688–1699.

Hausman, D. M. (2012). *Preference, value, choice, and welfare*. Cambridge University Press.

Henrich, J., Heine, S. J. & Norenzayan, A. (2010). The weirdest people in the world? *Behavioral and Brain Sciences*, 33(2–3), 1–75.

Hertwig, R. & Grüne-Yanoff, T. (2017). Nudging and boosting: steering or empowering good decisions. *Perspectives on Psychological Science*, 12(6), 1–14.

Hertwig, R. & Pedersen, A. P. (2016). Finding foundations for bounded and adaptive rationality. *Mind and Machines*, 26, 1–8.

Heukelom, F. (2014). *Behavioral economics. A history*. Cambridge University Press.

Heukelom, F. (2017a). Richard Thaler's behavioral economics. In R. Frantz, S.-H. Chen, K. Dopfer, F. Heukelom & S. Mousavi (Eds.), *Routledge Handbook of Behavioral Economics* (pp. 101–111). Routledge.

Heukelom, F. (2017b). Daniel Kahneman and the behavioral economics of cognitive mistakes. In R. Frantz, S.-H. Chen, K. Dopfer, F. Heukelom & S. Mousavi (Eds.), *Routledge handbook of behavioral economics* (pp. 112–128). Routledge.

Hirschman, A. O. (1970). *Exit, voice, and loyalty. Responses to decline in firms, organizations, and states*. Harvard University Press.

Hirschman, A. O. & Rothschild, M. (1973). The changing tolerance for income inequality in the course of economic development. *The Quarterly Journal of Economics*, 87(4), 544–566.

HL (2011). *Behaviour Change Report* (HL Paper 179, 2nd Report of Session 2010–12). Science and Technology Select Committee/House of Lords. http://www.parliament.uk/hlscience

Ho, T., Lim, N. & Camerer, C. F. (2006). Modelling the psychology of consumer and firm behavior with behavioural economics. *Journal of Marketing Research*, 43, 307–331.

Hodgkinson, G. P. & Healy, M. P. (2008). Cognition in organizations. *Annual Review of Psychology*, 59, 387–417.

Hoffrage, U., Hertwig, R. & Gigerenzer, G (2000). Hindsight bias: a by-product of knowledge updating? *Journal of Experimental Psychology: Learning, Memory, and Cognition*, 26(3), 566–581.

Hogg, M. A. & Vaughan, G. M. (2014). *Social Psychology* (7th ed.). Pearson Education.

Hosseini, H. (2017). George Katona's contributions to the start of behavioral economics. In R. Frantz, S.-H. Chen, K. Dopfer, F. Heukelom & S. Mousavi (Eds.), *Routledge handbook of behavioral economics* (pp. 129–138). Routledge.

Hunt, E. K. (1992). *History of economic thought: a critical perspective*. Harper Collins.

Ingrao, B. & Israel, G. (2015). *The invisible hand. Economic equilibrium in the history of science*. http://www.academia.edu

Inman, J. J., Peter, A. C. & Raghubir, P. (1997). Framing the deal: the role of restrictions in accentuating deal value. *The Journal of Consumer Research*, 24(1), 68–79.

Joule, R.-V. & Beauvois, J.-L. (2014). *Petit traité de manipulation à l'usage des honnêtes gens*. Presses Universitaires de Grenoble.

Just, D. R. (2014). *Introduction to behavioral economics. Noneconomic factors that shape economic decisions*. John Wiley and Sons.

Kahneman, D. (2005). Mappe di razionalità limitata: indagine sui giudizi e le scelte intuitivi. Nobel Lecture, 8 December 2002. In M. Motterlini & M. Piattelli (Eds.), *Critica della ragione economica. Tre saggi: Kahneman, McFadden, Smith* (pp. 77–140) (La cultura, 590). Il Saggiatore.

Kahneman, D. (2006). New challenges to the rationality assumption. In S. Lichtenstein & P. Slovic (Eds.), *The construction of preference* (pp. 487–503). Cambridge University Press.

Kahneman, D. (2011). *Thinking, fast and slow*. Farrar, Straus and Giroux.

Kahneman, D. & Tversky, A. (1979). Prospect theory: an analysis of decision under risk. *Econometrica*, 47(2), 263–291.

Kamleitner, B., Marckhgott, E. & Kirchler, E. (2018). Money management in households. In A. Lewis (Ed.), *The Cambridge handbook of psychology and economic behavior* (pp. 260–283, 2nd ed.). Cambridge University Press.

Kant, E. (2018). *Groundwork for the metaphysics of morals*. Edited and translated by Allen W. Wood with an updated translation, introduction, and notes (1st ed. 1785). Yale University Press.

Katsikopoulos, K. V. (2014). Bounded rationality: the two cultures. *Journal of Economic Methodology*, 21(4), 361–374.

Katsikopoulos, K. V. & Gigerenzer, G. (2008). One-reason decision-making: modelling violations of expected utility theory. *Journal of Risk and Uncertainty*, 37, 35–56.

Katsikopoulos, K. V., Şimşek, Ö., Buckmann, M. & Gigerenzer, G. (2020). *Classification in the wild. The science and art of transparent decision making*. The MIT Press.

Kattah, J. C., Talkad, A. V., Wang, D. Z., Hsieh, Y. H. & Newman-Toker, D. E. (2009). *HINTS to diagnose stroke in the acute vestibular syndrome: three-step bedside oculomotor examination more sensitive than early MRI diffusion-weighted imaging*. http//stroke.ahajournals.org

Keller, N. & Katsikopoulos, K. V. (2016). On the role of psychological heuristics in operational research; and a demonstration in military stability operations. *European Journal of Operational Research*, 249(3), 1063–1073.

Kirby, K. N. (1997). Bidding on the future: evidence against normative discounting of delayed rewards. *Journal of Experimental Psychology: General*, 126(1), 54–70.

Klein, S. (2015). *Il tempo, la sostanza di cui è fatta la vita*. Bollati Boringhieri.

Knight, F. H. (1964). *Risk, uncertainty and profits* (1st ed. 1921). Augustus M. Kelley Bookseller.

Koehler, J. J. (1996). The base rate fallacy reconsidered: descriptive, normative, and methodological challenges. *Behavioral and Brain Sciences*, 19, 1–17.

Kruglanski, A. W. & Gigerenzer, G. (2011). Intuitive and deliberate judgements are based on common principles. *Psychological Review*, 118 (1), 97–109.

Kurz-Milcke, E. & Gigerenzer, G. (2007). Heuristic decision making. *Marketing-JRM*, 1, 48–60.

Laibson, D. (1997). Golden eggs and hyperbolic discounting. *Quarterly Journal of Economics*, 112(2), 443–477.

Lane, D., Malerba, F. & Maxfield, R. (1996). Choice and action. *Journal of Evolutionary Economics*, 6, 43–67.

Lavoie, M. (1992). *Foundations of post-Keynesian economic analysis*. Edward Elgar Publishing.

Lavoie, M. (2014). *Post-Keynesian economics: new foundations*. Edward Elgar Publishing.

Lehrer, J. (2009). *How we decide*. Houghton Mifflin Harcourt.

Leland, J. W. (1994). Generalized similarity judgements: an alternative explanation for choice anomalies. *Journal of Risk and Uncertainty*, 9, 151–172.

Leland, J. W. (2002). Similarity judgments and anomalies in inter-temporal choice. *Economic Inquiry*, 40(4), 574–581.

Lenfant, J.-S. (2012). Indifference curves and the ordinalist revolution. *History of Political Economy*, 44(1), 113–155.

Levy, I. & Ehrlich, D. (2018). Neuroeconomics. In A. Lewis (Ed.), *The Cambridge handbook of psychology and economic behaviour* (pp. 627–649, 2nd ed.). Cambridge University Press.

Loewenstein, G. (1992). The fall and rise of psychological explanations in the economics of inter-temporal choice. In G. Loewenstein & J. Elster (Eds.), *Choice over time* (pp. 3–34). Russell Sage Foundation.

Loewenstein, G. (2009). Anticipation and the valuation of delayed consumption. In G. Lowenstein (Ed.), *Exotic preferences. Behavioral economics and human motivation* (pp. 385–409). Oxford University Press.

Loewenstein, G. & Prelec, D. (1992). Anomalies in inter-temporal choice: evidence and an interpretation. *Quarterly Journal of Economics*, 107(2), 573–597.

Loewenstein, G. & Prelec, D. (2009a). Anomalies in inter-temporal choice: evidence and an interpretation. In G. Lowenstein (Ed.), *Exotic preferences. Behavioral economics and human motivation* (pp. 411–440). Oxford University Press.

Loewenstein, G. & Prelec, D. (2009b). Preferences for sequences of outcomes. In G. Lowenstein (Ed.), *Exotic preferences. Behavioral economics and human motivation* (pp. 441–480). Oxford University Press.

Luan, S., Schooler, L. J. & Gigerenzer, G. (2011). A signal-detection analysis of fast-and-frugal trees. *Psychological Review*, 118(2), 316–338.

Luan, S., Schooler, L. J. & Gigerenzer, G. (2014). From perception to preference and on to inference: an approach-avoidance analysis of thresholds. *Psychological Review*, 121(3), 501–525.

Luan, S., Reb, J. & Gigerenzer, G. (2019). Ecological rationality: fast-and-frugal heuristics for managerial decision making under uncertainty. *Academy of Management Journal*, 62(6), 1735–1759.

Luyendijk, J. (2015). *Swimming with sharks: my journey into the worlds of bankers*. Guardian Faber Publishing.

Lyman, B. (1989). *A psychology of food. More than a matter of taste*. AVI Book/Van Nostrand Reinhold Company.

Marewski, J. N., Gaissmaier, W. & Gigerenzer, G. (2010a). We favor formal models of heuristics rather than lists of loose dichotomies: a reply to Evans and Over. *Cognitive Processing*, 11, 177–179.

Marewski, J. N., Gaissmaier, W., Schooler, L. J., Goldstein, D. G. & Gigerenzer, G. (2010b). From recognition to decisions: extending and testing recognition-based models for multialternative inference. *Psychonomic: Bulletin & Review*, 17(3), 287–309.

Martignon, L. & Hoffrage, U. (2002). Fast, frugal, and fit: simple heuristics for paired comparison. *Theory and Decision*, 52, 29–71.

Martignon, L., Vitouch, O., Takezawa, M. & Forster, M. R. (2003). Naive and yet enlightened: from natural frequencies to fast and frugal decision trees. In D. Hardman & L. Macchi (Eds.), *Thinking: psychological perspectives on reasoning, judgment and decision making* (pp. 189–211). John Wiley.

Martignon, L., Katsikopoulos, K. & Woike, J. K. (2012). Naïve, fast, and frugal trees for classification. In P. M. Todd, G. Gigenrenzer & ABC Research Group (Eds.), *Ecological rationality. Intelligence in the world* (pp. 360–378). Oxford University Press.

Marzilli, K. M., Ericson, K. M., Laibson, D. & Cohen, J. D. (2015). Earlier or later? Simple heuristics explain inter-temporal choices better than delay discounting does. *Psychological Science*, 26, 826–833.

Mazur, J. E. (1987). An adjusting procedure for studying delayed reinforcement. In M. L. Commons, J. E. Mazur, J. A. Nevin, H. Rachlin & R. J. Herrnstein (Eds.), *Quantitative analyses of behavior: the effect of delay and of intervening events on reinforcement value* (Vol. 5, pp. 55–73). Lawrence Erlbaum Associates.

McCammon, I. & Hägeli, P. (2004). *Comparing avalanche decision frameworks using accident data from the United States*. Paper presented at the International Snow Science Workshop, Jackson (WY). http://www.researchgate.net

McGraw, A. P., Mellers, B. & Tetlock, Ph. E. (2005). Expectations and emotions of Olympic athletes. *Journal of Experimental Social Psychology*, 41, 438–446.

Medvec, V. H., Madey, S. F. & Gilovich, T. (1995). When less is more: counterfactual thinking and satisfaction among Olympic medalists. *Journal of Personality and Social Psychology*, 69, 603–610.

Miller, J. B. & Sanjurjo, A. (2018). Surprised by the hot hand fallacy? A truth in the law of small numbers. *Econometrica*, 86(6), 2019–2047.

Mirowski, Ph. (1989). *More heat than light. Economics as social physics: physics as nature's economics*. Cambridge University Press.

Mirowski, Ph. (2002). *Machine dreams: economics becomes a cyborg science*. Cambridge University Press.

Mirowski, Ph. (2013). *Never let a serious crisis go to waste. How neoliberalism survived the financial meltdown*. Verso.

Mischel, W., Shoda, Y. & Rodriguez, M. I. (1992). Delay of gratification in children. In G. Loewenstein & J. Elster (Eds.), *Choice over time* (pp.147–164). Russell Sage Foundation.

Moffitt, T. E. (1993). Adolescence-limited and life-course-persistent antisocial behavior: a developmental taxonomy. *Psychological Review*, 100(4), 674–701.

Morgado, I. (2017). *Aprender, recordar y olvidar. Claves cerebrales de la memoria y la educación* (7th ed.). Ariel.

Morgado, I. (2019). *Deseo y placer. La ciencia de las motivaciones*. Ariel.

Morroni, M. (2006). *Knowledge, scale and transactions in the theory of the firm*. Cambridge University Press.

Morson, G. S. & Schapiro, M. (2017). *Cents and sensibility. What economics can learn from the humanities*. Princeton University Press.

Motterlini, M. (2006). *Economia emotiva. Che cosa si nasconde dietro and nostri conti quotidiani*. Rizzoli.

Motterlini, M. (2010). *Trampas mentales. Cómo defenderse de los engaños propios y ajenos*. Paidós.

Motterlini, M. (2014). *La psicoeconomia di Charlie Brown. Strategie per una società più felice*. RCS Libri.

Motterlini, M. & Guala, F. (2015). *Mente, mercati, decisioni*. Università Bocconi Editore.

Mousavi, S. (2017). Gerd Gigerenzer and Vernon Smith: ecological rationality of heuristics in psychology and economics. In R. Frantz, S.-H. Chen, K. Dopfer, F. Heukelom & S. Mousavi (Eds.), *Routledge handbook of behavioral economics* (pp. 88–100). Routledge.

Mousavi, S. & Gigerenzer, G. (2011). Revisiting the "error" in studies of cognitive errors. In D. A. Hofmann & M. Frese (Eds.), *Errors in organizations* (pp. 97–112). Routledge.

Mousavi, S. & Gigerenzer, G. (2014). Risk, uncertainty, and heuristics. *Journal of Business Research*, 67(8), 1671–1678.

Mousavi, S., Gigenrenzer, G. & Kheirandish, R. (2017). Rethinking behavioral economics through fast-and-frugal heuristics. In R. Frantz, S.-H. Chen, K. Dopfer, F. Heukelom & S. Mousavi (Eds.), *Routledge handbook of behavioral economics* (pp. 280–296). Routledge.

Nagel, R., Bayona, A., Kheirandish, R. & Mousavi, S. (2017). Reinhard Selten, the dualist. In R. Frantz, S.-H. Chen, K. Dopfer, F. Heukelom & S. Mousavi (Eds.), *Routledge handbook of behavioral economics* (pp. 66–87). Routledge.

Neth, H., Meder, B., Kothiyal, A. & Gingerenzer, G. (2013). *Homo heuristicus* in the financial world: from risk management to managing uncertainty. *Journal of Risk Management in Financial Institutions*, 7(2), 134–144.

Nisbett, R. E. (2016). *Mindware. Herramientas para pensar mejor*. Debate.

Noguera, J. A. & Tena, J. (2013). *Jon Elster. Un teòric social analític*. Universitat Oberta de Catalunya.

Nolan, J. M., Wesley Schultz, P., Cialdini, R. E., Goldstein, N. J. & Griskevicius, V. (2008). Normative social influence is under-detected. *Personality and Social Psychology Bulletin*, 34, 913–923.

Nowak, M. A. & Highfield, R. (2012). *Supercooperadores*. Ediciones B.

O'Donoghue, T. & Rabin, M. (2003). Self-awareness and self-control. In G. Loewenstein, D. Read & R. F. Baumeister (Eds.), *Economic and psychological perspectives on inter-temporal choice* (pp. 217–243). Russell Sage Foundation.

O'Neil, C. (2016). *Weapons of math destruction. How big data increases inequality and threatens democracy*. Crown.

Ortmann, A., Gigerenzer, G., Borges, B. & Goldstein, D. G. (2008). The recognition heuristic: a fast and frugal way to investment choice? In A. Plott & V. Smith (Eds.), *Handbook of experimental economic results* (Vol. I, pp. 993–1003). North-Holland.

Ostrom, E. (1990). *Governing the commons. The evolution of institutions for collective action*. Cambridge University Press.

Pachur, T., Todd, P. M., Gigerenzer, G., Schooler, L. J. & Goldstein, D. G. (2012). When is the recognition heuristic an adaptive tool? In P. M. Todd, G. Gigenrenzer & ABC Research Group (Eds.), *Ecological rationality. Intelligence in the world* (pp. 113–143). Oxford University Press.

Payne, J. W., Bettman, J. R. & Johnson, E. J. (1988). Adaptive strategy selection in decision making. *Journal of Experimental Psychology: Learning, Memory, and Cognition*, 14(3), 534–552.

Payne, J. W., Bettman, J. R. & Johnson, E. J. (1993). *The adaptive decision maker*. Cambridge University Press.

Piattelli-Palmarini, M. (1996). *Inevitable illusions: how mistakes of reason rule our minds*. Wiley.

Poundstone, W. (2010). *Priceless. The hidden psychology of value*. Oneworld Publications.

Prelec, D. & Bodmer, R. (2003). Self-signaling and self-control. In G. Loewenstein, D. Read & R. F. Baumeister (Eds.), *Economic and psychological perspectives on inter-temporal choice* (pp. 277–298). Russell Sage Foundation.

Prelec, D. & Loewenstein, G. (1997). Beyond time discounting. *Marketing Letters*, (8)1, 97–108.

Prelec, D. & Loewenstein, G. (2009). The red and the black: mental accounting of savings and debt. In G. Lowenstein (Ed.), *Exotic preferences. Behavioral economics and human motivation* (pp. 481–520). Oxford University Press.

Raab, M. & Gigerenzer, G. (2015). The power of simplicity: a fast-and-frugal heuristics approach to performance science. *Frontiers in Psychology*, 6, 1672.

Rabin, M. (1998). Psychology and economics. *Journal of Economic Literature*, (36)3, 11–46.

Rabin, M. (2013). Incorporating limited rationality into economics. *Journal of Economic Literature* (51)2, 528–543.

Rachlin, H. (2000). *The science of self-control*. Harvard University Press.

Rachlin, H. (2006). Notes on discounting. *Journal of the Experimental Analysis of Behavior*, 85(3), 425–435.

Raiffa, H. (1982). *The art and science of negotiation*. Harvard University Press.

Raiffa, H., Richardson, J. & Metcalfe, D. (2002). *Negotiation analysis. The science and art of collaborative decision making*. The Belknap Press of Harvard University Press.

Randall, A. (2011). *Risk and precaution*. Cambridge University Press.

Read, D., McDonald, R. & He, L. (2018). Inter-temporal choice. Choosing for the future. In A. Lewis (Ed.), *The Cambridge handbook of psychology and economic behaviour* (pp. 167–197, 2nd ed.). Cambridge University Press.

Reichlin, M. (2013). *L'utilitarismo*. Il Mulino.

Reiss, J. (2013). *Philosophy of economics. A contemporary introduction*. Routledge.

Rieskamp, J. & Dieckmann, A. (2012). Redundancy: environment structure that simple heuristics can exploit. In P. M. Todd, G. Gigenrenzer & ABC Research Group

(Eds.), *Ecological rationality. Intelligence in the world* (pp. 187–215). Oxford University Press.

Rizzo, M. J. (2019). Inconsistency is not pathological: a pragmatic perspective. *Mind & Society*, 18, 77–85.

Roberts, B. W., Walton, K. E. & Viechtbauer, W. (2006). Patterns of mean-level change in personality traits across the life course: a meta-analysis of longitudinal studies. *Psychological Bulletin*, 132(1), 1–25.

Roberts, S. & Pashler, H. (2000). How persuasive is a good fit? A comment on theory testing. *Psychological Review*, 107(2), 358–367.

Robinson, J. (1962). *Economic philosophy*. C. A. Watts & Co.

Roncaglia, A. (2005). *The wealth of ideas. A history of economic thought*. Cambridge University Press.

Rubinstein, A. (1998). *Modelling bounded rationality*. The MIT Press.

Rubinstein, A. (2003). "Economics and psychology"? The case of hyperbolic discounting. *International Economic Review*, 44 (4), 1207–1216.

Rusetski, A. (2014). Pricing by intuition: managerial choices with limited information. *Journal of Business Research*, 67(8), 1733–1743.

Russo, L. (2004). *The forgotten revolution. How science was born in 300 BC and why it had to be reborn*. Springer.

Rutherford, M. (1988). Learning and decision-making in economics and psychology: a methodological perspective. In P. E. Earl (Ed.), *Psychological economics. Development, tensions and prospects* (pp. 35–54). Kluwer.

Samuelson, L. (2005). *Foundations of human sociality*: a review essay. *Journal of Economic Literature*, 43(2), 488–497.

Sandel, M. J. (2009). *Justice: what's the right thing to do?* Farrar, Straus and Giroux.

Sandel, M. J. (2013). *What money can't buy: the moral limits of markets*. Penguin.

Schelling, T. C. (1992). Self-command: a new discipline. In G. Loewenstein & J. Elster (Eds.), *Choice over time* (pp. 167–176). Russell Sage Foundation.

Schelling, T. C. (2006a). *Micromotives and macrobehavior with a new preface and the Nobel lecture* (1st ed. 1978). W. W. Norton and Company.

Schelling, T. C. (2006b). Self-command in practice, in policy, and in a theory of rational choice. In T. C. Schelling, *Strategies of commitment and other essays* (pp. 63–81). Harvard University Press.

Schilirò, D. (2017). Psychology into economics: fast and frugal heuristics. *International Journal of Business Management and Economic Research*, 8(3), 934–939.

Scholten, M. & Read, D. (2010). The psychology of inter-temporal tradeoff. *Psychological Review*, 117(3), 925–944.

Scholten, M., Read, D. & Sanborn, A. (2014). Weighing outcomes by time or against time? Evaluation rules in inter-temporal choice. *Cognitive Science*, 38(3), 399–438.

Schooler, L. J. & Hertwig, R. (2005). How forgetting aids heuristic inference. *Psychological Review*, 112(3), 610–628.

Schwartz, B. (2016). *The paradox of choice. Why more is less*. HarperCollins.

Scitovsky, T. (1976). *The joyless economy. An inquiry into human satisfaction and consumer dissatisfaction*. Oxford University Press.

Seabright, P. (2005). *The company of strangers: a natural history of economic life*. Princeton University Press.

Sedlmeier, P. & Gigerenzer, G. (2001). Teaching Bayesian reasoning in less than two hours. *Journal of Experimental Psychology: General*, 130(3), 380–400.

Sedlmeier, P., Hertwig, R. & Gigenrenzer, G. (1998). Are judgements of the posi-
     tional frequencies of letters systematically biased due to availability? *Journal of
     Experimental Psychology: Learning, Memory, and Cognition*, 24(3), 754–770.
Selten, R. (1991). Evolution, learning, and economic behavior. *Games and Economic
     Behavior*, 3, 3–24.
Selten, R. (1998). Aspiration adaptation theory. *Journal of Mathematical Psychology*,
     42(2–3), 191–214.
Selten, R. (1999). *What is bounded rationality?* (SFB Discussion Paper B-454. Bonn,
     Uni Bonn). http://pdfs.semanticscholar.org/8237
Sent, E.-M. (2004). Behavioral economics: how psychology made its (limited) way
     back into economics. *History of Political Economy*, 36(4), 735–760.
Sent, E.-M. (2017). Herbert Simon's behavioral economics. In R. Frantz, S.-H. Chen,
     K. Dopfer, F. Heukelom & S. Mousavi (Eds.), *Routledge handbook of behavioral
     economics* (pp. 56–65). Routledge.
Serwe, S. & Fring, C. (2006). Who will win Wimbledon? The recognition heuristic in
     predicting sports events. *Journal of Behavioral Decision Making*, 19, 321–332.
Shefrin, H. M. & Thaler R. H. (1981). An economic theory of self-control. *Journal of
     Political Economy*, 89(2), 392–406.
Shotton, R. (2018). *The choice factory. How 25 behavioural biases influence the prod-
     ucts we decide to buy.* Harriman House.
Silk, J. B. (2005). The evolution of cooperation in primate groups. In H. Gintis, S.
     Bowles, R. Boyd & E. Fehr (Eds.), *Moral sentiment and material interests. The
     foundations of cooperation in economic life* (pp. 43–73). The MIT Press.
Silk, J. B. & House, B. R. (2011). Evolutionary foundations of human prosocial
     sentiments. *Proceedings of the National Academy of Sciences of the United States
     of America*, 108/supp. 2, 10910–10917. http://www.pnas.org/cgi/doi/10.1073/pnas
     .1100305108
Simon, H. A. (1954). Bandwagon and underdog effects and the possibility of election
     predictions. *The Public Opinion Quarterly*, 18(3), 245–253.
Simon, H. A. (1955). A behavioral model of rational choice. *The Quarterly Journal of
     Economics*, 69 (1), 99–118.
Simon, H. A. (1959). Theories of decision-making in economics and behavioral
     science. *The American Economic Review*, 49(3), 253–283.
Simon, H. A. (1987a). Bounded rationality. In J. Eatwell, M. Milgate & P. Newman
     (Eds.), *The new Palgrave. A dictionary of economics* (Vol. 1, A to D, pp. 266–268).
     The Macmillan Press.
Simon, H. A. (1987b). Satisficing. In J. Eatwell, M. Milgate & P. Newman (Eds.),
     The new Palgrave. A dictionary of economics (Vol. 4, Q to Z, pp. 243–245). The
     Macmillan Press.
Simon, H. A. (2000). Bounded rationality in social science: today and tomorrow. *Mind
     and Society*, 1, 25–39.
Skořepa, M. (2011). *Decision-making. A behavioral economic approach.*
     Palgrave-Macmillan.
Slovic, P., Peters, E., Finucane, M. L. & Macgregor, D. G. (2005). Affect, risk, and
     decision making. *Health Psychology*, 24(4 supp.), S35–S40.
Smith, A. (1981). *An inquiry into the nature and causes of the wealth of nations* (1st ed.
     1776). Liberty Classics.
Smith, A. (1994). *The theory of moral sentiments* (1st ed. 1759). Liberty Classics.
Smith, V. L. (2008). *Rationality in economics. Constructivist and ecological forms.*
     Cambridge University Press.

Sofo, F., Colapinto, C., Sofo, M. & Ammirato, S. (2013). *Adaptive decision making and intellectual styles*. Springer.

Solomon, M. R. (2015). *Consumer behavior. Buying, having, and being*. Pearson Education.

Soman, D., Ainslie, G., Frederick, S., Li, X., Lynch, J., Moreau, P., Mitchell, A., Read, D., Sawyer, A., Trope, Y., Wertenbroch, K. & Zauberman, G. (2005). The psychology of inter-temporal discounting: why are distant events valued differently from proximal ones? *Marketing Letters*, 13(3/4), 347–360.

Sorokowska, A. et al. (2017). Preferred interpersonal distances: a global comparison. *Journal of Cross-Cultural Psychology*, 48(4), 577–592.

Spetzler, C., Winter, H. & Meyer, J. (2016). *Decision quality. Value creation from better business decisions*. Wiley.

Stanovich, K. E. & West, R. F. (2000). Individual differences in reasoning: implications for the rationality debate? *Behavioral and Brain Sciences*, 23, 645–726.

Steedman, I. (1989). Economic theory and intrinsically non-autonomous preferences and beliefs. In I. Steedman, *From exploitation to altruism* (pp. 205–221). Polity Press.

Stevens, J. R. (2016). Inter-temporal similarity: discounting as a last resort. *Journal of Behavioral Decision Making*, 29, 12–24.

Stevens, J. R. & Soh, L.-K. (2018). Predicting similarity judgments in inter-temporal choice with machine learning. *Psychonomic Bulletin Review*, 25, 627–635.

Sunstein, C. R. (2009). *On rumors: how falsehoods spread, why we believe them, what can be done*. Allen Lane.

Szmigin, I. & Piacentini, M. (2015). *Consumer behaviour*. Oxford University Press.

Taleb, N. N. (2007). *The black swan: the impact of the highly improbable*. Random House.

Tetlock, Ph. (2005). *Expert political judgement: how good is it? How can we know?* Princeton University Press.

Thaler, R. H. (1992). The ultimatum game. In R. H. Thaler, *The winner's curse. Paradoxes and anomalies of economic life* (pp. 21–35). Princeton University Press.

Thaler, R. H. (2015). *Misbehaving. How economics became behavioural*. Allen Lane.

Thaler, R. H. (2016). Behavioral economics: past, present, and future. *American Economic Review*, 106 (7), 1577–1600.

Thaler, R. H. & Loewenstein, G. (1992). Inter-temporal choice. In R. H. Thaler, *The winner's curse. Paradoxes and anomalies of economic life* (pp. 92–106). Princeton University Press.

Thaler, R. H. & Sunstein, C. R. (2008). *Nudge. Improving decisions about health, wealth, and happiness*. Yale University Press.

Thaler, R. H. & Tversky, A. (1992). Preference reversals. In R. H. Thaler, *The winner's curse. Paradoxes and anomalies of economic life* (pp. 79–91). Princeton University Press.

Todd, P. M. & Gigerenzer, G. (2000). Précis of *Simple heuristics that make us smart*. *Behavioral and Brain Sciences*, 23, 727–780.

Todd, P. M. & Gigerenzer, G. (2012). What is ecological rationality? In P. M. Todd, G. Gigenrenzer & ABC Research Group (Eds.), *Ecological rationality. Intelligence in the world* (pp. 3–30). Oxford University Press.

Tomer, J. F. (2017). *Advanced introduction to behavioral economics*. Edward Elgar Publishing.

Trentman, F. (2016). *Empire of things. How we became a world of consumers, from the fifteenth century to the twenty-first*. Allen Lane.

Tversky, A. & Kahneman, D. (1986). Rational choice and the framing of decisions. *The Journal of Business*, 59(4), 251–278.

Tversky, A. & Kahneman, D. (1992). Advances in prospect theory: cumulative representation of uncertainty. *Journal of Risk and Uncertainty*, 5(4), 297–323.

Tversky, A. & Kahneman, D. (2018a). Judgement under uncertainty: heuristics and biases. In E. Shafir (Ed.), *The essential Tversky* (1st ed. 1974, pp. 1–18). The MIT Press.

Tversky, A. & Kahneman, D. (2018b). Rational choice and the framing of decisions. In E. Shafir (Ed.), *The essential Tversky* (1st ed. 1974, pp. 127–154). The MIT Press.

Tversky, A., Slovic, P. & Kahneman, D. (1990). The causes of preference reversal. *The American Economic Review*, 80(1), 204–217.

Ubel, P. A. (2008). *Free market madness. Why human nature is at odds with economics and why it matters.* Harvard Business Press.

Urminsky, O. & Zauberman, G. (2016). The psychology of inter-temporal preferences. In G. Keren & G. Wu (Eds.), *The Wiley Blackwell handbook of judgment and decision making* (Vol. I, pp. 141–180). Wiley-Blackwell.

Vercelli, A. (2002). Uncertainty, rationality and learning: a Keynesian perspective. In D. S. Dow & J. Hillard (Eds.), *Keynes, uncertainty and the global economy* (pp. 88–105). Edward Elgar Publishing.

Viale, R. (2018). *Oltre il nudge. Libertà di scelta, felicità e comportamento* (Saggi 872). Il Mulino.

Vlaev, I., Chater, N., Stewart, N. & Brown, G. D. A. (2011). Does the brain calculate value? *Trends in Cognitive Sciences*, 15(11), 546–554.

Vohra, R. V. & Krishnamurthi, L. (2012). *Principles of pricing. An analytical approach.* Cambridge University Press.

Von Neumann, J. & Morgenstern, O. (1953). *Theory of games and economic behavior.* Princeton University Press. http://jmvidal.cse.sc.edu/library/neumann44a.pdf

Vosoughi, S., Roy, D. & Aral, S. (2018). The spread of true and false news online. *Science*, 359 (6380), 1146–1151.

Wakker, P. P. (2010). *Prospect theory for risk and ambiguity.* Cambridge University Press.

Wärneryd, K. (1982). The life and work of George Katona. *Journal of Economic Psychology*, 2(1), 1–31.

Watt-Smith, T. (2016). *The book of human emotions. An encyclopedia of feeling from anger to wanderlust.* Wellcome Collection.

Wilke, A. & Clark Barrett, H. (2009). The hot hand phenomenon as a cognitive adaptation to clumped resources. *Evolution and Human Behavior*, 30(3), 161–169.

Wilkinson, N. (2008). *An introduction to behavioral economics.* Palgrave Macmillan.

Wilkinson, N. & Klaes, M. (2012). *An introduction to behavioral economics* (2nd ed.). Palgrave Macmillan.

Wübben, M. & Wangenheim, F. v. (2008). Instant customer base analysis: managerial heuristics often "get it right". *Journal of Marketing*, 72, 82–93.

Yee, M., Dahan, E., Hauser, J. & Orlin, J. B. (2007). Greedoid-based noncompensatory inference. *Marketing Science*, 26(4), 532–549.

Index

paradox 16
and prices 19

Walras, L. 21
wants 74